AF352466

GENERATIONS OF EMPIRE

Generations of Empire

*Youth from Ottoman to Italian Rule
in the Mediterranean*

ANDREAS GUIDI

UNIVERSITY OF TORONTO PRESS
Toronto Buffalo London

ISBN 978-1-4875-4127-9 (cloth)   ISBN 978-1-4875-4129-3 (EPUB)
ISBN 978-1-4875-4128-6 (PDF)

Toronto Italian Studies

Library and Archives Canada Cataloguing in Publication

Title: Generations of empire : youth from Ottoman to Italian rule in the
  Mediterranean / Andreas Guidi.
Names: Guidi, Andreas, author.
Series: Toronto Italian studies.
Description: Series statement: Toronto Italian studies | Includes bibliographical
  references and index.
Identifiers: Canadiana (print) 20220148392 | Canadiana (ebook) 20220148759 |
  ISBN 9781487541279 (hardcover) | ISBN 9781487541293 (EPUB) |
  ISBN 9781487541286 (PDF)
Subjects: LCSH: Youth – Greece – Rhodes (Island) – History – 20th century. | LCSH:
  Youth – Political activity – Greece – Rhodes (Island) – History – 20th century. |
  LCSH: Youth – Greece – Rhodes (Island) – Economic conditions – 20th century. |
  LCSH: Students – Greece – Rhodes (Island) – History – 20th century. | LCSH:
  Families – Greece – Rhodes (Island) – History – 20th century. | LCSH: Italians –
  Greece – Rhodes (Island) – History – 20th century. | LCSH: Rhodes (Greece :
  Island) – Social life and customs – 20th century.
Classification: LCC HQ799.G92 R56 2022 | DDC 305.23509495/870904 – dc23

This book has been published with the assistance of the École des Hautes Études
en Sciences Sociales – Centre d'Études Turques, Ottomanes, Balkaniques et
Centrasiatiques and the University of Konstanz – Centre for Cultural Inquiry.

We wish to acknowledge the land on which the University of Toronto Press
operates. This land is the traditional territory of the Wendat, the Anishnaabeg, the
Haudenosaunee, the Métis, and the Mississaugas of the Credit First Nation.

University of Toronto Press acknowledges the financial assistance to its publishing
program of the Canada Council for the Arts and the Ontario Arts Council, an agency
of the Government of Ontario.

Contents

Maps, Figures, and Tables

Maps

Figures

Tables

Acknowledgments

I was 20 years old when, in the summer of 2007, I visited Rhodes for the first time. The town's history, just like the beauty of its nature and monuments, captivated me from the beginning. At that time, however, I had no idea that this place would later be so central in my thoughts and words for almost ten years, nor that I would eventually publish a book about Rhodes to discuss Mediterranean and imperial history. This is the result of a long journey. It would not have been possible without the wonderful support and inspiration of many friends and colleagues, whom I feel lucky to have had by my side along the way.

My first thought of gratitude goes to my PhD advisors Hannes Grandits and Nathalie Clayer. Hannes's passion and perspicacity have shaped my love for history, and he believed in this research project since the first time we discussed it in Berlin. Nathalie welcomed me in Paris, and I cannot thank her enough for her dedication, her encouragement, her friendship, and everything I learned from her.

Next to these two intellectual guiding lights, I am indebted to friends with whom I had innumerable discussions. They made academic nomadism feel like a world with multiple homes. At the Humboldt University in Berlin, I learned a lot from the participants of the *Kolloquium* on Southeast-European History and the convivial *Postkolloquium* at the *Café Chagall* between 2012 and 2018. I am particularly grateful to Fernando Zamola, Ruža Fotiadis, Nikos Papadogiannis, Konrad Petrovszky, Robert Lučić, Đorđe Tomić, Janis Nalbadidacis, Thomas Porena, Veronika Hager, and Jovo Miladinović. At the *École des Hautes Études en Sciences Sociales* (EHESS) in Paris, between 2015 and 2019, I found an incredibly enriching atmosphere. I had never-ending writing (and chatting) sessions in the *Salle des Doctorants* of the Center for Ottoman, Turkish, Balkan, and Central Asian Studies (CETOBaC). I also attended with many of them the CETOBaC research seminars followed by nice apéros at *Le Raspail*. Special thanks to Gabriel Doyle (a dearest friend and a globetrotter whose curiosity always inspires me), Elif Becan (a real sister-in-arms inside and outside academia), Antonis Nasis (a brilliant mind and a *rembetiko* maestro who also bore with me during our *colocation*), Zeynep Bursa-Millet, Ece Zerman, and Lucie Drechselovà. I also thank my long time sister-friends Nora Illanes, Anna Chiara Mezzasalma, and Agathe Bernier-Monod simply for being so wonderful. They were always ready to help, listen, work together, and host me in Berlin and Paris. As you open this book, my friends, raise your glass to the fun and unforgettable moments we had the chance to spend together!

The project took its shape thanks to the opportunities I had to discuss it in several seminars and workshops. I thank all those who invited me to share the preliminary results of my work and, in particular, Christian Voss (Berlin), Christine-Isabel Schröder (Bochum), Oliver-Jens Schmitt (Vienna), Thomas Gallant (San Diego), Efi Avdela (Rethymno), as well as Emmanuel Szurek, Fabio Giomi, Xavier Bougarel, Bernard Lory, Claire Zalc, and Morgane Labbé (Paris).

Many friends and colleagues helped me through invaluable comments and remarks at all stages of the manuscript. Warmest thanks to Marc Aymes, Naomi R. Cohen, Aron Rodrigue, Alexandre Toumarkine, Alexander Nützenadel, Andreas Eckert, Malte Fuhrmann, Roberta Pergher, Pamela Ballinger, M'hamed Oualdi, Nazan Maksudyan, Manuel Borutta, Fernando Esposito, Clara Frysztacka, Jonathan Lohnes, Carolyn Taratko, Jonas Hock, Laura Linzmeier, Sarah Nimführ, Jan-Christoph Maschelke, Filippo Espinoza and Luca Castiglioni (two experts on the history of the Italian Dodecanese), and Nisrine Rahal. My book owes a lot to your advice, and I hope you can recognize in this work some of the paintbrush strokes that you inspired.

My access to the sources was made possible by the work and knowledge of many librarians and archivists, without whom any historian would be lost at sea. I cannot adequately express my gratitude to Irini Toliou, the directress of the Greek State Archives in Rhodes, who guided me with patience and trust every day during my stays with her assistants Maria Papanikolaou and Evangelia. I was extremely lucky to cross Marco Clementi's path as he was in Rhodes doing an excellent job for the *Carabinieri* collection of the same archive. Marco introduced me to this valuable collection when I had just begun my research, and the discussions with him were a turning point. Papas Michalis welcomed me at the archive of the Metropolitan See of Rhodes, Carmen Cohen at the Jewish Museum, Chrysanthi Karakiza-Papatharrenou at the gymnasium Venetokleion, and Yusuf Bey at the Hafiz Ahmed Ağa Library. Frà Gabriele Pomatto guided me at the archives of the *Fratelli delle Scuole Cristiane* in Turin, as Francis Ricousse did at the congregation's generalate in Rome. In Paris, I worked at the archives of the *Alliance Israélite Universelle* with the help of Rose Levyne. I also thank the staff at the Town Hall of Rhodes, the Ottoman Archives of Istanbul, the Central State Archives and the Archive of the Ministry of Foreign Affairs in Rome, the French Diplomatic Archives in Nantes, and the State Archives in Vienna. The staff at the Italian National Library in Florence, the Center for Contemporary Jewish Documentation in Milan, and the Central Zionist Archives in Tel-Aviv assisted me with online requests for specific documents. Moreover, I am indebted to all those who shared with me primary sources and stories about Rhodes, and especially Constanze Kolbe, Leyla von Mende, Aron Hasson, Claude Benatar, Ben Levy, Joe Bogdanich, and Theologos Tsigaros.

Without funding from public institutions, this journey would have never started. I acknowledge the support of the Humboldt Research Track scholarship by the Humboldt University in Berlin in the earliest phase of my research and by the Elsa Neumann Scholarship for doctoral students of the Bundesland Berlin. I had the honour to obtain a fellowship at the Doctoral Program *"Construire les differences/Unterschiede denken"* financed by the French-German University as well as mobility grants by the EHESS and the CETOBaC.

As I moved towards the book manuscript, Stephen Shapiro kindly expressed his interest in acquiring it for University of Toronto Press, and he has been an impeccable and supportive editor. I also thank the three anonymous readers whom Stephen invited to guide me in improving the manuscript with valuable comments, as well as the anonymous reader of UTP's manuscript review committee. Two student assistants at the University of Konstanz helped me prepare the manuscript: Basile Desvignes assisted me with the footnotes, while Naemi Haberkorn worked on the bibliography's format and prepared the index. I thank these promising students and wish them all the best for their future career. The Center for Cultural Inquiry at the University of Konstanz and the CETOBaC contributed to the book's publication with a generous grant, and I thank both institutions for their support.

Some persons deserve not only gratitude, but also a special mention. During my research, I met three men who were born in Rhodes almost at the same time, in the early 1930s: Nuri Alayalı, who still lives there, Pasquale Cacopardi, now in Piacenza (Italy), and Nick Bogdanich, whom I met by chance in Rhodes and who lives in Vancouver. They have probably never met each other, although I have always wondered whether they might have played football, gone to the cinema, or swum together and with other kids in the last years of the period I discuss in this book. The long conversations I had with each of them, their similar smiles and tears when remembering their life, the photographs that they showed me and the impressive memory they received as a gift were surely among the most rewarding aspects about conducting this research. As they agreed to share their lifeworld with me, these witnesses made me touch, hear, and see the history that I was investigating and trying to put into words, and I feel privileged to have had this experience.

I dedicate this book to my family. To my partner Zeynep Ertuğrul for being a source of love, strength, and inspiration – an elixir of life, my *Bengisu*. To my mother Deanna, my sister Alessia, and my brother Enrico for their love and all they have done and still do to support me and care for each other.

Washington, DC, March 2022

Abbreviations

Archives and Sources

AAPP	Affari Politici (Political Issues)
ACS	Archivio Centrale dello Stato (Central State Archives)
ADS MUN	Archeio tis Dimogerontias Symis (Archive of the Elders Council of Symi)
AIMR	Archeio tis Ieras Mitropolis Rodou (Archive of the Holy Metropolis of Rhodes)
AIU	Alliance Israélite Universelle
AMEGLIO	Carte Ameglio (Ameglio Papers)
AMIA CMT	Asociación Mutual Israelita Argentina, Centro Marc Tucnow (Argentine-Jewish Mutual Association, Marc Tucnow Center)
ASDMAE	Archivio Storico-Diplomatico del Ministero degli Affari Esteri (Historical-Diplomatic Archives of the Ministry of Foreign Affairs)
BCA	Başbakanlık Cumhuriyet Arşivi (The Prime Minister's Republican Archive)
BEO	Babıali Evrak Odası (Record Office of the Sublime Porte)
BOA	Başbakanlık Osmanlı Arşivi (The Prime Minister's Ottoman Archives)
CADN	Centre des Archives Diplomatiques de Nantes

CDEC	Centro di Documentazione Ebraica Contemporanea (Center for Contemporary Jewish Documentation)
CEMLA	Centro de Estudios Migratorios Latinoamericanos (Latin American Center for Migration Studies)
CZA	Central Zionist Archives
DH	Dahiliye (Ottoman Ministry of the Interior)
DR LIX	Dimos Rodou Lixiarcheio (Registry Office of the Municipality of Rhodes)
EIF PR	The Statue of Liberty – Ellis Island Foundation Passenger Records
ENIO	École Normale Israélite Orientale (Israelitic Oriental Teacher Training School)
FF	Fogli di famiglia (Family Certificates)
FRATRES	Federazione Rodia delle Associazioni Turistiche, Ricreative e Sportive (Rhodian Federation of Tourism, Recreational, and Sport Associations)
FSC	Fratelli delle Scuole Cristiane (Brothers of the Christian Schools)
GAB	Gabinetto (Office)
GAK DOD	Genika Archeia tou Kratous Nomou Dodekanisou (General State Archives of the Prefecture of the Dodecanese)
GAM	Gamoi (Weddings)
GC	Greenberg Center
HUS	Hususi (Special Matters)
ID	İdare (Administration)
IDD	Italiki Dioikisi Dodekanisou (Italian Administration of the Dodecanese)
II	Informazioni Italiani (Information on Italians)
ILHAA CENS	Islamic Library Hafiz Ahmed Ağa Census
IM	Isole Minori (Minor Islands)
IN	İddianame (Bills of Indictment)

ITA DIK	Italika Dikastiria (Italian Tribunals)
JDC NY AR	American Jewish Joint Distribution Committee New York Archives
KMS	Kalem-i Mahsûs (Private Secretarial Staff of the Ministry of the Interior)
MF	Maarif Nezareti (Ministry of Education)
MKT	Mektubî Kalem(i) (Secretarial Staff)
MKT MHM	Muhimme Kalemi Evraki (Documents from the Staff on Urgent Matters)
MRF	Mostra della Rivoluzione Fascista (Exhibition of the Fascist Revolution)
MTV	Mütenevvi Maruzat (Various Requests)
ÖStA HHStA GKA	Österreichisches Staatsarchiv, Haus-, Hof-, und Staatsarchiv, Gesandschafts- und Konsulatsarchive (Austrian State Archive, Embassies and Consulates Archives)
OTH	Othomaniko (Ottoman)
PCPA	Pasquale Cacopardi's Personal Archive
PNF	Partito Nazionale Fascista (National Fascist Party)
PO	Publications Officielles (Official Publications)
PRK AZN	(Perakende) Adliye ve Mezahib Nezareti Maruzatı (Requests to the Ministry of Justice and Confessions)
PS	Pubblica Sicurezza (Public Security)
RM	Religiosi Musulmani (Muslim Religious)
RRCC	Carabinieri Reali (Royal *Carabinieri*)
SIT POL PROV	Situazione Politica nelle Province (Political Situation in the Provinces)
SP	Schedati Politici (Politically Dangerous Filed Persons)
SYS	Siyasi Kısım (Political Section)
TFR I A	Rumeli Müfettişliği Sadâret (Inspectorate for Rumelia, Papers of the Grand Vizier)
TR	Tourkiko (Turkish Archive)

UH MGCJS	University of Hartford, The Maurice Greenberg Center for Jewish Studies
US NA CS 1940 ED	United States National Archives 1940 Census, Enumeration District
USC SF VHA	University of Southern California Shoah Foundation Visual History Archive
UWL OHC	University of Washington Library Oral History Collections
VENETOKLEIO	Archive of the Gymnasium *Venetokleion*
Y	Yıldız (Yıldız Palace Collection)
YSU SVV	Youngstown State University Steel Valley Voices

Others

AOI	Africa Orientale Italiana (Italian East Africa)
ASR	Associazione Sportiva Rodia (Rhodian Sport Association)
CUP	Committee of Union and Progress
DG	Disposizione Governatoriale (Governor's Decree)
GER	Gioventù Ebraica di Rodi (Jewish Youth of Rhodes)
GIL	Gioventù Italiana del Littorio (Italian Youth of the *Littorio*)
GUF	Gruppi Universitari Fascisti (Fascist University Students Groups)
LUCE	L'Unione Cinematografica Educativa (Educational Cinematographic Union)
MVSN	Milizia Volontaria per la Sicurezza Nazionale (Voluntary Militia for National Security)
ONB	Opera Nazionale Balilla (National *Balilla* Organization)
OND	Opera Nazionale Dopolavoro (National Recreational Organization)
SAIFE	Società Anonima Italiana Fruttindustria Egea (Anonymous Italian Aegean Company for Fruit Industry)

Notes on Transliteration, Dates, and Names

When using Ottoman words of common usage and not quoting a text (e.g. "vilayet," "İdadiye") I used the current Turkish spelling. Whenever referring directly to a document in Ottoman Turkish, I adopted the *International Journal of Middle East Studies* transliteration system.

For Greek, both in its *katharevousa* and *dimotiki* versions, I adopted a standard simplified transliteration based on the International Organization for Standardization.

Proper names are often spelled incoherently in the sources, especially when the same person appears in documents in Ottoman, Greek, French, and Italian sources (e.g. the following versions of the same surname: Aya Kacika, Agiaktsikas, Ajacatsicas, Aiacatzica). I generally used the one found in the document I mainly refer to. I kept the Turkish, Greek, or Ladino/Hebrew first names (e.g. Durmuş, Panagiotis, Bohor) when the same people appear in sources in different languages.

For toponyms, I generally adopted the version in use when the source in question was created (e.g. "Lero"). When the place is of common usage, I adopted the English version (e.g. "Smyrna").

Concerning dates, I converted the Ottoman *Hicri* and *Rumi* calendars as well as the Julian Orthodox dates into the Gregorian calendar (*Miladi Takvim*), for the sake of reading fluency.

When I referred to particularly sensitive private information retrieved exclusively from material not yet fully available to the public, I opted for an anonymized version of the surname (e.g. "Eirini A.)

Map 1. The Eastern Mediterranean, 1910.

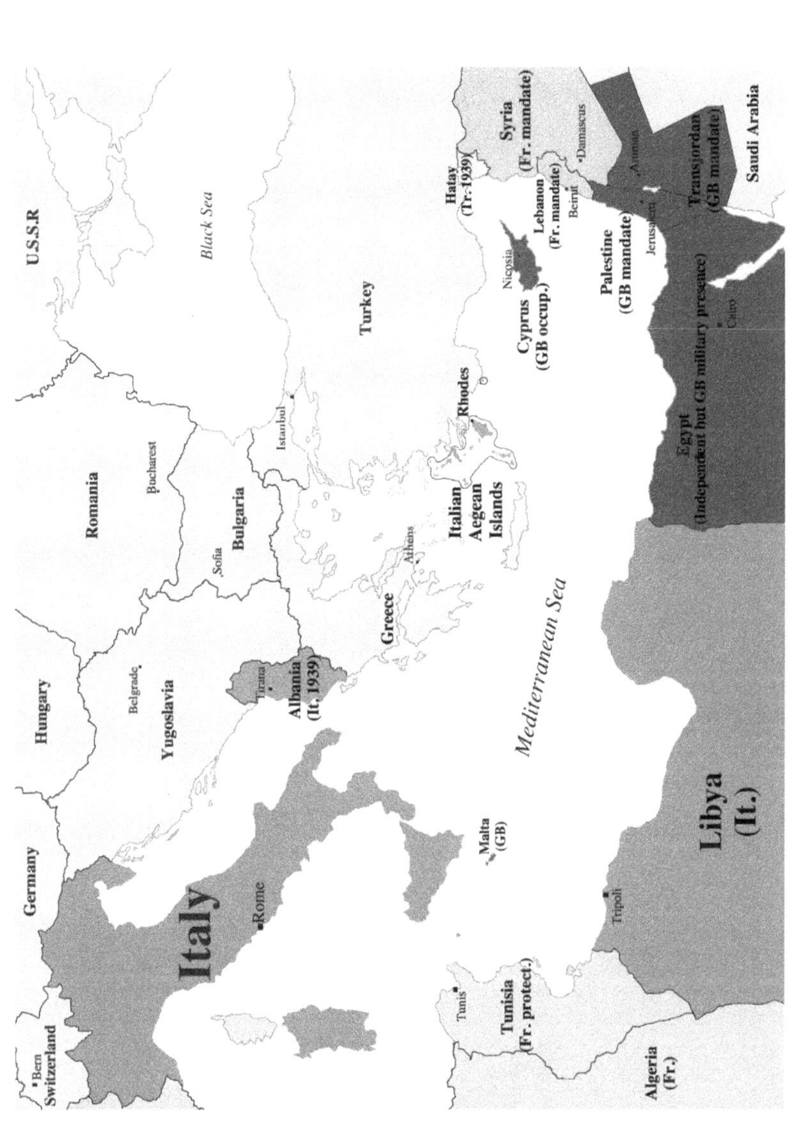

Map 2. The Eastern Mediterranean, 1938.

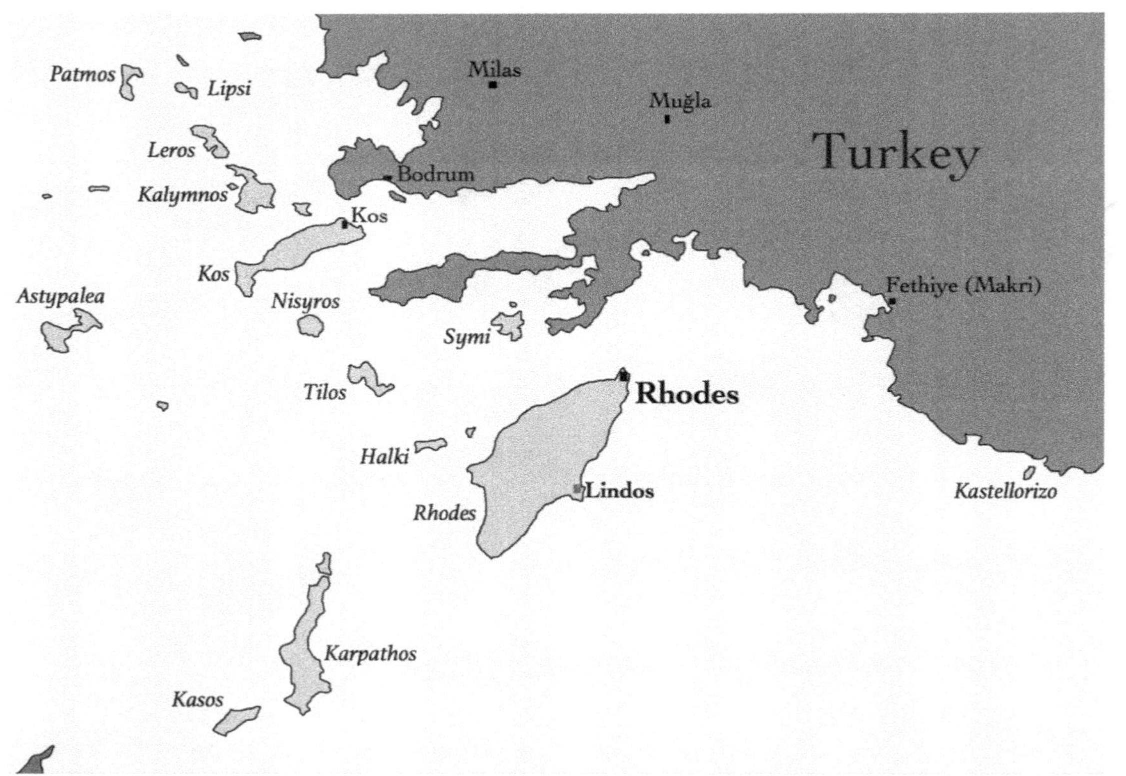

Map 3. The *Possedimento* of the Italian Aegean Islands.

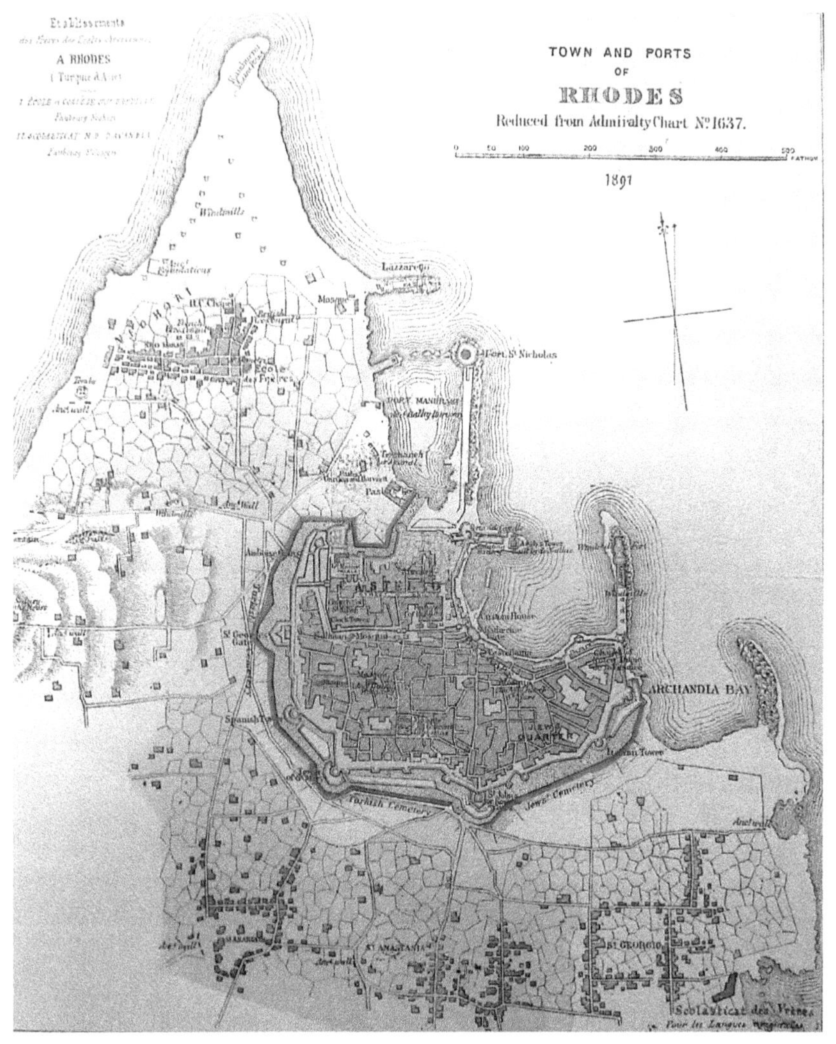

Map 4. British map of Ottoman Rhodes, 1891. FSC ROMA 560 4.

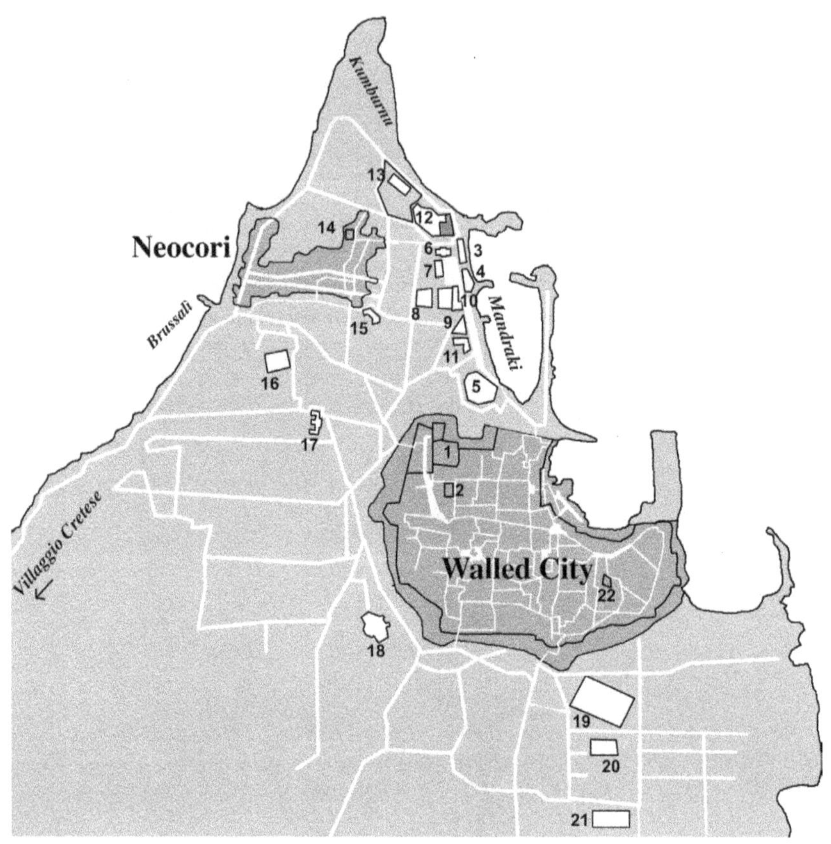

Map 5. Architectural landmarks of 1930s Rhodes.

Built before 1912:

1) Palace of the Grand Master; 2) *İdadiye* High School; 12) Murad Reis Tekke; 14) *Santa Maria della Vittoria* Catholic Church (and Monastery); 20) Gymnasium *Venetokleion*; 21) Orthodox Metropolitan Church; 22) *Kahal Shalom* Synagogue.

Built during Italian rule:

3) Governor's Palace; 4) Saint John of the Knights Catholic Church; 5) New Market; 6) *Teatro Puccini*; 7) *Casa del Fascio*; 8) Military Barracks *"Principe"*; 9) Courthouse; 10) *Cinema San Giorgio*; 11) *Circolo Italia*; 13) *Grand Hotel delle Rose*; 15) *Regio Istituto Maschile* High School; 16) Royal Hospital; 17) *Regio Istituto Femminile* High School; 18) Military Barracks *"Regina Elena"*; 19) Stadium *"Arena del Sole."*

GENERATIONS OF EMPIRE

Introduction

"Long live the *Duce*, Long live the New Imperial Italy." This graffiti appeared in an alley of Rhodes around 1927, next to Mussolini's austere portrait.[1] At that time, the Italian flag waved above a town dotted with mosques, synagogues, and churches. From the windows of his brand-new palace on the Rhodes waterfront, the Italian colonial governor of the islands known as the Dodecanese could look at the mighty mountains of Anatolia, shimmering in purple tones across a few kilometres of deep blue water, so much closer than Italy's shores. Outside the building, Rhodians of all ages, classes, and confessions used to stroll and chat about their everyday life: news about weddings, gossip about schoolmates, job opportunities and football games, fortunes and misfortunes of their relatives abroad. As they walked by the governor's palace, some of them might also have talked – or rather whispered – about their views on Italian colonial rule.

Fifty years after its creation as a unified state, the Kingdom of Italy had occupied Rhodes, ending the Ottoman Sultans' four-centuries-long rule over the town and the homonymous island. This happened as a side operation during the Italo-Ottoman war of 1911–12, in which Italian troops invaded Tripolitania and Cyrenaica, two regions in today's Libya. The conquest of some among the few territories left in the European scramble for Africa had boosted Italy's imperialism in the Mediterranean.[2] After early hesitations about the durability of the occupation in the Aegean, Rhodes acquired its importance as an outpost countering French and British interests in the Levant.[3] In 1923, after eleven years of military occupation, Rome's sovereignty over the *Isole Italiane dell'Egeo* (Italian Aegean Islands) was recognized by the Treaty of Lausanne, which also removed the Ottoman Empire from world maps. Starting in November 1922, the discussions in Lausanne were the first performance for Mussolini's diplomacy, since the *Duce* had seized power in

Figure 0.1. The Rhodes waterfront, 1934. "Rodi, 1934," AKON/Österreichische Nationalbibliothek, AK081_404.

Rome only a few weeks earlier. The birth of fascist colonialism in the Eastern Mediterranean corresponded to the Ottoman demise.

Once the centre of an Ottoman province, Rhodes became the centre of a *Possedimento*, literally a "possession" of Italy's Mediterranean empire. Yet, what did sovereignty in a post-Ottoman colonial setting imply? What attitude did the "new imperial Italy" adopt towards its subjects in social, cultural, and political terms? In his well-known verdict on the *Risorgimento*, Italy's state- and nation-building project in the nineteenth century, the Italian intellectual Massimo d'Azeglio lamented that, while Italy had been created, Italians were yet to be made.[4] This bittersweet formula from the 1860s resonated in time beyond unification, expressing a tension between state formation and nation-building reaching into the twentieth century. It also resonated in space beyond the Italian peninsula since the *Risorgimento*'s national myth nourished Rome's imperial ambitions.

The Italian Aegean Islands were part of an empire that reached its widest sovereign extension on the eve of the Second World War with the annexation of Albania. After 1918, this empire included former Habsburg territories coveted by Italian irredentism like South-Tyrol, the Julian March, Istria, Fiume, and Zara. In Africa, before the First World War Italy ruled over Eritrea, Somalia, and, since 1911, Libya. Mussolini's proudest conquest was Ethiopia, a state invaded in 1935 causing a wave of international protests. This expansionist drive changed the meaning of "Italy" and of "Italians." They did not anymore only refer to national, but also to imperial belonging. Transposed to Rhodes, a post-Ottoman town marked by confessional and linguistic diversity, d'Azeglio's quote points to a crucial challenge faced by Italy and other modern empires, namely, how to negotiate inclusion and separation in their colonies.[5] While Italy expanded, should Rhodians too be made into "Italians"? While Mussolini claimed that fascism was the quintessence of Italianness, could Rhodians too become fascists?

In 1929, in the middle of his mandate as civil governor of Rhodes (1923–36), Mario Lago voiced his opinion about the integration of Dodecanesian subjects into the Fascist Party:

Fascism means patriotism squared, and I seriously do not believe that people who have become Italian subjects only five years ago can seriously belong to it. They, who have a mentality which is not yet assimilated into ours, who, even if they lived in a politically amorphous atmosphere, have been accustomed for centuries to a secret pride of race and religion … The new generation will doubtlessly provide elements of quite different patriotic spirit, and therefore, while I am not convinced of the need for welcoming local subjects into Fascism, I am developing the *Opera dei Balilla* in the Aegean to attract indigenous youth (*giovinetti*). We will certainly make good Fascists out of them.[6]

In the governor's statement, the colonial subjects strolling under his palace's windows were a claylike object mouldable according to his regime's wishes. Still, Lago admitted that young Rhodians were not ready to become good fascist Italians. His "new generation" could only be a future achievement. The palace in which he wrote this letter, like many other buildings in town, might have been brand new, but the Ottoman legacy weighed over the government's efforts to shape the local society.

Italian imperial rule in Rhodes therefore cultivated a sense of generational discontinuity, separating the local youth's experiences from the experiences of their parents, who had grown up in Ottoman times. To create new patriotic "indigenous" subjects, colonial difference had to be harmonized with fascist indoctrination. But a hierarchization based on that difference and an assimilation based on fascist ideology acted as counterweights to each other. Reaching a balance was a hard, if not impossible task for Italian rule. Despite his self-confidence, the Italian governor was not a scientist experimenting in a laboratory, giving life to a perfect creature. The colonial state was necessarily responsive to challenges originating from the population it ruled.

We can thus invert the original questions: how did a former Ottoman society experience Italian colonialism? In his novel "The Viceroys" (1894), Federico de Roberto reflected on the shift from Bourbonic to Italian rule in Sicily during the *Risorgimento*. One of the protagonists, a nobleman, sardonically stated that, after Italy had been "made," his family would simply have to mind their "own business."[7] Even if we blunted this sentence's cynicism, it would still fit the post-Ottoman setting of Rhodes. Colonial rule depended on how resources, relationships, and social statuses – the "business" writ large – were handled from below. "New generations" also resulted from negotiations within families and in spheres of society that political authorities aimed to pervade.

Lago was not the first to refer to generations and youth with a political purpose. In 1908, before the Italian flag first waved above the walled town of Rhodes, a military revolution instigated by the Young Turks, an oppositional movement formed in the 1880s, shook the Ottoman state. A few months later, a local newspaper close to the Young Turks summoned a "new generation" of "enlightened youth" (*münevver el-efkār gencler)* whose right and duty was to live in the spirit of the newly introduced Ottoman Constitution and break with Sultan Abdülhamid II's authoritarianism.[8] The Young Turks shared Lago's anxiety about creating new imperial subjects. For both, "new generations" were to reinforce the link between Rhodes and the state, projecting a ruling authority in the future and demarcating this authority's specificities from the past. This destabilizes a viewpoint anchored in the history of Italian colonialism and introduces an alternative lead. What if Lago's ambition to create a new generation drew from processes already at work before 1923? What if fascist colonialism had taken over issues linked to rule and subjecthood originating in the late Ottoman period?

Generations of Empire combines four objectives to engage with these questions. The main one is a change of *framing* towards thinking Italian colonialism as post-Ottoman history, which I define as imperial consequence. A study on how an imperial province turned into a colonial territory allows us to situate Rhodes at an underexplored junction of Ottoman and Italian, but also Mediterranean and global imperial history. In the nineteenth and twentieth centuries, colonial administrations throughout the world acquired their specificities through the encounter with pre-existing structures. In Rhodes, Italian authorities emphasized their own rationality and efficacy in contrast to Ottoman backwardness. Yet, Ottoman institutions, social statuses, and forms of belonging reverberated after the Sultan's rule ended, creating challenges but also opportunities for fascist colonialism. The Italian occupation suspended a feverish redefinition of the relationship between the state and communal institutions based on confession which marked the last years of the Ottoman rule. Still, it also preserved these communities in a post-Ottoman regional environment that considered them obsolete.

The book argues that Italian colonial rule favoured imperial continuities through its management of diversity in the 1920s, sparing resources that a fascist tabula rasa would have required. This became a problem in the 1930s as fascism's assimilationist and militaristic aims implied the state's deeper penetration in its Mediterranean possession. Guided by the anxiety that future citizens would remain outside sovereign control, all modern empires struggled to establish new relationships between state and society. Seen from Rhodes, this process appeared during the Young Turk constitutional experience after 1908, then during Italy's military occupation, Lago's reforms inspired by the Treaty of Lausanne and, eventually, the more aggressive fascistization of colonial rule in the 1930s. None of this provided a durable answer to how state authority should increase its control by breaking with the past while maintaining the politics of difference so crucial for every empire. In this sense, late

Ottoman rule in Rhodes is an integral part of a broader imperial consequence essential to understand fascist colonialism.

As a second objective, imperial continuities offer a new *perspective* on
the reconfiguration of the Mediterranean in the early twentieth century.
A series of conflicts, the "Greater War" between 1911 and 1923, accelerated the end of the Ottoman Empire.[9] At the same time, persisting
warfare produced an earthquake in the region's political and territorial configurations. The Greater War's outcome saw fascist colonialism
engage with other expanding Mediterranean powers. France and Britain encircled Italian Libya through Tunisia and Egypt and secured a
dominant position in the Levant. In turn, the Italian Dodecanese lied
between Republican Turkey – itself a state emerging from the Ottoman
demise – and Greece. This raised the governors' anxieties about irredentist feelings among the Orthodox and, to a minor extent, Muslim
Dodecanesians.

Today, territorial tensions between Greece and Turkey in the Aegean
inform Mediterranean politics, while colonial legacies reinforce the
divide between the sea's northern and southern shores. Militarized
borders, together with asymmetries in terms of economic exchanges
and migration flows between Europe and Africa as well as the Middle
East, challenge any idea of Mediterranean "unity." Apart from a past
marked by economic expropriation, racist policies, and cultural oppression of Mediterranean peoples, colonialism reverberates in memorial
and archival disputes, as the case of French rule in Algeria shows.[10] Yet,
colonialism in the region was one turn in a longer, connected history
of modern empires across these divides. The book embeds local forces
in Ottoman and Italian Rhodes in a modern Mediterranean marked by
the expansion of capitalism, innovations in the cultural and educational
domain, emigration and settler colonialism, world wars, and travelling
ideologies.[11] Moreover, the Ottoman and Italian states in Rhodes drew
from repertoires of rule ranging from autocratic monarchism to constitutionalism, from military governments to fascism. These regimes
appeared in the same period throughout the world. Zooming in on
Rhodes allows to address the macro-processes influencing imperial
transformations by valuing local knowledge and archives. Discussing
webs of personal relationships in a transimperial setting in flux thus
brings global history and microhistory closer to each other.[12]

Thirdly, the book investigates transimperial history through a *prism*
that reflects interactions between governments, confessional communities, and families. *Generations of Empire* approaches communities as
institutions mutating from Ottoman to Italian rule instead of taking
fixed collectivities – "the" Muslims, Orthodox, or Jews of Rhodes – as

exclusive units of analysis. All communities mediated between the state and the population they claimed to represent. They struggled to maintain the authority that imperial governments assigned to them while the same governments increased state interference in the local society, and while their coreligionists' families sensed the allure of centrifugal references. Sociopolitical change crossed confessional boundaries and most families moved in an environment not delimited by their communal belonging. The book narrates the trajectories of families and individuals of all confessions. It reflects this diversity by drawing from archival sources in eight languages, from police records to the press, from school reports to oral histories. This wide range of primary sources is the key to approach empires as containers for interactions involving mediation with and stimuli from local realities.

To investigate the motives of those interactions, lastly, the book's *foci* are the notions of "generation" and "youth." Today, next to a widespread use in advertising and merchandising, these terms are associated with activism spanning across the political spectrum, from "Youth for Climate Action" to "Generation Identity." Scholars use them as analytical categories for collectivities acting as a motor, or a product, of historical processes. While the notion of youth figured prominently in late Ottoman politics and in the fascist regime, this book sets itself apart by using youth and generations as interpretive tools rather than essentialized categories that make history. Rhodian families experienced youth under different regimes and sovereignties. Alike institutions around them, these families talked about youth and generations through a range of meanings that went beyond the Young Turk or fascist rhetoric around these terms. Actors mobilized youth and generations to situate themselves in a changing environment and to make sense of new trends and habits. This reveals everyday implications and polyphonic perceptions of imperial rule. Understanding the circumstances under which these notions mattered unearths the intersections between the shift from Ottoman to Italian sovereignty and changes in how resources were transmitted, how roles were demarcated, and how the locals reflected on the past's legacy, on present challenges, and on future scenarios.

The book's chapters investigate domains in which imperial transformations and generational dynamics interrelate: politics, the family, education, work and leisure, and mobility. Deciphering the nexus between state formation and social change through the interconnections among these fields, but also their specificities, sharpens and diversifies our image of empires, colonialism, fascism, and nationalism. The book covers the late years of Sultan Abdülhamid's rule and the Ottoman constitutional regime after 1908, followed by Italian military occupation

(1912–23) and the fascistization of Italy's sovereign rule from the 1920s
to the 1930s. It also offers an insight into the Second World War, the
arrival of German troops and the deportation of local Jews coordinated
with the Italian authorities.[13] The imperial coda sets in with the end
of Italian rule in 1945, the two years of British Military administration
and the annexation by Greece. Let us now move on into our journey by
highlighting the benefits of this transimperial periodization.

Rethinking the Imperial Consequence

Preserving elements of an earlier system is a marker of empires "turning
conquest into governing."[14] In the modern imperial history of Rhodes,
continuities outweigh ruptures. Continuity does not mean immutabil-
ity or linearity but adapting repertoires of rule. Ottoman elements made
Italian rule just as Italian rule *un*made them.

Calls for narratives framed as the "after-empire" or imperial "legacies" bloomed in the 1990s to investigate the emergence of nation-states
across area studies.[15] As Maria Todorova put it, Ottoman legacy combined "continuity" – persistence of infrastructure, modes of socialization, multi-confessional population – and "perception" – references to
the Ottoman past to claim legitimacy by successor polities.[16] Focused on
areas formerly part of the Ottoman, Habsburg, and Romanov empires,
these calls have rarely been met by works on empire-into-empire
transformations breaking the fixed periodization based on changes
of sovereignty.[17] Past imperial polities often merely echo in the post-
imperial rulers' leading voice. Since ruptures of sovereignty are central in this approach, their "after" still determines the interpretation
of what existed "before." More recent studies unearthed the motives
behind imperial continuities. As Mary D. Lewis argues for French
Tunisia, "indirect rule" and the preservation of the Bey's sovereignty
was a necessity to combine expansionism with Great Powers balance
and fragmented local jurisdictions.[18] Focusing on Bosnia, Leyla Amzi-
Erdogdular has shown that Muslim intellectuals experienced Habsburg
rule as an opportunity to continue debates on modernity which originated in Ottoman structures.[19]

The history of colonial and imperial Italy has been only marginally
studied with this approach, and it has long remained in the shadow of
narratives centred on the nation-state.[20] However, as Stephanie Malia
Hom and Pamela Ballinger recently argued, Italy's "imperial formations"
and its "long decolonization" are still underlying present structures
of integration and exclusion.[21] This is a symptom of renewed interest
in Italy's imperial and colonial past. Rhodes has its own marginality in

the historiography of Italian colonialism, partly since the Aegean *Possedimento* had an ambiguous juridical status "between a colony and a province of the kingdom."[22] Nicholas Doumanis writes of "colonizers" and "colonized" as an asymmetry of power between Italians and Dodecanesians which coexisted with cultural affinity.[23] Nicola Labanca defined the *Possedimento* as a "white colony" with a softer racial hierarchization compared to African colonies in terms of citizenship regimes and communal autonomy.[24] These differences resulted from a complex relationship between nation and empire in Italian history. Italy is often described as a nation-state which belatedly developed imperialism to reinforce its own nationalism. Roberta Pergher analyzed fascism as a "nation-empire" to illustrate demographic politics tying together new borderlands and colonies.[25] That Italy became an empire by engaging with pre-existing empires remains a neglected aspect which this book sets out to explore.

From Italy's nineteenth-century occupations in the Red Sea to the atrocities against anticolonial resistance in Libya until the 1930s, Italian colonialism collided with the Ottoman state's ambitions, it seized Ottoman territories, and it faced Ottoman legacies in those territories. The Dodecanese is a refraction of this larger picture. After 1912, ruling Rhodes meant to domesticate Ottoman institutions, to increase interference in a society shaped by the Ottoman past, and to neutralize circulations linking Rhodes to the post-Ottoman Mediterranean.[26] Whereas Karen Barkey urged to investigate the "consequences of Empire" for nation-states, this book proposes a decisive step forward.[27] Fascist colonialism was, literally, a "consequence" (Lat. *con-sequor*, follow-together) of precolonial conditions because it faced problems related to imperial rule that had already challenged the Ottoman state.

Just like histories of Mediterranean colonialism can reconsider their periodization and include the late Ottoman period, histories of the Ottoman Empire can extend towards colonial transformations. The Italian presence in Rhodes was shorter compared to post-Ottoman settings under British or French control, such as Egypt or Algeria. Still, the imperial consequence was not just the result of a short adjustment period. Until the late 1930s, fascist colonialism in Rhodes invested into continuities with Ottoman elements while presenting itself as a "reforming" and "modernizing" force. As a result, sources of the Ottoman and Italian periods dialogue with each other, sometimes separated by long distances, sometimes covered by the same dust in Rhodes's archives. Lending our eyes to documents from both periods enhances our understanding of modern empires, moving from separation towards interrelation.

Palimpsests of Empire

In 1888, Rhodes became the centre of the Vilayet of the Archipelago, also known as Vilayet of the White Sea (from Ottoman *Cezāyir-i Baḥr-i Sefīd*) including other Aegean islands like Mytilene, Chios, and Karpathos.[28] It is difficult to infer Rhodes town's population from Ottoman sources, since they often used other units of measure. In 1885, the *kaza* (a district corresponding to the judge's jurisdiction) of Rhodes included the whole island plus other islets. It had 4,903 Muslim, 2,660 Jewish, and 19,533 Christian inhabitants.[29] Greek speaking Orthodox were the large majority on minor islands and in Rhodes's villages. Only a few hundred Muslims and even fewer Jews resided in those areas, while confessions were remarkably balanced in Rhodes town. A 1917 census by the Italian military recorded 5,715 Muslims, 4,031 Orthodox, and 3,277 Jews in town, later growing to, respectively, 6,461, 5,654, and 4,038 in 1922.[30] While these proportions did not change dramatically, Catholics grew from 300 to several thousand from the 1920s onwards through immigration from Asia Minor and Italy. Most metropolitan Italians in town were traders, artisans, and civil servants, while many soldiers stayed there at the end of their service. Overall, the population of Rhodes town grew from approximately 14,000 in 1917 to 25,000 in 1936.[31]

While the town expanded, precolonial realities continued to mark everyday life. In late 1920s Rhodes, one family had an inheritance case firstly processed by a religious Jewish tribunal deliberating already before 1912 and, subsequently, by Italian state courts. Another family sent their children to a Muslim primary school founded in Ottoman times and, later, to an Italian Royal secondary school. A football team called *Fascio* played against *Diagoras*, a club created within the Ottoman Orthodox community in 1905. The Italian mail delivered to a Jewish family news from Argentina, where their relatives had emigrated at the dawn of the twentieth century. Such glimpses reflect the social and confessional diversity persisting under Italian rule. They are also palimpsests, traces of an Ottoman past not erased but reconfigured through additions. Each is also part of a longer paper trail. By unearthing Ottoman sources, we can reconstruct these palimpsests and reassess the colonial archival script.

According to Lago's "new generation," colonial youth should diverge from the "amorphous" politics that surrounded their ancestors. Lago caricaturized Ottoman society as the prehistory of his enlightened governance. Whereas he attributed to himself the virtue of enhancing a dormant population, his policies tackled a vibrant Ottoman legacy. As Marc Aymes has illustrated with regard to Cyprus, the Ottoman

Figure 0.2. A view of the Walled City of Rhodes, 1934. "Rodi, Quartier[e] Turco, 1934," AKON/Österreichische Nationalbibliothek, AK076_101.

"Province" was a dynamic space marked by circulations with imperial territories and foreign countries.[32] Rhodes was a transit port on the routes of the Levant. Travelers from Istanbul or Smyrna heading for Lebanon, Palestine, or Egypt would likely stop there. Next to numerous European travelogues, late Ottoman personalities described their itineraries in popular journals.[33] At the turn of the twentieth century, the increased exposure of new media like magazines and photographs led empires to represent themselves as civilizing forces, and the Ottomans were no exception.[34] The state intensified its presence in the provinces while these became more visible in the empire.[35] The vilayet's *salnameler* (yearbooks), listed the bureaucrats roster and the accomplished "works of just pride" (*mefharet*) such as repairing mosques, building an admiralty, a military hospital, and a soup-kitchen.[36] Public interventions were exalted by conflating the fate of Rhodes with the Ottoman order: the state as a guarantee of security, prosperity, and justice.[37]

Recent scholarship underlined Italian investments in public works and tourism to make Rhodes a "showcase" or an "emblem of colonial and Fascist modernity in the Mediterranean." This discourse resonated in Italy and reinforced the myth of empire.[38] Fascist colonialism praised the town's "Latin" architecture next to the "Mediterranean" style of its new buildings. The Foro Italico, where the governor's palace stood, became an austere esplanade outside the walled city that wished to compete with Rhodes's medieval grandeur and Ottoman monuments.[39] In so doing, Italian rule overemphasized its divergence from the past, although the rhetoric of imperial civilization was a stratagem already used by the Ottomans.[40] Framing state intervention into a broader periodization decentres discourses of colonial "modernity." New schools, cultural associations, and censuses claimed to be a novelty in the interactions between the state and its subjects. Italian colonialism shared these claims with the late Ottoman state, but it articulated them through its own variations on the theme of imperial rule.

Political Representation

Structural reforms to regulate the subjects' rights and duties preoccupied all modern empires. In late Ottoman political history, Rhodes seems peripheral because the reforms as well as the turbulence leading to the state's dissolution originated elsewhere. Yet, the island was an important destination for *sürgün* (or *nefiy*), the Ottoman political banishment, including of illustrious intellectuals like Namık Kemal, Ahmed Midhat Efendi, and Ebüzziya Tevfik Bey. Many of them, known as Young Ottomans, demanded steps towards liberalism and constitutionalism beyond the mid-nineteenth-century administrative reforms subsumed under the term *Tanzimat*.[41]

The empire had briefly experienced a constitutional regime between 1876 and 1878. After a disastrous war against Russia and a debt crisis, Sultan Abdülhamid II (1876–1909) abolished the constitution and pursued an authoritarian centralization.[42] Galvanized by the later constitutionalist momentum of the 1900s that also involved Russia and Iran, the Young Turks gained the army's support, a decisive force against Abdülhamid.[43] One morning in the summer of 1908, Rhodes woke up to the news of the Young Turks' military putsch in Istanbul which reintroduced the constitutional regime.

After 1908, the constitutional empire blended cultural effervescence with a backlash of state interference in the provinces. Ottoman parliamentary elections allowed a segment of the male population to choose their state representatives. In Rhodes as in other provinces, factionalism coexisted with the valorization of multi-confessional patriotism in the name of the freedom and fraternity that the constitution promised to Ottoman citizens.[44] Yet, the second elections of 1912 were suspended due to rumours of an imminent Italian invasion. Soon after their arrival in Rhodes, Italian military governors used repression and banishment to neutralize the risks of disorder resulting from the accelerated politicization of the last Ottoman years. After 1923, colonial rule limited elections to the local confessional communities, always surveilled by informants and police. The suspension of constitutional parliamentarism lasted longer than most contemporaries would have expected in 1912. From Italian military occupation to a fascist system antinomic to representative democracy, Rhodians would again vote for a parliament, the Greek one, only after the Second World War and the end of Italian rule.[45]

State integration also related to military service and citizenship. The Young Turks extended conscription to non-Muslims, with poor effects, in 1909.[46] In the early 1930s, Governor Lago saw military service as a precondition for local men to upgrade from subjecthood to citizenship. Conscription into the Italian army was debated until the Second World War, but it never applied to Dodecanesian subjects.[47] Whereas for the Young Turks citizenship *implied* military duty, for fascist colonialism volunteering in the army *enabled* citizenship.

After 1908, a more precise citizenship regulation tightened the bonds between the Ottoman state and its population.[48] Under Italian sovereignty, in turn, most Rhodians had a status defined as *cittadinanza* or *sudditanza italiana egea* (Italian Aegean citizenship/subjecthood). Based on the Treaty of Lausanne and on decrees coordinated between Rhodes and Rome, this replaced political rights with the notion of "personal status" (*statuto personale*) granting religious communal jurisdiction in issues such as inheritance and divorce.[49] Sources at times equal the term "subjecthood" with "citizenship," although they never question a difference between metropolitan Italian citizenship and the legal condition of Dodecanesians. In 1939, Lago's successor Cesare Maria De Vecchi drafted an eleventh-hour project to replace Aegean subjecthood with full citizenship, since he considered the former "the highest hurdle for assimilation." This unrealized plan reflected growing militarism and antisemitism in Italy. It foresaw conscription in the case of war, while the Jews, "subject to the legislation in force in the Kingdom," namely the antisemitic Racial Laws, would not be spared persecution.[50] Neither Ottoman nor Italian rulers proved capable of mobilizing a large portion of the population in an imperial province turning into a colonial possession, nor to create a lasting system of representation tying them to the empire's centre.

The Post-Ottoman Mediterranean and Fascist Colonialism

While they regulated inclusion and exclusion in state structures, Ottoman and Italian rulers acted on a broader Mediterranean stage. Already in 1887, the British antiquarian Cecil Torr included a prophecy in his erudite history of Rhodes. Attesting the "decline" of the Ottomans, he stated that the town's future would "be determined by its strategic value to a Mediterranean Power with interests in Egypt against a hostile Power in Asia Minor."[51] Torr likely considered Britain or France the only naval powers capable of seizing Ottoman territory. Very few, at that time, could anticipate Italy's occupation in the Aegean. Yet, twenty-five years later, the Italo-Ottoman war brought Rhodes into the history of Mediterranean colonialism.

A Railroad Switch of Empire

The war of 1911–12 which changed the fate of Rhodes was an intersection of imperial trajectories. For Rome, it meant "accept[ing] the challenge of imperial competition" while for the Ottomans it was an exacerbation of this competition that accelerated state disintegration.[52] As the Italians faced difficulties in advancing beyond Libya's coast, they started swift naval operations in the Mediterranean to pressure the Ottomans towards peace negotiations. After seizing other Aegean islands, on 4 May 1912, General Giovanni Ameglio entered Rhodes town. Within a few days, he forced the last Ottoman pockets of resistance to surrender. Among Ameglio's first decisions, he deported to Italy hundreds of soldiers and dozens of civilians considered close to the Young Turks.[53] The civilians' ambiguous status between prisoners of war and political banished conflated military and colonial violence: disarming the war enemy paired up with impacting local politics, which anticipated Italian rule's longer-term aims.[54]

The Treaty of Ouchy of November 1912 ended the Italo-Ottoman War. It foresaw Ottoman withdrawal from Tripolitania and Cyrenaica in exchange for returning the Aegean islands under the Sultan's control. The concomitant First Balkan War opened another front for the Ottomans and froze this treaty's implementation. Italian troops remained on the Aegean islands, although Ameglio himself considered evacuating them "for future interests in the Levant, for the prestige of our army, for the good reputation of Italy."[55] The Italian military occupation coexisted with Ottoman sovereignty, a situation similar to other empire-into-empire transformations such as British Cyprus (1878–1914) and Habsburg Bosnia (1878–1908).

At the outbreak of the First World War, while Rome remained neutral, Rhodes was still under a "pawn occupation" (1912–15). From August 1915 onwards, as Italy and the Ottoman Empire were belligerent enemies, this turned it into a "war occupation," although no front combat affected Rhodes.[56] The First World War ended with a victory for Rome and a catastrophe for Istanbul. Italian and Greek troops occupied Ottoman Western Anatolia. The two allies negotiated the unrealized Tittoni-Venizelos Agreement in 1919, through which Italy pledged to cede the Dodecanese to Greece except for Rhodes, provided the very unlikely scenario of Britain renouncing Cyprus.[57]

The Greater War afflicted the Dodecanese with scarcity and political repression, but Rhodes was in a sort of hurricane's eye. The occupation acted as a buffer in a decade of internecine "provincial violence on a grand scale" in the Aegean, which shattered a centuries-long multi-confessional coexistence on its shores.[58] In the autumn of 1922, diplomatic negotiations at Lausanne wove together the destinies of the Aegean, Italy, and the Middle East. In September, the Greek invasion of Anatolia had turned into a retreat as Mustafa Kemal's Turkish militias counterattacked. The Great Fire of Smyrna which followed was a death knell for Greek expansionist ambitions, but also for the millennial Orthodox (*Rum*) presence in Anatolia. The Lausanne Treaty forcedly displaced more than a million to Greece while more than 350,000 Muslims crossed the Aegean in the opposite direction.[59] Instead of partition into states or zones of influences, as the victorious Entente had envisioned, Anatolia remained united as a new republican and nationalized Turkey, a step which also validated the Italian occupation of Rhodes.

Rome ruled over a Mediterranean territory marked by rivalries with the French and British empires with which, however, cooperation remained possible.[60] From Cyprus to Egypt, Tunisia, and Lebanon, Italy's former war allies elaborated statehood in form of colonies, mandates, and protectorates. The common denominator was the constant anxiety about anticolonial unrest. But, hampered by the Greater War, "liberal" Italy could not define a blueprint of rule in Rhodes to counter this risk. This happened only when sovereignty allowed fascism to seize the new "imperial possibilities" created by the world conflict.[61] The decade of military occupation was, in all its uncertainty, a railroad switch separating Young Turk and fascist colonial rule. The Young Turks had tried to solve the thorny issue of governing difference by increasing their provinces' integration in the Ottoman state. In turn, fascist colonialism avoided an egalitarian integration in Italian metropolitan structures while building its colonial instruments of rule.

Enter Fascist Colonialism

While the ashes in Smyrna were still warm, in October 1922, Mussolini received a government mandate by King Vittorio Emanuele, who considered the fascist leader a needed force of stability. In Rome and in Italian provinces, in borderlands and in the colonies, fascism assimilated into state authority. From its centre, the new regime wished to create an Italian "new (wo)man," which would embody what scholars called fascism's "cultural" or even "anthropological revolution."[62] Whereas this echoes Lago's "new generation," fascism in Rhodes had to adapt to the post-Ottoman Mediterranean while exporting these visions. Paraphrasing Thomas Kühn's study on Yemen ruled by "colonial Ottomanism," Italian rule in Rhodes was less marked by colonial fascism than by fascist colonialism.[63] In other words, colonial politics of difference remained more urgent than fascist ideological penetration.

Fascism further racialized Italian nationalism while it inherited a management of colonial difference that had existed before 1922. Compared to settings under French or British control, the absence of revolts and mass violence characterized early Italian rule in Rhodes. However, Italy promulgated the antisemitic "Laws for the Defense of the Race" in 1938. The criteria for the persecution of Rhodian Jews were negotiated by governor De Vecchi with Rome and the local Jewish community. Many Jews left for the few destinations still accessible, such as Central Africa, where they were welcomed by relatives and friends.[64] Those who remained, with few exceptions, were deported in July 1944. The last phase of Italian rule pushed Rhodes into the unmixing of peoples that characterized late and post-imperial polities.[65] This genocidal vio-lence was unprecedented, but its conditions of possibility were rooted in the trajectory of fascist colonialism. It was the apex of an imperialism that progressively – and not abruptly in 1938 or 1944 – cherished mili-tarism, racism, and police surveillance.

Since its onset, fascist colonialism feared nationalism linked to neigh-bouring Greece and, to a minor extent, Turkey. Building colonial gov-ernance and order implied hampering the circulation of people and resources outside Italian control.[66] Emphasizing the insularity of Rhodes was essential to neutralize alternative references and connections that, as in most islands, tended to escape the "isolation" prompted by state rule. Lago exploited insularity to surveil the mobility of colonial sub-jects and unwelcomed individuals. At the same time, he fostered the Italian presence through settler colonies of woodcutters and farmers like Campochiaro and Peveragno Rodio.[67] The regime showcased these colonies in newsreels which also displayed the exotic Mediterranean allure of Rhodes. The exoticization of Aegean islands later combined with the emphasis on local traces of the Roman and Christian past, particularly evident in Rhodes town. This legitimized a fascist empire projected towards the future and neutralized the impression that for-eign influence existed in its territory.[68] In fact, the interwar Mediterra-nean generated and fostered other ideologies like Revisionist Zionism, Kemalist nationalism, and Greek Irredentism, that the colonial govern-ment feared and repressed until its end. Fascism was thus not the only political reference towards which colonial subjects positioned them-selves. Rather, it was the only one tolerated by Italian rule.

Yet, what was the civil governors' understanding of fascism? While eight military governors succeeded one another between 1912 and 1921, only two civil governors – Lago and De Vecchi – ruled Rhodes between 1923 and 1940 in the name of Italian sovereignty.[69] The dif-ferences between the two have shaped a controversial interpretation of fascism in the Dodecanese. Luca Pignataro has relativized fascism contrasting Lago's tempered rationalism with De Vecchi's ideological and emphatical aggressivity, thus also contrasting a positive evalua-tion of Italian colonialism with its (moderately) negative later devel-opment.[70] This differentiation resonates in the memory of Greeks and Jews who lived under Italian rule, as argued by Nicholas Doumanis.[71] Valerie McGuire expanded this debate by describing these memories as the ambivalent result of, on the one hand, the locals' positive per-ception of everyday interactions with Italians and their culture and, on the other hand, interactions with the Italian state negatively associated with fascism.[72]

Even by turning from memories to archival sources, differences between Lago and De Vecchi cannot be overlooked. This, however, corresponds to the variety that one would find within the fascist apparatus in the metropole as well as among successive colonial administrators in other empires. Reading Italian rule with a focus on Lago and De Vecchi as Janus-faced fascist colonialism would fall short due to a "great men" bias. The local society did not change only based on the governors' attitude, and fascist colonialism in Rhodes evolved within a broader shift. Mussolini's regime increased its expansionism from the mid-1930s onwards, which also corresponded to the Fascist Party's growing grip on society, in Italy as well as in the colonies. In Rhodes, De Vecchi's rigid interpretation of fascism did not undo Lago's governance. It built upon its principle – minimizing disorder and unloyalty – adapting to changing circumstances on the ground, in state politics, and in regional geopolitics. Reinforcing state juridical institutions, dissolving communal schools and associations, and banishing political opponents marked the late 1930s, but Lago already achieved them before De Vecchi arrived in Rhodes.

Until the Second World War, fascism in Rhodes produced a considerably lesser degree of physical violence compared to most Italian towns but also colonies. At the same time, as Filippo Espinoza has argued, Rhodes was ruled through discrimination between collaborators and antagonists as well as through state-driven capitalism alike other Italian provinces.[73] Fascism can neither be downsized as accessory nor essentialized as totalitarian. It was a mighty force adapting to and influenced by the local setting. The book discusses fascism as a marker of colonial difference, a militant institution, and a language of power that had to make its way into the local fabric. Adult Italian citizens were entitled to join the National Fascist Party while colonial subjects could only support it. As spearhead of *Italianità*, party militancy reinforced the members' privileged position at the intersection of citizenship, religion, and ethnicity. For the rest, fascism consolidated the subalternity of Aegean subjects, regardless of their ideological orientation.

Yet, these subjects did not remain indifferent. The semantics of fascism characterized petitions to the colonial government requesting material aid. Rhodians could also creatively appropriate fascist motives to discredit someone through rumours that were occasionally intercepted by the police. Fascism thus generated many examples fitting James C. Scott's notion of infrapolitics, the "circumspect struggles" through which subjects engaged with the rulers' supremacy and ideas.[74] The locals could associate fascism with the Italian occupation in toto, ranging from hyperbolic support to overt despisal. In sum, although the party progressively gained importance, integration into fascism never became a reality for the whole population. Reinforcing the difference between rulers and ruled, fascism was the "new generation's" horizon: it pointed to its destiny while being impossible to reach.

Seen from the 1930s, Torr's 1887 prediction was not wrong after all. Fascist Italy had become a Mediterranean power with expansionist ambitions in North Africa and it rivalled other states in the Aegean. Yet, what the British scholar had called the "fate" of Rhodes was not limited to geopolitics. In most reports sent by Italian governors from 1912 to the Second World War, the assessment of the situation on the ground occupied a central place. Sovereignty in a post-Ottoman colony implied engaging with local power structures and with the population's expectations.

A Rule of Interaction between the State, Communities, and Families

When Governor Lago invoked a "new generation," he addressed the question of how colonial subjects should be "welcomed" in the Fascist Party. He anticipated that youth would prefer fascism over identifications based on "race and religion." In Rhodes and other post-Ottoman settings, like Habsburg Bosnia, emphasizing generations and youth as collectives reinforced boundaries of belonging, be it as confessional, ideological, or national communities.[75] Lago's statement leaves unsaid that his rule reinforced "race and religion" institutionally. He saw confessional communities as the direct bond of loyalty linking the state to colonial subjects. Italian rule arguably relied more on communal institutions than late Ottoman administration, while it expanded the surveillance on the communities' notables and associations.

Colonial state governance was a gameboard where communities and families were players, not pawns. Confessional boundaries were a rule within this game, albeit not relevant enough to determine its outcome. The book therefore includes actors and institutions of all confessions, stressing how similar challenges posed by state governance could lead to different reactions. In certain cases, identifying as a Jew, an Orthodox, or a Muslim was an important marker for parents and children, pupils and teachers, notables and workers. In others, communal belonging remained marginal compared to gender, class, kinship, and profession. Including communities and families in the narrative illustrates who, why, and how conformed or diverged from the norms prescribed by successive state regimes as these regimes sought a balance between politics of difference and a more direct control over their population. In this sense, Alf Lüdtke's notion of rule as "social praxis" is inspiring to investigate multilayered relations of power and differentiated responses to domination.[76] Communities drew their legitimacy from being intermediary institutions between government and families. All three forces produced cohesion and fragmentation, which also transformed the function of communal mediation.

Reframing Communities across Empires

The diversity of the population of Rhodes implies asking to which extent interactions were divided along confessional lines. Communities are *one*, yet not the only dimension that shaped social bonds. Ottoman and Italian rulers adapted their approaches to communal institutions through time. To different degrees in its provinces, the late Ottoman Empire was marked by sectarianism and confessionalization.[77] Ottoman communities were local instances of empire-wide autonomy structures which gained visibility after the revolution of 1908.[78] In Rhodes, there existed Orthodox and Jewish communal bodies, while the fewer Catholics, be they Roman, Armenian, or Syriac, did not have equivalent structures. With or without an official institution called community, the identification with a confessional category could be a "parallel and mutually nurturing" process in regard to the Ottoman state. After 1908, its constitutional regime – at first – promoted coexistence as an aggregative force.[79] It is no surprise that, in 1909, the newspaper in Greek *Rodos* opened with the slogan "Long live the Constitution" next to an article discussing communal reforms.[80]

Communal bonds persisted after the end of Ottoman rule, although the juridical and political notion of community underwent a transformation.[81] Post-Ottoman states referred to the previous *"millet* system" with different attitudes towards local realities.[82] In general, colonial and national states turned communities into majorities and minorities.[83] On the contrary, Italian rule in Rhodes mostly avoided those terms.[84] Only partially explicable through the town's demographic balance in confessional terms, this resulted from Italian colonial anxieties after the First World War. The governors perceived the dangers encoded in the new language of national belonging, legitimacy, and anti-imperialism of the "Wilsonian moment."[85] Talking about majorities and minorities could associate "Orthodox" with "Greeks" and "Muslims" with "Turks," nourishing irredentism and discrediting the colonial denominations of "Dodecanesians" or "Aegeans." Preexisting communities were instrumentalized based on the belief that holding a colonial setting to a stage "before the nation" would neutralize anti-imperialism.[86]

In 1930, Lago redefined the communities' statutes, also introducing a "Muslim Community" unconceivable for the Ottoman state that saw Sunni Islam as its official religion.[87] Like other colonial powers, Italy promised "autonomy" and "respect" for confessional institutions and demanded their strict obedience in return.[88] Communal leaders accepted this bargain and stabilized fascist colonialism. They were not entitled to elaborate own visions of fascism, but they reiterated its legitimacy and its idea that alternative identifications were to be eradicated. The persecution of Rhodian Jews proved this transaction's volatility. While Lago cultivated a special bond with Jewish notables, state antisemitism in the late 1930s dramatically changed this relationship. Despite efforts by the community, expulsions and the eventual deportation of 1944 did not spare local Jews. Colonial communal structures served the rulers' control though separation more than the protection or the autonomy of the population.

The relationship between communities and families was more complex to handle for the rulers. While many subjects complied with the colonial order, others challenged it by pursuing interactions and identifications beyond the community and the government's reach. When Rhodians praised Italian rule in the community's newspapers, or when they enrolled in communal sport clubs, fascist colonialism's ruling scheme seemed to work. As soon as they criticized communal institutions or circumvented the political immobility implied in colonial subjecthood, Italian rulers felt threatened. Eventually, Lago's wish that Rhodians become both legally subaltern subjects and fervent supporters of fascist rule proved not viable.

Communal belonging in Rhodes also left a trace in memorial and historiographical narratives, which Alexis Rappas has defined as "soliloquies" of separated collectivities.[89] Some authors have aimed at preserving forgotten spaces of Turkishness outside Anatolia. Others have focused on the Jews of Rhodes and blend memoirs, folklore, and history, stressing good relations with the Ottoman and Italian authorities with hints to tension with the Orthodox population. A different corpus emphasizes foreign domination over local Greeks, connoted as *tourkokratia* and *italokratia*. The trope of the "foreign yoke" echoes irredentist pamphlets published before 1945, which reclaimed the Dodecanese, including Rhodes, as exclusively Greek. They depict the Orthodox population as both victim and resistant vis-à-vis two regimes favouring local Jews over Greeks.[90] Most of these narratives ignore or neglect each other, arguing for the coherence of each community as part of broader Turkish, Jewish, or Greek collective identities.

Studies on intercommunality in (post-)Ottoman studies offer an alternative to soliloquies, although they risk overemphasizing the relevance of communal belonging for human interactions.[91] Individuals are not *atomic* representatives of a group called community, just as communities are not *molecular* representatives of these individuals. For instance, "the Orthodox community" as an analytical category does not overlap with "the Orthodox" as a collectivity, and vice versa. As "communalist" organizers channelled resources within the community to foster collective belonging, this led to diverse outcomes ranging from enthusiasm to indifference to criticism.[92] Retracing how all communities oscillated between cohesion and fragmentation, and how this interplayed with imperial and international sociopolitical transformations, allows us to move beyond a state-centred approach without essentializing communities as the perimeter of historical analysis.

Policing and Profiling

Bringing governance, communities, and everyday life closer to each other reveals appropriation, negotiation, and contestation of political projects. In sum, these outcomes are what Alf Lüdtke called the actors' *Eigensinn*.[93] However, the state was in a privileged position vis-à-vis other forces. As Martin Thomas argued, colonial governance was anxious when facing little-known local realities. The state tackled this problem by laboriously collecting information. One of the pivotal tasks of colonial bureaucracy was policing, which proved the colonial state's "closer interest in the family lives of their citizenry."[94] A novelty of the Italian period was surveillance through the *Carabinieri*. This royal police corps arrived in Rhodes in 1912, but a dramatic rise in their production of documents occurred after 1932. Their archive has recently been recovered and this book explores it in its breadth.[95] Although the *Carabinieri*'s reports circulated only within government structures, the police communicated colonial order through visible interference in everyday situations, similar to other settings like German Southwest Africa.[96] Some local informants and translators worked for an institution that maintained a rigid colonial hierarchization as part of the Italian army. The *Carabinieri* covered political surveillance and criminal investigations, but also issued passports or hunting permits, business licenses, residence permits for foreign nationals.

Before and after 1912, other institutions partook in this process of profiling, aimed at reconstruing life trajectories and social relationships. Whether in the case of an Ottoman schoolteacher asking a pupil to describe his relationship with parents and friends, or a teenager interrogated by the Italian tribunal for a petty crime, institutions needed information about individuals who, through different modalities, responded to this demand. The documents produced by profiling the local population are the "tear in the fabric of time," to follow Arlette Farge's formulation. They shed light on relations of power beyond a narrow understanding of politics. The fragments of the actors' voices reveal how imperial institutions reached down to the intimate sphere.[97]

Central to profiling was "morality," an important notion for Ottoman society which Italian rule further bureaucratized. The colonial police included a judgment on *condotta morale* (moral conduct) next to *condotta politica* in the individual file called *specchietto informativo*. In these exchanges, the authorities focused on generational bonds to gather information about an individual's social environment. Were Rhodians economically dependent on their parents? Did sentimental and sexual relationships with peers impact their "reputation" in the eyes of the neighbourhood or the community? How did they raise their children? This intimate knowledge was not always retrieved through spies or informants. Individuals also described generational bonds voluntarily to make their own situation comprehensible to the authorities. Talking in terms of generations and youth allowed institutions and families to make sense of each other, negotiating integration and exclusion in a changing social order.

Generations, Youth, and Political Change

Governor Lago knew that building a new colonial society would primarily target the "indigenous youth." Although the term "indigenous" demarcated colonized from colonizers, all children could access fascist youth organizations until the age of 21. Coming of legal age ended this hybridity, as locals were (generally) excluded from full Italian citizenship and membership in the Fascist Party. The governor's statement quoted above is an outstanding case of authorities explicitly discussing generations and youth. The omnipresence of these terms in the political language until today proves their flexibility. Regimes and media around the world use them for different messages. Yet, generations and youth, like all notions, have their own historicity. They gained relevance in societies undergoing rapid sociopolitical transformations.

Generations as Socialization

In the period discussed in this book, European thinkers like Wilhelm Pinder and Karl Mannheim invented the "problem" of generations to interpret the rhythm underlying social and cultural change. Casting a long shadow on the humanities and the social sciences, they conceived of generations as units of analysis, collectivities that made – and were made by – history.[98] By entering a dialogue with scholarship on generations in the Ottoman and post-Ottoman world, *Generations of Empire* has a hermeneutical rather than essentializing approach.[99] History is not forcibly made by reified generations (such as the "lost generation," the "boomers," or the "millennials"), but it can be explained through generational dynamics.[100]

This differentiation links generational dynamics with the process of socialization, addressed by other thinkers of the early twentieth century like Georg Simmel, who investigated the complexity of modern life. Socialization is the set of interactions (*Wechselwirkungen*) through which individuals become part of collectivities.[101] In this process, they do not only actively *socialize,* they are also *socialized* by institutions. The domestic, the communal, and the governmental sphere concurred in determining norms of socialization and sanctioning their transgression. Generations were rarely mentioned explicitly in Rhodes but, when this was the case, pivotal issues like boundaries of belonging or social stratification were at stake. For Young Turks and fascist alike, "new generations" reflected a load of ideology and loyalty that they placed upon the youth's shoulders. Beyond these motives, generational dynamics worked as a middle ground between the individual and the collective. Exploring this middle ground reveals how authorities, communities, and families coped with their own apprehensions. Studying interactions beyond explicit references to a "new generation" helps understand what the "new imperial Italy" actually was and how it emerged from an Ottoman environment.

Youth between Words and Groups

The normative character of generational dynamics often involves the notion of youth. But what do actors mean when they use this word? Youth has a long history as a nationalist or anti-imperial mobilizing motive. It stretches through the nineteenth and twentieth centuries from Giuseppe Mazzini's revolutionary club *Giovane Italia* against the Habsburgs to Frantz Fanon's appeal to the "Youth of Africa, Madagascar, and the West Indies" joining forces against French colonialism.[102] Youth fuelled radical movements through the idea of a generational rupture. Oftentimes, however, it was a notion mobilized by elders from the outside to de-legitimize these movements and highlight their lack of experience.[103] The historiography of youth has an increasingly transnational agenda in which, however, the category of empire still lags behind.[104] Visions of youth in fact originated within modern empires and, by voicing dissent, demands of reforms, or ideological adherence, they reflected the social, political, and cultural transformations of those empires.

Ottoman history contains crucial references to youth, like the Young Ottomans and the Young Turks' movements. As to fascism, the party's anthem was entitled "Youth" (*Giovinezza*), which symptomizes how its leaders instrumentalized a generational conflict to nourish a "myth of youth." This built on previous influences but exacerbated the cult of violence and death, as Sven Reichardt has illustrated.[105] Yet, fascism did not celebrate youth without qualification. In her study on Venice, Kate Ferris has shown how the virtues of youth were glorified only inasmuch as they strengthened the Fascist Party, repressing diverging youth voices and practices.[106] But state-driven projects did not have a monopoly on the connotation of youth. Accordingly, one would search in vain for specificities of Rhodian youth as a coherent collective, or as a reflection of Ottoman or Italian youth. A Young Turk newspaper, an Italian colonial governor, an Orthodox student, a rabbi, or a Muslim notable might have used the term youth with quite different aims. Yet, all considered it socially and politically relevant, be it as an object to mould, a responsibility to claim, or a symptom to criticize. Rhodes was a permeable space in which the notion of youth evolved through external impulses processed locally. Youth was therefore a *situational* term used in contingent configurations with different meanings.

Speaking of youth did not define what youth was and was not. Pierre Bourdieu famously stated that youth "is nothing but a word" concealing distinctions in terms of class, race, and gender.[107] Henri Lefebvre suggested that the idealization of youth originates more from "the guilty conscience of the elders" than it is cherished by youths themselves, although the latter can appropriate it.[108] While we usually attach anxiety, inquietude, and explorative experiences to youth, these feelings were equally relevant to adult institutions. Luisa Passerini argued that youth represented "a metaphor of social change" for different state regimes.[109] By shifting the view towards our transimperial narrative, this formula can be paraphrased. Youth emphasized – positively or negatively – the change of social metaphors through which state, communities, and families interpreted their condition: a uniform provided by the state versus a badge venerated autonomously by local students, virtuous marriage versus vicious promiscuity, formative schools versus dangerous streets, healthy bodies versus debauched night-cafés, overseas emigration versus the transmission of customs. Youth was a *correlative* term determining the value of such concepts and objects when it connected them to belonging and loyalty.

New travelling ideas and political transformations impacted socialization patterns through an increased attention on youth. When political change occurs, in general, the more negative the perception of the recent past, the more positive the expectation of the near future and vice versa, depending on whether one considers the winners or the losers' perspective within this change. One way or another, institutions speaking of youth claimed their present legitimacy by expanding it into the future or rooting it into the past. Be it the "enlightened" youth of Ottoman constitutionalist forces or the "indigenous" youth mobilized by Lago, this term embodied hopes and anxieties within a changing relationship between state and society. Youth was, therefore, a *projective* term. By revealing situational negotiations, correlations between concepts and norms, and projections of legitimacy into the future and into the past, youth is much more than a simple word, yet less than a coherent group.

Generations of Empire discusses generational dynamics and youth to interpret the imperial consequence from Ottoman to Italian rule in five fields of socialization. Chapter 1 makes the case for a more diversified approach to the field of political identification and mobilization. It describes how the Young Turks merged the idea of a "new generation" of youth with innovations in imperial rule to establish a rupture with Abdülhamid's reign, an example of the *functional* feature of generational dynamics mobilized for political purposes. In the same period, the expansion of political participation and an incepting elite circulation caused a juvenilization of politics. This preceded the politicization of youth emerging during the Italian military occupation. Italian authorities attached youth to exaltation and risks of disorder against their effort to gain control over communal institutions. After a decade of institutional transformation following the Treaty of Lausanne, the politicization of youth reappeared in the 1930s. Alternative identifications circulating in the post-Ottoman Mediterranean, such as Revisionist Zionism, Kemalism, and Greek irredentism, came to be identified as youth movements and were not tolerated by the colonial authorities. Early fascist activism, in turn, missed the mobilization of youth observable in Italy. Only as a part of the ruling apparatus did fascism reach to youth from above. Until the Second World War, fascism remained caught in the dilemma of combining hierarchization based on colonial difference with the indoctrination of loyal subjects. In so doing, it often betrayed the local youth's hopes of equality expressed through their voluntary fascist militancy.

State and communal institutions in Rhodes raised their ambitions to pervade different domains of youth socialization. In chapter 2, the book turns to the family as a container for generational dynamics. Family segmentation based on age and lineage shaped the circulation of resources, which in turn reproduced social structures.[110] I inquire into this *transmissional* feature of generations through the analysis of population censuses, family certificates, life memoirs, hand-out requests, as well as dowry and inheritance juridical documents. The chapter describes how family structures remained relatively stable until the Second World War, although generational roles were constantly negotiated reflecting a changing sociopolitical reality. Italian rule increased the bureaucratization of marriage, which persisted as a norm but resulted from situations ranging from affection to calculations and violence against women. The monetization of the living space increased legal disputes among kin and favoured the nuclearization of households. These disputes had a generational dimension and were managed by a plural jurisdiction based on confession next to Italian state tribunals, until communal courts were abolished in the late 1930s. As they raised state interference in family issues, colonial authorities faced the appropriation of these tighter bonds by the local population. Families traded expressions of loyalty to fascism for material aid by the authorities, establishing a convergence between the fate of the kin and that of the state.

In chapter 3, the book addresses the domain of education. It focuses on secondary schools, a novelty of the late Ottoman period. State and communal institutions as well as missionaries and foreign organizations created a semantic link between youth and students. These schools proposed a new notion of education merging knowledge, manners, and idea(l)s. By transferring parent-child relationships into school socialization and teacher-pupil relationship into the family, educational institutions also tackled the notions of morality and communal belonging. This highlights the *relational* feature of generational dynamics, namely how demarcation based on age and roles resonated in broader collectivities than those interacting directly. After 1923, Italian rule aimed to remove foreign influences and italanize the schools' personnel and diplomas. This did not erase the circulation of students abroad that colonial governors feared as the origin of uncontrolled politicization. Indeed, schools had been sites of unrest even before the beginning of Italian sovereignty. During the military occupation, students protested and interpreted the Greater War's turmoil by addressing local, regional, and even global politics.

Negotiations at school also related to changing conditions for work and leisure, analysed in chapter 4. Communities and authorities were interested in the productive and non-productive activities of the population to establish a gendered notion of "morality." For women, it meant modest sexuality constrained by patriarchy. For men, it meant the absence of idleness, debts, and addiction. Italian rule raised pressure on family-owned companies, who adapted from generation to generation to a colonial economic space and the authorities' political control. This pressure also applied to precarious labour and unemployment, connoted as "vagrancy," "vice," and "idleness." Lower class families requested the colonial government's intervention to "correct" their children misbehaviour, although the authorities generally pushed the responsibility of virtuous upbringing back to parents. Communities put (limited) material efforts aimed at securing a smooth transition from school to work, while notables voiced their coreligionists' moral decay as a youth problem. Young women's precarious labour such as domestic service and sex work gained momentum during Italian rule due to the inflow of men from Italy. Official documents often did not recognize these occupations and subsumed them under the term "housewife," while they regulated the sex market through increased police control. The chapter also discusses football, a new leisure activity which brought about new representations of masculine youth. Amateur societies and teams came under the control of communal structures and were later domesticated by state institutions, until fascism increased its role in the management of sports in the 1930s.

Chapter 5 looks at Rhodes as a space marked by forms of mobility which redefined belonging to the community and the nation. Its first part focuses on how Jewish and Orthodox emigrants from Rhodes who left mostly in the last Ottoman years handled the bonds with their homeland while establishing new communal institutions overseas. Norms of family building and upbringing aimed at keeping the migrants within the boundaries of the respective community. This happened despite the proximity which characterized many Orthodox and Jews prior to departure and during the first years abroad. The second part of the chapter discusses how metropolitan citizens and former Italian *protégés* from Anatolia settled in Rhodes and were integrated in the Italian national-imperial body politic. The paradox was that precisely those embodying *Italianità* often intermarried with local women, blurring colonial hierarchies within the family. Involvement in the Fascist Party compensated to some extent the "anomy" of exogamy and economic difficulties. The expectation to mould future generations of settlers reinforcing Italian superiority was as urgent as disciplining these settlers' socialization in the present.

A fascist new generation, like the one invoked by Young Turks decades earlier, did not materialize because the war catastrophe connected with the regime's growing militarism brought Italian rule to an end. The Second World War produced the non-healing wound of the Holocaust while the history of empires in Rhodes faded through the annexation by the Greek nation-state. The epilogue sketches this imperial coda through personal trajectories discussed along generational dynamics. The "new imperial Italy" shaped the history, the landscape, and the memory of Rhodes, but it encountered constraints from below and from outside related to making "new imperial Italians." Facing the challenge to domesticate a post-Ottoman setting in a regional context in flux, Italian state authorities did not sacrifice a colonial mindset based on difference on the altar of political integration in their dictatorial empire.

Chapter One

The Emergence of Youth as a Political Category

In July 1908, the Young Turk movement initiated a revolution in the Ottoman Empire that led to the reintroduction of a constitutional regime. This heterogenous galaxy composed of Turkish nationalists and liberals, proponents of centralization and decentralization, non-Muslim radical activists and military officers had coalesced in the previous years united by their opposition to Sultan Abdülhamid II's authoritarian rule. The Yung Turks were not a popular, but rather an elite movement. Once in power, however, they were capable of conflating some of the problems of what they considered the Ottoman *ancien régime* in a discourse addressing large segments of the empire's society.[1] As diverse as these groupings and their specific agendas were, it is no wonder that the dawn of the new constitutional regime saw effervescent discussions about the future of the state which rapidly expanded from centres like Istanbul and Salonica to the provinces of the Ottoman Empire.

A few months after the constitution had been re-established, in May 1909, the first issue of the Rhodian newspaper *Afitāb* published a column that praised the new regime and directly addressed youth: "Hey, enlightened youth, thou shall not forget! A whetstone from the roots of the generations' (*ceẓur-i nesliñ*) … future has heralded you in front of humanity like excellent blossoms (*şkūfe-i muzāyā gibi*)." The article exhorted youth to activism, claiming that "it is not the past glory (*fahr-ı māmża*), but the traces of the zeal (*āṣār-ı gayret*) prepared by present efforts (*sa 'y-ı mā fi el-ḥāl*)" which prove a generation's virtue. Its author, signing as M. Nuri, stressed the importance of an education jointly developing brains (*dimāg*) and hearts (*ḳalb*). While mentioning youth and future generations, the column also referred to a recently passed Law on vagrancy (*Serserī niẓāmnāmesi*) in order to stigmatize those who "spend their lives in coffeehouses." By contrast, it praised the "holy work(s)" (*ā 'māl-ı muḳaddese*) beneficial to the "fatherland's prosperity" and to "national progress." Education and productivity were part of an equation in which state politics were a central factor. The new constitutional administration (*idāre-yi meşrūṭe*) would vitalize a state compared to a living organism. The Ottoman "enlightened youth" would have to contribute with their zeal, since the "right to be public citizens" (*teba 'a-yi ma 'rūfe olmak ḥakkı*), recently enacted by the new regime, was per se not sufficient for the state's virtuous development.[2]

In those early months after the revolution, the Young Turks did not become a cohesive, one-sided political force. Their movement displayed differences causing rivalries and frictions. Altogether, however, it succeeded in transforming politics from Istanbul, the centre of the empire where many Young Turk leading personalities had studied in elite schools. They did not confine their ambitions to structural novelties like a parliament and a constitution. They aimed to reinforce the state's grip on the population and to inspire among the latter a stronger attachment to the empire. Bearing the notion in their very name, the Young Turks emphasized youth as an "autonomous force," a "new generation" (*nesl-i cedīd*) blossoming on the ashes of Hamidian despotism.[3] The leaders of the constitutional regime invested in youth to foster Ottoman nation-building, militarism, and competition with rival states. The political turbulence in the empire created a tension between past and future, instability and hope, which also translated into generational tensions. Despite a stronger bond, politics in the main centres of the empire differed from politics in provinces like Rhodes, where explicit mentions of youth related to the new Ottoman political climate, such as the *Afitāb* column, remained exceptional.

The Italian invasion of 1912 severed the direct link between the "excellent blossoms" mentioned in that article and the Ottoman Empire's fate. A decade later, Italy equally experienced a tectonic change in state politics with the establishment of the first government led by Benito Mussolini. It was under this same government dominated by the Fascist Party that Italy obtained sovereignty over the Dodecanese in 1923. In the following years, the colonial authorities were in charge of transferring indoctrination from the metropole, where youth had been pivotal in Mussolini's mobilization of the masses, to the Aegean *Possedimento*.

In 1937, the government's newspaper *Il Messaggero di Rodi*, published a report on the *Leva fascista* festivities. This yearly event marked the passage of cohorts from one section of the fascist youth organization to the next. The newspaper's cover quoted the *Duce* stating that "fascist Italy entrusts you [youth] with its grandeur and its victory."[4] In the same issue, a local commentator highlighted the value of youth: "We can say without ostentation that we are proud of being among ranks of very strapping (*gagliarda*) youth educated, in the purest sense of the word, in the fascist ethics and fully aware of the tasks and goals that the Regime intends to achieve to create new generations of soldiers citizens, fully worth of the new imperial fatherland."[5]

Reading this article together with the 1909 *Afitāb* piece reveals a striking imperial consequence. Fascists and Young Turks alike exhorted local youth as the engine of imperial rule. The fascist dictatorial and expansionist empire in 1937 was surely a different framework from the Young Turks' empire venturing into a constitutional regime in order not to collapse in 1909. Yet, fascist propaganda claimed to fulfil hopes which resembled those raised thirty years earlier by the Young Turks: marking a break with the past while laying stable foundations for the future. Mobilizing youth from above during political transformations was part of an early twentieth-century transnational Zeitgeist. If the new generations of "excellent blossoms" could appear and wither at different points in time and in specific looks, the notion of youth was the common root of several regimes: it was meant to strengthen the bond between the state and its society acting like the glue tying together a plant and its soil. Still, Young Turks and fascists knew that such pompous images of youth as "new (wo)men" and "new generations" did not imply an effective control over a population marked by social and confessional diversity.

The generational approach to politics proposed in this chapter is far from the idea that Rhodians simply shifted from being "Young Turks" to becoming "Young Fascists." Reflecting on generational dynamics and representations of youth tackles the gap between entities imagined by state regimes and the impact of these regimes within family relationships. The rhetoric mobilization of youth was one thing, another thing was the implication of this mobilization in personal interactions and life trajectories. Bearing this distinction in mind allows us to describe the transformation of political commitment within imperial polities, as Rhodes changed from an Ottoman province into a fascist colony. This chapter investigates how Rhodians appropriated the political climate of their time in terms of participation, negotiation, and dissent. Moreover, it expands the look on political activism in Rhodes beyond ruling and mobilizing forces such as the Committee of Union and Progress (CUP) or the Fascist Party. Without downplaying an asymmetry of power in which Ottoman and Italian state authorities were dominant, the chapter ventures in webs of social bonds to understand why youth mattered "on the ground." It illustrates what meaning was attached to this notion, and what repercussions being the child or the parent of a person involved in politics could have up and down the generational ladder.

The chapter argues that Rhodes experienced an incepting juvenilization of politics in the last Ottoman years which evolved into a politicization of youth during Italian rule. As in other settings around the globe in the early twentieth century, youth became a political category under colonial rule. Politics were not necessarily or simply *made* by young actors, but they were now *pertinent* to youth. This notion expanded to a synonym of both activism and loyalty.[6]

The late Ottoman years saw the emergence of new forms of mobilization and representation in the provinces. The rupture with the past was legitimized by elders by stressing a juvenilization of the political language louder than the actual voice of youngsters. This prepared the stage for early Italian military governors to interpret politics in the new territory in terms of "youth" and "elders." The politically vibrant 1910s were marked by the rise of factionalism in the Ottoman state, warfare in the region, and the military occupation in Rhodes, which increased the pressure on existing power relations. Reciprocal denouncements, the substitution of religious leaders, and banishments all point to a turmoil that affected governors and notables alike. Although the young "excellent blossoms" in Rhodes did not bear the fruits that Ottoman constitutionalists had hoped for, youth in Rhodes remained a notion which refracted the twilight, rather than the sudden demise, of the Ottoman Mediterranean and its imperial politics. During the Greater War (1912–23), Italian authorities considered the politicization of Rhodian youth a danger for public order. Yet, they did not ascribe to youngsters the capacity to elaborate political ideas autonomously. The military governors were most concerned about how adults in persisting Young Turk and surging Greek irredentist networks manipulated youth.

After Lausanne, fascist colonial rule assumed that local politics, understood as a polyphonic field, should not exist. Lago claimed to base his government on the "respect" of local religious communities. This respect implied that loyal and local communities were the political perimeter for the adult population. Beyond communities, political activism was a domain reserved to Italian full citizens, the only category entitled to join the Fascist Party. The communalization fostered by Italian rule, however, was not only a preservation of Ottoman organization of difference. It was also an originally colonial tool to isolate what, already before 1923, had emerged as a political field receptive to outer influences. In the 1920s, Italian rule made politics more ideologically charged and pervasive in the public sphere. Public and official statements, supported by the *Messaggero,* propagated a cultural revolution in the name of *Italianità.* The room left for the autonomous expressions of the local youth shrank. Moreover, the interference of neighbouring states like Turkey and Greece was feeble. Both these newborn republican polities were more preoccupied with internal instability than with exerting influence on the population of Rhodes.

The colonial ruling scheme of "local and loyal" surely brought results, especially compared to other Mediterranean settings like Syria or Cyprus, where anticolonial movements erupted in organized revolts. Yet, the 1930s revealed that Rhodes remained exposed to the Eastern Mediterranean political arena. Rhodians responded to other nationalist movements, all of which attached a special value to youth. They all intersected with the authority of fascism in Rhodes and provoked its reaction. Some Muslim youth were receptive to Mustafa Kemal's Turkish nationalism. Jewish youth elaborated an original synthesis of Zionism and fascism with a strong sense of male peer solidarity, creating a conflict with the community's elders. Orthodox youth confronted the authorities even more explicitly by refusing to obey new assimilationist policies after the new governor De Vecchi arrived in Rhodes.

These almost simultaneous movements had different motives and degrees of antagonism with regard to Italian rule. Moreover, each gathered youngsters identifying with the respective confessional or ethnic category. Still, discussing them together underscores a significant shift in the politicization of youth in a colonial, post-Ottoman setting. Compared to the 1910s, Italian authorities now acknowledged youth in Rhodes as an autonomous, and therefore dangerous political entity capable of challenging the politically fossilized communal institutions. Although these movements remained minoritarian and ephemeral, they reveal the boundaries set by fascist colonialism to youth politicization as well as the broader horizons emerging among local youth. The salience of youth was reflexive for the authorities: the more fascist colonialism was preoccupied with bringing youth under its control, the more it became alarmed by signs of divergence, therefore interpreting alternative allegiances as a problem of youth.

Facing these potentially divergent identifications, colonial rule had little answers other than repression and indoctrination. The *Carabinieri* had the essential task of surveilling and intervening with admonitions and sanctions, massively raising the authorities' interference in the everyday interactions of the locals. This authoritarian attitude, observable since 1912 but increasing significantly in the late 1930s, contributed to the perception that the end of fascism would mean the simultaneous collapse of Italian rule in the Dodecanese. The very emergence of fascism in Rhodes happened differently than in the metropole. Juvenile practices and symbols of fascist violence in post-war Italy, which turned fascism from a street movement to a ruling party, were barely relevant in Rhodes. Embedded in colonial sovereignty from the start, fascism operated as an institution from above, rather than founding its original legitimacy on youth activism.

Since access to the Fascist Party was reserved to Italian citizens, local youth whose parents were not part of this category could only partake in fascism activism until 21 years of age. This is where the main dilemma of fascist colonialism in a post-Ottoman context emerged. Granting continuity from youth to adulthood in terms of affiliation to fascism would contrast the colonial hierarchy established in Rhodes based on the imperial consequence with precolonial Ottoman structures. If fascism was the quintessential expression of *Italianità*, could it be shared equally with colonial subjects? Lago used youth as the elusive way out from the dilemma of how to foster support of fascism while keeping the separation between Italians and "indigenous" subjects in terms of citizenship, confession, and – increasingly – race. Youth thus became a conundrum of colonial rule, a litmus test for both the management of difference and for ideological propaganda. Talking "youth" and "new generations" legitimized Italian rule by projecting a solution to this dilemma in the future. In so doing, fascist colonialism replicated the problems faced by late Ottoman politicians and communal leaders, which culminated in the constitutional period after 1908.

The Juvenilization of Politics in Late Ottoman Rhodes

At the turn of the twentieth century, a new connection between provincial and state politics in the Ottoman Empire laid the groundwork for a later politicization of youth under Italian rule. Although youth did not provoke significant debates and polarization in Rhodes in Ottoman times, young actors were not aloof from political ideas circulating across the empire. Until 1912, the town was one of the main banishment destinations for Ottomans accused of political nuisance and rebellion. Depending on these accusations' gravity, some served their banishment in the dungeons, while others could at least spend part of their day in the sunlight so generously shining over the island. The banished included several students from the Imperial School for Civil Administration (*Mekteb-i Mülkiye*), a particularly politicized site in the empire's centre where opposition to Sultan Abdülhamid's autocracy proliferated.[7] Shortly after the Young Turks' revolution of July 1908, the new government proclaimed a general amnesty for political prisoners.[8] Nonetheless, it was not easy for the new authorities to ascertain why these students had been banished by the previous regime. The Ministry of the Interior and the *vali* (governor) often generally referred to "political crimes" (*politik tuhmetiyle*) committed before being sent to Rhodes.[9] Concerning the Young Turks' influence in Rhodes before 1908, primary sources are scarce.[10] Although some Rhodians might have had bonds with the Young Turk opposition, their impact on local politics cannot be confirmed by material from the Ottoman ministries or European consulates' archives. Even investigations concerning an alleged "Armenian committee" in 1896 ended with no results.[11] Thus, it seems that no effectively organized dissidents operated in Rhodes before 1908.

Although Rhodes was not an oppositional foyer, political ideas circulated as locals mingled with banished individuals or fugitives. In 1901, Rodoslu Mehmet Şevket, a Jewish convert to Islam, was profiled as a political suspect in the correspondence between the *vali* of Rhodes and the Sultan's palace. Şevket, repeatedly referred to as "youth" (*genc*), had helped an officer, İsmail Hakkı Paşa, to escape from Rhodes after the latter had broken out from prison.[12] In his memoirs, İsmail described Şevket as an "intelligent and freedom-loving young man." In 1900, the 20-year-old had recently graduated from the state secondary school and was a regular visitor of the Qadirī Sufi lodge.[13] Although Şevket was only three years younger than İsmail Hakkı, the sources only stress the former's youthfulness. Youth arguably stood for lack of experience in terms of political commitment as opposed to İsmail Hakkı's own trajectory. The officer stated that Şevket helped him "as a human duty," without political motives.[14] Yet, ten years later, Şevket was in Istanbul at meetings organized by the Ottoman Liberals, including the now deputy of Amasya İsmail Hakkı, who had become his patron.[15] Şevket is mentioned again in March 1912, accused of "daring to use insults against the current government and harming religion" (*hükümet-i ḥāżire 'aleyhinde ve dīne doḳunacaḳ tefevvuhāta ictisār ilmesinden dolayı*) through propaganda for the liberal "Freedom and Accord Party" (*Ḥürriyet ve İ'tilāf Fırḳası*).[16] Şevket's politicization thus occurred as a double opposition against Abdülhamid and against the CUP, arguably the most organized faction of the Young Turks before and after 1908.

Next to Şevket, other Rhodian Muslims entered state politics in the crucial decades that led to the demise of the empire. At least three members of the first Turkish National Assembly in Ankara were born there, but they did not have any significant impact on the local political field before or during the Italian military occupation.[17] What, then, did a career in late Ottoman provincial power structures require? Building on the *Tanzimat* administrative reforms, late nineteenth-century Hamidian rule was marked by the expansion of state activities at the local level and an increase in formalized participation.[18] Factionalism was a part of this process, albeit mostly bound to economic and social patronage rather than (explicit) ideologies. Thus, the main factor required to enter provincial administration as an elected member during the Hamidian period was wealth. Converting economic into political power was a point of arrival rather than of departure in a notable's life trajectory.

But did political careers resist the shift from Ottoman to Italian rule, passing from one generation to the next? The rosters of the elected secular members of the Hamidian provincial and municipal councils (*Meclis-i İdāre-yi Vilāyet* and *Belediye Dā'iresi*) stemming from the available issues of the Ottoman yearbooks called *salnameler* suggest some trajectories to follow, especially for those non-Muslims whose identity is easier to retrieve thanks to the mentioned surname:

Table 1.1. Members of the Provincial Council of Rhodes 1893–1903.

1893	Mehmed Ali Ağa, Mehmed Ali Efendi, Haci Pandelli Efendi, **Anastas Dimitriadi Efendi**
1894	Dadieli Mehmed Ali Efendi, Mehmed Ali Efendi, Haci Pandelli Efendi, **Anastas Dimitriadi Efendi**
1898	Sheih Abdullah Efendi, Mahmud Efendi, **Anastas Dimitriadi Efendi**, Dimistoni (?) Efendi
1900–1	Edhem Efendi, Mahmud Efendi, **Anastas Dimitriadis Efendi, Nikolaos Fraraki Efendi**
1903	Edhem Efendi, Mahmud Efendi, Yani Venetokli Efendi, Ilya Efendi

Table 1.2. Members of the Municipal Council of Rhodes 1893–1903.

1893–4	Reis Ismail Hakki Efendi, Haci Mehmed Ağa, Murad Efendi, **Nikolaki Linardi [Fraraki]Efendi**, Panagi Paraskeva Efendi, **Salomon Efendi**
1898	Reis Haci Hüseyin Efendi, Sadik Efendi, Mehmed Ali Efendi, Murad Efendi, Bogaz Efendi, Panagi Paraskeva Efendi, Dimitri Cuvalla Efendi
1900–1	Reis Hakki Efendi, Haci Hafiz Ismail Asim Efendi, YusSuf Efendi, Behcet Efendi, **Salomon Alhadef Efendi, Spiro Paraskeva Efendi**, Andon Kacika [Agiakatsikas?][19]
1903	Reis Ismail Hakki Efendi, Mahmud Efendi, Haci Yussuf Efendi, Behcet Efendi, **Salomon Alhadef Efendi, Spiro Paraskeva Efendi**, Andon Kacika Efendi

Source: Data for both tables are taken from: *Sālnāme* C 1893; *Sālnāme* C 1894; *Sālnāme* C 1898; *Sālnāme* C 1900; *Sālnāme* C 1901; *Sālnāme* C 1903.

All the individuals highlighted in tables 1.1 and 1.2 were prominent traders. Spiros Paraskevas's son Michalis studied engineering in Athens but often returned to Rhodes. In the early 1930s, he was filed by the Italian police as a member of the Greek Irredentist society called *Gioventù Dodecanesina* (Dodecanesian Youth), active in the Greek capital.[20] Anastasios Dimitriadis's son Manolis remained active in the later

Italian administration as town council secretary (*segretario comunale*) in 1920, which was certainly not an upgrade towards a more prestigious administrative post compared to his father's.[21] The same can be said for the Alhadeff family, the wealthiest traders and bankers of Rhodes. Salomon's first son Acher gave up leading the family's business in favour of his brother Joseph.[22] He compensated this withdrawal with a role in the Jewish Communal Council in the early 1920s which was, however, less prestigious than the one held by Salomon.[23] Even if the family's business and banking expanded during Italian rule, its members could not convert economic into political capital, since they had no access to a career broader than the communal level.

Lastly, Nikolaos Frarakis, agent of the Greek shipping company *Panteleon*, moved from offices in the Municipal Council, to the Provincial and then to the Communal Council (*Dimagerontia*), which shows a durable influence on Orthodox electors.[24] In 1913, Nikolaos's son Theodoros was a member of the *Dimagerontia* and one of the signatories of a letter addressed to Prince Luigi Amedeo of Savoy, who visited the island, asking for the union of Rhodes with "motherland Greece."[25] This made the Italian authorities suspicious and marked a shift in the family's place in the political field. The Frarakis reoriented their sphere of influence from communal institutions to one based on the Greek citizenship, which most of them acquired after Lausanne. A foreigner in a colonial setting, Theodoros was a close friend of the Greek vice-consul Nikolaos Karajannis, while his daughter married a Greek diplomat working between Smyrna and Athens.[26] No one among the third generation Frarakis entered the Orthodox Communal Council. The only member profiled by the Italian authorities in terms of political activism was Theodoros's nephew Nikolaos, who had moved to Athens for his studies. The police regretted that "he has never felt sympathy for Italy," "used expressions hostile to Italian rule in the Dodecanese," and pursued "a cunning propaganda against our national interests among his compatriots in Athens."[27]

These trajectories reflected the changing state administration in the late Ottoman Empire. Provincial notables, sitting next to non-elected religious leaders in the councils, fostered a stronger bond between the state and communal structures.[28] Abdülhamid II's expanding state counterbalanced these elected stakeholders' influence through the control of appointed civil servants who circulated in the empire. The main function of imperial schools such as the *Mekteb-i Mülkiye* was to mould a loyal youth formed in the centre, which the Porte could later appoint as "wandering" administrators. At the same time, elected notables took advantage of this link to central power to promote urban and provincial development that strengthened their interests.

In certain provincial centres, like Beirut, the local councils consolidated a political class that maintained their status from the Hamidian to the Second Constitutional period and even beyond the end of the Ottoman rule.[29] In Rhodes, on the contrary, post-Ottoman fascist colonialism created obstacles for such generational continuity due to the shrinking perimeter of political participation it allowed and its increased surveillance on communities. This caused a downgrade of political capital across time, or even the withdrawal from institutional politics. Yet, the change of sovereignty was not the only factor preventing generational continuity. Already before 1912, the Ottoman constitutional regime fostered competition and brought new actors on the stage of provincial politics.

During the feverish summer of 1908, from his elegant mansion in an alley of Neocori, a neighbourhood outside the walled city, the French vice-consul in Rhodes wrote almost day-to-day accounts of the Young Turk Revolution. Demonstrations started on 31 July and targeted persons accused of being Hamidian spies and persecutors, such as the head of the gendarmerie.[30] The situation degenerated rapidly and the French diplomat wrote about a "complete anarchy" with orders arriving from the CUP Section in Salonica instead of the Porte in Istanbul.[31] The vice-consul mentioned a "mob" (*foule*) composed of mostly "Muslims" and "Jews," whereas he described the unnamed main agitators as coming from the "lower classes."[32]

Soon afterwards, the Municipal Council was called to vote for the representative of Rhodes at the Ottoman Parliament. The choice fell on a doctor from the village of Vati, Theodoros Konstantinidis. He was a compromise between a "Muslim" faction – who would have elected a CUP sympathizer – and Orthodox electors. The latter were themselves divided into a faction led by the metropolitan bishop and another led by delegates from the villages.[33] Konstantinidis, allegedly a former member of the secret Macedonian Committee, was not a charismatic politician. He could not speak fluent Ottoman Turkish, did not belong to a notable family, and, although close to the Liberal Party, he was elected as an independent. Being only 34 years old, Konstantinidis nevertheless exemplifies the circulation of Ottoman political elites: high-rank state offices had become accessible to a younger *homo novus* through the constitutional regime change.[34]

The Young Turks increased their intrusive force in local politics after crushing a countercoup in Istanbul led by conservative forces on 31 March 1909, which led to Abdülhamid's deposition. Stronger control on the emerging provincial press and the purge of civil servants – most notably the *vali* in early September 1909 – were phenomena observable in other Ottoman provinces, where a new political vocabulary went hand in hand with an intensified struggle for power.[35] Apart from the already mentioned *Afitāb*, the newspaper *Rodos*, founded in 1909 and printed in Greek, wrote of intercommunal harmony in the name of the Ottoman Constitution. When the discourse moved to communal issues such as school fees and the foundation of the Orthodox gymnasium *Venetokleion*, "youth" (*neolaia*) was evoked as the "generation in which both the Church and the Nation (*genos*) rightly place many hopes."[36] In fact, in such turbulent times, youth did not represent the hopes *of*, but rather the hopes *for* the Church and the Nation – presumably referring to the Orthodox element within the Ottoman state – to remain legitimate players in the future political field.

Another change in the relationship between state and communities concerned the army. In 1909, military service became mandatory for all male Ottoman subjects, irrespective of religion. This draft reform aimed at linking coming of age with a stronger allegiance to the state. Reactions were mixed, with non-Muslim intellectuals debating notions of citizenship and *millet* belonging, including the proposal of forming separate Orthodox battalions in the imperial army.[37] In Rhodes, the decree on conscription was read out at the walled city's main square in mid-January 1910 by the religious communal authorities in the presence of the governor. The speech reported by *Rodos* contained recurring references to liberty (*eleutheria*), equality (*isotis*), and fraternity (*adelfotis*).[38] As the French consul in Smyrna reported, the measure was to target only those born between 1883 and 1888, and the diplomat stressed his doubts that more than the half of those eligible would actually be recruited.[39] Indeed, the Ottoman conscription reform of 1909 did not dramatically alter the composition of the army, which remained largely composed of "Anatolian Muslim peasants."[40]

However, many Rhodians perceived conscription as a universal measure. Vittorio Alhadeff recalled the reaction of his uncle Acher, aged 24 at the time: "All young men, absolutely all of them, had to give in to the hated and feared *askerlik* for three years! The case of uncle Acher was particularly pathetic … [H]e really fell ill, deeply depressed, and he had a dramatic crisis of hopelessness … All this happened while my sister Amélie and all her Jewish classmates at the *Alliance* [*Israélite Universelle*] School sang in choir the patriotic song imposed to all schools by the Young Turks: 'Oh, Turkey, yes, you are my fatherland!'"[41] The experience of military service for non-Muslims changed from generation to generation. Acher's father Salomon could pay the exemption tax known as *bedel*, while Vittorio himself was later exempted since he had the second class Italian *cittadinanza egea*. In 1909, the Alhadeffs mobilized their network to avoid Acher's conscription. Bension Menashe, a board member of their company and teacher at the Ottoman high-school (*İdadiye*), successfully asked one of his former students, an influential Young Turk in Istanbul, to intercede.

Yet, not all the wealthy non-Muslims were reluctant. In March 1910, *Rodos* dedicated an article to Orthodox and Jewish recruits of the 1883 cohort. Among the ten names (four Orthodox and six Jews) one finds representatives of the Frarakis and the Menashes, whose families, as shown above, were well integrated into the Hamidian local administration.[42] In general, though, conscription provoked mistrust, fear, and refusal. When relatives of Orthodox reservists wanted to follow them until Marmaris in Anatolia, where they would start their service, a "violent discussion" emerged with some CUP members, and an anonymous writing on a wall directed against the Party appeared in Rhodes in the aftermath: "You have removed Abdülhamid but not the tyranny. You are not worth a Constitution, Long Live Republican France!"[43]

In the following months, meetings animated by the president of the Civil Court Cemil Bey – a prominent CUP member who had recently arrived in Rhodes – instigated the population against merchants owning the Greek citizenship. This was a refraction of the empire-wide anti-Greek boycott following the political crisis in Crete and the fear of its annexation by Greece.[44] The tension persisted throughout the autumn of 1911, when Italy declared war against the Ottoman Empire. The director of the Jewish school remarked that "chauvinism has begun to penetrate into the masses."[45] The CUP wanted to deliver weapons to civilians to defend the island from an Italian attack, although only some lower class Muslim Cretan refugees allegedly responded to this call.[46] The *vali* eventually disarmed the civilians but the atmosphere before the second Ottoman parliamentary elections, due in May 1912, remained conflictual. The trope of equality among communities (*milel*) now turned into an electoral dispute. As the French vice-consul argued, the CUP maneuvered to have five Muslim delegates next to five Orthodox in the local council that would elect the deputy for the Ottoman assembly.[47] However, the elections were suspended since the Italian troops were already threatening the island.

A few months after the Italian invasion, the Ottoman Ministry of the Interior sent the Egyptian doctor Ahmed Fuad Bey incognito to Rhodes to investigate the situation. In his report, Fuad mentioned the qadi Şakir Efendi as an ally of the new rulers, adding that "his hostility is particularly well known to youth and [CUP] Unionists (*genclere ve ittihâdcılara*)."[48] This is the earliest account I have found mentioning youth as a collective force of local politics, not only as a metaphor or an individual marker. Compared to the Şevket described as "youth" in 1901, a shift had occurred. Under Hamidian rule, youth stood for lack of experience and awareness in politics. In 1912 it was a label attached to Young Turk radical elements opposed to the new rulers.

Why was this term suddenly part of the political spectrum right at the end of Ottoman rule? The Second Constitutional Period was not only a moment of institutional change, it also impacted the way individuals were socialized in politics and how politics was discussed. A circulation of elites between the provincial and the state level gave younger individuals without an influential family background access to important positions. In public statements, "youth" mostly referred to political instability. It blended inquietude for the fading of established structures and hopes for the future, whereas it was basically never used by activists in first person. The inception of such juvenilization of politics, however, did not correspond to a diffuse politicization of youth. The conditions of possibility for the latter were nonetheless in place by 1912: the expansion of the local press, an easier access to elected positions for other professional categories than landowners and wealthy traders, as well as state propaganda penetrating schools. All three factors persisted under Italian rule, which added an even more intrusive system of surveillance and repression against political activities. Ahmed Fuad's remark on the "youth" partisans of the CUP is therefore a perfect junction between the Ottoman and the Italian periods. It marks the beginning of a phase in which youth became the most sensible – both troublesome and valuable – category of activists.

Military Governors and "Exalted" Youth

When his troops seized Rhodes in May 1912, Giovanni Ameglio's priority was to maintain "public order" among the population. This also implied collecting information about the new territory's social and political fabric, that the Italian governor knew only superficially. To him, for example, the Young Turks were a quite protean and general category through which he described politicized individuals in Rhodes. Nor was Ameglio the only Italian on the spot trying to make sense of local politics.

Ten days after the town's occupation, Luigi Ambrosini, a reporter of the newspaper *La Stampa*, arrived from Libya. In a long article, he described his encounter with a man aged 25, whom he ironically labelled the "Old Turk." This character was portrayed as a "young man" with a "not quite reassuring" "boy face," claiming to be "a Turk of the 'ancien régime' persecuted for political reasons, who came into our service to help us hunt soldiers still hidden in town." Animated by "fanaticism," this young man nonetheless inspired sympathy among Italian troops.[49] The impressionistic article emphasizing youth reveals the inquietude and curiosity that the Italians developed vis-à-vis local society. The "young Old Turk's" portrait is also symmetric to Ahmed Fuad's remark on the "youngsters" close to the CUP mentioned in the previous section. Political "fanaticism" was now associated with youth, since politics produced uncertainty through rapid and unstable transformations. Following other informants' hints, Ameglio arrested Ottoman civil servants and public figures. Already on 8 May, a naval officer telegraphed to Rome that "one vali, two secretaries, five officers, ninety-nine soldiers, nine gendarmes, fourteen Young Turks and one expelled individual" had been embarked to Italy, where they would be kept as prisoners and hostages until the end of the Italo-Ottoman War.[50]

Soon after this epuration, the Italian military administration was concerned with other, more troublesome agitators. In September 1912, the governor spoke to the lawyer Venetoklis, an Orthodox notable whom we will meet again in chapter 3. Venetoklis described his local coreligionists as consisting of the "bourgeois youth" (*gioventù borghese*), the "adult bourgeoisie" (*classe adulta borghese*), and the "rural classes" (*classi rurali*). This is how Ameglio summarized this distinction between the former two categories when reporting the conversation:

1) The mentality of the bourgeois youth, just graduated from school and who has spent some time in Greece. These youths of idealist character, educated to hate the Turk and to the centuries long aspiration of the Hellenic race, are imbued with the ideal of the annexation of the island by Greece. Not caring about the real interest of the country and even less about the requisites of politics, they only think of this dream, without considering anything else.
2) The mentality of the adult bourgeoisie. The representatives of this category, who only care about their individual benefit, are in favour of granting autonomy to the island. They hope that this form of government will make it easy for them to seize power and obtain eminent and lucrative appointments. This mentality finds many adepts among the aforementioned class of adults since it mirrors the moderate nature of Hellenic patriotism, by which current Greek politics are animated, and to which this bourgeoisie adheres. It would not be difficult, considering the interest-oriented feelings of this class, to change its mentality.[51]

Early Italian rule distinguished "youth" and "adulthood" in terms of different political visions resulting from, respectively, intellectual and economic capital. Contrary to Lago's later remarks, Venetoklis and Ameglio suggested that it would be easier to change the adults', rather than the youth's mentality.

Later in 1912, the Balkan Wars further amplified the politicization of some Rhodians.[52] This is when youth was considered responsive to transnational politics. Ameglio and his successors realized that the occupation of the Dodecanese and the ongoing Greek military conquests had opened a "Dodecanese question" for islanders based in Greece and Egypt. No armed uprising against the Italian occupation appeared, but some Orthodox volunteers, simply labelled by the governor as "youngsters" (*giovinetti*), allegedly left Rhodes in 1912 to fight in Macedonia.[53]

Venetoklis's generational interpretation of politics echoed in Ameglio's repressive measures. In November, the governor stated that Mayor Savvas Pavlidis's son, described as an "exalted youngster" (*giovane esaltato*), had sent a telegraph from Athens "praising the [Greek army's] victories wishing that the Aegean islands will soon be free from any yoke."[54] Pavlidis senior had been elected president of the Municipal Council of Rhodes in 1911, prevailing over the CUP candidate.[55] Another lawyer, Server Efendi, had accused him of being a radical Young Turk by quoting the pro-CUP newspaper *Ḥaḳ*, which praised Pavlidis's "patriotism" (*ḥamiyet-i vaṭaniye*) against the Italians.[56] Considered loyal by the occupiers, Pavlidis was nonetheless a member of the *Dimagerontia* organizing unofficial referenda in the occupied villages and minor islands to demand the *Enosis*, the union with Greece.[57]

In such turbulent atmosphere, deciphering political attitudes required looking beyond the individual level and into kinship bonds. In February 1913, Ameglio banished Pavlidis and one of his sons.[58] Only a few weeks later, another son, Pavlos, was accused of spreading the rumour that Italy would give back the Dodecanese to the Ottomans, in order to incite the Orthodox peasants to revolt.[59] Pavlos had just arrived in Rhodes from Istanbul, where he was studying at the "American School."[60] With an ironic remark, the French vice-consul commented on Ameglio's "monomania" for every sign of "Hellenic propaganda" among youth: "Whatever dangerous can a child (*enfant*) aged 18 undertake in a place where one cannot make a step without facing armed soldiers?"[61] The Pavlidis case also confirms the local politicians' devaluation from Ottoman to Italian rule, here due to repressive measures. Before withdrawing from politics, Savvas became president of the Orthodox Communal Council (now called *Koinotiko Symvoulio*) in the 1920s, downgrading his former position as mayor, while his sons remained aloof from politics.[62]

In other instances, the youth worrying military governors were not children of prominent notables, but nameless figures profiled as "fanatics" and "agitators." In February 1913, when some "intellectuals" spread rumours of a Great Powers agreement about Greece's annexation of Rhodes, the governor mentioned forty "youngsters, budding students" (*ragazzi, studentelli in erba*) celebrating at the Orthodox metropolitan see.[63] Similarly, a few days earlier, a religious procession turned into a demonstration for the *Enosis*. A police officer reported that Demetrios Anastasiadis, the gymnasium's headmaster, instigated the crowd, but that three "youngsters" (*giovani*) were the "unruliest" (*riottosi*) protagonists.[64] Not claimed by the actors themselves, this youth referred to the discovery of the political landscape of Rhodes by anxious authorities. Ideology and activism were interpreted through the notion of youth, albeit a youth manipulated by elders. It was still the latter who appeared as a threat to Italian rule in a regional setting in flux.

The decade of war following the Italian seizure of Rhodes marked a rapid politicization of youth in Rhodes. At the same time, the trope of youth shifted from Ottoman politics to broader Mediterranean and, eventually, post-Ottoman scenarios. As early as September 1914, the French vice-consul reported that "thirty young men (*jeunes gens*) left for Constantinople to enrol in the Turkish army hoping to start a campaign against Russia."[65] The radicalization of young Muslim volunteers kept the pace with the atmosphere in the Ottoman Empire. After establishing a dictatorship in 1913, the CUP organized paramilitary youth organizations as an instrument of nationalist propaganda later to be mobilized for the war efforts.[66] Italian occupation prevented this development in Rhodes, but military voluntarism existed and concerned local Orthodox as well. In June 1915, the French diplomat reported that "several Greeks from the islands came to the consulate and asked to be sent as volunteers to the Dardanelles," although, in this case, no specific age was reported.[67] Warfare also reinforced press censorship, mail and police surveillance, bans on movement between the islands, and expulsions, particularly of some Muslim notables considered linked to the CUP, who were banished to the island of Karpathos in 1916.[68] Political turbulence marked the relationship between Italian state authorities and the population. Yet, it also shook local communal institutions with repercussions reaching beyond the end of Italian military occupation.

Fragmented Communities and Travelling Ideologies

Even after the first waves of repression against Muslim political activists in 1912 and 1916, the military governors' reports suggested that the CUP was still influential in town and that allegiance to it still divided the Muslim population. General Elia noted in 1919 that the

Muslim "conservatives" were headed by the mufti and "included the most prominent and wealthiest notables," all favourable to the occupiers. The qadi Ferid Bey, whom the CUP had sent to Rhodes from Aydın in 1914, led the local Young Turks, a faction that was rapidly falling from grace in Anatolia after the defeat in the First World War.[69]

Within the Orthodox community, a new leader appeared in that same year with the appointment of Metropolitan Bishop Apostolos, who declared his loyalty to the Italian occupiers straight after his arrival.[70] During the military occupation, however, Apostolos had an ambivalent political stance. At times, he was stigmatized by the hardliner Greek nationalists as a collaborator. Still, he never enjoyed the full trust of the Italian authorities either, who were convinced that he might become the leader of the same Greek nationalists. Later in the 1920s, Apostolos eventually supported Mario Lago's unfinished project to establish an autocephalous Dodecanese Orthodox Church.[71]

Given the overall dramatic transformation of political rhetoric and loyalties which the Aegean and, more broadly, the Mediterranean region underwent between the Italo-Ottoman War and the Treaty of Lausanne, the fragmentation of communities in Rhodes is not surprising. It even appears as a "softer" process of adaptation to changing state authorities compared to other settings. This fragmentation also emerged in form of school protests at the Ottoman state high-school and the Orthodox communal gymnasium in 1915 and 1919 respectively, as will be illustrated in chapter 3. However, the Italian military authorities, not yet sovereign in Rhodes, did not interpret them as an urgent danger in terms of confrontation with local youth.

Jewish institutions were also facing new ideas and a diversification of political groupings. In 1922, the director of the *Alliance Israélite Universelle's* boys school complained about a "denigration campaign" by some teachers. These were inspired by Wolfgang von Weisl, an Austrian journalist and a leading figure of a new current of Zionism criticizing the British Mandate for Palestine. Weisl spent some time in Rhodes on his way to Palestine.[72] In his article for the *Wiener Morgenzeitung*, he described the condition of the town and its Jewish community. Although he stressed that military governors had gained the locals' trust, he claimed that "the youth particularly suffered" from post-war hardship. Himself only 26 years old, the Zionist activist was eager to raise the Rhodian Jews' enthusiasm for his project: making Rhodes a temporary colony for the *chaluzim* (Zionist pioneers) waiting in European or Balkan cities for the permission to settle in Palestine. Weisl gave lectures in Italian in a crowded synagogue and admitted that his audience had no idea of the Zionist cause. Still, he could convince Bohor Israel, teacher at the *Alliance* school, to lead a section of the Jewish National Fund.[73] Israel had the support of two influential notables, David Gaon and the former Communal Council president Rahamin Cohen, who sponsored the foundation of a Zionist society.

Although Weisl's account is enthusiastic, this project had a quite limited influence on the community's power relations. The Zionist society nonetheless reveals a delicate moment in the political transformation of Rhodes. The Ottoman demise had become a concrete scenario, but Lago's administration had not yet begun. Weisl's followers discussed about whether the society should be affiliated to the Zionist Federation of Greece, of Italy, or of "the Orient." Eventually, the newborn committee opted for Italy in line with diplomatic developments, although the World Zionist Organization first sent propaganda material in French, the language hundreds of Rhodian Jews learned at school.[74] Moreover, some had their own view of Zionism. Interested in the project, they pointed out that Rhodes, governed for centuries by the same empire that ruled over Jerusalem, was already a part of *Erez Israel* and not of the *Goluth* (land of exile), thus asking for being affiliated directly to the Zionist organization in Palestine.[75] These lively debates were symptomatic of a widespread anxiety for the future of the Jewish community, which again mobilized the notion of youth.

The notables were caught in a delicate redefinition of loyalty and worried about their legitimacy in the new colonial regime. In 1924, the grand rabbi complained that many parents sent their children to non-Jewish schools. He spoke of youth by addressing an older generation: "Our youth includes a large number of youngsters who completely ignore our religion, our principles, our history, and our traditions ... You [the parents] should think for a moment, that you, who have learnt something about religion, basically do not observe the recommendations of our Law. You are not capable of understanding anything, or only very little about the prayers you say. Nothing, or very little you know about our history, our Bible, our traditions. I imagine, then, what will become of your sons and daughters, innocent souls, delicate plants which constitute our hopes of tomorrow." Here, youth is a bone of contention between the families and the community: "If, during their tender age, your children are not able to learn in your houses and in the schools what JUDAISM is, it is certain that, once they become men, they will find the word Israelite ridiculous and will do anything to get rid of it. The immense pain and the moral suffering we feel by watching so many youth of our confession, youth of talent, of knowledge, of merit, become little by little stranger to Judaism is already enough for us."[76] The rabbi's speech tied together hopes and fears about tradition and novelty. A link between the past and the future, youth signalled a corrective intervention by parents and institutions necessary to grant the community's stability in the present.

Meanwhile, the Muslim community was exposed to the rise of Turkish nationalism in Anatolia. Already in March 1922, before the Treaty of Lausanne, Mustafa Kemal had sent Celaleddin Azif Bey to Rhodes as a "representative," since he could not yet be appointed as a consul.[77] The Kemalists could also count on local agents, who drew the Italian authorities' attention. Regent Governor Albertazzi invalidated the election of Şevket Müderiszade as the head of the Muslim Communal Council in 1922. Müderiszade, former *kaymakam* of Karpathos, was an experienced politician deemed a dangerous mediator between Ankara and the Muslims of Rhodes.[78] These repressive measures, however, did not neutralize a faction within the Muslim communal institutions that sided with the Turkish government on issues such as the reform of the local *vakıf* properties or the nationality option related to the Treaty of Lausanne.[79] In February 1927, the Consul Celal(eddin) Bey's influence grew to the extent that Lago reported to the Italian ambassador to Turkey about his espionage and anti-Italian propaganda. The governor, supported by the Fascist Party, countered this with stronger surveillance.[80] While Italian authorities invested in the control of communal leaders, Ankara leveraged the local Muslims' kinship, property, and business bonds with Anatolia to raise its influence.

The Orthodox community too had to position itself towards the post-Ottoman scenario. Between the end of the First World War and the Treaty of Lausanne, several Dodecanesians based abroad, such as Skevos Zervos from Kalymnos and Michael Volonakis from Symi, aimed at convincing foreign governments that the Dodecanese should be awarded to Greece.[81] While their pamphlets circulated, associations of Dodecanesians were founded by emigrants in Greece, Egypt, and the United States. These circles worried the Italian authorities due to the allure they exerted on emigrants, especially from the minor islands. Already in 1922, the Italian ambassador in Athens complained about the illicit enrolment of Aegean subjects in the Greek army during the Asia Minor Campaign.[82] Student sections developed within these associations, especially at the University of Athens, the main study destination for Orthodox Dodecanesians. In 1926, an "Association of Dodecanesian Students" sent a resolution to the president of the University of Rome denouncing the abusive treatment of their coreligionists by the colonial authorities.[83] One year later, Bishop Apostolos was wounded during an ambush. The Italian police concluded that the author of the attack was the priest Sava Magnataci, from Asia Minor. Magnataci had arrived in Rhodes only in

1923, but the authorities were worried by his links to the Dodecanesian circles in Alexandria and even more in Athens, where an association called "Dodecanesian Youth" boosted anti-Italian propaganda.[84]

In the 1920s, all communities were affected by a fragmentation reflecting the making of a post-Ottoman Mediterranean. Zionism emerged among Jews, Kemalist nationalism among Muslims, while Greek irredentism perturbed the metropolitan bishop's cooperation with the authorities. Against this backdrop, Governor Lago's attempt to (re)build communal structures as loyal instruments of rule was a specific interpretation of the Ottoman legacy. Italian colonial rule faced the fact that sovereignty alone could not isolate Rhodes from its regional political environment. What happened in other sites of the Mediterranean directly affected local communities. This caused anxiety concerning the authority of the fascist colonial state. Violent repression could deteriorate diplomatic relationships with neighbouring Greece or Turkey but a stronger control over communities was needed to avoid the expansion of alternative identifications. Lago's statement about the "new generation" can be seen in a different light in this regard. Italian colonial rule used this trope to legitimize the government's action while hoping that dangerous bonds with outer political movements, implicitly acknowledged as a threat, would vanish in the future. Later developments proved how misplaced this perception was.

Colonial Youth Allured by Nationalism

In the 1930s, the Mediterranean was part of a global landscape of political ideas and movements that emphasized the value of youth. From fascist Italy to the Soviet Union, from the Lebanese *Kataeb* Party to the Popular Front in France, from Nazi Germany to imperial Japan, movements in power as well as in the opposition stressed that a disciplined and militant youth was the key to political success. This formula reverberated in Rhodes, where fascist colonialism implanted its youth organizations based on the model of the Italian peninsula. Italian rule did not tolerate the creation of institutions outside its control and surveillance. And yet, groups of local youth were attracted by Revisionist Zionism, Kemalism, and Greek irredentism, movements for which youth was just as important as for the fascists. A look from Rhodes contributes to the history of political activism in the Mediterranean by highlighting the travelling feature of these ideas as they collided with fascist colonial rule, rather than the top-down mobilization emanating from their respective centres.[85]

Revisionist Zionism significantly expanded in Rhodes in 1935. The complexity of this movement in terms of intellectual and geopolitical implications goes beyond the scope of this section, which limits itself to a few general observations before addressing more closely the politicization of youth in Rhodes.[86] From 1931 onwards, this right-wing Zionist faction led by Vladimir Jabotinsky increased the contacts with Mussolini's fascist apparatus. This resulted from ideological affinities such as the idea of a nationalist and authoritarian society without class conflicts. However, their proximity also built on geopolitics. Even before the foundation of the Revisionist Party in 1925, Jabotinsky's Zionism harshly criticized the British Mandate for Palestine. His opposition to Britain appealed to Mussolini's need for allies in an inter-imperial rivalry with London. Lastly, it was youth which brought the Revisionists in the orbit of fascism. Mussolini's co-optation of youth from the early squads to disciplined party sections served Jabotinsky as a model towards the creation of his envisioned Jewish state. The most evident example of this convergence of interests was the establishment of a Zionist naval academy in Civitavecchia, near Rome, in 1934, coordinated by the Revisionist youth organization *Betar*, which Jabotinsky had founded, even before the party, in 1923.[87]

The intellectual centre of the Italian Revisionists was Milan, where the lawyer Leone Carpi propagated Jabotinsky's ideas of fascist-Zionist synergy. His friend Renato Coen, a teacher from Parma who worked at the Italian Jewish schools in Rhodes, politicized a group of students, ten of whom subscribed to the Revisionist Party. The *Carabinieri* stated that Coen was disappointed after being "hampered by the elders" of the community who were cautious with regard to Zionism, and that he consequently "turned his actions towards the youth."[88] Several youngsters in Rhodes responded with interest and became the movement's multiplicators. Their voice stressed allegiance to Italy and the colonial authorities, which coexisted with an intransigent attitude towards communal leaders. In November 1935, some pupils at the Jewish school wearing the *Betar* badge claimed their affiliation to Revisionism against other Zionist currents, like the association founded by Bohor Israel in 1922, which was still active but of no significant importance. They also opposed the headmaster's admonition "not to do politics at schools," causing his concern "about the moral affection this [doctrine] can exert on adolescents … by exciting their fantasies with visions of things that they are not mature enough to understand."[89]

In 1936, this tension became a proper generational conflict between the Communal Council and the young Revisionists. The community's president Hizkia Franco wrote severe words in an article for the Jewish newspaper *El Boletin*, censored by the *Carabinieri* just before its publication: "This propaganda is directed by inexpert youth, who do not scout for party members among mature people and developed men, capable of assuming responsibility for their opinions, but among the neighbourhood's youth, a prey likely to fall into the movement's net. They have nothing better to do than to spread the movement among our school pupils, whose lips still smell of their mothers' milk." Franco urged parental and communal authority to intervene: "In our view, they commit a serious sin, let us even say a crime. What was, until now, the consequence of this active propaganda among our school's pupils? Indiscipline, insubordination, and even revolt! … We invite these children's fathers and all reasonable men in our Community to consider this propaganda with all necessary importance and attention … [W]e have decided to fight them overtly and with all our spirit's strength to extirpate it from our Community."[90]

This excerpt echoes the grand rabbi's 1924 speech addressing Jewish parents, but the focus switched from religion towards communal politics. More importantly, Revisionist Zionism was interpreted as a movement *only* pertinent to youth, be it in the role of propagators or infantilized receptors.[91] Although the article was not published, the Revisionist activists knew about Franco's hostility. A few weeks earlier, they had published a column on the Milanese newspaper *L'idea sionistica*, edited by Leone Carpi. By refusing the accusations of dividing the Jews, the anonymous author attacked the community's leaders precisely by reverting the condescending trope of education, claiming that youth knew more about politics than did elder notables.[92]

Despite their allegiance to fascism and Italy, these activists challenged a key element of colonial rule. In 1936, an influential local fascist scolded one of them by claiming that "Revisionism and fascism are not compatible and that he should choose between belonging to the Italian party and the Jewish one [*sic!*]." They reacted with a letter to the Fascist Party's local section and to the police arguing that Revisionism worked in the interest of fascism, that their ideologies were perfectly compatible, and that strong bonds existed in Italy between the activists and the regime. It was a natural conclusion for them to state that they were proud to militate in fascist youth organizations.[93]

Colonial authorities knew little about Revisionist Zionism, and the police had to inquire about its features and relationship with fascism. Since other police stations in Italy did not contradict the youngsters' claims, the government in Rhodes privileged a "soft" (*colle buone*) intercession by Hizkia Franco, upon whom Lago arguably relied more than on the other communities' leaders.[94] The scheme of fascist colonialism, according to which obedience and order could be achieved by disciplining communal institutions, did not work so smoothly in this case. The

Betar followers continued their activities, which prompted the police to intervene in a more "resolute way." The governor made clear that he "does not want and cannot tolerate" the movement since it could provoke "scissions in the little local Jewish element."[95] In the summer of 1936, through the joint intervention of police and community leaders, the Zionist youngsters eventually stopped their agitation.

The stress on youth in this movement did not imply that only a narrow range of teenage cohorts partook in it. One of the main activists, Giuseppe Levi, was born in Rhodes in 1907. He is among the youngsters in figure 1.1 (first standing from the right) posing around a menorah placard, the symbol of Jabotinsky's *Betar*. In 1934, Levi was profiled as "loyal, frank, and docile, of good economic and social condition … devoted and obsequious" towards the authorities. He ran a photography equipment shop and was considered the best boxer in Rhodes. One year later, in line with the reform passed by Lago, he even applied for military service to acquire full Italian citizenship. Calling him a young man while he was almost 30 years old confirms that youth was not only an age-related, but also a political marker, since it was taken to signify the whole Revisionist movement. A youth diverging from the goals of fascist colonialism was the boundary that the authorities did not allow to cross. The police explicated this with a harsh but unequivocal comment: "Jews in Rhodes are respected in terms of religion, but they should not engage in politics, be it Zionist or anti-Zionist." In 1937, now a full Italian citizen, Levi applied for entering the Fascist Party. The police remarked that he had "always shown patriotic sentiments and favourable to our institutions." Very soon, though, his economic condition worsened, he closed his store and found a job as a delivery man, ironically at the company run by Hizkia Franco, the Revisionists' main enemy.[96]

Levi's trajectory shows that Zionism and fascism were not incompatible in the eyes of "young" activists, but the authorities were not willing to let this synthesis amplify youth politicization outside their control. The Zionists' activism was not ideologically dangerous, but it was divisive for the community, which was the sole tolerated political space under colonial rule. Only when he fitted the "indigenous youth" envisioned by Lago could Levi be "welcomed" within the fascist colonial body politic. And yet, neither adhesion to fascism devoid of Revisionist nuances, nor military service and upgrade in terms of citizenship could grant local Jews a chance of survival during the persecution inaugurated by the Racial Laws of 1938 and the deportation of 1944. Levi's death in Auschwitz in 1944 is the dramatic reminder of the frail attachment which fascist colonialism conceded to its Jewish colonial subjects.

Figure 1.1. Followers of Revisionist Zionism in Rhodes, 1936. Courtesy of the Rhodes Jewish Historical Foundation and Aron Hasson

While Jewish youth joined the Revisionist movement, Muslim youth were increasingly addressed by the Turkish consul in Rhodes, who sought to interfere in communal affairs in the Italian colony through propaganda for the Kemalist regime. In 1934, the consul informed Ankara about a confidential conversation between Lago and the community leaders. The governor complained that many Muslims from Rhodes pursued their secondary and higher education in Turkey instead of remaining on the island or moving to Italy: "Some of the Turkish youth owning the Italian [Aegean] citizenship who study in Turkey are impregnated with fanatical sentiments (*taşkın hislerle*) and I observe with great sadness that they occasionally produce unpleasant incidents … I gave a resolute order to discipline them. I recommend that Muslim youth do not give rise to these incidents … I do not want this kind of unpleasant incidents to disturb the atmosphere in Rhodes. Give advice to your youth."[97] Lago also added that the parents of Muslim youth willing to study in Turkey should be warned, while the consul remarked that even the sons of some notables continued their studies there. Muslim youth's mobility to Turkey was not only a matter of education, but also of political socialization. The challenge for Lago was how to deal with these post-Ottoman Muslim subjects within his colonial rule and an expanding nationalism that (re)created bonds between Rhodes and neighbouring Turkey.

These considerations affected individual life trajectories. Celaleddin Sünger, born in Rhodes in 1912, seemed to adhere to Lago's envisioned "new generation" of loyal colonial subjects. He studied at the local Italian state schools with brilliant results, entered fascist youth organizations, and was even selected for a student delegation who travelled to Italy to pay homage to Prince Umberto in 1929. After his studies, he ran a bookstore but found a part-time clerk job at the Muslim community. In 1934, when the Turkish consul Hasan Sözen hired him as interpreter, the Italian police reported a "fast metamorphosis." Sünger had allegedly become a "fanatic supporter of the Turkish nationalist ambitions" including irredentist claims on the Dodecanese.[98]

The Turkish consulate was indeed a site of Muslim youth politicization, as its receptions involved men in their late teens and early twenties.[99] Sözen's successor as a consul, Cavit Erçin, discouraged Muslim families from enrolling their children in fascist organizations. He also propagated that emigration to Turkey would improve the youth's economic condition in light of the stagnation in Rhodes.[100] But the authorities knew that politicization was not simply a matter of the consuls' intrigues. Youth like Sünger had interiorized this message and further spread it among peers: "his propaganda conquered the spirit of many young Muslims of Rhodes, to whom he suggested that Kemalist Turkey was the promised land."[101]

A few months later, in 1936, the police caught Sünger taking pictures of a food factory in Rhodes, which they interpreted as espionage. The police found a letter in which Sünger insulted the mufti of Rhodes, another sign of how communities were fragmented along generational lines. Based on these accusations, the authorities banished him to Italy, only a few weeks after his engagement.[102] He spent two years in a village in Basilicata begging for pardon and lamenting his "great material and spiritual desolation." Sünger's attachment to Turkish nationalism did not prevent him from sending an admiring petition directly to the *Duce* asking for mercy, in vain. He could return to Rhodes only in 1938 and, soon afterwards, he moved to Turkey and applied for Turkish citizenship, joined by his mother and brother.[103] Seen as a *Bildungsroman*, Sünger's trajectory turned from everything a colonial governor could wish for to everything he would worry about. He changed from being close to the loyal "indigenous youth" of "good fascists" to becoming a fifth column of foreign nationalism working against Lago's "new generation." Even if Sünger did not show any overt opposition to fascism or Italian rule, suspicions of nationalist propaganda led to its banishment. In the eyes of fascist colonialism, there was no place for heterogenous allegiances involving foreign governments.

Compared to the Muslim and the Jewish, unrest among the Orthodox youth reveals a stronger continuity of political motives with the 1910s. Declarations of attachment to Greece and the conflict around the clergy's position towards Italian rule persisted in a latent tension which could escalate and be amplified through the Dodecanesian diaspora. In April 1934, a brawl broke out in the village of Salakos, leaving two dead and several wounded. What the *Messaggero* described as an accident due to alcohol abuse and rivalry between two factions provoked a considerable echo abroad.[104] The French press published a *dépêche* and other reports in the following weeks.[105] The news of a "massacre" committed by the Italian police reached the Dodecanesian Orthodox community in Egypt. Their Alexandrian newspaper *Dodekanisos* published a letter sent by the association Dodecanesian Youth to Mussolini, urging the *Duce* to stop violence in the Aegean.[106]

Dodekanisos regularly propagated the union with Greece through a stress on youth as a symbol of nationalist aspirations. These motives circulated even beyond the Mediterranean. A few weeks later, a new section of the Dodecanesian Youth opened in New York, following those in Athens and Alexandria, claiming that the "bloody events at Salakos" were behind its foundation.[107] Rather than an autonomous initiative of youngsters, the Dodecanesian Youth was a political trope projected in the future to legitimize present action by the elders. The latter remained important actors, as one comment *on*, rather than *by* youth explained in the newspaper: "everywhere, youth shall depart in the first line of the struggle, bravely marching forward with vitality in their prime. This will be reinvigorating for [us] the elders on our perilous path, who are despairing (*dia tous apodyspetountas eis ston trachi dromos mas parilikas*), and whose wise advice and the experience shall not be overlooked."[108] Lago's priority was the surveillance of the few intellectuals and activists from the diaspora who regularly visited Rhodes. As the police put it: "without overestimating the danger, it is appropriate to keep the eyes open."[109]

The *Carabinieri*'s eyes were certainly open on youth activism interpreted as Greek irredentism appearing in Rhodes. In January 1935, two teenagers, Giorgio S. and Giovanni T., were arrested for an anonymous leafleting campaign insulting and menacing, among others, the metropolitan bishop, the gymnasium headmaster, and the newspaper *Rodiaki*'s director. The two boys signed their leaflets as "whole Rhodes" and addressed their enemies as "traitors." The police suspected their fathers, already known as "philhellenes," of being behind this act targeting those personalities accused of being pro-Italian. A report stated that "it cannot be assumed that the two youngsters have acted on their own initiative."[110]

Two years later, the new governor De Vecchi banned the berets worn by the students at the gymnasium *Venetokleion*, since he considered them a nationalist symbol. The police condescendingly reported that many students gave back their berets in "scenes of fanaticism, weeping and kissing the badges."[111] In fact, these berets were above all a form of identification with the school. For instance, there is no mention of any link to the uniform introduced in those years by General Ioannis Metaxas in Greece. His "Fourth of August" dictatorship was in fact inspired by fascist Italy's mobilization of youth. Metaxas put his "National Youth Organization" (*Ethniki Organosis Neolaias*) at the centre of the regime's iconology, while at least until 1938 he did not lose occasions to stress his country's friendship with Italy.[112] Rather than allegiance to Greece as a state regime, the Orthodox youth's politicization in Rhodes blended local dynamics with irredentism circulating transnationally in the diaspora.

The "beret issue" escalated into overt resistance against fascist colonialism's ideological assimilation. A few days after the ban, the school headmaster announced that all pupils were to take part in the fascist celebration of the Foundation of Rome (*Natale di Roma*) on 21 April

1937. One student, Eleftherios M., stood up and declared: "we will not take part in the ceremony and, from this moment, we are on strike … Mr. Headmaster, didn't you always tell us that we are Greeks?"[113] Afterwards, he left the classroom followed by all his classmates. A group of them started a discussion in the schoolyard aimed at persuading all students to strike, also threatening the younger ones with retaliation should they refuse to join. In the end, almost forty students boycotted the celebration. This spectacular protest, left unmentioned by the *Messaggero*, caused seven arrests. All involved students were cautioned, and the three main agitators were expelled from all the schools of the Dodecanese.[114] This contributed to De Vecchi's decision of shutting down the *Venetokleion*, which remained closed until the German military pushed for its reopening during the Second World War.[115]

For the first time, the police considered the protest an independent initiative by the students: "Any external or parental interference in the students' rebellious determination should be excluded, and, thus, such determination must have received a strong affirmation among some of the pupils."[116] This episode was an explicit sign of hostility to fascism. When the authorities pressured the teachers to have the pupils enter the *Gioventù Italiana del Littorio* (GIL), which had just replaced the *Opera Nazionale Balilla* (ONB), only seven among them did. One of the students expelled after the boycott, Savvas Vrouchos, shared an anti-colonial, Greek nationalist inclination with his brother Michalis.[117] The latter partook in the British secret operation "Erratic" aimed at destabilizing Italian rule during the Second World War by using local informants.[118] Arrested and executed by the Germans in September 1944 in his early twenties, Michalis (and his companion Giorgios Kostaridis) counts as a patriotic martyr in Rhodes's collective memory until today.

The 1930s were the decisive moment for the politicization of youth in Rhodes. Revisionist Zionism, Kemalism, and Greek irredentism gained visibility in this colonial setting and involved issues of education and mobility, highlighting power relations between state authorities, communal leaders, and youth. Although these political currents appeared almost simultaneously, ideological differences mattered: whereas the Revisionists displayed a strong identification with fascism, Turkish nationalists were not manifestly hostile to fascist rule, while Greek irredentists opposed the Italian regime more directly by denouncing the occupation of the islands. Moreover, their irradiation differed: the Revisionists' main contacts were in the Italian Kingdom, Kemalism was fostered by a representative of a foreign state, while Greek irredentism established links with the diaspora. Yet, these movements shared the hostility to the communal-colonial order which was supported by notables of the respective confession.

All actors involved were discontent with the constraints this order posed to their professional, intellectual, and political development, as their horizon reached beyond the boundaries of colonialism. Lago's governance did not empower this ambitious local youth. His priority remained the elder notables' allegiance and the indivisibility of colonial communities. Integrating youth into fascism was a means to this end. The anxiety about youth "fanaticism" resulted from the impossibility that these youth be patriotic and colonized at the same time. Some youth stuck in this dilemma, like Giuseppe Levi, Celaleddin Sünger, and Savvas Vrouchos, were most receptive to alternative identifications circulating in Rhodes. Growing up in a colonial setting, their trajectories intersected with fascism's endeavours to transfer its dictatorial hegemony over youth to this part of the post-Ottoman Mediterranean, a process for which the manpower of local activists was as vital as it was hard to discipline.

Fascist Activism in a Colonial Setting

In the aftermath of the First World War, while communal institutions experienced turmoil and Italy assured durable control over the Dodecanese, fascism arrived in Rhodes. Fascist activists could count on slogans and practices that characterized the movement in the metropolitan areas of the Kingdom. Once in power, fascism expanded the field of youth political activism with novelties such as summer camps, parades, and uniforms, all embedded in colonial imaginaries such as the myth of *Italianità* and of a Mediterranean Empire. Until the end of Italian rule, these were central in legitimizing the *Italianità* of Rhodes and they were a pillar of the colonial repertoire of governance.

The structure of the party blended colonial and metropolitan features: in 1927, the Rhodes section moved from being under the supervision of the *Fasci* abroad towards integration in the National Fascist Party. It was thus formally more connected to metropolitan administration than the very *Possedimento* government, since Governor Lago embodied the link to the state mainly through the Ministry of Foreign Affairs.[119] Fascism had to adapt to the local setting, first and foremost regarding the conditions of access to the party. Since only full Italian citizens could join it, the authorities faced the paradox of investing into the fascistization of a colonized youth destined to remain at the margins of fascist adult structures. The challenge was to foster the population's loyalty and keep citizenship and racial boundaries upright at the same time. But fascism was more than an element of governmental rule. This section explores it as a reference that actors appropriated to position themselves in the political field of the Italian colony.

The earliest available mention of fascism in Rhodes is a meeting advertised in the *Messaggero* in October 1921 by the *Fascio di Combattimento*, as the movement's sections were called before their transformation into a national party a few weeks later, validated by a congress in Rome. The fact that "members (*soci*) and participants (*aderenti*)" were urged to gather privately for "information of utmost importance," suggests that the association was created earlier but still lacked a proper agenda.[120] In early November, the *Fascio* figured prominently in the *Messaggero di Rodi* with a message commemorating the Unknown Soldier (*Milite Ignoto*), a symbol of Italy's victory in the First World War.[121] In those early months, fascists in Rhodes stood under Governor Alessandro De Bosdari's (1921–2) protection and favour, although his own attitude towards fascism was rather lukewarm.[122] The fascists in Rhodes displayed an aggressive masculinity modelled on the exaltation of soldiering life similar to the squads (*squadracce*), even though the low degree of physical violence in the Aegean was not comparable to most metropolitan settings.

The most salient episode was a raid at the local farmers' market in October 1922. Arriving in the early morning, a group of fascists threatened the vendors, seized their produce, and sold it at a lower price. More than fifty vendors denounced this act to the mayor. Whereas De Bosdari promised an "exemplary punishment" for the perpetrators, nothing is known about his measures and the episode was silenced by the press.[123] Local fascists also claimed to grant material aid to the population during the post-war hardship. Already in August 1922, they invited "all compatriots who happen to be unemployed to show up at the party's office and submit a regular request of employment" to "facilitate the procedure of hiring."[124] Another relief initiative occurred in September 1922, right after the Great Fire of Smyrna. The local party section funded a committee called *"Pro Profughi Italiani di Smirne"* aimed at aiding the incoming refugees.[125] The Government of Rhodes donated 2,000 lire, Governor De Bosdari as a private person 1,000, and the section of the *Fascio* 500.[126] This initiative confirms the special bond that fascism built with Italian citizens from Asia Minor, as illustrated more in depth in chapter 5, even before the establishment of Mussolini's regime in Rome.

In Italy, early fascism coupled a core of young male activists with an omnipresent "appeal to youthfulness" in its mobilizing discourse.[127] In a colonial setting like Libya, squads of young fascists arrived from Italy as early as 1923 and their violence against the population "threatened to upset delicate colonial hierarchies" that bound local institutions to Italian state control.[128] By contrast, young fascists were not prominent in Rhodes, and adult men led the movement. Vincenzo Rao, the first local leader, was 35 years old at the time of the marketplace raid. He had studied law in Sicily and worked as a low-rank civil servant in his hometown before the First World War. Only after moving to Rhodes, in 1921, he opened a lawyer office "hoping to improve his economic situation," as the Italian police remarked. Rao was one of the many Italian men who came to Rhodes without large sums of money, investment ambitions, or career experiences. Yet, he had a considerable social capital. Rao was in the executive board of the *Lega Italiana*, a cultural institution that, in territories acquired after the First World War, propagated the legitimacy of Italian rule.[129] In later years, Rao was known as a "libertine" neglecting his wife and regularly visiting brothels with his son Liborio.[130] He had debts with women who maintained him, with local private individuals, banks, and companies. Even his clients complained about his lack of professionalism in several court cases.[131] Rao managed to live above his means while his reputation worsened. His party activism did not improve his economic status, and yet his role as first director of the *Fascio* and of the *Lega Italiana* granted him the authorities' favour when he faced his creditors' complaints. Rao did not hold prestigious functions in the party after fascist functionaries sent from Italy replaced local activists. Nor did his son Liborio, born in 1912, profit from his father's militancy. He had occasional jobs in the movie industry in Rome and in Rhodes. Alike his father's, Liborio's morality was considered reproachable due to affairs with married women and to insolvency problems.[132] Liborio became a member of the Fascist Party in 1934 but did not cover any key role in local structures.

Another participant in the marketplace raid, Francesco Mellone, was born in 1878 in the region of Puglia. After serving as a brigadier for the *Carabinieri*, he settled in Rhodes in the early years of the occupation because of "lack of fortune" (*poca fortuna*) in Italy, according to the police. In 1920, he married an Orthodox woman of humble origins from Symi, who was nineteen years younger than him. Mellone was neither a prominent political figure, nor a member of the economic elite. He worked for the Italian Mail and, contrary to Rao, was "esteemed by his directors for his reliability, confidentiality, and industriousness." Despite his average social status, early activism in the Fascist Party combined with his past in the *Carabinieri* assured him assistance and protection in terms of jobs at state institutions. Mellone even received a homage after his death in 1939. Government and party structures sent a funeral wreath and the *Messaggero* dedicated an article to his burial, including the fascist ritual of the "call" (*appello*) in his honour.[133]

Mellone left four daughters and one son, born between 1921 and 1933. The first-born Luisa entered the *Fascio Femminile*, the female section of the party, in 1938.[134] A few months earlier, two Orthodox students bullied Mellone's son near his house. When Mellone's wife intervened, the two boys insulted her and shouted that she should "better go and see how [her] daughters let the students kiss them under the Brussali pier."[135] When she reported to the police, Luisa's mother claimed that the reason behind this altercation was that her son was a fascist *Balilla* and his sisters were "daughters of Italians." The boys' sexist accusations corresponded to the police's remarks on Luisa's bad moral reputation, stressed in a later report.[136] Moreover, the two boys attended the *Venetokleion* which, a few weeks earlier, had been the stage of the incidents described above, while Luisa studied at the Italian *Regio Istituto*. Attending these schools was perceived as a marker of political – and national – belonging. Luisa embodied a "hybrid" *Italianità* as a descendant of an interconfessional marriage. And yet, she was identified with the fascist occupier and insulted by young neighbours unsympathetic towards colonial rule. The dispute escalated into a political issue partly because one of the boys' father was considered an anti-Italian informant of the Greek consul.[137]

Giacinto Landriscina also took part in the 1922 fascist raid at the market. Landriscina was born in Rhodes in 1892 and, in 1911, he was arrested with the accusation of raping an Orthodox woman, spending some weeks in jail.[138] He then worked as interpreter for the *Carabinieri* between 1916 and 1918. After joining the *Fascio* in 1921, Landriscina was later expelled from the party due to "indiscipline" and was only allowed to enter minor organizations such as its sports club. Landriscina had frequent trouble with the local police, mostly due to insolvency and money smuggling. He was also accused of having an illicit relationship with a Catholic woman from Smyrna and was morally stigmatized as a regular visitor of brothels.[139] His sons Francesco and Constantino, born in 1918 and 1919, did not inherit any privileged status within the Fascist Party, and they replicated their father's transgressive profile.[140] Only after many infractions did the authorities intervene to place Landriscina senior on the list of "socially dangerous persons."[141] Francesco remained in Rhodes after the mobilization of 1940, while Constantino and the youngest son Antonio (b. 1921) served in the Italian army in Greece and North Africa respectively.[142]

The Landriscinas' trajectory bears similarities with the Raos: well-known figures in public, they had an overall bad reputation for the authorities which, however, rarely intervened against them. The colonial authorities had a convergence of interest with the Fascist Party since they needed residents with full citizenship who could represent sovereign and ideological authority at once. In exchange, early fascist activists could benefit from tolerance for transgressive behaviour and, oftentimes, obtain a decent public employment. These two advantages, then, were more easily transmittable to their children than economic, intellectual, or prestige improvement through militancy in the party.

The Limits of Integration into Fascism

Lacking young activists in its beginnings, the Fascist Party in Rhodes was concerned about how to attract youth as a colonial ruling structure. This problem also resonated among local observers recognizing control over youth as a crucial stake for legitimacy. On 7 May 1928, an article titled "Fascism and Youth" appeared in *Selām*, a local newspaper in (Ottoman) Turkish surveilled by the authorities as a favourable "element of propaganda" among Muslims.[143] By stressing the importance of statism (*devletçilik*) for "*Senyor*" Mussolini, the column claimed that "the state, being the model for the future and the life of the nation, takes the youth, generator of the future, under its wing without constraints and rivals."[144] According to the article, fascism should win the youth's support by overcoming other references such as the Catholic Church and illegal parties. Fascism was thus a force competing against others in the political field. Although the mentioned competitors did not threaten colonial rule in Rhodes, moulding colonial youth as a disciplined but voluntary reflection of fascist values was easier said than done.

The authorities were confronted with the question of the integration into fascist organizations for citizens above 21 years of age. As Lago stated in 1929: "the indigenous youth's … inclusion in these *Fasci* poses a political problem: some particularly deceitful and cunning elements may act against the regime … And I should add that the Aegean *fasci* would be quite inhomogeneous if, next to the fellow citizens from the Kingdom (*regnicoli*), they were to host Dodecanesians not compelled to military service."[145] Lago's statement highlights the dilemma mentioned in the introduction. If fascist colonialism wanted to control youth through fascism, what would be left of the separation between metropolitan and "indigenous" subjects? Boosting identification with fascism among the local youth before they reached the age of majority suspended the problem of how to integrate them as adults on equal footing as *regnicoli*, the metropolitan citizens. Fascism's interference in education can also be explained through this motive.

From 1928 onwards, the religious instructors at the Italian schools of Rhodes supervised a summer camp organized for Fascist youth groups. At Fileremo Hill, fifteen kilometres southwest of Rhodes Town, the instructors were to provide "physical and moral assistance" with "order and serenity."[146] The camping was later renamed from "Lago" to "Ave Dux," and moved to the mountainous area of Prophet Ilias, where the governor had his summer chalet. A leaflet from 1935 informs us on a daily routine in which male participants performed recreational (singing, music, playing), religious (mess), and educational activities, with some moments dedicated to politicized acts of patriotism and militarism (flag-raising, changing of the guard, etc.).[147] Youth summer camps existed in Italy and in other countries, combining preoccupations with children's health with moral dressing and political mobilization.[148] In Rhodes, their fascist container created a bond between the participants and the governor, as Lago used to be present at the closing reception for the participants and their families.[149]

Lago also used the Fascist Party's youth activities to connect Rhodes with other localities in Italy and the Mediterranean. In 1931, a cruise of *Avanguardisti* sailed from Naples to Jerusalem via Istanbul, and the stop in Rhodes showcased the progress achieved through investments in colonial infrastructure.[150] Four years later, Rhodes hosted a *Balilla* delegation from the Fascist Party Section of Egypt.[151] These events linked metropolitan fascism with settings where large communities of Italian citizens resided. The colonial setting of Rhodes represented not only a geographical, but also a symbolical station between these worlds reinforcing the idea of a continuous *Italianità* bolstered by fascism in the Mediterranean.

In Rhodes as elsewhere in the Kingdom, boys joined the *Figli della Lupa* (the "Sons of the She-Wolf," the symbol of Rome, 6 to 8 years of age), the *Balilla* (8 to 14), the *Avanguardisti* (14 to18), and the *Giovani fascisti* (18 to 21). The female equivalents were the *Figlie della Lupa* ("Daughters of the She-Wolf," 6 to 8), the *Piccole Italiane* ("Little Italians," 8 to 13), *Giovani Italiane* (13 to 18) and the *Giovani fasciste* (18 to 21). These corps were accessible to all children, regardless of their parents' citizenship status. Quantitative and nominative sources are scarce, but sons of *regnicoli* are predominant in rosters dated 1927. However, they also included Catholics from Rhodes and Smyrna, Armenians and Jews, as well as a smaller number of Muslims and Orthodox.[152] The ethno-confessional composition did not change significantly throughout the 1930s, and the presence of different categories in terms of their parents' citizenship and confession, although marginal, confirms that fascism was not an exclusive domain of metropolitan Italian settlers.[153]

Nonetheless, preserving the colonial hierarchy was more urgent than integrating the entire population into party structures.

Italian rule did not claim this in public. Statements like the one on the "new generation" had no place in the *Messaggero*, which silenced and neuralized colonial separation when reporting events involving fascist youth. Its articles praised Italian civilization, its fascist grandeur as well as youth virtues such as sense of duty, discipline, industriousness, patriotism. By reading its daily front page, one would have believed that Rhodes was part of the Italian Peninsula. References to the communities were mostly relegated to the section *Dentro e fuori le mura* ("Inside and outside the City Walls"). Communities appeared rarely, mostly when the newspaper stressed the cohesive and at the same time diverse scenery of fascist celebrations in which youth were to represent their respective confessional group. This was the fiction of a smooth fascistization beyond colonial separation. Lago's dilemma of the "new generation" was not to be heard and negotiated by those whom the governor claimed to target.

Anxiety about controlling colonial youth gained momentum in the late 1930s. When the ONB's successor GIL was founded in 1937, De Vecchi distributed 306 membership cards, uniforms, and sport clothes to attract Dodecanesian children of all confessions. This contributed to a growth in membership reaching 1,846 (1,192 male and 754 female members) for the whole Aegean section of the party.[154] De Vecchi's thrust had some effect. One Orthodox participant at the 1938 *Balilla* Summer Camp sent the governor a thankful letter after returning home. "I became," he wrote, "more tempered in the spirit and the body. But apart from the moral and physical gains which I acquired in the seven days at the camp, I could realize with my own eyes everything that the fascist government does for the Italian youth, even in these islands of the newborn empire."[155]

This appropriation of imperial rhetoric when addressing the authorities is striking. It is certainly the expression of a broader feeling among the youth in Rhodes for whom fascism corresponded to the promise of living Italy's imperial dream. Yet this promise was ambivalent. What does "Italian youth" mean in the boy's letter? Did he see himself as part of it? Since the authorities did not lose a single occasion to emphasize the values of Italian youth by avoiding the question of colonial separation, children and adolescents in Rhodes might well aspire to become Italians. They likely knew, though, that as adults they would be categorized as not fully belonging to the Italian body politic. Such appropriation coexisted with resilience, scepticism, and even hostility towards fascist affiliation. Valerie McGuire reported the testimony of Manolis

Despotakis, who stood out for its marks at school but refused to enter the *Balilla*. He cunningly told the teachers that his mother needed him for the housework to avoid taking part in the *Balilla*'s activities.[156]

The *Carabinieri* archive abounds with documents in which "youth" and "fascism" related to each other in everyday interactions. Politics was projected onto intimate and everyday issues and its language reprocessed to negotiate and even subvert relations of power without frontally challenging the rulers, a pattern in which generational categories were central. For instance, identifying a family with fascism underlined their support for Italian rule, which in turn might discredit them. Comissa C. had married an Italian citizen and Fascist Party member in the mid-1920s, although the couple broke up a few years later. In 1938, she had a relationship with her neighbour Nicola Z., aged 17, although the latter's tutor disapproved of her. Comissa took her revenge when she told the authorities that the tutor had given Nicola a "bad" advice: "Don't subscribe to the fascio, because after the upcoming uprising, they (the Italians), will have to leave the Dodecanese and the state that will occupy the islands will ruin anyone registered in the Fascio ... It is a matter of days."[157] Nicola, who wanted to join the *Giovani Fascisti*, claimed that the woman had made up these sentences. Whosever standpoint one accepts, this exchange reveals that (geo-)politics and future scenarios interplayed with private disputes.

Similarly, Pietro C., an Orthodox worker, reported a quarrel between his wife and a neighbour to the police:

> While I was sleeping at home ... we suddenly woke up because our neighbour Marco M., drunk, swore against us and our son, *Giovane Fascista*, Nicola C., aged 23, who was absent because he lives at his fiancée's. He said to my wife from his courtyard, which is just next to ours: "Bootlicker, you speak about the rumours of the neighbours everywhere you go." My wife Diamanti replied to this sentence: "Shut up, because my son is a fascist and I will have you punished!" To this, M. replied: "You think you scare me because your son is a fascist? I don't fear anybody, I shit on him and his black shirt! ... Don't even mention fascism, because if your son is a fascist, I am a communist!"[158]

The police did not pursue Marco and warned the couple not to "speculate on the basis of the reputation they enjoy through their sentiments of *Italianità*."[159] Being a fascist's parent was displayed as social prestige, also to compensate a poor economic condition. Pietro's son, aged 23, went through the full "curriculum" of fascist youth organizations while only two of Marco's children aged 10 and 7 were members of the younger *Piccole Italiane* and the *Balilla* respectively. His older children worked at the age of 11 (labourer, helping his father) and 13 (domestic servant) and were not part of any fascist organization. Thus, the threat "Shut up, *because* my son is a fascist" interiorized a hierarchy that saw fascism as the most powerful authority. However, this hierarchy did not always operate as the actors thought. The official rhetoric urged lower class colonial subjects to express attachment to Italy. But away from the spotlight, the police did not allow them to boast about their superiority vis-à-vis other colonial subjects in the name of *Italianità*. Excessive attachment to Italy showed in private issues among Aegean subjects could be interpreted as insidious for public order and for the colonial politics of difference separating them from metropolitan Italians.

The Orthodox woman quoted above referred to an "uprising" and the "departure" of Italians from the Dodecanese in a rather trivial conversation. This was a symptom of a politically tense atmosphere in the late 1930s. It echoed De Vecchi's push for fascistization, the surge of state antisemitism in Italy, the regime's militarism, and geopolitical rivalry with neighbouring countries such as Greece and Turkey. The expansion of fascist youth organizations was part of this process. In a letter to the Party's central in Rome dated January 1939, the new PNF provincial secretary (*Segretario Federale*) Attilio Romano expressed his opinion on Rhodes:

> I would like to introduce you to the necessity of extending the obligation of pre-military instruction to the subjects of the Italian Aegean Islands with the aim of a higher endeavour of political and spiritual penetration. In so doing, we will have a recruitment of more than 5,000 souls, inexorably converging towards the light of Fascism … To exclude young subjects, whom we mould in the crucible of faith of the Italian School, from the moral and human right of … pre-military education, means to lose them.

Blending pragmatism, idealism and vulgar antisemitism, Romano reverted Lago's approach:

> by refusing them, we push them away from our spirit and, when they turn 18, we deliver them to the corrupting action of the [Orthodox] priests, who still support Greek irredentism. During the three years of pre-military education, with an ardent postulate of *Italianità*, a healthy work of depuration can be carried out, which assigns to the rising generation the sacred tasks of Fascism. Only through youth educated in Fascism will it be possible to set the *Possedimento* free from the ignoble marketplace of the Jewish-Masonic capitalism that has branches in all the sectors of life in Rhodes.[160]

Romano's statement reiterated Lago's project of a "new generation" strengthening fascism and *Italianità*. Both knew that fascist colonial rule could neither fully include nor fully exclude local individuals. Voicing an aggressive assimilation into fascism, Romano put his finger on Lago's dilemma. Eleven years after Lago's statement quoted in the book's introduction, "indigenous youth" had not yet become the "new generation" of good fascists, and a colonial mindset based on cooperation with local religious and communal elites was insufficient to control youth. Romano thus unveiled a latent problem of fascist colonialism. Military expansionism needed manpower from the colony, but the Treaty of Lausanne's legacy and the following citizenship reforms had made exemption from conscription a cornerstone of fascism colonialism. The ambivalent status of the Aegean *Possedimento*, ruled through politics of difference but not comparable to African colonies according to Italy's civilizational and racial categories, made fascism tend towards assimilation into the Italian army rather than the creation of separate colonial troops such as the Eritrean *Ascari*.

Eventually, though, this exemption continued throughout the Second World War, and the Italian authorities even refused requests of voluntary enrolment by local subjects.[161] A part of the local population sincerely believed in the Fascist Empire, hoping for the same rights and duties as metropolitan Italians. In 1935, Leon Levy left Rhodes for a short training in Sardinia, before being sent to fight in the Spanish Civil War, where soldiers and Blackshirts, the fascist (para)military corps of the *Milizia Volontaria per la Sicurezza Nazionale* (MVSN), engaged in mixed battalions on Francisco Franco's side.[162] Ideological sympathy for fascism was not a central motive for this Jewish volunteer.[163] Writing to his uncle Raphael Capeluto, Levy described his decision and his experience in the army as follows: "Dear Uncle, I was idle, and not having work, I was compelled to enlist in the Army. The hard times that my family went through were not enough and I had to leave them to suffer and to waste my youth in the military life at a great distance from my family."[164]

Giuseppe Hasson had a similar background. When his father died in 1935, he worked as an accountant for an Italian company based in Rhodes, earning an average salary. Soldiering as a volunteer was an occasion to have a higher income and send his widowed and destitute mother a part of his salary, since his siblings either lived abroad or had humble occupations such as grocer or carpenter in Rhodes. Upon returning from Spain in 1939, Hasson took back his job, but the situation of Rhodian Jews had changed dramatically due to the infamous Italian Racial Laws of November 1938. These were supposed to strip Italian citizenship from Jews who had obtained it after 1919, creating discussions between Rhodes and Rome on how to implement this denaturalization and expulsion in the *Possedimento*.[165] Since Hasson was not only full citizen, but also had received military honours for his service in Spain, his request of exemption from the anti-Jewish measures was accepted. He converted to Catholicism in May 1940 and obtained a passport to Spain, although his paper trail ends with a stay in Naples one year later.[166]

Hasson's conversion and military service protected him from persecution. This was not the case for other Jews who were too young to apply for full citizenship despite their attachment to fascism and Italy. Gini Alhadeff recalled how her father Carlo (b. 1924) "learned to wear a black shirt and hat, and to extend his right arm in a fascist salute." After going through all youth sections from the *Figli della Lupa* to the *Avanguardisti*, he was targeted by the Racial Laws: "My father remembers feeling afraid, paying attention to what was being said. On the one hand, he was still under the influence of the fascist movement; on the other, he was a dirty Jew. 'At that age,' he said, 'you think you're the shit – that everyone is right and you are wrong.'"[167] Age was a crucial factor of distinction in a masculinized and hierarchical political socialization, as fascism imposed a rigid obedience on its young followers. For Alhadeff and other young Jewish activists, this led to a sense of inferiority and incredulity when the regime changed from treating them as politically valuable to persecuting them based on their race. Similarly, the orphan Morris Sciarcon "probably had thought of being adopted by fascism from which he now felt forever repudiated," as his son Andrea recalled.[168]

In some cases, expulsions from the GIL resulted from a conflict between communal and national identification. Raimondo Hanan was born in Buenos Aires in 1918 but he studied at the Italian schools of Rhodes. The police profiled him as a "good-mannered young man, serious and respectful, showing attachment to our institutions" when he applied for entering the *Giovani Fascisti*.[169] On 2 October 1936, Raimondo was attending the public broadcasting of Mussolini's speech on the first anniversary of the invasion of Ethiopia, when he quarrelled with another *Giovane Fascista*, son of a metropolitan citizen. The latter scolded Raimondo since he wore civil clothes as a sign of pious respect for the Rosh Hashanah festivity instead of the mandatory Blackshirt fascist uniform. The situation degenerated in a brawl and Raimondo was expelled shortly afterwards for "indiscipline, incorrigibility, and absence of fascist faith."[170]

Pressure to enter fascist youth organizations grew parallel to Italy's imperial ambitions, culminating in the late 1930s. Voluntary integration in the GIL coexisted with increasing scepticism and the feeling that this affiliation could produce a conflict with other spheres of socialization, be it the school, the neighbourhood, the family, or the community. Next to promises of imperial grandeur that Aegean subjects could dream of but hardly live as protagonists, fascist activism offered a high but unstable social capital that could vanish either by sudden and arbitrary expulsion from Party organizations or by larger scale events such as the Racial Laws. At the eve of the Second World War, the political field constructed by fascist colonialism in Rhodes left little space for strategies other than indoctrination, assimilation, racial discrimination, displacement of dissidents, and widespread police surveillance. Under these circumstances, without ever granting alternative political references to the youth it governed, how could Italian imperial rule successfully foster its legitimacy and end differently than in the catastrophe of war and persecution that fascism contributed to create?

***

In May 1940, a few weeks before Italy entered Second World War against France and Great Britain, the French vice-consul had complained that a group of "young people" led by members of the Fascist University Students Groups (GUF) had gathered at his residence and shouted slogans against France, before throwing stones at the windows of the British consulate.[171] Compared to the situation of 1909 presented at the beginning of this chapter, the Aegean regional setting had profoundly changed. It is possible that, after the Young Turks called for youth to regenerate imperial rule in the name of constitutionalism thirty years earlier, some local youngsters resisted against the Italian invasion in May 1912, but no available sources point to such successful mobilization. On the eve of the Second World War, fascism now used its own youth organizations to project European rivalries into a colonial setting. Taken together, the late Ottoman and Italian period reveal that bringing the youth under state control was a persisting challenge for imperial authorities, although the politicization of youth appeared only after 1912.

Fascist colonialism shared with the Young Turks the idea of building an imperial mindset which would require a new balance between indoctrination and politics of difference in their attitude towards communities. Notables and religious authorities were rather accommodating with rulers of both periods, never acting as leaders of dissent, also because state pressure on them effectively prevented this danger. For the same reason, they were criticized by those who understood their function as the neutralization of politics. Late Ottoman communities were a platform where local aspirations to participate in politics tended towards state integration, as demonstrated by an increasingly competitive atmosphere in the Second Constitutional Period. By contrast, Italian colonial communities served the purpose of separating integration into state politics reserved to full citizens from the "indigenous" affairs. When considered together, these two directions hampered strong continuities in terms of political family "dynasties": political pressure made it hard to hold to important offices in both the Ottoman and the Italian periods. Whereas De Vecchi's push for fascistization represents the culmination of state efforts, the Second World War and the end of Italian rule did not allow for a transformation of "indigenous youth" into fascist Italian patriots, just like the Italo-Ottoman War and the decade of conflicts in the 1910s made the ideological mobilization of the masses as envisioned by the Young Turks ephemeral.

Yet, wrapping up the political history of youth in Rhodes only based on state projects conceals the variety of references appropriated by those targeted as youth. The chapter has shown that some Jews interpreted Zionism as the possibility that Rhodes be part of *Erez Israel* while others later embraced Jabotinsky's Revisionism. Some Orthodox irredentists demanded *Enosis* with Greece as a benevolent act following Italy's "liberation" from Ottoman rule while others later claimed their national belonging through resistance against fascist Italianization. Some Muslims stressed their allegiance to the Ottoman Empire during its military effort at Gallipoli, while others later flirted with the nationalization of politics in Kemalist Turkey. Despite their differences and distance in time, these attitudes prove that the attempts to isolate Rhodes as an impermeable outpost of Italian colonialism could not succeed. Youth intersected with ideology but also with the appropriation of national and spatial categories of belonging. This allowed local actors to define their place in a Mediterranean world marked by the Ottoman collapse and by new forms of nationalism.

Such polyphonic representation of politics does not downplay fascism's indoctrination in Rhodes, it rather points to the limits of interpreting fascism as a monolithic entity without competitors, which is how authorities liked to describe it in public statements. Yet, polyphony applies beyond competing ideologies. It allows for an interpretation of the late Ottoman and the Italian colonial political field as intersecting with other domains of youth socialization. Our journey into the imperial consequence will now continue towards the domestic sphere to discuss how families acted as a container of generational dynamics connected to the transformation of communal structures and state rule.

Chapter Two

Where Families and Empires Meet

In March 1995, Pasquale Cacopardi, a resident of Piacenza (Italy) but Rhodian by birth, published a lively account of his childhood in 1930s Rhodes in a magazine about Sephardic culture. Only a couple of weeks later, Pasquale received a letter from Nice, France, by Leon Alhadeff, also originally from Rhodes.[1] Leon rejoiced over discovering to be Pasquale's distant cousin. This letter tells the story of a family bond between two men who never met, corresponding fifty years after the end of Italian rule and even longer after they had left Rhodes. The shared experience of a childhood spent in the Italian Aegean colony before the Second World War compensated the distance in space and time. Yet, the letter ended with a bittersweet tone: "I imagine how sorrowful it must have been for your mother to live so many years with a feeling of reclusion, without any family contact, and then to pass away with such resentment. Should you happen to be around here let me know, so I could be delighted to greet a new cousin among others scattered around the world."[2]

Memories of the parents' trajectories recomposed a familial mosaic that displacement had "scattered around the world." But this distance was not only caused by mobility. Why did Pasquale's mother lose family contacts? Pasquale was the first-born son of Antonino Cacopardi, a Catholic Italian citizen, and Violetta (Zimbul) Mizrahi, a Rhodian Jew. Antonino had moved from Sicily to Rhodes around 1927 after completing his military service. Five years later, as he worked for a beer import company, he met Violetta and promised to marry her. Shortly afterwards, she got pregnant and a scandal arose in her family. She decided to leave her parents' place and move to Antonino's flat. At that point, the accounts gathered in Antonino's police file diverge as to whether she had willingly abandoned her parents or whether they had wanted her to leave to lower the economic burden on their humble household. Other relatives demanded a way out of this uncomfortable situation. Violetta's brother Sadoc sent a letter to Rhodes from the Belgian Congo, where he had moved some years earlier like many local Jews. He urged Antonino to marry Violetta and settle the issue: "You ought to be aware of the sorrow that this event is causing us, above all to our elderly parents that my sister had to leave due to her actual condition and without a legal act of union, which would give you the right to live together ... You know that in Europe too, where minds are more open, similar cases trouble family life, even more in a small town like Rhodes."[3]

Encouraged by the Italian police, Antonino agreed to recognize the child as the "son of an unknown woman," claiming his right and responsibility to "take care, the way he will deem more appropriate, of his nurture, education, and upbringing." Nonetheless, he refused to marry Violetta and tried to persuade her to move back to the paternal home.[4] In the meantime, Violetta gave birth and recognized Pasquale. One year later, as Violetta turned 21, she was entitled to marry without her parents' consent, and Antonino agreed to "regularize" the situation. After being baptized and renamed Maria, she married him in October 1934 at the Catholic Church of Santa Maria della Vittoria. Her conversion further deteriorated the relationship with her Jewish family. Violetta lived in a nuclear household with her husband and children, and later hired an Orthodox domestic servant from a nearby island. Pasquale, however, continued to visit his maternal grandparents. The family even moved back to Violetta's parental home after her mother's death to look after the old widower. Only amid the Second World War did Violetta move to Sicily with their children to join her husband, who had already left Rhodes.[5]

The Cacopardis' trajectory left a remarkable paper trail. Their story includes social and political factors which transformed family bonds during the shift from Ottoman to Italian rule in Rhodes: the immigration of Italian men pursuing new occupations, their intermarriage with local women, local men's emigration overseas, disputes over the legal recognition of marriage by religious and state institutions, the establishment of nuclear households later including domestic servants, the *Carabinieri*'s interference in private affairs. Moreover, Maria/Violetta, who grew up as a Jew and a non-metropolitan subject, would have been discriminated by the antisemitic Racial Laws promulgated in Fascist Italy in 1938 had she not acquired the Italian citizenship and converted to Catholicism through her wedding.[6] This rescued her from an almost certain deportation in the summer of 1944, since she left for Sicily when it was almost impossible for Jews to find shelter.

In a few lines of a letter, in a few pages of an archival file, family trajectories weave into major historic developments. Echoes of a global dispersal resonate within domestic walls. What keeps these scales together, the micro and the macro, state and society, the mobile and the local, is the story of a local Jewish woman's encounter with a Catholic newcomer. Theirs is also the interwoven story of an Ottoman and an Italian family, which makes it a symbolic reflection of the political changes discussed in this book. For Maria and Antonino, like for other couples of any confession, the process of family building was neither linear nor simple while navigating imperial transformations. Engagement, marriage, procreation, and parenthood were the result of conflicts and compromises. These generational dynamics were *transmissional*, since they influenced the circulation of resources and roles. Partners negotiated with each other but also with their relatives as well as with communal and state authorities in charge of recognizing legal acts. All sides described generational bonds in terms of "care," "sacrifice," but also "break," "crisis," and "scandal," charging them with social and moral values. This chapter asks how family socialization changed during a colonial turn in imperial governance. It is concerned with how mobility and economy in the late and post-Ottoman Mediterranean impacted the family, and how we can locate fascism as a force within this change.

The family is not simply the receiving end of social and political change but also one of its propellers. Changes in family roles and the organization of the household can quickly become issues discussed by institutions and governments.[7] Colonial rule brought about an increased interference of political authorities in generational dynamics within family affairs. Conversely, families appropriated the political meaning attached to the representations of kin and household. Italian colonial bureaucracy intervened along a hierarchization based on gender, race, and citizenship, but also reflecting a tighter relationship between state and families in the metropole.[8] In Rhodes, whereas the Ottoman *vali* around 1900 could well not be concerned by who married whom, the Italian *governatore* forty years later became an active stakeholder in family issues, supported by the colonial police and the judiciary institutions. Despite this difference, the imperial consequence was manifest in the way Italian authorities acknowledged the verdicts by the local religious courts of the Ottoman period, in line with the special personal status that they granted to Aegean colonial subjects. This created a strong analogy between the Aegean and the "Libyan citizenship," since the personal status included customs like divorce and polygamy (the latter being extremely rare in Rhodes), that were not admitted by Italian metropolitan law.[9]

Not only did family issues define Italian Aegean subjecthood, they also marked a certain reciprocity vis-à-vis other post-Ottoman realities. Such reciprocity was a legacy of the Treaty of Lausanne, which granted a special personal status to non-Muslim minorities in republican Turkey.[10] Generational dynamics within the family were handled locally, but they reveal how each state interpreted population politics in the post-Ottoman Mediterranean. Dealing with family issues exposed different politics of difference in the region, for instance by justifying special criteria through the notion of "minorities" in Turkey while referring to "communities" in Rhodes. The previous Ottoman predominance of religious communal jurisdiction related to marriage and inheritance partially yielded to civil state institutions during Italian rule over the islands. Yet, the colonial governors were aware of the impossibility – and the inconvenience – of monopolizing the management of the family. Instead of building a monolithic legal polity and erasing communal courts, Italian rule increasingly interfered in the communal jurisdiction that it kept alive.

While new laws and institutions emerged in early twentieth-century Rhodes, the percentage of married couples among the local population and the age at marriage did not profoundly change. Family structures were not shattered by political transformations, but the latter required intense negotiation to adapt to new circumstances. A more direct interaction with the authorities is visible in the documents related to diverse pre-conjugal relationships. These included gendered violence, social pressure based on the notion of reputation, mediation by peers, parents, and communal institutions, but also a wide range of sentiments which nuance a dichotomy between "arranged" and "love" unions. Marriage applications introduced in the 1930s became a bureaucratic device to profile the local population by investigating the couples' life trajectories and their social environment. Interference from above coexisted with efforts from below to cope with the fragmentation of the family as an economic unit. This was in turn related to mobility. Outflows starting in the last Ottoman years as well as inflows gaining momentum under Italian rule caused separation within large families and a redistribution of the living space available in town, often leading to legal disputes concerning its usage. The resulting household nuclearization intersected with the monetization of rented estate property. It especially concerned new couples in which the husband was an employee, a craftsman, or a small trader. Moreover, the lower classes faced precarious sources of income, frequently addressing the authorities with petitions. During Italian rule, these requests reveal a creative elaboration of family roles and bonds to obtain material aid. Especially women mobilized the notion of morality and appropriated the plurality of legal systems responsible for family issues in the colonial setting. Many also used the language of the rulers, including Mussolini's aggressive imperialist rhetoric of the 1930s. Describing the own family through solid and virtuous generational bonds emphasized a convergence between the domestic realm and Italy's imperial mission.

We are used to think of the family as the central container of generational dynamics. According to the segmentation based on age and lineage, we mostly discuss our family tree as consisting of children and parents, youth and elders, siblings and partners. The conflation of interest and emotions related to the nodes that keep a family tree grow and extend makes the family "a key referential grid for the social imaginary."[11] Entire states, nations, but also companies and associations have been described through similes related to the family. In turn, historians often describe individuals with formulas such as "the daughter of a middle-class bureaucrat" or "the son of peasants." But how does such social status impact generational bonds in the family? How do actors perform these bonds and represent them outside the household? The chapter discusses family as a flexible notion, including household and kinship, linking these questions with two premises. First, families move through historical transformations both as a unit and as the sum of their members' individual trajectories. Second, life experiences are as important as collective categories and quantitative data when interpreting the relationship between families and authorities.

The correlation between the terms family, kinship, and household became evident during my research as I found a "family picture" on the Rhodes Jewish Museum's website. Fascinated by the many generations appearing in figure 2.1, I also realized the problems of defining family relationships. Were these persons all kin? Did they live under the same roof? How did they manage family resources? As studies on late Ottoman family photography have demonstrated, these artefacts are as precious as difficult to handle when it comes to reconstruct lives and experiences behind the studio scenery.[12] Yet, in this case, the comment by a descendant offers several hints:

Figure 2.1. The Angel family in early twentieth-century Rhodes. Courtesy of the Rhodes Jewish Historical Foundation and Aron Hasson.

This is a family shot of grandmother Angel before she and children left for Seattle, grandfather Angel and uncle Moshe were already in Seattle. Among the people in the picture ... are neighbours of grandmother Angel. I was told they were of the Capelluto family, and Aunty Bohora was part of that family. Front row, left to right; uncle Avner (with cap); uncle Ray (the baby); young boy probably of the Capelluto family; uncle Joseph, at the far right, wearing a fez, (who wasn't admitted to the US because he had a disease (tinyas); he was sent back to Rhodes, eventually married and had 4 children. He died in 1943. his wife and children were deported by the Nazis in 1944 and were murdered at Auschwitz). Middle row, left to right; Aunty Victoria; Unknown; grandmother Angel; to her immediate left, standing beside her, is Bohora Rosa Capelluto, who was to become wife of our uncle Moshe; the woman and two children are probably also of Aunty Bohora's family; on the far right is aunty Luna. Back row, left to right: Ralph Angel ... he's wearing a fez and has his hand on his chest.[13]

This description confirms that a "family picture" was often not indicative of residential units or kin. It could exclude members who were already in the United States, while it included prospective members like Rosa Capelluto and, most likely, her parents (in the top-right corner).[14] A "family picture" is easy to put in a frame as a static object, yet family itself is a fluid subject changing through space and time, impacted by historical events and mobility which make *our* framing an infinite process. Some of the names (but not all of those mentioned in the comment) appear in the passenger record of a ship arriving in New York from Fiume in November 1911, and they are recorded as heading for Seattle to Behora's (Boulissa's) brother-in-law Morris Cohen.[15] Moreover, Joseph Angel's fate is confirmed by a document issued by the Italian authorities in the 1930s and updated until 1944. By working as a boatman, he became the head of a new household including his wife and children, his brother-in-law and mother-in-law, as well as a niece. He was thus the only member of the Angel family who remained in Rhodes until the Second World War.[16]

Like the Cacopardis, the Angels are a kaleidoscope of local and global dynamics, which is why framing the family is more than an exercise in genealogy. In this chapter, singular family stories (and memories) meet the imaginary and bureaucratic classification of the family as a general category. The difference between these two aspects is essential, but so is exploring their intertwining. Generational bonds within the family are made and unmade by actors while they face both norms and their transgression. Be it in the case of negotiation of marriage, heritage, or domestic roles, norms were reflected in representations of the family but acquired their value precisely because they were frequently transgressed. While a number of voices commented on transgression and norms, government institutions collected information to classify family structures, which is best illustrated by population censuses.

Bureaucratic Knowledge about Marriage and Celibacy

Marriage is commonly assumed to be a crucial step in the family and life cycle, separating youth from adulthood. Already in the nineteenth century, Georg Simmel underlined its complexity as a combination of "erotic as well as economic, religious as well as social interests, interests of power and of individual formation."[17] All these features produced a wide range of outcomes that altogether made marriage the norm for adult socialization in early twentieth-century Rhodes. A good marriage required adapting to innovations related to education and mobility. The director of the local *Alliance* school commented in 1906 that Jewish girls "became aware of the appreciable benefits that education provides them, especially if they will emigrate, because they will be able to marry more easily."[18] Next to migration, commentators stressed the importance of marriage for strengthening tradition. In this case, marriage was mostly considered a union within confessional boundaries. In the essay "*O Gamos*" (The marriage), published on the local yearbook *Rodiakon Imerologion* in 1912, an Orthodox doctor argued that marriage "deserves being considered a sacred institution by religion, and inviolable by the state regulations."[19] Some fifteen years later, the local newspaper *Selām* published articles on "The family in contemporary social relations" (*'aṣrī mu'āşerette 'ā'ile*) which described a still patriarchal, yet more "modern" family based on affections and solidarity.[20] These were vernacular expressions within the broader discourse linking families, religious institutions, and governments that circulated globally, including in the Ottoman Empire and Italy.

Debates on marriage in Ottoman society gained momentum in the mid-nineteenth century, turning from a trope in novels to a political controversy on civilization.[21] During the First World War, when Rhodes was already quite out of reach for Ottoman state interference, previous debates on marriage precipitated in the 1917 Law of Family Rights. The Committee of Union and Progress's authoritarian government established legal normativity "for family life and gender relations."[22] This discourse mostly concerned the role of women, welcoming new modes of affective socialization but also imposing new moral constraints.[23] A parallel development occurred in early twentieth-century Italy, where neo-paternalistic family policies emerged. The value of marriage was reaffirmed as the cornerstone of procreation and morality against the rather non-interventionist strategy of earlier governments. Thus, the way was paved for fascism's conservative turn in family policies from the mid-1920s onwards, which was also a result of the regime's pacification with the Catholic Church.[24] Representations of the "man-as-husband" developed already in nineteenth-century Italy at the intersection of nationalist and medical discourses.[25] After the First World War, the character of "family man" produced a masculine persona not confined to domestic practices, and Italian fathers were seen as carriers of the new fascist order.[26]

The family was not only categorized through laws and commentaries, but also through bureaucratic quantitative information. The only preserved state census records available dating prior to the arrival of Italian troops are two draft registers (*müsvedde defterleri*) of the 1905–6 Ottoman census.[27] These documents offer an insight into the tendency towards marriage and celibacy across age and gender distinction. Among the two *mahalle* recorded, Hudayi in the walled city recurs in a later census, thus allowing for a diachronic discussion.[28] Several social strata ranging from estate owners (*aṣḥāb-ı emlāk*) to custom officials (*rüsūmāt me'mūrleri*) to (agricultural) labourers (*rençberler*) appear in Hudayi's ninety Muslim *hāneler*, an ambivalent term in between "households" and "residences."[29]

Concerning women, data from 1905 reveal that marriage became a concrete possibility around 15 years of age, although more than 50 per cent of women above that age were "nubile" (*bākire*, also meaning "virgin") or *seyībe*, a term for singles which could mean "no longer a virgin" as well as "widow." However, if one considers women over 25, 94 per cent were recorded as married (*mütāhele*), which suggest that being single at that age was exceptional and considered anomic. Among men, the youngest husband in 1905 was 22 years old. In a sample of 107 men above that age, 36 per cent were listed as single (*mücerred*), although this term does not distinguish widowers from bachelors. A wedding around the age of 35 was clearly less frequent for men. Moreover, as many as 60 per cent of men aged between 22 and 35 were single. Thus, there was more pressure on women than on men for an "early" marriage at the dawn of the twentieth century. The opposite holds true for a second and/or a "late" marriage: in case of widowhood, men were more susceptible to find a new spouse.

This snapshot of 1905 can be compared with the 1922 census of Hudayi organized by the Italian governor and the local confessional authorities.[30] There was no relevant change in the early modal age for marriage, the youngest wife being 16 and the youngest husband 20. A drop from 22.5 per cent to 13 per cent for nubile women over 15, however, shows a slight increase in early marriage for Muslim women before the end of Italian military occupation. Material scarcity, insecurity due to warfare around Rhodes – albeit without the massive mobilization of men that characterized the Ottoman Empire – but also a growing negotiation power in family building by Ottoman Muslim women made marriage a subsistence strategy aimed at sharing and optimizing resources among families.[31]

A further layer of analysis that includes other confessional categories can be added through the family certificates (*fogli di famiglia*) preserved at the town hall of Rhodes.[32] These certificates were (most likely) produced since the late 1920s and updated until 1945, with occasional entries in Greek for the post-war period.[33] I have sampled forty households of each confession (Muslim, Orthodox, Jewish, and Catholic) in which at least the head of household or his/her spouse were born between 1884 and 1914, in order to have more coherent data for the period under scrutiny. The youngest bride in this sample was again 15 years old, yet the youngest husband was 24, the latter marking a significant increase (+4) from the 1922 census but converging with the one from 1905. The increase in age at marriage in European settings has been associated with structural transformations such as industrialization and accelerated social mobility.[34] In the case of Rhodes, it is more accurate to speak of a diversification and specialization of the occupational world, as will be illustrated below. Furthermore, a convergence with previous patterns could occur: the family certificates provide the same percentage (22 per cent) of unmarried women for all confessions over 15 years of age as in 1905, while there was only a slight increase in unmarried women over 25 (8 per cent). Data also reveal a lower rate of unmarried men (19 per cent) in comparison to 1905 and 1922, while bachelors over thirty dropped significantly to 8 per cent. In the previous three decades, thousands of men, especially Jews and Orthodox, left Rhodes to seek working opportunities or to gain specialized skills increasingly needed to pursue a profession. Many got married abroad or postponed their marriage. At the same time, it was easier and more urgent to get married once they returned on the island with more resources, which partially explains the low rate of unmarried men in the 1930s.

The 1930s family sheets also provide clues as to what degree marriage and celibacy ratios differed along confessional lines:

Table 2.1. Celibacy according to confession around 1940, in per cent.

	Bachelorettes over 20	Bachelors over 24
Catholics	9%	20%
Muslims	12%	22%
Jewish	14%	19%
Orthodox	17%	10%

As table 2.1 shows, Catholics, Muslims, and Jews present convergent trends in terms of male and, to a slightly lesser extent, female celibacy. The only category at odds with the rest are the Orthodox. Their proportions are reversed, with a higher rate of single women than men. This specificity is again a result of mobility from the surroundings of Rhodes town to faraway destinations. Emigration from the villages of Rhodes as well as nearby islands concerned primarily Orthodox men, while many of their sisters opted for short distance mobility to Rhodes town. There, many women found an occupation, for instance as servants (25 per cent of single Orthodox women over 20 in the census), which delayed or precluded their marriage.

The interdependence of mobility and nuptiality is striking: the higher male mobility of one confessional category *from* Rhodes and its surroundings, the *higher* female celibacy, since women had more competitors and fewer match chances among coreligionists. Reversely, the high mobility of Catholic men from the Italian Peninsula *to* Rhodes resulted in *low* rates of female celibacy. In general, marriage and celibacy patterns seem to exclude a significant demographic rupture. Yet, these figures conceal the manifold paths leading to new unions. A look at life trajectories and at the conditions under which marriage occurred can make this picture more dynamic and diversified.

Reputation, Affection, and Violence

Marriage implies the circulation and repartition of capital among families, which affects their social status. Especially for wealthier families in Rhodes, having a "good" son- or daughter-in-law was a matter of concern, given the greater resources at stake. This had a gendered dimension related to the unbalance of power between men and women, which often produced pressure on the latter. Marriage bonds, moreover, created human connections between Rhodes and a broader space, and the political transformations in the Aegean region implied new possibilities and constraints. Thus, Şevket Müderiszade, the former *kaymakam* of Karpathos, pursued personal interests through his daughters' marriage with well-off and politically influential families in Antalya and Makri (Fethiye), in Anatolia. A few years after the beginning of Italian occupation, these unions allowed Şevket to reduce the Italian authorities' control on his progeny and to maintain his bonds to Kemalist personalities, who in turn saw him as an informal representative of the Turkish government in Rhodes, as mentioned in the previous chapter.[35]

Political and economic calculations often did not bear the expected fruits. Vittorio Alhadeff, descendant of one among the wealthiest families of Rhodes, recalled his parents' concerns for his sister Amélie, aged 21, in his memoirs. They thought, "that there was no worth match for her in Rhodes."[36] Consequently a part of the family moved to Milan after the First World War to expand networks in the most vibrant Italian city *and* to find a husband for Amélie. All Jewish Milanese families were eager to "open wide the doors of the Community" to the Alhadeffs through this marriage, but Amélie's father did not consent. The woman, the "first victim of this situation," eventually married "a Rhodian living in Paris, of excellent lineage, good-looking, of impressive appearance, but loaded with even more impressive debts, which he hurried to pay using Amélie's dowry."[37]

Beyond reinforcing networks as well as confessional and social cohesion, marriage was the normative moral framework of fertility. Mothering out of wedlock like in the Cacopardis' case remained, however, a frequent issue. Documents from the Italian criminal courts reveal cases of families ready to commit infanticide or induce an abortion, considered illegal under Italian law. These were extreme options to save the family's reputation by risking the mother's life, and they especially occurred when she was still in her teens, when she was considered single, or when her partner belonged to another confessional group.[38] Eirini A., the daughter of an unskilled worker, got pregnant in 1939 when she was 23. After some visits, her doctor belatedly proscribed a drug for abortions, which eventually caused her death by septicaemia. The doctor was prosecuted for the double crime of causing the illegal abortion and the woman's death. Before the judge, he stated that he had suspected Eirini's pregnancy since her first visit. Still, he had "to throw off any suspicion" in front of her family and her fiancé – who was not recognized as such by her parents – even when, short before dying,

Eirini showed him the half-expelled foetus "with great caution" afraid of her family's judgment.[39]

Handling extra-conjugal fertility varied significantly depending on the social position of those involved. The French citizen François V., a clerk at the British consulate of Rhodes, got engaged in October 1933 with a Catholic woman, Cécile T., niece of a former French vice-consul.[40] Retrospectively compiling his personal dossier, the *Carabinieri* reported that: "The wedding did not take place because Ms. T., hearing about the immoral life pursued by V., returned to her relatives in France. V., a passive homosexual, was friends with many public drivers, who often blackmailed him … He had a daughter some years ago with his servant Calliope C. … Aware of her rights and of the weakness of V.'s mind, she placed herself as a mistress in the apartment and insisted that V. hire a servant for her."[41] Social distinction, gender, age, and reputation all conflated in this report: it concerned an "illicit" relationship between a man with high economic and social capital who was stigmatized for his homosexuality and a woman of humble social background; the man was a foreign subject and therefore less exposed to the authorities' interference; the couple were already over 30 when their daughter was born; the woman came from a village on Kos, and did not have many relatives around her in Rhodes who could stigmatize her conduct. In fact, François V. could "regularize" his union by marrying Calliope C. in 1938. They had two daughters, with whom they emigrated to France in 1941.[42]

The authorities were more prone to intervene when generational conflicts within the family could raise a public scandal, and this frequently targeted lower class families. In 1933, Concetta Bogdanich, a Catholic aged 21 born in Smyrna, had a love affair with a certain Gino, which caused a violent clash with her parents. The *Messaggero di Rodi* publicly denounced the "young girl's" (*fanciulla*) attempt to commit suicide in an article claiming "the simple aim of moral disinfection."[43] Such moral pressure by the authorities was not omnipresent, and sentimental bonds often led to engagement and marriage without frictions.

Historians have described "love marriage" as "a radical intrusion by the individual into the hegemony of family groups" in late Ottoman society.[44] In fact, the boundaries between these individuals and their families or between "arranged" and "love" marriages in early twentieth-century Rhodes were fuzzy. Many matches originated in between these two poles, ranging from cases of "bride theft" to pragmatism facing the scarcity of potential spouses.[45] In a book published in the 1990s, some Sephardic women from Rhodes narrated how their conjugal match came into being decades earlier. The egg-seller's daughter Iojevet

Huniú (Cugno), described her elder sister's difficulties due to the massive emigration of Jewish men, as she eventually "got married … for the sake of convenience, simply, as most of the people." Sarina Alhadeff, born in 1910, got engaged with Celebi Galante, who had emigrated to Buenos Aires to live with an uncle. After some years, when Celebi was 26, he sent a photo to his mother in Rhodes, who showed it to Sarina, her neighbour. Sarina remembered Celebi as "lank and awkward (*flaquito y desgarbado*) adolescent" before his departure, when the two used to exchange looks on the street. When she saw his picture eight years later, he appeared to her as a "fine young man" (*buen mozo*) and even a proper "man" (*hombre*). In a letter, Celebi asked Sarina if she would "become [his] life companion," and they got engaged within a month. Soon after, Sarina recalled, "he came to marry me here [in Rhodes] and took my dowry with me."[46]

Another narrator, the orphan Rebecca Huniú (Cugno), moved from Bodrum to Rhodes in 1918 to join her grandparents. The economic scarcity during the First World War had heavily affected them, who made a living as street vendors. When she was 21, strolling along the Mandraki (or Mandracchio) waterfront, Rebecca was noticed by a man sitting with a distant relative of hers. Shortly after, the man declared his engagement intentions first to her grandparents, and then to Rebecca. Her grandparents approved of him: "[They] showed a great interest for this young man, whose family they knew: according to what they told me, he was a good man, hard-working, a serious man; he would make me happy without doubts, and granny told me again 'You'll see Rebekita, if he comes from a good family, you don't need to worry'."[47] Retrospectively, she confessed that she "knew nothing about life" back then but also that she fell in love and was reciprocated by her husband. Rebecca accepted the proposal and got married, after which the couple moved to Argentina, where her husband had already spent some years.[48]

These stories connect coming of age and emigration, resulting in a quite egalitarian engagement driven by affection and facilitated by the mediation of friends and relatives who knew where to find candidates. Mandraki, a promenade stretching from the north-western tip of the walled city until the governmental buildings of the Foro Italico, was a prominent site for sentimental encounters. It is remembered by Vittorio Alhadeff as a "fiancés exhibition" (*foire aux fiancés*) and in the short stories by the local writer Antonis Vratsalis as "bride market" (*nifopazaro*) where individuals of all confessions "scouted" for possible partners.[49] As these terms suggest, wealth mattered significantly. Potential partners were to be acquired against a better life prospect. The less economic capital available, the narrower the range of options and candidates to consider before taking a decision.

These negotiations coexisted with violence. Cases of marriage arranged after rape were far from exceptional. In 1918, a muleteer raped a peasant's daughter and allegedly promised to marry her straight after the crime. When her father heard about the accident, he pushed her to take some drugs and abort but, according to her attestation before the judge, the woman opposed this and kept the baby. Moreover, when the girl told her mother about her pregnancy, the latter expelled her from home and forced her to spend the night at her assaulter's place to convince him to get married. The girl begged her rapist in tears saying that "she would be happy even with only a few days of marriage, to save her honour."[50] Since he did not accept this desperate request, the girl's mother appealed to the religious court demanding that the qadi force the sexual offender to marry her daughter.

During the Italian military occupation, such disputes could be handled by both the state criminal and the local religious tribunals. In this case, while the former pursued an investigation for rape, the Muslim communal court was concerned with how to regularize the union and settle the dowry issue. Since no agreement was found at the religious tribunal due to the man's mother veto on the marriage "for economic inequality" between the families, the rapist was sentenced to two years of prison by the Italian court. At this point, his family opted for a settlement and agreed on the marriage. The state tribunal decided to suspend the punishment, acquit the man and close the case when his wife declared to have: "pardoned her husband for the act of violence she suffered and have been totally satisfied by him concerning the dowry and other financial provisions related to marriage, according to local customs."[51]

Italian authorities were not passive observers in negotiations between the couple and their families. In the 1930s, in order to validate a union before the civil authorities, couples had to submit an application and receive a Single Status Certificate (*Certificato di stato libero*) and a Health Certificate (*Certificato medico*) issued by private or public doctors. These documents reveal a special attention on tuberculosis, syphilis, and other sexually transmittable diseases, as well as on certifying "complete mental faculties."[52] The trend towards state control continued under Governor De Vecchi. Confessional tribunals were eventually abolished as juridical authorities except for religious issues in November 1938, which also marked the beginning of anti-Jewish persecution.[53] Two further decrees aimed at the standardization of marriage based on Italian law beyond confessional differences. These decisions prioritized the ordinary state tribunals before the Muslim, Orthodox, and Jewish authorities in litigations.[54] It thus became mandatory to present an application at the Town Hall and to publish the marriage act. Thirdly, a homogenous wedding rite by the religious ministers would remind that marriage:

> imposes upon the spouses the mutual obligation of co-residence, marital fidelity, assistance, that the husband is the head of the household; that he has the

duty to protect the wife and keep her with him, providing her what vital needs require, according to his resources; and that the wife should as well contribute to the husband alimony if the latter does not have sufficient resources.[55]

Such interference of state institutions reached its peak during the Second World War. The Registry Office (*Anagrafe*) of Rhodes could start investigations on couples applying for marriage. They did not only supply information on the two individuals, but also on their relatives' political, moral, and socio-economic profile. Some cases stand out for their blend of sentimental, political, and bureaucratic issues. In 1943, the 17-year-old Arghirulla M. wrote to the vice-governor (using the third person) "appropriately authorized by her parents," begging him to:

> authorize her to marry the young Augusto R. ... aged 25, Italian metropolitan citizen, with whom she has been engaged for over two years. He has already carnally abused the girl. The mentioned fiancé has himself submitted a request to marry the undersigned Arghirulla, but the *Carabinieri Reali* have given a negative response because, based on false information delivered by envious and malevolent people, they have reported wrongly about the conduct of the undersigned, who, on the contrary, has kept a very reserved and honest conduct.[56]

The report issued by the authorities is strikingly detailed. It described even the life of the potential groom before he had moved to Rhodes. Most reports contained information about the two families in terms of religion, race, occupation, monthly income and value of property, marital status, place of residence and birth, criminal record including pending causes, as well as remarks like "currently detained in the local prison" or "not inclined to work." The government thus filed and mapped the population in the domain of family bonds and capital, a policy already practiced by the *Carabinieri* regarding mobility (the issue of passports), professions (the issue of work and business permits), and politics (the files on suspects and influential personalities).

Individuals at the threshold of conjugal life could be profiled in these documents as "youth," and this notion was mostly used to connote the social condition of their family. It was not a definite marker in terms of age, civil status, or parenting and rather related to roles and behaviour within familial structures. Pregnancy or marriage did not *per se* mark the end of youth as much as the conditions in which affection, reputation, and violence appeared in the making of a new family. The more a union adhered to the normativity envisioned by the institutions, the more likely a wedding or a child's birth could be considered a sound watershed between youth and adulthood.

A Changing Household Organization

After marriage, families reorganized the domestic space, a process recorded by the authorities in census data, since these classified the population using the household as a unit of measure. Although the censuses' detailed information is valuable, these sources imply certain problems. The vocabulary of a census tends to naturalize and objectify the family, and its classification conceals relations of power and emotional relationships within a family.[57] Moreover, in most cases, a census is but a snapshot. Even by juxtaposing documents from the same locality dating back to different years, it is difficult to render the "developmental cycle" which leads individuals to reside in different household types throughout their life.[58] Despite these limits, retrieving a detailed census can be a starting point to interrogate the link between state bureaucracy and the factors impacting changing family trajectories.

According to the Hudayi *mahalle* census of 1905–6, Rhodes had a rate of solitary (10 per cent) and extended (17 per cent) households comparable to other Ottoman cities like Istanbul or Damascus, although it stood out for the high number of nuclear/simple (51 per cent) and non-conjugal (13 per cent) as well as for a low number of multiple (9 per cent) households.[59] A look at later censuses in Rhodes reveals an interesting dynamic during the Italian occupation:

Figure 2.2. Evolution of household types in Rhodes 1905–40, in per cent.

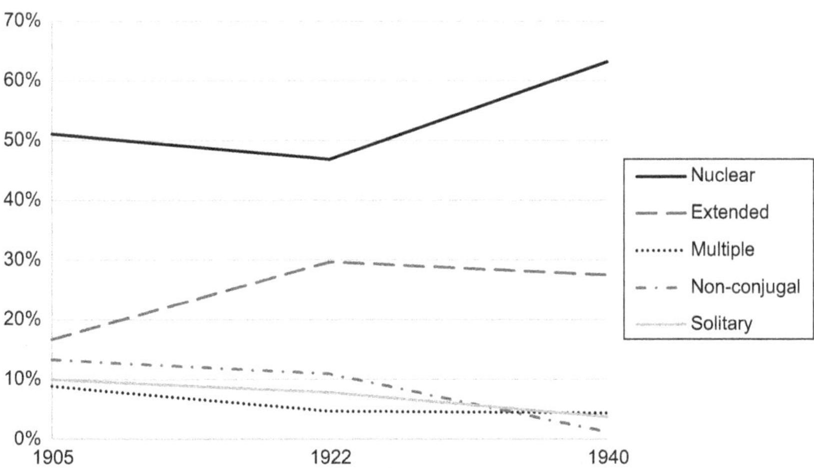

Figure 2.2 shows a trend inversion for nuclear and extended households, which converge and then diverge through symmetric trajectories. While nuclear households slightly declined from 1905 to 1922, extended ones grew and reached closer to the former. Between 1922 and 1939, however, the nuclear type rose way beyond the earliest score to almost two-thirds of the total, whereas extended households stagnated under 30 per cent.

The decade of warfare in the region between 1912 and 1922, despite marriage rates not decreasing overall, caused economic constraints to founding new conjugal residential units. Moreover, until the end of the 1920s, Rhodes saw an increasing number of departures and arrivals. The emigration of young men resulted in the fragmentation of family bonds, which destabilized the marriage market. Whereas in Rhodes and on nearby islands it became easier to find a spouse for men, emigration made the competition harder among women.[60] Many single women entered a relative's household or became domestic servants, leading to a growth of the extended household type. Households with servants increased from zero in 1905 to 10 per cent in 1922, back to 7 per cent in the late 1930s.

Between the second and third census the striking "re-nuclearization" of households primarily concerned those with a male head under 45:

Table 2.2. Household types for household heads younger than 45, ca. 1905–40, in per cent.

	1905	1940
Nuclear	41.4%	65.1%
Extended	27.5%	20.9%

Towards the end of the 1930s, it was therefore more common for recently married couples to form nuclear households. Younger couples were less exposed to residential proximity to their relatives, although this alone does imply a larger autonomy of the "younger" from the "elder."

Figure 2.3 shows a strong similarity among Catholic, Jewish, and Muslim households, while the Orthodox display a more balanced picture. This exception is related to the demographic imbalance of men and women in the sample. Whereas the ratio is almost equal for Catholics (103 women and 100 men), Muslims (90/89), and Jews

Figure 2.3. Household types according to head's confession around 1940, in per cent.

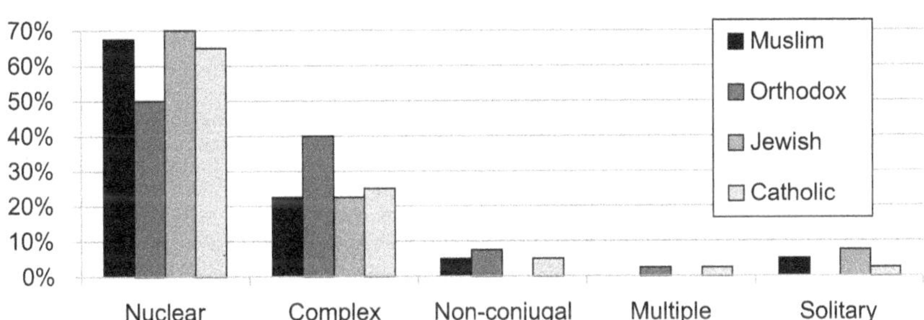

(92/91), Orthodox women outnumber men by 110 to 95. Again, this is explainable by the vast emigration of Orthodox men from smaller Dodecanese islands, including many sponge fishers and traders, which complicated marriage plans for Orthodox women.[61] Those not working as servants often joined their married relatives' household.

Compared to confession, as figure 2.4 illustrates, occupation was a clearer factor of distinction for residential patterns. Extended households were widespread among big-traders, professionals (lawyers, doctors, etc.) and landowners. In turn, the nuclear type dominated in the primary sector (peasants/farmers), among workers and craftsmen. As a consequence, the economically better-off children were more exposed to intergenerational control through everyday contacts with uncles, aunts, grandparents, as well as servants, while the poorer more often resided with their siblings and parents only.

Professional categories were themselves changing in the period under scrutiny. Small traders/shopkeepers and self-employed (including lesser specialized professionals such as mechanics, drivers, electricians, etc.) display a more balanced ratio between simple and extended households. These occupations were linked to technological innovation and circulation of new consumer goods. Intergenerational discontinuity was more likely, since such occupations were hardly available to these men's parents. These categories were also overrepresented among mobile individuals. Many self-employed and small traders moved to Rhodes from Asia Minor and Italy, like the already mentioned Cacopardi, who made a living in the beer trade.

Figure 2.4. Household types according to head's occupation around 1940, in per cent.

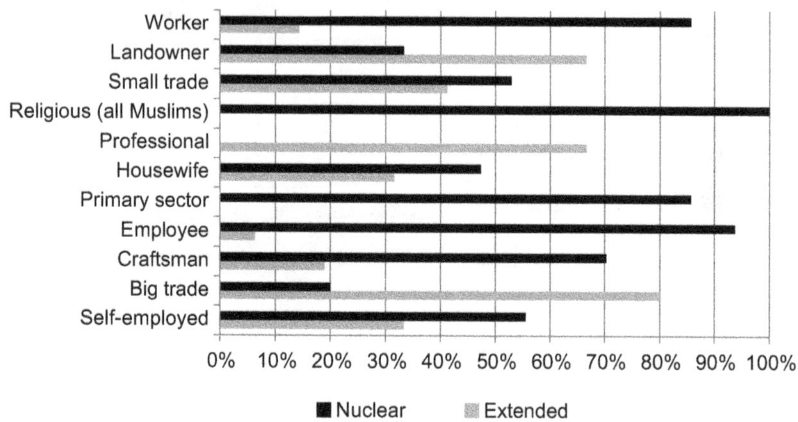

Mostly unmarried and without parents, these newcomers had lower chances of including relatives in their household. Antonino and Maria's family sheet lists them as a nuclear household in the early 1930s, although they later hosted an Orthodox servant from Symi. Moreover, Antonino's brother Francesco also figures in the certificate but as "temporarily in Messina."[62] Frequent mobility thus complicates the picture. As a general observation, though, household re-nuclearization in 1930s Rhodes is best explained by combining age, cross-confessional differentiation of occupations, and mobility. It concerned above all young couples of the lower classes who had recently moved to Rhodes.

Difficulties in the labour market and family fragmentation due to mobility were also visible through a more direct communication between the population and state authorities through the requests of material aid. Petitions were already known in the Ottoman period. One particular type of request concerned state allocations as *ma 'işet* (alimony, sustenance) which could be granted to families of banished individuals. Especially families displaced to Rhodes from rural areas of the empire received a monthly (*ma 'āş*) or daily (*yevmīye*) handout. This measure could be extended across generational lines to the men's wives, sons, daughters, and even cousins, and the state could sustain the relatives even after the death of the banished.[63] When the Yemenite Müşir Şakir Paşa died in his vilayet of origin in 1909 after several years spent as a deportee in Rhodes, the Ottoman Ministry of the Interior received a petition from a certain Muhammed Nasır El-Necdi. The request concerned the children of Şakir's stepmother, who were born in the Aegean town and were "left alone" (*kimsesiz kaldıkları*). El-Necdi proposed either transferring them to Yemen or "assuring them an alimony in form of the allocation of their father's lately expired allowance."[64] Although separated by distance and death, these family bonds could be emphasized by relatives and their intermediaries as sound and solid in order to request a state handout, even if the banished had been considered a danger for the state.

While handouts requests remained quantitatively marginal in Ottoman times and during Italian military occupation, they increased after 1923 and especially in the 1930s. Changes in local and regional politics affected how families portrayed themselves in front of the state. Parallel to the imperialist rhetoric in Italy in the years of the Ethiopian Campaign, petitions mobilized a language in which the fate of the family and that of the state were increasingly interconnected. In 1937, Paolina R., a Catholic born in Smyrna, addressed the governor asking for aid in order to pay the debts accumulated in the flat she leased from a Muslim woman:

> I am not asking for a favour but for an act of Fascist justice for someone who has faith in His Excellency: I am poor and have no economic resources from anybody … My [future] son-in-law was and still is my source of maintenance, not just mine but of us all who expect from him everything we need to make a living. I could have had my daughter married last December but my son-in-law's sudden duty in the army hampered wedding plans … I am eager to see my daughter marry a good Italian as my son-in-law, since he served for more than six years as a volunteer in the Royal Navy and was a volunteer in the AOI [*Africa Orientale Italiana*], but my economic situation paralyses me to the extent that I always had to postpone this purpose to better times.

Paolina also expressed her admiration for Governor De Vecchi who, just like her family, had been trying to help Italy's empire in Rhodes and elsewhere: "I consider His Excellency my saviour and advocate, who has always shown steely Italian discipline both in Somalia and in the Aegean, full of [anti-Italian] fanatics. It is this justice that I invoke to my aid and, having great, rather unwavering faith in it, I salute you the Fascist way (*fascisticamente*) … Post Scriptum: I also want to have the honour to see my daughter donate a *Balilla* to the Fatherland, this is my dream as a good Italian."[65]

After an investigation on Paolina's family, the *Carabinieri* refused to grant the handout. They described her family as composed of her husband, from whom she lived separately "because of her bad conduct," and her children Giuseppe (painter, 28, married, with children), Giovanni (employee, 27, married with children), Anna (housewife, 23, single), Nicola (employee, 22, bachelor), Antonietta, (apprentice tailor, 13).[66] Paolina did not mention the married children in her petition, maybe since they were not on good terms or in close contact with her. Nonetheless, her petition translated family bonds into an imagined fascist household. Evoking the future son-in-law and *Balilla* grandson created a convergence between her family and the regime's fortune. Arranging a good marriage with a fascist or providing the state with good loyal youth were seen as acts of loyalty deserving a transaction. This also applied to non-Catholic colonial subjects, who sought to find a common ground with the authorities.[67] However, the question of "moral and political conduct" was often part of the equation, and a negative judgment by the police could outweigh a passionate representation of attachment to the state.

Women often petitioned by representing themselves as guardians of generational solidarity. This role occasionally belonged to the youngest member of the household, like in the case of Frossini P., aged 12:

> I know Italy aids destitute and poor children. This is why I write to you begging on my knees: My father left his children nine years ago. We are descendants of an honourable family. My dad was a school headmaster when he got married, at the beginning it was quite fine, then he was downgraded to a simple teacher. He often did not feed us, he went to a hotel and beat up mom and us … He smashed everything at home and took mom's money … He was removed from school and hung around without work … I have a brother and a sister, my mom is weak and ill, just as my sister. One brother, aged 24, what could he do? He works as hard as a porter. What can he do? He doesn't earn much, now life is expensive, our resources are not enough.

Since generational solidarity was not enough to survive economically, Frossini addressed the governor as a last resource, not only as a donor, but also as an employer: "I beg you infinitely, take me, feed me, place me as a servant for your daughters … I will eat the leftovers, I am fine with just a little. Thus, I will have more motivation in my study, I will always go to the Italian school and will learn the beautiful language, I can't write anything better."[68] Frossini's awareness of family and gender roles is remarkable, and her petition was successful. Abandonment and violence could be represented as unity and sacrifice through the action of female relatives who displayed attachment to the authorities.

These petitions are not primarily important for their outcome (most of them were rejected), but as pieces of "social poetics" through which individuals appropriated an unprecedented convergence between the self, the family, and the state in the late phase of Italian rule.[69] Different generations of women from the lower classes displayed their subjectivity to receive material aid. Relations of power were not subverted, nor any significant emancipation or integration obtained. Rather, petitions consolidated gender, generational, and political hierarchies. Women's subalternity was directly associated to primary needs, such as alimony and housing, two elements particularly impacted by changes in the local economy.

The Monetization of the Domestic Space

Parallel to the development of banking, cash and bills circulated increasingly in Rhodes at the turn of the twentieth century, changing the way people paid and were paid for work.[70] Monetization did not imply an improvement in economic status, since money was often obtained by loans causing further indebtment. Still, it changed the way people provided and obtained access to a home. More and more objects and services had a price, and so did the living space, which was increasingly managed as a rentable resource. This was interrelated with the household nuclearization described above. In a sample of eighteen change of residence certificates (*denunzie di cambiamento di abitazione*) from 1936, nuclear households (72 per cent) are overrepresented among tenants.[71] Family certificates from the 1930s also show more diverse tenants in neighbourhoods previously characterized by strong ethno-confessional cohesion and called accordingly. Next to the "Jewish quarter" or *Juderia*, the urban area where the effects of emigration was most visible, one interesting case concerns the "Cretan Village."

From 1898 onwards, hundreds of Muslim refugees (*muhacirler*) came to Rhodes from Crete escaping clashes with Christians. As elsewhere in the empire, most *muhacirler* were socially marginalized, although in Rhodes they were not involved in a vortex of mutual violence with local Christians as was the case in Anatolia.[72] They were resettled in a suburb named Hamidiye after Sultan Abdülhamid, known as Villaggio Cretese after 1912 and as Kritika until today.[73] As several *muhacirler* moved to other neighbourhoods or left Rhodes, the same area came to host lower class Italian speaking Catholics who arrived in Rhodes from Western Anatolia in the 1920s due to the hostile atmosphere towards foreigners in Turkey. Many settled in the humble houses of the Villaggio Cretese, facing a similar condition of scarcity and marginalization as the Muslim *muhacirler*. Monetization was thus correlated with an increase in nuclear households and migration. Those who left Rhodes also left living space available. Those who arrived were ready to pay for it, creating a convergence of interests.

The monetization of the living space impacted the generational distribution and circulation of resources. In 1928, Rebecca B. was taken to court by her sons, who accused her of not fairly distributing the rent shares from one of the apartments that she had inherited from her husband. During the trial, she defended herself by stating: "That since the death of my deceased husband and father of the claimants, named Perahia A., I do not own any property from which I can obtain alimony. That, according to the Mosaic Law … the claimants … are obliged to provide me with the alimony and other necessities. That the claimants never provided me with an alimony since the death of their father and thus I am forced to obtain it by renting the houses in question."[74] The management of rentable real estate was embedded into changing relations of property involving kin, generations, and gender.[75] In replying to their mother's claim, the brothers described themselves as "family men" and lamented that only their three sisters had been given the usufruct of one house each plus the shares of a fourth one, while the fifth house was rented to cover their mother's alimony. They also invoked the Mosaic Law to argue that male descendants are exempted from providing alimonies if their parents own rentable properties.[76]

A similar case refers to a Muslim family. Nuri S. was sued by his half-sister Zeineb for breaking into her portion of their house, which she had locked up during her absence. They had inherited the house together with three other brothers in 1898. Nuri, who was providing his siblings and stepmother with an alimony, left the house in 1900, while Zeineb got married and left for Istanbul in 1905. Thus, no descendants used the family house, which was let to three different tenants between 1905 and 1920. At first, the revenues were given to Zeineb's aunt, and only later managed by Nuri himself, who raised 240 Italian lire of net profit in ten years. He declared to be ready to divide it "among the five siblings and the mother," but used this argument to countercharge Zeineb about the objects she kept in her room: "Mr. President, please! Ask Zeineb, where did she find all that furniture? From which trader did she buy it? Where did she find all that money? If she has obtained it from our father, we, the other siblings, also have our rights upon it … At first, Zeineb was supposed to move to my place, but because of her bad conduct (*condotta disonesta*) I did not accept her and did not give her a dowry for her wedding, this is why she is charging me, to take revenge on me."[77] Obligations of family solidarity, such as providing a sister with a dowry, were acknowledged as a norm but could also be refused based on "bad morality," causing familial strives. Transactions were not always transparent or regulated by a legal document, as Nuri raised doubts about Zeineb's money "informally" received from their father.

To avoid such disputes, especially wealthy families could impose clauses concerning descendants, siblings, or even servants in their last will, as in the case of Étienne M.:

1) I want my sister Adèle P. to have the lifelong right to personally inhabit the house located in Mixi [part of nowadays Ialyssos, southeast of Rhodes town] in the property which belongs half to Henri M. and the other half to myself, a house she is currently occupying. She will not have, of course, the right to let this house for rent to anyone, neither for a fee nor free of charge.
2) I want my three servants Eftichia, Irini and Youlia M. to have the right, if they wish, to inhabit either the house in Neocori or the one in Mixi ... during one year after my death, but they will certainly not have the right to let the houses in question, neither totally nor partially.[78]

Even within the same family different attitudes towards rentable property could emerge. Alice M., a member of a less wealthy branch of Étienne's family, was filed by a creditor who claimed property rights on a real estate that she had inherited. She had decided to let the house in order to be able to pay back the debt instalments contracted to finance her brother's high-school studies in Beirut.[79] Although the risk of indebtment grew, this monetization allowed for new forms of solidarity within the same generation of the family, as the rent money passed from one spouse to the other and eventually to the latter's sibling. Yet, quite often, the negotiations caused by monetization created disputes with consequences beyond the domestic walls, pushing communities and state authorities to prove the reach of their jurisdiction.

Dowry and Inheritance as a Test for Governance

In Ottoman times, most lawsuits related to inheritance and dowry were dealt with by the respective religious tribunals. However, as Avi Rubin noted, "legal pluralism" was a relevant marker of late Ottoman sovereignty. A grey zone between the domain of state civil courts and that of religious tribunals presented both confusion and opportunities to

Ottoman subjects.[80] This continued during the Italian occupation, when pending cases would involve colonial state authorities and communal tribunals as well. In general, state courts did not interfere with dowry and inheritance agreements, but rather with infractions related to their consequences, as in the case of Nuri and Zeineb's lawsuit described above. The judiciary system in Rhodes evolved during Italian sovereign rule. While Lago preserved the Muslim religious courts, in 1924 he abolished the function of qadi, transferred his jurisdiction to the mufti – who, traditionally, had served as a legal expert rather than a proper judge – and added an Italian magistrate to two Muslim members in the local religious tribunal.[81] Even if confessional laws were responsible for solving most cases related to dowry and inheritance, the "customary" norms that actors referred to were not always clear.

We still know little about marriage and inheritance customs in early twentieth-century Rhodes, since the literature available, especially for Muslims and Jews, reduces family life to folklore, highlighting the ceremonial aspects of marriage with an impersonal account marked by a vague historicity and the stress on one exclusive community.[82] As anthropological fieldwork in the Dodecanese gained momentum from the 1960s onwards, it mostly addressed villages or minor islands and only dealt with the Orthodox population. Michael Herzfeld elaborated on the hermeneutic problem around the notion of "dowry" (*proika*) among the villagers of Pefkoi on the island of Rhodes. This term was ambiguously perceived between its legal and its customary meaning, either too narrowly or too vaguely corresponding to a non-real-estate endowment without full possession by the bride.[83] Irini Toundassaki added further elements applicable to Rhodes: the diversity in terms of inheritance patterns existing even within one island in the Dodecanese; the importance of property transmission on two "genealogical lines distinguished by sex"; the fragmentation of inheritance customs during the twentieth century, with an increasing conformity in regard to a broader Greek "continental" dimension; the reorientation, rather than the collapse, of these practices' value in line with social change, most notably with the monetization of dowry.[84]

Real estate was a bone of contention precisely because it was heavily affected by monetization. Family property was often bilocated, used and managed between town and countryside.[85] However, the value of real estate was generally higher in town, and rural estate acquired by inheritance or dowry was often sold to invest money in an urban residence.[86] Urbanization in early twentieth-century Rhodes was a gradual adaptation to a new setting requiring a flexible management of properties and also causing a higher risk of disputes among relatives.

Especially among Orthodox families, dowry was more important than inheritance and could include items traded for lifelong protection, cohabitation, and/or alimony. In 1897, Nikolaos V. married Theodosia K., probably an orphan, under the condition that he "also bring her aunt Marigo K. into his home and he maintain and nourish and shelter her as his mother until her death." The aunt, probably a widow, brought an icon into the new house, an item usually transferred from mothers to first-born daughters.[87] A dispute arose when Marigo moved the icon into a church on a Bright Friday. After her death in 1913, her nephew-in-law Nikolaos claimed that the icon belonged to his household, while Marigo's brother considered it a donation to the church. These transactions were ambivalent as to who ultimately owned the property (Marigo or Theodosia? Nikolaos or the church?). This matrilineal dowry did not exclude a growing interference of the male line in the generational transmission of capital, as it was the two men who brought the issue before the tribunal, where Nikolaos's claim was eventually accepted.[88] Moreover, cash dowry was perceived as a threat for family's cohesion because it "could be disposed of by an unscrupulous or wastrel husband," who could invest the dowry money in his own business.[89] In one case from 1913, an Orthodox woman claimed back one hundred golden Napoleons, which her dead husband had invested in a company with an associate. She therefore acted both as bride – the vehicle of the original dowry – and as heir – the recipient of her husband's capital.[90]

Among non-Orthodox families, capital circulation relied more on inheritance than on dowry. For Muslims, successive division of property in shares followed Sharia principles combining kinship, gender, and generational categories. The trader Haci H. Ağa died in 1897: his two sons received 70 shares each, followed by his wife E. Hanum (40 shares, 1/8), and his four daughters (35 each, the half of a male descendant's share). Since one daugther, Hadice, died before the property had been divided, her shares were again distributed between Haci H.'s grandchildren, namely Hadice's two sons (14 each) and her daughter (7).[91] Capital could move up and down the generational ladder, and proportions were more important than the nature of the property, often omitted in the documents. Complex schemes could appear such as in the case of the baker Nuri, shown in table 2.3. When he died in 1922, he left his property to his father exclusively. However, a second partition occurred when his father died and left Nuri's mother, brothers, and sister as beneficiaries of the original 144 shares.

The increasing cases of arbitration by the civil tribunal during the Italian occupation show the subsidiarity of the judiciary system available

Table 2.3. Nuri bin Haci M.'s inheritance partition, 1922–7.[92]

Nuri bin Haci M. (†) 144 shares	Mustafa (son) 34	Hafiz Fevzi (brother) 6
	Celal (son) 34	Salih (brother) 6
	Haci M. (father †) 24	Mehmed (brother) 6
	Taliat (wife) 18 (1/8)	Scerife (mother) 3 (1/8)
	Hamide (daughter) 17	Sidica (sister) 3
	Saadet (daughter) 17	

to the Muslim population. Such plurality continued even after the Sharia was abolished in other post-Ottoman states like Kemalist Turkey in the mid-1920s.[93] This could raise legal confusion for families moving between Rhodes and Asia Minor. In 1927, the civil court of Köyceğiz decreed the inheritance partition concerning a man from Rhodes who had moved to Dalyan, Turkey. The court communicated the decision to both the Muslim Community and the Italian authorities in Rhodes. In this case, his widow received 2/8 of the inheritance and the rest was divided equally – contrary to the "customary" Sharia pattern – between the son and the daughter, both minors.[94]

Coexisting legal codes allowed for negotiation, but also hierarchization, between families, religious institutions, and state authorities. Italian state interference in family issues gained momentum with the decree no. 14 of 1930, which delegated the appeal procedures of local subjects to the "ordinary" second instance of the Italian courts of Rhodes.[95] But there were other paths than state tribunals to discuss these issues. In 1932, Hüriye M., a Turkish citizen, sent a petition to the mufti of Rhodes in order to ask for a pension handout after being abandoned by his well-off husband Mehmed. This request eventually landed on Governor Lago's desk:

After opting for the Turkish citizenship, my husband has left me here with my children to go and live with a woman of bad morals (*bed-ahlāḳ*) … The Turkish consul, whom I had addressed, harshly replied 'I can't do anything about it' … Since I am a Muslim, shouldn't the religious authorities protect me, regardless of my nationality? Only because the consul has no juridical authority here, will the fate of all Muslims with Turkish citizenship depend only on the consciousness of the husband and of the woman? Would this mean that there is no authority willing to protect a woman repudiated in such an offensive way? Doesn't a situation like this have consequences from the point of view of morality and public security?[96]

Once again, a woman from the lower classes constructed a continuity between the familial, the communal, and the governmental spheres calling for civil and religious authorities to find a solution for her needs. The Turkish consul contacted by the Italian authorities agreed on her request, while the mufti complained about the fact that Turkish citizens in Rhodes appealed to the Sharia, with which they were more familiar from past experiences, and not to the Turkish civil jurisdiction. The Italian authorities wanted colonial subjects to stick to the double system of local Muslim and state Italian courts.[97]

As part of the imperial consequence, Italian rule took over the Ottoman Young Turks' attempt to "match Sharia and governmentality."[98] The Italians adapted their response to legal pluralism in family issues to fit a colonial mindset. This implied the preservation of religious tribunals for their subjects but also pushing foreign citizens towards foreign, non-religious judicial authority. Hüriye's petition revealed the confusion resulting from cases where gender, confession, citizenship, and residence interplayed. Lago did not respond to her message but accepted his secretary's initiative to inform the mufti, who in turn informed Hüriye that she could recur to Italian tribunals. Rather than unloosing a gordian knot with an authoritative decision, Italian rule reasserted the necessity to keep margins of interpretation in the jurisdictional authority divided between community administration, state power, and foreign institutions. These interstices in the relationship with the families joint with a case-by-case attitude were meant to hamper the possibility that family affairs and generational dynamics become a matter of "public security" a real risk that the petitioner cunningly made explicit to draw attention on her request.

***

Colonial governors in Rhodes adapted and innovated their policies by building upon previous Ottoman structures. Accordingly, legal subsidiarity had to be constructed vis-à-vis local dynamics. The encounter with the situations and needs of families from Rhodes represented, as Alexis Rappas has noted, the "domestic foundations" in which regulations for the transmission of capital within and across generations emerged and reinforced colonial authority.[99] Ambitions to control the family, however, implied dealing with complicated and diverse situations involving the redefinition of generational relationships. While the bureaucratization of family life during the Italian period concerned the entire population, more delicate cases of abandonment, scarcity of resources, and domestic violence were sensed as anomy and social disorder especially in regard to the lower classes. This pushed the authorities to intervene more frequently and aggressively when poorer families were involved.

The *Messaggero*'s public denunciation in the name of "moral disinfection," mentioned above, was an exceptional case. However, it strikingly reveals how fascist colonialism went further than Ottoman rule in interfering in the familial realm, which also meant than this realm was more exposed to public judgments. At the same time, most of this interference happened discretely. The police often surveilled and intervened underneath the level of legal disputes before a matter of "morality and public security" could address and challenge the jurisdictional framework of Italian colonial rule.

The marriage applications from the late 1930s are the best example of how the state aimed at knowing, and therefore controlling, the socialization of local families. Criteria such as health, the social, and even the racial profile of the new couple were instruments outside the focus of Ottoman state bureaucrats. The colonial period's tighter communication between political power and families was double-edged. Governors might have been delighted to be praised as "saviours," or to read how local subjects exalted fascism imperialism and Italy's grandeur in exchange for subsistence aid. Yet, they surely felt anxious when other subjects addressed their confusion regarding the legal system at work. The main danger posed to "public security" by family issues emerges from Hüriye M.'s letter, namely that an entity beyond Italian jurisdiction – the Turkish consul – could exert influence on Italian subjects as a concurring force in the post-Ottoman Mediterranean. The same issue was even more urgent when children of local families stepped outside the domestic walls to be socialized at school. In this case, not only generational dynamics, but also representations of youth played an important role in how governors, communities, and families redefined the relationship between state and society.

Chapter Three

New Schools, or How Youth Became Students

In June 1969, Pope Paul VI welcomed an alumni delegation of the former "Italian schools of Rhodes." The magazine in French *Informations Lassaliennes*, published by the congregation *Frères des Écoles Chrétiennes* which had run the schools, described the event as follows: "The meeting gathered around one hundred representatives of different graduation years, but fervent messages of solidarity coming from Africa, Asia, and America brought the larger adhesion of those who had remained far away ... Everyone who managed to come to Rome took care of bringing the own contribution of remembrance: joyful schoolyears memories, stirred memories of deceased friends and relatives – killed during the war or exterminated in the lager – comforting memories of testimonies of real friendship among classmates."[1] The Rome reunion took place twenty-two years after the school in Rhodes had been closed. Bonds created at school were reactivated as a "community of experience" despite the alumni' diverse trajectories and locations.[2] Jewish students had been deported to Auschwitz-Birkenau in 1944, Italian metropolitan citizens had moved to Italy after the war, many Orthodox and Muslim classmates had remained in Rhodes.

The magazine's retrospective narration simplifies the history of the school in question. What became the "Italian schools" of Rhodes was an institution founded in Ottoman times, in 1889, through a donation by the local British subject of Maltese origins, the Catholic Henry Ducci. The school was run by francophone religious teachers, commonly called *Frères*, until 1922. Following the international recognition of Italian sovereignty over the Dodecanese, it was placed under the colonial government's control. The *Frères* school maintained a privileged reputation thanks to its Catholic character – appealing to the Italian rulers – and its economic resources. For the same reason, the Italian governors chose it to establish a new type of secondary school, the *Regio Istituto Maschile*.

This shift resulted in the coexistence of religious and civil teachers and, alike most Italian schools of the period, a symbiosis with the Fascist Party.

The *Frères* school was not the only institution of this level in Rhodes. Other secondary schools were an important novelty of the late Ottoman period. All of them faced similar challenges in terms of resources and management. However, each had a different curriculum and a different agenda, and they were treated differently by the successive state authorities. The Italian colonial government transformed the Ottoman state secondary school *Mekteb-i idadi* – literally "preparatory school," commonly referred to as *idadiye* – into a communal institution renamed *Scuole Turche* (sometimes referred to as *Scuole Mussulmane*), thus breaking the bond that formerly tied it to equivalent Ottoman state schools throughout the empire. The boys and girls' schools of the *Alliance Israélite Universelle*, which had significantly impacted the Jewish community at the dawn of the twentieth century, became the *Scuole Ebraiche*. Here, the priority for Italian rule was to erase the French influence that had characterized this institution until the mid-1920s. The *Gymnasion Venetokleion*, founded before the beginning of Italian occupation by the Orthodox community, kept its communitarian character until 1937, when, as discussed in chapter 1, it was closed because fascist authorities considered it a nest of Greek nationalist propaganda. It reopened during the Second World War and it is the only one among these institutions still existing today in Rhodes as a Greek public school.

This chapter investigates the transformation of schooling in a setting turning from an Ottoman province into an Italian colony. Schools are a privileged object to study a state-society relationship in flux through the experiences and the semantics of youth. The trajectories of local schools summarized above show the Italian colonial government's interest in controlling the educational domain by isolating it from dangerous links with foreign countries. Schools also reveal the imperial consequence in the making of fascist colonialism. Governor Mario Lago did not erase but rather accomodated the plurality of Ottoman provincial education under his control. Italian rule thus took over challenges related to educational innovations that had emerged before 1912.

In late Ottoman Rhodes, state ministries, communities, transnational donors, foreign institutions, and religious missions participated in expanding school infrastructure but also aimed at regulating this educational market. In 1896, an Ottoman inspector general of education expressed his concern about sons of peasants attending state secondary schools. He proposed to raise the tuition fee in order to hamper access to this level of education to "ordinary people" and stop the "impropriety of educational equality."[3] The Ottoman Empire regulated access to its new schools while propagating its legitimacy as an "educator state" through a more direct bond with the population.[4] Moreover, it countered centrifugal tendencies and Western encroachments by increasing surveillance over schools run by the empire's confessional communities.[5] Sultan Abdülhamid also reinforced state culture in this domain by elaborating principles of scientific education containing Islamic elements. After 1908, the Young Turks pushed for raising the visibility of the state in schools as a sign of rupture with the Hamidian past. A more effective propaganda, they thought, would gain the loyalty of the empire's subjects beyond confessional boundaries. In 1909, the inspector of education for the Vilayet of the Archipelago addressed the students at the *Alliance* school in Rhodes, exhorting them to not neglect the language of the "Fatherland, the Turkish language," since it could enable them to "become deputies, governors or even ministers."[6]

In the same period, the Italian state accelerated the establishment of schools in the Mediterranean to provide a broader offer of "national" education for the large communities of emigrants in the Levant. Italy considered this expanding infrastructure a necessary move in an imperialist game dominated by France and Britain. At the turn of the twentieth century, investments in schools were inseparable from the imperialist ambitions cherished by prime ministers like Francesco Crispi, which also implied a more aggressive colonialist militarism in Africa.[7] This challenge gained momentum when fascism pragmatically sought a synthesis between Catholic religious infrastructure, the political indoctrination of emigrants, and the Italian influence on other communities intercepted from rival imperial powers.[8]

Whereas missionary institutions in Rhodes before 1923 were influenced by French cultural imperialism, Italian sovereign rule in the Aegean could redefine the balance of power by combining fascistization and Italianization. Although the regime in Italy had a complicated and at times conflictual relationship with the Catholic Church and its institutions well into the 1930s, the colonial setting enabled a rather harmonious cooperation between the government and the clergy. As soon as the main childhood and youth organization linked to the Fascist Party, the *Opera Nazionale Balilla* (ONB), was created in 1926, some of its local activities were assigned to the supervision of the now Italian religious instructors of the *Regio Istituto*. As the chronicle of the school notes: "We [the teachers] did not hesitate to assume [this supervision], both because it was a task completely in line with the directive of the higher ranks, and because, if left in other hands, it would have led astray from us a significant number of pupils who, thanks to this association, approach us to a larger extent."[9] The ONB and the school missionaries needed local children as human capital to reinforce their legitimacy in front of other schools. The colonial government saw their synergy as a way to optimize resources and showcase Italian superiority in the educational domain. Like the Ottoman government, however, the fascist regime's investments in education went hand in hand with regulating access to it. The Gentile School Reform of 1923, valid for the Aegean possessions as well, remodelled tuitions and exams. As Patrizia Dogliani has argued, this restricted the chances of educational trajectories leading to elite positions in the fascist state, which negatively affected the lower classes and women.[10]

In the early twentieth century, most states aimed at reinforcing their grip on secondary education.[11] Studies on education during Hamidian and Young Turk rule, as well on fascist education, have focused on questions of loyalty and dissent towards these regimes, highlighting propaganda and indoctrination. The students targeted as "new (wo)men" reacted differently, ranging from enthusiasm to a widespread resilience or even aversion preparing the ground for these regimes' "ideological bankruptcy."[12] In the case of fascism, even prominent personalities like Achille Starace lamented in 1935 that pupils perceived the regime's schools as "emptied of any educative content and of any ideal illumination."[13] For Italian African colonies, historians have illustrated how indoctrination coexisted with pervasive racism, which prevented the formation of local elites.[14] Like the Young Turks did with regards to the Hamidian period, Italian fascists advocated a rupture with the past. They accelerated the statalization of schooling, prompted by the need to create loyal cadres who could serve the state, while preserving elements of difference that characterized imperial rule. Yet, what happens when we test these assessments with the evolution of governance in Rhodes, highlighting the Ottoman provincial instead of the state scale of analysis, or shifting the perspective on Italian colonialism and fascism from state policies towards interactions with local realities marked by religious diversity? In fact, state intervention does not appear as the only force at play. It coexisted with notables' and communal institutions' efforts to channel the students' socialization towards their orbit. This process engendered negotiations with local families, which brings the question of schooling as experience prominently into the picture.

Even before the late nineteenth century, several primary schools existed in Rhodes and other villages of the island. On the contrary, until the 1920s, new secondary schools could be found only in Rhodes town. Inhabitants of villages and minor islands around Rhodes were less exposed to the increase of literacy and schooling, which remained markers of the urban space. A comparison between the neighbourhood censuses of 1905 and 1922 used in chapter 2 provides some elements about this increase. In 1905, only 22 per cent of the Hudayi neighbourhood households had a (male) member marked as *"okur yazar"* (reads and writes), while in 1922 almost each unit had one member (including some women) for which the officer noted *"taḥṣīli: vardır"* (he/she received an education). These categories disappear in the family certificates from the 1930s, which might indicate that basic literacy was, if not taken for granted, no longer a relevant marker of social distinction.[15] Managing secondary schools in Rhodes town mattered precisely because this higher level of education would influence the later trajectories of the students, potentially opening a better horizon for a family's social position.

For the period under scrutiny, most students in secondary schools were the first in their families who had access to these institutions. Secondary schools were therefore not only an object of governance, but also a site of socialization around which new generational dynamics within families and new representations of youth intersected with political transformations from Ottoman to Italian rule. School institutions shared the idea of a new, "progressive" education in line with the needs of local society. This education actually reached far beyond school desks and books. Before 1912, communal schools expanded their allure to broader segments of the population. Adult commentators stressed the importance of education and conflated it with a virtuous image of youth, which resulted into the new profile of youth-as-students.

Since schooling gained visibility and recognition as a site of socialization, state officials became eager to raise their influence and visibility in all schools. Between 1908 and 1923, educational institutions increasingly became permeable to politics. But such permeability was not just steered by powers from above. Episodes of school unrest in the 1910s reveal that local students could as well interpret the regional political turbulence of the Greater War through their own visions, expressing loyalty to the Ottoman Empire or demanding the *Enosis* with Greece. In this crucial long decade for Aegean politics, they took stances on local, national, and international issues, before Italian sovereign rule profoundly altered schooling infrastructure.

In 1920s Rhodes, secondary schools acquired a new dimension, becoming a test for the governability of a colonial territory. Lago recognized the necessity to mould generations through schooling and align youth-as-students to the government's interests. To some extent, this strategy was successful, as the Italian schools attracted students of all confessions like their predecessors, the *Frères* school. Yet the gap between the authorities' vision and the socio-economic reality on the ground complicated the scenario. The Italian secondary schools did not serve a massively expanding access to secondary education, but rather the consolidation of the cultural hierarchy between rulers and ruled and the erasure of external interference. Lago's 1926 school reform encouraged diversity and even hybridity through courses mixing Italian and local languages like Greek and Turkish, in fact similarly to late Ottoman curricula at public schools that included Greek but also French. The idea of Italian superiority in providing education and, more generally, culture, was a pillar of colonial rule.[16] Yet, whereas elements of foreign administration in local schools were largely neutralized, influences from outside in terms of personnel, material, and programs at communal schools continued to cause anxiety well into the 1930s, especially concerning the Orthodox gymnasium. Although communities gradually lost authority in educational issues, Italian state schools did not monopolize the trajectories of the population. Several wealthier families, the main target of co-optation in the eyes of the colonial regime, often continued to send their children abroad bypassing Italian education.

At the same time, new pedagogic methods changed codes of behaviour and discipline. At communal and state schools alike, pupils were targeted directly, but teachers and directors also aimed to impact their parents' upbringing. School institutions discussed and criticized parental authority by referring to the lower classes, often using a patronizing tone. This reveals the *relational* feature of generational dynamics, since parent-child relationships was transferred and instrumentalized outside the home and the family. Yet, material conditions mattered as much as commentaries. Scarcity of resources led local families to a pragmatic approach towards secondary schools. The number of pupils rose while high dropouts continued throughout the period, reflecting changing conditions of access and tuitions.

Beyond numbers, the transformation of the local school landscape was a major cultural turn for the population. This is how the director of the *Alliance* boys school reflected on his casual encounter with a graduate in 1919:

In this moment we are undergoing such a period of moral evolution as the history of our community has never recorded so far … The good deeds of the *Alliance*'s work become evident today in all their breadth; The taste for learning, the thirst for becoming educated, the desire of all fathers for completing and finalizing their sons' education becomes in Rhodes, above all among our coreligionists, a question of fashion, an urging need that takes precedence over everything else … Eighteen years have passed [since the foundation of the school], the curtain rises, what a change! One does no longer recognize the scene, neither the actors, nor the spectators, not even the setting, so radical has been the transformation! … [A] young gentleman, dressed up smartly, introduces himself very politely, he – I can assure you – takes off his hat and asks for having a word with you in very good French – *"C'est vous Victor?"* (his name is not Haim anymore, this is too archaic).[17]

The use of a French instead of a Hebrew first name is a telling example of a student's perception of how schooling shaped his personality and horizon. Even more important is the idea of secondary schooling as "fashion," namely adaptation to changing norms. As sites of moral "orthopaedics" where students were supposed to interiorize discipline, along Foucault's definition, schools left room open to both conformity to and contestation of behavioural norms.[18]

School governance and school socialization are therefore two interdependent elements. The former does not simply determine the latter, it also evolves as a response to situation on the ground and to students' initiatives. This became particularly visible during the already mentioned episodes of students unrest in Rhodes in the 1910s. A close reading of local events reveal that the politicization of schools was interwoven with notions of discipline and sexuality, which could be appropriated by students to criticize authorities and take political stances. To understand these new political subjectivities and the claims to public visibility among students, it is important to reinsert the precolonial innovations in the educational domain and the central role that communal institutions played in it.

Education between Home and Community

For Jewish and Orthodox communities throughout the Ottoman Empire, schools were an established and quintessential element of the self-administration "privilege" granted by the state to its non-Muslim subjects.[19] Yet, before the period under study, the grip of the local communities on their coreligionists was often limited to primary education. Those who wished to continue their studies would often have to move away from their homes. Emmanouil Kalambichis was born in a peasants family in the village of Malona in 1882, where he attended a primary school run by the Orthodox community. Noticing Kalambichis's high motivation, his teacher offered him private lessons in exchange for aid in classes for the younger pupils. The instructor helped Kalambichis prepare for the admission exam at the prestigious school *Pythagoreio* on the island of Samos. He "made it possible" (*katorthose*) that Kalambichis be accepted thanks to a "word of recommendation" (*logo diafimisis*), "whereas no one, even from the city school in Rhodes, could be admitted" there.[20] The talented pupil later became a journalist, a teacher, and prominent member of the Orthodox Communal Council. However, such trajectories were, by far, an exception. Only the elite could generally afford the mobility and expenses required by secondary schooling.

The aftermath of the Young Turk Revolution opened new possibilities in terms of freedom of the press and association for communal institutions in the provinces, leading to what Bedross Der Matossian called the Ottoman "formation of public sphere."[21] In January 1909, the Orthodox institutions of Rhodes laid the cornerstone of the gymnasium *Venetokleion*, the first secondary school founded by this community. The building was located in the suburb of St. Anastasia, south of the walled city and next to the Metropolis, the episcopal see. A donation by the orthodox notable Minos Venetoklis was essential for the school's foundation. Venetoklis was born in Rhodes but he was mostly based in the booming commercial environment of early twentieth-century Alexandria, where he had made a fortune as a lawyer.[22] Venetoklis made a speech about the humble spirit that guided him for his homeland's (*patrida*) sake: "I paid the minimum tribute of gratitude, by doing away with a part of the [school] expenses and tuitions due in the city that alimented [me] and from where I drew the first sources of education ... Like many others, actually, even I was aware since my childhood of the absence of a secondary educational institution (*anoterou ekpaideutiriou parechontos*), providing the youth with all knowledge available, to make them strong enough to courageously face the numerous necessities of their life." Venetoklis had a utilitarian attitude towards education and saw himself as a cultural engineer optimizing the human resources already available: "I noticed that the youth of our Homeland is thirsty for education (*paideia*), which ... can produce men excelling in every science, art, industry, and craft, men valuable for themselves, valuable for the families (*oikeous*), but above all valuable for the Homeland, which draws from those men its hopes and fortune. This is because, as we all know, the prosperity of the individual entails the prosperity of the families, and that of the families entails that of the entire society."[23]

The generational transmission of resources is an implicit but central element in his speech. Venetoklis constructed a parallel between parental and communal responsibility in terms of educating youth. A new school in town could reduce the expenses for families that would send their children to local schools instead of other cities. This would make secondary education accessible to those who could not afford it. In return, the new youth-as-students would develop skills and bring benefits to their families and communities.

The *Venetokleion* channelled within communal boundaries the educational trajectories of the Orthodox population. Schooling also made the authority of religious and civil personalities visible to the students on a daily basis in a formative moment of their life. This was evident since the foundational ceremony, which opened with the sanctification with holy water followed by a speech by the metropolitan bishop. The Patriarch of Constantinople, whose permission had been necessary for the construction approval by the Ottoman Ministry of the Interior, had sent a message that was read out during the event.[24] After Venetoklis, the floor was given to the Town School's (*Astiki Scholi*) director Dimitrios Anastasiadis, who would become the *Venetokleion*'s headmaster, and then to Giorgios Georgiadis, a lawyer and president of *Diagoras*, the most active gymnastic club of Rhodes.[25] Interestingly, both Georgiadis and Anastasiadis were among the few who had had the economic possibilities to pursue their secondary education away from Rhodes, and they were now involved in the efforts to bring it closer to their younger townsmen.[26]

Many Ottoman authorities were also present, such as the vilayet's director of education Musa Bey, the vali Ali Ekrem, and the director of the vilayet's press office Şevket Efendi.[27] Secular and religious, communal and governmental features were complementary forces targeting the students and their families towards a new idea of education. Through initiatives aimed at increasing their grip on the population, communities saw themselves as part of a broader cultural and political collectivity. Georgiadis was identified by his contemporaries as a fervent "patriot" intellectual.[28] His speech at the foundational ceremony referred to a glorious past of the city's culture contrasting with the recent "dark era" (*skoteinis epochis*) marked by intellectual "desolation" (*erimoseos*) and "illiteracy" (*amathias*). This would come to an end in a *patrida* "enlightened" (*fotisthisomeni*) by the new school.[29] For Venetoklis and Georgiadis alike, the *patrida* in question was Ottoman Rhodes. Still, the school also encapsulated a vital bond with the Hellenic world that included Greece as a neighbouring state and the politically active Orthodox diaspora, most notably in Egypt. This bond, still embryonic in 1909, would gain political importance during Italian rule, as already discussed in chapter 1.

A closer look at other recurring terms can highlight the innovative character of this school towards creating youth-as-students. The Greek terms *paideia* and *ekpaideusis*, salient in Venetoklis's speech, are usually translated as "education," although their meanings are more nuanced. Equivalent to the Ottoman *terbiye* and *tahsil*, they distinguish "upbringing" from "instruction." As a third element recurring in the speeches, the notion of *morfosis* – semantically close to the German *Bildung* – denotes an intellectual outcome, the formation of the self through schooling. *Morfosis* was a marker of respect and distinction emphasizing the social capital of education, especially in the case of return to the family's rural setting with a diploma.[30] Whereas schools primarily provided *ekpaideusis* and *morfosis*, a broader discussion on *paideia* gathered momentum in those years as it contested and innovated the role of traditional schooling in shaping generational relations.[31] *Paideia* accordingly included the discipline of behaviour and emotions, which was part of the civilization discourse of the nineteenth and twentieth centuries.[32] A sound environment at home, the notions learned at school, and good manners in public therefore converged in the idea of education for youth-as-students.

Education was a vast semantic field in motion and resonating globally. A further example of how these ideas circulated in Rhodes is Süleyman Kaşlıoğlu's library. Born in Rhodes in 1884, he graduated in the Al-Azhar religious university in Cairo and was appointed teacher of natural sciences (*ulum-u tabiye*) at the Rhodes *idadiye* in 1914. Kaşlıoğlu became the local mufti in 1936 and his tenure lasted until his death in 1974.[33] The mufti owned a copy of Zekeriya Sertel's "*Hayāt ve şebāb*" (Life and Youth), published in 1911. Sertel was an intellectual active in post-1908 Salonica, he was integrated in Young Turk networks and wrote this essay at the age of 20. According to Sertel, youth is endowed with a mission: "The future belongs to the youth (*istiḳbāl gencleriñdir*). Consequently, youth is the element that demands the most favorable attention for every nation that is concerned for the future of the family ... For this reason, the civilized nations (*millel-i mütemeddine*) that want to take their future under warranty and security strive above all to 'raise (*yetişdirmeğe*) the youth.' The schools shall provide the student with all the profitable scholarly and scientific advancement ... [E]very day they should lay down a new further achievement, and the books offer what guides them in their life."[34] Sertel exposed his idea of youth education beyond schools in specific book sections on personal (*şahṣiye*), intellectual (*fikriye*), corporal (*bedeniye*), national (*miliye*) and social (*ictimā'ye*) upbringing (*terbiye*), to which the "moral" (*ahlāḳiye*), a term recurring in the text, should be added. We cannot ascertain how a religious intellectual like Kaşlıoğlu perceived the positivist stance of Sertel's book. However, other influential personalities in Rhodes adopted these notions. Bension Menashe worked as French teacher at the *İdadiye* while being in the Alhadeff Bank's board.[35] In 1926, the newspaper *Selām* published a series based on Menashe's earlier lectures entitled "The education issue" (*Terbiye baḥsı*). By reiterating the trope of "future generations" (*ensāl-i ātiye*) as a hope for the virtuous development of society, Menashe claimed that "a child's education is not confined to the courses he or she attends at school."[36]

The value of education as a mixture of instruction and upbringing invoked the children's behaviour at home. Since most parents in the early twentieth century had not attended secondary education, they were in a subaltern position vis-à-vis their children's teachers in terms of cultural capital. This does not imply that children automatically interiorized the notion of education propagated at school and refused parental upbringing. Still, school instruction implied the effective reiteration of principles learned in the classroom but aimed to be implemented outside the school gates. At the admission exam of 1912 for the *École Normale Israélite Orientale* in Paris (ENIO), where the best *Alliance* graduates were further trained, the candidates were asked to write a dissertation in French on the following subject: "Describe the portrait of a good student (personal care, care for clothing, care for the notebooks, exactitude and attention in the classroom, politeness towards the teachers)." The essays are strikingly similar, and a candidate from Rhodes wrote: "Of all my acquaintances, my best friend is Jean ... He is extremely clean because he knows that cleanness prevents diseases, and thanks to it he is vigorous and strong. We can see Jean wash himself in the morning before going to school, brush his clothes ... Jean is polite, affable, kind, helpful, and lenient with his classmates." The author also discussed Jean's virtues through a specific example: "One day, for an issue that I have forgotten, the teacher inflicted a collective punishment on the whole classroom, since the culprit who deserved this punishment did not declare himself. Jean knew the culprit quite well, but he did not denounce him. The following day, to our great surprise, the teacher cancelled the punishment because, he said, the culprit had declared himself." Continuities between good behaviour at school and at home were also highlighted:

In the classroom, Jean is always attentive and obedient. He always listens to the teacher's advice and never skips lessons. Jean is kind toward his teacher, because it is from him that [Jean] receives his instruction, it is him who develops [Jean's] intelligence ... From this I draw the conclusion that not only we should respect our parents and the elderly, but also our teachers, since there is a proverb for children that says "The teacher is a second father for the children he instructs." Thus, when Jean will grow up, he will be respectful toward the others, a benefactor to humanity and all people.[37]

An *Alliance* student could reproduce the institution's discourse on education through several elements: a generational hierarchy in which students respect teachers and parents; affection and emulation among peers oriented towards the more virtuous; a notion of education including hygiene, attention, and obedience; the value of solidarity instead of selfishness; continuity between good manners at school and moral integrity during adulthood.[38] In this discourse, an ideal profile of youth-as-students did not require a stress on social differences. Indeed, the *Alliance* school sent its best male and female students to Paris with a scholarship regardless of their parents' wealth and gender. This was meant to support the students' motivation, and the reports positively emphasize the sacrifices made by their lower class parents.[39] Yet, the *Alliance*'s personnel clearly displayed a moralizing attitude towards poorer families in the reports that they regularly sent to the Paris headquarters. One directress stated that lower class girls were deemed worth of "solicitude" since "the *Alliance* is the[ir] only place of salvation."[40]

In state and communal schools alike, students were to educate their parents in their domestic environment, thus being a "crucial point of contact between state planners and its citizenry."[41] Students also linked communal and missionary instructors and the collectivities these addressed. In this process as well, the discourse on education was mostly produced and propagated by the intellectual elite to change the socialization of lower class families. An inevitably condescending attitude could create frictions between educational institutions and parents, which were common at *Alliance* schools. In 1903, the girls school's headmaster narrated this episode:

> Lately, a girl stole a pair of scissors, it took me one hour to have her confess that the item in question did not belong to her ... [and] she has been punished. The following day, her mom came to the school claiming that the scissors belong to her daughter. Having shown her the gravity of her conduct, she replied to me: "can someone who embezzles such a worthless item be called a thief?" New lesson for the mom: "Good woman! ... Today your daughter is young, she steals a little item. Tomorrow, she will grow up and will steal something more valuable." As a reply, she just said *"kissmet"* [Arabic/Turkish for "it's fate!"]. People are fatalist here in the Orient.[42]

Another director of the same school described the impact of parent-child relationships by contrasting it with the moralizing function of schooling:

> Almost the totality of fathers and mothers from Rhodes did not attend any school ... The quarrels in the marriage are frequent here. They happen in front of the children, who take part supporting either the father or the mother. And these parents, cause of evil, often come and complain to us about the bad conduct of their children ... The father is sometimes respected only when he threatens with beating. Fathers and mothers do not have any authority on their children. Within fifteen days, four pupils, four girls, have left school rather than undergoing a little punishment decided by a teacher due to their bad behavior in the classroom. And the parents ... have not managed to put their girls back on the right track.[43]

Undisciplined parenting was considered an obstacle to the civilizing endeavour of new schools. Children thus became the vector bringing the authority of the teachers – and the institutions above them – into the domestic walls. They helped propagate a virtuous socialization in their family. A distinctive feature of school instruction in regard to parental and domestic upbringing was literacy. Textbooks, notes on blackboards, class rosters, notebooks, exams, and diplomas were the written elements reinforcing the transmission of new behavioural codes. These items became familiar to an increasing number of students but not necessarily to their parents.

Schools also contributed significantly to the expansion of printed material in Rhodes beyond schools. Beside the first local newspapers which appeared at the turn of the twentieth century – sold next to those arriving from Smyrna and Istanbul – the yearbooks (*salnameler*) of the Ministry of Education record four "Muslim" libraries in 1901 with 1,249 books.[44] Jewish religious learning centres (*yeshivot*) had their own libraries. As Vittorio Alhadeff recalls, however, their visitors mainly consisted of "old and pious bearded Jews" and they were hardly appealing to youth.[45] Alhadeff was among the few children who could use a well-equipped library at home, a marker of the wealthiest Ottomans.[46] The majority of his peers did not have access to the domestic consumption of books and magazines. Aware of the situation, school boards provided their pupils with new reading rooms, which in turn widened the perception of schools as morally safe places opposed to the stigmatization of lower class homes as spaces outside their enlightenment. The *Alliance* school imported hundreds of books from France. Its directors appreciated that reading "enormously interests" the pupils and considered the library a leisure site where youth could "stay away from bad relations and bad examples."[47] Other school libraries existed at the *Frères* school, and at the *Venetokleion*, the latter consisting of books sent from Egypt by the Venetoklis family.[48] These innovations upgraded literacy from the primary schools' compulsory training towards more complex intellectual notions, criteria of morality, and ideas of belonging that secondary schools offered. The access to these novelties, however, remained confronted with the economic possibilities of Rhodian families.

A Diverse Educational Market

In 1883, the Ottoman state established a public secondary school for boys in Rhodes. It consisted of a lower (*rüşdiye*) and a higher section called *idadiye*, a term often used for the school as a whole. Prior to this date, secondary schooling was not an option on the island. Other educational centres like Smyrna, Samos, Istanbul, and Athens were mostly reserved to the economic elite of Rhodes, who could afford boarding schooling for their children. The *idadiye* in Rhodes was among the first of its kind founded outside Istanbul in the Ottoman Empire.[49] Its origin is linked to the educational reformer Ahmed Midhat Efendi, exiled to Rhodes in the 1870s.[50] During his banishment, the Ottoman intellectual experimented new methods to replace religious instructors at local schools, thus anticipating the expansion of the *idadiye* model in the provinces as prescribed in the imperial Educational Bill of 1869.[51] This boys school had a curriculum of five to seven years, the higher grades existing or not according to the oscillating number of graduates above the fifth.[52] It was located next to the monumental Palace of the Grand Master, Rhodes's most majestic landmark built in the Middle Ages by the Knights Hospitaller. The non-boarding institution hosted approximately 150 pupils. These were mainly Muslims, while Jews were the largest confessional minority, amounting to 15 per cent on average.[53] A yearly, relatively low fee was to be paid in three rates starting from the fourth grade. The exempted students' quota rose significantly from 20 per cent in 1909 to 53 per cent in 1911 and 58 per cent in 1912. This suggests an intention to raise accessibility for families with low income, although the number of students fluctuated minimally.[54] The Ottoman state opened a secondary school in Rhodes before foreign or missionary institutions of this kind appeared in town. Contrary to the pattern highlighted by historians for other provinces, which points to a reaction against foreign influence, the foundation of Rhodes's *idadiye* was primarily aimed at the standardization of provincial education according to a model developed in the centre.

A few years after the *İdadiye*'s foundation, the *Frères* inaugurated the already mentioned Catholic *Collège de St. Jean*.[55] The French vice-consul contributed financially after the initial donation by Henry Ducci. Before the school's opening, the diplomat stated that it would host "around forty pupils, of which more than the half of French nationality." Its purpose was to "give to well-bred children (*enfants de famille*), an education that could later lead them to the high school diploma." The vice-consul added that "the parents would like to separate the school for tuition payers from the school for non-payers."[56] The wealthier families preferred to hamper school socialization across class boundaries. Although this separation did not occur, the directors of the *Frères* school preserved the elitist status of the school in the following decades. The tuition was the highest among secondary schools in Rhodes[57] and was paid by the majority of the students.[58] At the same time, the *Frères* aimed at attracting a larger number of pupils of all confessions, who could act as disseminators of *francophonie* in the Levant. Figure 3.1 shows the balanced distribution of pupils according to their confession, especially during the Italian occupation:

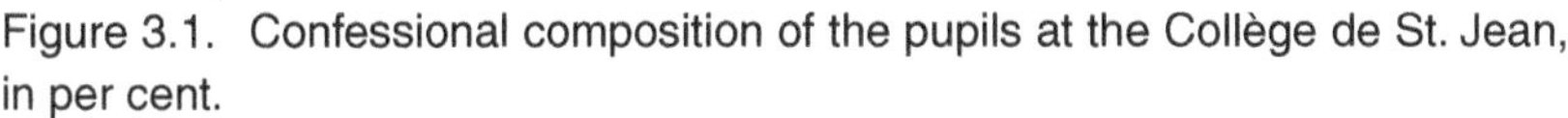

Figure 3.1. Confessional composition of the pupils at the Collège de St. Jean, in per cent.

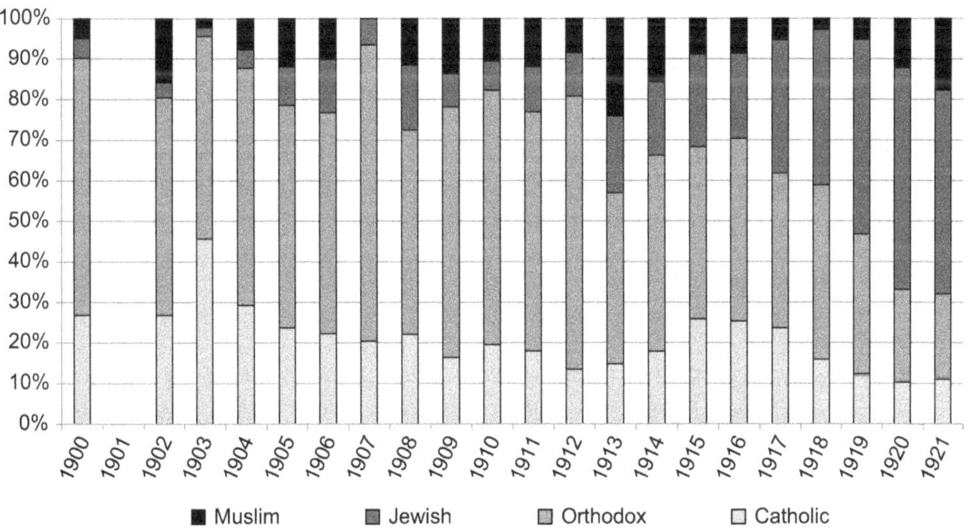

Source: FSC ROMA 560 1. Diagramme du College; Kladaki-Menemenli and Freris, Istoria, 82.

As will be shown in chapter 5, the decade 1905–15 corresponded to a wave of mass emigration for Jewish families. This partially explains that more Jewish pupils could later afford the tuition through the remittances sent to Rhodes by their older relatives. Meanwhile, the opening of the *Venetokleion* in 1910 led to a decrease in the number of Orthodox students. In 1901, the Franciscan *Soeurs du Sacré Coeur* of Gemona opened a Catholic school for girls also partly financed by the French government. Almost all female pupils were admitted without a fee, although the decreasing rate of those exempted (90 per cent in 1905, 68 per cent in 1910), is yet another sign of the social distinction promoted by Catholic schools.[59]

The French influence also characterized the *Alliance* school, which opened a non-boarding section for boys in 1901 and one for girls one year later. The *École de Garçons* hosted approximately one hundred pupils and offered language courses in Hebrew, Ottoman, and French.[60] One among the most acknowledged Ottoman Jewish intellectuals of the time, Avram Galante, prompted the school's foundation. During his appointment in the board of a local *Talmud Torah* school, he convinced communal notables to ask for support from the *Alliance* in Paris, while Baron Rothschild offered a donation during his 1903 stay in Rhodes.[61] The *Alliance* aimed at moulding young Sephardim who could harmonize French cultural superiority, Jewish humanism, and integration in the Ottoman state.[62] In other cities, this agenda exacerbated factionalism, although the situation in Rhodes was relatively calm. Disagreement on organizational and financial issues could emerge, however, between the Communal Council and the directors, who were sent to Rhodes from other Sephardic communities of the Mediterranean.[63]

The tuition issue saw the *Alliance* school in competition with the still existing and less expensive *Talmud Torah*, which the francophone institution considered inadequate because of their religious nature and backward teaching methods. At the opposite end, the *Alliance* rivalled the more expensive, but also more prestigious *Frères* school. In 1910, the director decided to admit children of "very poor" parents for free at the Jewish community's expenses, while the others would pay "according to their parents' wealth" between ten and thirty piastres monthly.[64] This strategy was far from effective, since the director complained in the same letter about the community's deplorable finances. The communal revenues derived from taxes imposed on Jewish families according to their local properties, excluding the fortune made by emigrants.[65] Remittances flowed directly to these emigrants' relatives, who could more easily afford to send their children to the Catholic school. While trying to reach the broadest possible number of students, the *Alliance* school aimed at keeping the brilliant ones away from its Catholic rivals. In 1921, the director bitterly noted that "more than eighty students" had changed school before the end of the curriculum.[66]

Debates on tuition among communal leaders and families also concerned the *Venetokleion*. Straight after its opening in 1910, the newspaper *Nea Rodos* reported discussions within the Orthodox community's Educational Commission about whether the new institution should become a commercial school or a gymnasium. This highlighted a tension between an education more oriented towards the humanities – considered more suitable to develop a sense of cultural belonging and intellectual prestige – and one focused on technical skills, later only available at the Italian *Regio Istituto*, more alluring for the families' material prospects but also for the community's economic development. When the gymnasium option prevailed, it became urgent to demand donations to establish a fourth grade to complete the curriculum offer.[67] Many villagers apparently hesitated to enrol their children at the *Venetokleion* because the main outcome they saw in the diploma was a career as teacher, which they did not consider as particularly attractive in terms of economic upgrade. As *Nea Rodos* reiterated in 1913:

> No student is admitted to the gymnasium for free, not even considering all the possible certificates, because the guarantee of support of students in need will not continue until the completion of university, which will result in the youth's incomplete studies (*imimatheian*) and, consequently, the failure on the practical level (*apotichian tou praktikou stadiou*).[68]

These financial concerns led to the decision that no student be exempted from tuition.[69]

While discussions continued within communal institutions, the Italian occupation of 1912 raised the question of how schooling should contribute to building bonds between Italian authorities and local families. In fact, the Italian military governors did not venture in significant experiments towards an Italianization of schools. They were aware of the risks that this could provoke in terms of conflict with local notables within the uncertainty caused by ongoing warfare and the persisting Ottoman sovereignty.[70] In terms of programs, the governors only introduced Italian language courses for youths and adults organized by the military in the evening, but also some hours in the "Turkish," "Orthodox" and "Jewish" schools' curricula.[71] Only in 1917 did the coordinator of the Italian evening school call for the establishment of a regular secondary institution.[72] In 1922, after the government had opened a primary and a technical school, the prestigious French Catholic College eventually turned into an Italian secondary school.[73]

Figure 3.2 shows some of the first students attending what was commonly referred to as "Italian Schools." The photograph was taken in 1923, the first schoolyear after French instructors had ceded their functions to Italian personnel led by Friar Clemente (Giuseppe Piola), sitting in the middle. This transition happened during intense diplomatic discussions over the future of the Dodecanese at the Lausanne Conference.[74] The recognition of Italian sovereignty allowed for the redefinition of this school and the establishment of its female equivalent. The status and curricula of the *Regi Istituti* – *Maschile* and *Femminile* – were defined more precisely in 1926. They were not run by the Ministry of Education but jointly by the Ministry of Foreign Affairs and the National Association Supporting Italian Missionaries (ANSMI). Their status resembled many extraterritorial Italian schools, hence the preferred term "Royal" (*Regi*) instead of "State schools." The school also changed location, moving to a new building, south of the Neocori neighbourhood. The *Istituti* contained a technical and commercial school, a humanities

Figure 3.2. The Italian schools in Rhodes, second grade of the technical curriculum, 1923. FSC TORINO 791 3468.

gymnasium, and a preparatory school for teachers. In 1922, during the transitory phase in which the *Frères* school had a technical curriculum run by Italian religious teachers, a few girls sat in the same classrooms as boys.[75] Yet, in the second half of the 1920s, as the missionaries Sisters of Ivrea reinforced their presence in the Italian schools, girls could opt between a separate gymnasium and the teacher-training curriculum.[76] Concerning the tuition, the monthly fee in the first years was the highest in Rhodes, as during its French administration.[77]

All these schools blended secular and religious elements but generally moved away from pre-existing confessional training. The late nineteenth and the early twentieth century saw the decline of Muslim religious training centres such as the *medrese* or the *dergâh* of Sufi congregations.[78] In the nineteenth century, four *dergâhlar* in Rhodes included training and occasional teaching as primary schools, but sources from the late Ottoman and the Italian period do not mention them as relevant sites of religious education.[79] The Catholic *Scolasticat* for religious training remained active from 1890 to 1922 and mostly hosted students from France who stayed in Rhodes for a few years only.[80] This trend shows an interesting exception in the case of Jewish institutions. Governor Lago founded a *Collegio Rabbinico* to attract future Jewish religious scholars from the Eastern Mediterranean and Southeast Europe, challenging France's influence.[81] Lago engaged in feverish fundraising and negotiations with the Jewish community in Italy and Italian consuls in the Levant. Not only financial, but also organizational problems made a promising initiative only little effective. The *Collegio* had a total of fifteen to twenty full graduates, of whom only three became rabbis. Governor De Vecchi closed it in 1938 just before the promulgation of the Racial Laws in Italy.[82]

Regulating the educational market was surely one of the fronts on which governmental institutions and communities engaged to shape Rhodes's society. Yet, not a single secondary school was founded simply as a result of local initiatives. The *Frères* school originated from a local donation but hosted foreign personnel. The *Alliance* had foreign donors, directors and supervision but interacted with the local Communal Council. The *Venetokleion's* donors lived in Egypt, although the board and the personnel were local. The *İdadiye*, lastly, was under the Ottoman ministry's control and was later run by a board of local notables under strict surveillance by the Italian authorities. The interactions between students, teachers, and authorities had local consequences, but they were situated in a broader political space surrounding Rhodes.

Moreover, secondary schools did not rely on stable teaching methods, curricula, and programs. This is particularly true for the *Alliance*, the *Venetokleion*, and the Italian schools, but the *İdadiye* and the *Frères* schools also underwent frequent modifications. Above all, financial scarcity hampered the establishment of higher classes to fulfil the original curriculum. As late as 1921, the director of the *Alliance* proposed to welcome the graduates of the first grade (the highest) in the following school year offering them "two or three classes a day" in order to complete the curriculum, given that the school could not afford hiring personnel for a proper *"cours supérieur."*[83] Additionally, although several dozens of students attended the early grades, frequent dropouts characterized all schools.[84]

Overall, diplomas did not become more accessible to poorer families, nor were schools guided by an egalitarian principle that was consequently implemented. The *Frères* school presents only a slight increase from six graduates in 1909 to nine in 1922, most of whom came from wealthy families.[85] At the *İdadiye*, thirteen students attended the highest class in 1900 and sixteen in 1922, while the *Alliance* boys school had only sixteen in 1921.[86] Lastly, the *Venetokleion* grew from seven graduates in 1913 to twenty-seven in 1922, although this number stagnated until 1933 and dropped significantly in the mid-1930s, with a decrease in sons of peasants/farmers compared to liberal professions. The increase in graduates of the early 1920s partly resulted from the admissions of girls in mixed classes at the *Venetokleion*.[87] For both girls and boys, being a *Venetokleion* graduate still counted as a factor of social distinction and even "class segmentation" in the name of the already mentioned notion of *morfosis*.[88]

Once they obtained sovereignty over Rhodes, the Italian authorities realized that the state would have to weigh more in regulating these economic and social aspects of secondary schooling since schools were considered a site where loyalty could be fostered. A decisive turning point was Lago's educational reform of 1926. The reform implied that criteria elaborated by the Italian Ministry of Education for the final exam be the only valid framework for communal schools, which implied, among others, that Italian professors sit in the examining commission.[89] The reform draft, elaborated by Lago's consultant Pietro Egidi, points to the colonial government's expectations of an atrophy of private and communitarian schools in favour of Italian institutions and their uniform school system.[90] As the governor explained in 1928: "We can easily anticipate that, within five or ten years, the whole new generation of Dodecanesians will be familiar with the Italian language, and will be sensibly adapting to our culture ... The teachers attend more and more our summer preparatory courses for the Italian language exam, and they attend the additional didactic courses at our state schools."

Lago, though, was also aware that colonial rule had to prioritize some urgent goals:

> while the teaching profession is important, especially to shape the future generations in the Dodecanese, it is maybe the most modest one. The bourgeoisie cadres (*borghesia dirigente*) of the Orthodox population consists of traders, doctors, lawyers, and other liberal professions. We cannot influence much the culture of the trading class, since only a few traders and companies require specific school diplomas. However, our Technical Institute is growing, and for sure the technical degree (*titolo di ragioniere*) will be increasingly appreciated. This government demands it, and will demand it even more in the future, for the admission to some employments.

"Future generations" were the unit of measure to evaluate the successful penetration of Italian culture in Rhodes. This future had to be rosy also because the colonial youth's present, in terms of loyalty, was not. In the same letter, Lago regretted that the graduates of the *Venetokleion* could obtain a diploma recognized by the Greek state. Hence, many of them moved to Athens to attend university. The main danger, Lago argued, were the nationalist ideas that they could spread in the Dodecanese: "Youth who, during their stay in the *Possedimento* stood out for docility and sympathy come back, during summer holidays, animated by incoercible acrimony, thus forcing this Government to rigorous measures that sadden their families and themselves once youthful exaltation has expired, as they start to reflect on their future."[91] Youth embodied the anxiety that the socialization of the colonial population could deviate from the authorities' control. The Italian project for youth-as-students aimed at localizing the local upper class's educational trajectories to turn potential nationalists into docile subjects.

Lago also negotiated with Rome, to no avail, the possibility to open a university in Rhodes. While he had an almost unlimited decisional power on local matters, goals demanding significant financial commitment from the state were difficult to achieve.[92] Following episodes of unrest in the mid-1930s, illustrated in chapter 1, his successor De Vecchi chose a more aggressive strategy by introducing the "State school" (*Scuola di stato*) making the Aegean *Possedimento* subject to the same regulation as the Italian Kingdom. Increased state interference would "discipline private [communal] training and establish an efficient regulation and inspective control over every degree and type of instruction."[93]

Was this assimilationist strategy effective? An increase in graduates is indeed observable at Italian schools in figure 3.3:

Figure 3.3. Number of internal candidates admitted to the final exams in the Italian schools.

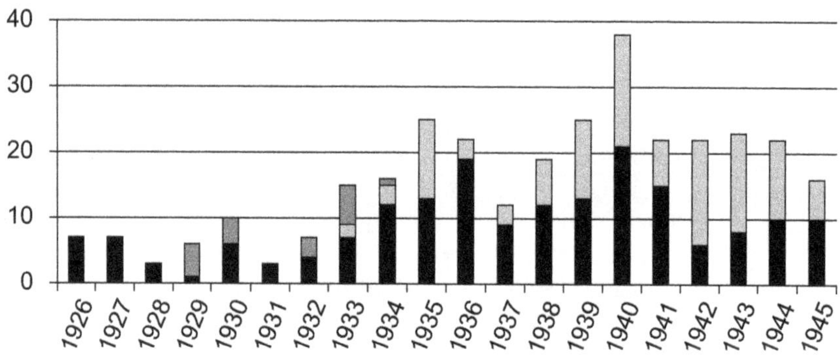

▨ Scientific High School Diploma *(Maturità Scientifica)*
▢ Classical High School Diploma *(Maturità Classica)*
■ Chartered Accountant Qualification *(Abilitazione Tecnica alla Ragioneria)*

Source: Statistics found in: FSC TORINO 786 3421; 787 3425; 789 3438. All but three students were boys. Concerning girls, the only available data point to fifteen candidates for the Teacher Training High School Diploma (*Maturità Magistrale*) in 1933, listed next to seventeen male candidates.

However, the trend is already observable in 1933, and the peak of 1940 looks more like an exception considering that the rate dropped again under the score of 1935 in the following years, also due to the outbreak of the Second World War. These numbers were not only the result of the authorities' policies, they also originated in economic dynamics concerning both the students' families and the school institutions.

If we move from numbers and governmental reforms to life trajectories, the impact of innovations in the domain of secondary schooling appears under a different light. For many graduates, a diploma offered opportunities inaccessible to their parents, or at least an upgrade within the same occupational sector. The *Alliance* and ENIO graduate Jacques Moussafir founded his own trading company in Paris, while his father, also active in commerce, only had the status of employee.[94] Such upgrade could also relate to intellectual occupations often overlapping with mobility from a rural to an urban milieu. The son of a peasant/farmer (*georgos*) Christodoulos Papachristodoulou became an influential teacher and historian upon graduation from the *Venetokleion* with excellent marks (*arista*) in 1922.[95] Yet, completing a secondary school curriculum also required economic calculations and sacrifices on the side of families. Two sons of the destitute Isaac and Joya Hanan emigrated to the United States in the early twentieth century as teenagers, after only a few years spent at the Jewish primary school. With the money sent to Rhodes, the family paid for other children's journeys to America. The family thus invested in only one daughter, Rachel, based on her intellectual skills. She attended the whole curriculum of the *Alliance* school and eventually worked as a teacher assistant.[96]

Such success stories concern few students compared to those who left school without obtaining diplomas. Families generally maintained a pragmatic approach vis-à-vis secondary schooling, which was a difficult commitment in times of material scarcity and intense mobility inbound and outbound. In 1922, Friar Clemente, first Italian director of the former *Frères'* school, commented that: "The locals … don't see in their studies more than a means to entering trade … Young Rhodians aspiring to more are very rare … Among the Italians (sons of clerks or army officers) some, two right now, prefer the gymnasium. But there is a reason for this as well: the dad thinks he will soon return to Italy, where his child will continue on this path."[97]

For many families, the main obstacle to schooling was poverty, and the material aid as provided by philanthropic societies founded in late Ottoman years was one of the few options to recur to. The societies *Ergani Athina* and the *Filoptochos Adelfotis* were managed within the Orthodox community, *B'nai B'rith* was their Jewish counterpart, while the *Fukaraperver Cemiyeti* was founded through the initiative of Muslim notables. These associations offered aid to poor children, although this communal patronage was mainly confined to primary schools. Little changed in this regard in the 1920s, when the Italian authorities established the *Patronato Scolastico* to reinforce the role of the state, including for the Catholic population not represented by the communities. While this aid did not generally concern secondary institutions, Lago introduced four yearly scholarships of 600 lire in 1923 and 1924, not surprisingly reserved to students at the Italian school and its technical-commercial curriculum.[98] Another way to facilitate access to school was to exempt families from the tuition fee. Yet, in this case too, the efforts were rather meagre. In 1924, only twelve students at the Italian secondary school were allowed to attend classes without tuition.[99] Even this exemption was hardly enough for a family with scarce economic capital to afford the expenses for school material. Moreover, schooling meant that their children contributed less, if at all, to the household's economic productivity or to domestic work.

For these reasons, some families in need addressed the local government as a potential sponsor. Their petitions to the governor, however, rarely met with success. In 1924, Markos T. asked for a handout for his son, aged fourteen, a graduate from the *Alliance* school (one of the rare cases of Orthodox students at the Jewish institution), to complete his studies at the new Italian schools of Rhodes. The destitute father addressed the governor as "Saviour," "Pole Star," and pledged to pray for "the Grandeur of the Glorious and Mighty Italy in the interest of Civilization and Humanity." Unfortunately for Markos, a police informer reported that his wife's relatives were hostile to Italy, refusing several Italian officers' marriage proposal to their daughters.[100] We cannot know if this report was decisive for rejecting the request. Be it as it may, in a new interplay of private and public affairs during fascist colonial rule, generational dynamics tied together family issues, chances in education, and political loyalty.

A sign of this trend is the local section of the Fascist Party's increasing influence in the allocation of scholarships in the 1930s. The party managed thirty-two of the forty-two scholarships allocated to secondary school students in 1941.[101] Apart from these grants, exceptional handouts left a narrow, yet viable space for negotiation to the petitioners. As shown in chapter 2, fascism changed the language of petitions and created a convergence between families and the state. This is how the Muslim girl Mensure Ö. asked for a governmental mediation to raise her father's salary and keep her siblings enrolled at school: "His Excellence, we are four siblings, of whom I am the eldest, being 15 years old. All four of us attend the Italian Schools and we are members of the *Fascio* [youth sections] … His Excellence, we, belonging to a different religion, will pray our Common God heartedly and according to our custom for the health of His Excellence, His family, and our Italian Fatherland."[102] Many Rhodian families saw secondary schooling as an important opportunity, but simply could not afford it. Even by attending only a part of the curriculum, pupils dropping out obtained precious skills to face the requirements of an evolving labour market based on new competences such as computation, grammar, and basics of accounting, whereas the final degree itself remained an exclusive symbol of social distinction.

Despite the Italian governors' efforts in keeping educational trajectories within colonial control, the wealthiest local families often sent their children away from Rhodes to complete secondary and higher education. Vittorio Alhadeff enrolled in the Parisian *Lycée Lakanal* in 1921 after graduating from the *Frères* school. As mentioned in chapter 2, the Alhadeffs were eager to make the best out of the political change from Ottoman to Italian rule by expanding business in Italy. Thus, Alhadeff first considered pursuing his university studies in Paris, but he eventually enrolled in the Faculty of Law in Pavia following his father's insistent advice.[103] The tension concerning the persisting French influence on school graduates from the Eastern Mediterranean continued as late as 1932. Several students from Rhodes were reported to attend the francophone Lazarist College in Santorini, while wealthy Catholic families inquired through the French vice-consulate in Rhodes into the possibility to enter Catholic schools in Beirut.[104] For a few others, on the contrary, higher education in Italy fulfilled Governor Lago's expectation to divert colonial subjects from foreign influence. A few dozen Dodecanesians followed Lago's encouragement to study in Pisa in the early 1930s, but their experiences were marked by economic scarcity and political surveillance.[105]

Compared to Ottoman times, especially Orthodox and Muslim youth studying abroad became an urgent political problem, since cross-border connections raised the authorities' suspicions of unloyalty. Their mobility implying the allure of foreign diplomas would hamper fascist colonialism's efforts to steer its subjects' transition from the educational to the professional realm. Even though the Italian authorities aimed at co-opting the local elite, their concerns and sanctions largely applied to lower class students who usually did not pursue higher education but attended secondary schools elsewhere thanks to kinship support. Aged fourteen, Mustafa Müderiszade, son of a night watchman, moved to Istanbul in 1935 to complete his curriculum at a Turkish secondary school while living at his aunt's. The Italian police put him under strict surveillance, and he was suspected of trading cash illegally, until he was eventually denied to land at Rhodes harbour in 1938.[106] His trajectory shows that youth-as-students were not just an object to mould, but also a thorn in the authorities' side as soon as they ventured out of the latter's control. In Rhodes, signs of students' politicization emerged already during Italian military occupation, and they were closely related to transformations in late Ottoman schooling experiences.

Discipline, Sexuality, and Politics at School

At all the institutions mentioned above, schooling implied repetitive everyday interactions between pupils and teachers based on appreciations or reproaches. Discipline was therefore a cornerstone of education. Punishing or praising a student could remain a trivial occurrence, but it could also expose the "room for manoeuvre" binding students and teachers, teachers and directors, as well as directors and authorities, thus acquiring a much broader dimension.[107] In line with the complexity embedded in the notion of education, behaviour at school was not limited to intellectual performance and involved notions of morality and obedience.

Sources such as the *tekdīr i 'lānları* (punishment certificates) from the *İdadiye*, the *poinologia* (penalty records) from the *Venetokleion*, and the reports on *conduite* from the *Alliance* school reveal the link between discipline and sexuality in regulating and performing school sociability. The imperial consequence in Rhodes added an increasing politicization of the educational realm to this link. Documents on discipline concerning the *Frères* school are rare. Vittorio Alhadeff's memoirs, however, inform us that, in the late 1910s, corporal punishment through the stick (*canne*) coexisted with the more "constructive" measure of giving extra loads of work such as the memorization of literary texts.[108] More material is available from the *Venetokleion*. When students were sanctioned, they had to apologize in front of the teacher.[109] A shift at the Orthodox gymnasium is noticeable in the penalty records of the school year 1916–17. A clear and brief summary of the reasons behind the punishment was included together with rather uniform disciplining measures. Students were punished for infractions like "behaving improperly" (*feromenos aoraios*) in the classroom, "absence from classes," or being "insulting to the teachers." The punishments, often collective, went from three to eight days of suspension, up to three days of detention at school and/or the deduction of five points in conduct (*vathmos tis diagogis*).[110] There was no evident distinction between boys and girls, although the tendency to subversion among the latter acquires a particular dimension as it was sanctioned in a classroom environment dominated by male teachers and pupils. The orphan Magdalini A. was expelled indeterminately (yet later reintegrated) for her being "cause of unrest (*proxenos tarachis*) in the classroom" and showing "signs of disobedience and impudence."[111]

The system of conduct points at the *Venetokleion* most probably derives from the Ottoman state regulations in use at the *İdadiye*, which allocated fifty credits on "morals" (*ahlak*). At any infraction, they could be deducted with remarks remaining in the student's personal record until the diploma.[112] Penalty records from the *İdadiye* have been preserved for the years 1905 to 1908. These documents offer a vivid portrait of student life. For instance, a Jewish student from the fourth class, Avram, was the victim of bullying. The teachers identified a classmate, Nacib, as the main culprit, who was punished with the "abatement of five credits in conduct" and temporary expulsion from school, also because he had already been punished previously for coming to school armed with a dagger.[113] Avram's classmates also bullied him with sexual references to his sister, spreading "calumnies" (*iftirā*) in order to seek revenge for a penalty that one of them had received upon being denounced to the teacher.[114] The responsible, Faik, was suspended from school for a week.[115] The bullies also feminized Avram by talking to him condescendingly as an object of desire only to reinforce the boundaries of their masculinity from which he was to be excluded.[116]

Contrary to the Orthodox schools, the *İdadiye* students were asked to give their version of the story when such incidents occurred. Investigating commissions consisting mainly of teachers filed a report after collecting notes from all the youngsters involved, occasionally through questions such as "Why did you run away [from school], who was with you? Where did you walk around?."[117] This was part of the rigid discipline of Hamidian state schools, but the students were involved as witnesses and negotiators in the reconstruction of events.[118] Among decisions by commissions, school regulations (*mekteb talimātı*), and detailed reports, the students' voice was recorded and preserved in its autonomy. They were considered agents with their own motivations, ethical code and, since many notes describe their activities beyond the school walls, their use of free time. The Ottoman *İdadiye* was therefore a space where male teenagers made first experiences in presenting themselves as accountable in front of authorities.

One frequent issue was the carrying of weapons (knives and occasionally even guns) to school. In January 1912, a boy called Uruf stabbed a classmate in the thigh with a pocket-knife. He had found the weapon at home, while his father was carving a horseshoe (*na'il*) on both his arms as a "sign of heroism." The boy said to his father "I will also take a knife and carve a horseshoe, or maybe I will stab someone." His father, a lower class gendarme and *muhacir* from Crete, considered this an expression of "Cretan bravery" and did nothing to prevent the plan. The teachers strongly condemned such bad parental influence. Alike teachers at the *Alliance,* they asserted that a youngster's evil deed pointed to even greater harm during adulthood. The report concluded by requesting from the Directorate of Education that Uruf be sent to a reformatory (*ıslahhāne*) and be removed from the school roster.[119] Such extreme intervention by school authorities related to a boy's emulation of his father in terms of aggressive masculinity, fearing that undisciplined and lower class youth were but criminal adults *in nuce.* The gravity of Uruf's deed excluded any attempt to reeducate him at school and the report emphasized the importance of morality to correct bad education.

The Hamidian period characterized schools discipline through a "ritualistic approach to corporal punishment"[120] Yet, already in the months preceding the Young Turks' Revolution, the vilayet's director of education sent detailed instructions to the head of the *İdadiye* demanding less repressive and more constructive methods to prevent misconduct and react to it.[121] School institutions in Rhodes voiced the necessity to raise children in a sound atmosphere even beyond the family control more frequently after the revolution of 1908, as in Uruf's case. This form of state surveillance during the Second Constitutional Period also affected communal schools. In a note to the rabbi of Rhodes from June 1910, the vilayet's director of education complained that some students at the *Alliance* school "had been excessively beaten." He stressed that such measures were "strictly prohibited by the government" and officially admonished the rabbi.[122] Nonetheless, similar episodes occurred again only a few weeks later, forcing the authorities to threaten with "legal action" against the school in case of further complaints by parents or tutors.[123] The *Alliance* school directors also denounced some instructors who used physical violence on students and, in line with the headquarters in Paris, criticized the use of the stick (*baton*) outside the schools by both parents and rabbis.[124] Persuasive rather than repressive methods to correct misbehaviour were considered a form of civilized and enlightened education, in which self-appreciation but also shame were equally important cognitive processes. This would reform school sociability by having the virtuous pupils influence the vicious through emulation. Consequently, teachers placed "undisciplined and lazy" students in "quarantine" at separate desks instead of threatening them with violence.[125] In so doing, the *Alliance* saw pupils as belonging to a life stage clearly different from adulthood, thus legitimizing the teachers' intervention as a form of protection.

In the students' life outside school as well, a strict sexual discipline, especially for female adolescents, described "street life" as a dangerous spatial and moral category. The public space was a third dimension beside school and home.[126] The girls' "hanging around," "speaking loud on the street, bursting out laughing in people's face" were interpreted as signs of bad behaviour and exposure to sexuality, to be corrected in the classroom.[127] Attempts to discipline the pupils' everyday life were not only punitive. During the First World War, the *Alliance* girl school's directress proposed to open a broidery workshop inspired by the voluntary association *Ergani Athina*, founded a few years earlier by Orthodox women.[128] The aim was to "keep unemployed [Jewish] young girls busy" based on the principle that "misery and idleness lead to vice" and parents might instigate girls to commit "dishonest acts."[129]

Despite concerns related to "promiscuity," the lack of financial and human resources at the *Alliance* school occasionally led to mixed classes, especially in the early 1910s. This situation was not new at the *Alliance*, which ran thirty-seven mixed schools, approximately 25 per cent of the total, in the region.[130] Nonetheless, having boys and girls in the same class was considered abnormal and morally reprehensible. Madame Graziani, the school directress in the 1910s, noted that by hosting both sexes "in the same building, the shock is unavoidable."[131] She particularly regretted being forced to send young female instructors to the boys school, where they had to take care of pupils only three or four years younger than them.[132] All these efforts aimed at constructing youth-as-students by stressing morality, intellectual development, and good manners through the separation of the sexes.

While teachers fostered a reformed school socialization, episodes of sexual harassment were frequent and could also concern non-teaching personnel, such as janitors.[133] Sexual abuses on pupils could lead to arguments about discipline measures, which in turn could have broader consequences in specific situations of political turmoil. In the winter of 1914–15, a scandal occurred at the *İdadiye*. Less than three years had passed since the occupation of the island by Italian troops. Greece had, in the meantime, annexed Ottoman territories and the Committee of Union and Progress in power in Istanbul had plunged the empire into the First World War. The "Turkish" school, as the Italian authorities referred to it, became affected by politicization based on sympathy for the fate of the Ottoman Empire. In March 1915, amid the crucial battle at Gallipoli in which the Sultan's army resisted a major Allied offensive, the Ottoman journal *Ceride-yi 'ilmiye* published a report on war aid donations (*i'āne-yi harbiye*) which included a contribution by "the students of the *İdadiye* under the guidance of the vice-director of education Mehmet Kadri."[134]

Yet, beside this sign of patriotism, the situation was tense at the Ottoman school. A few weeks earlier, one of the substitute teachers, Ahmet Tevfik, was fired by the qadi of Rhodes, who oversaw education matters during the military occupation. Tevfik had previously accused another teacher, Kjanan (Kenan) Efendi, of "pederasty," and the latter replied with an attestation addressed to the school's investigation commission. This document reveals details on the intimacy that teachers and pupils could reach:

> One day, I saw the seventh grader Ziya Efendi son of Mehmet Ali Efendi at the coffeehouse. He was wondering whether to attend the classes or not, and I encouraged him to attend. It would be good for him and he would quickly receive his diploma. I invited him to come to my place and discuss the question to solve the difficulties together with Hassan Efendi [the chief janitor], who visits me in the evening … Ziya came with the sixth grader Mehmet Galip Efendi and … we told him to come in for a matter of courtesy … A third evening Ziya again came with Mehmet, and after half an

hour also Mahir son of Şevket, but they obviously did not say anything, so we let them in.

In his defence, the teacher explained that he knew the boundaries of his proximity with students: "The next morning, I told Hassan Efendi that, although we had invited only Ziya, he had come on two evenings with Mehmet and Mahir, and that was not fair. Not judging it appropriate to send them away, Hassan and I decided to go to the market in the evening to avoid these visits, and since then no meeting took place."[135] Whereas parents are completely absent from this picture, in the same attestation Kjanan claimed that students of the higher grades were inciting their younger colleagues to rebel against some teachers and even "held meetings in coffeehouses and other gatherings to make propaganda" against him. Only one day after he sent the letter, students from the fifth, sixth, and seventh grades sent a petition to the investigation commission and listed ten complaints and questions including: criticism of the appointments of several teachers; accusations of bad morality against teachers and janitors; attacks on the already mentioned Bension Menashe, teacher of French, who "has been receiving his salary for two months without teaching"; regrets that the investigation had treated the students as culprits instead of victims; protests against forced custody at school on Fridays, considered an expedient of morally corrupt teachers to sexually abuse the students while the school was closed; accusations against Mehmet Kadri of not having offered enough preparation for the upcoming final exams and of having stolen some maps from schools imported from Europe to embellish his house.

The students presented themselves as an active collectivity of peers, aware of their own rights as well as the duties of the older generation. The entanglement of discipline, sexuality and politics was appropriated and narrated by the very students: they regretted that Rhodes "has lived under the enemy occupation for three years" and that the mismanagement of the school "has provoked in us, who will draw the reins of the Fatherland tomorrow, a sense of rebellion and hatred."[136] This episode also brought to the surface a latent polarization among teachers and board members. The Italian authorities interpreted this as a friction between the "old Turks" (guided by the mufti, the local religious leader), the "young Turks" (led by the qadi, the judge of the communal tribunal), and the "separatist young Turks," siding against the second faction mostly for personal issues. Since the vice-director Mehmet Kadri, close to the mufti, was a target of the students' attacks, it is unlikely that the activists were among those participating in the war aid donation that he organized short after this incident. Whereas

Ottoman patriotism was common to both actions, a discipline affair revealed political divisions resonating throughout the empire.[137]

A similar dynamic occurred at the *Venetokleion* in early 1919. In a likewise delicate moment, Greek nationalists were lobbying for annexations in the Aegean at Versailles. In May, Prime Minister Venizelos would command Greek soldiers to land in Ottoman Smyrna. In Rhodes too, the atmosphere was tense. On Easter Sunday, the Italian army killed a priest and a peasant woman in the village of Villanova. With many others, they had demonstrated against the Italian repression of gatherings in favour of the *Enosis*.[138] Short before this incident, in February, the trader and member of the Communal Council (*Eforia*) Giorgios Katsouris complained that his son had been suspended from school "simply for a remark towards the gymnastics teacher."[139] Supported by the metropolitan bishop, Katsouris pressured the *Venetokleion*'s director, Iordanis Papadopoulos, who, however, did not cancel the punishment. The director was sent for at the Metropolis, dismissed, and even beaten up by Katsouris. Perceiving that the tension in the Orthodox community was growing, the Italian authorities increased the *Carabinieri* presence in town, ordering them to "stay neutral," although the police appreciated the headmaster's commitment "not to serve philhellenic propaganda."[140]

The situation escalated when a group of students rallied at the headmaster's house to show him their support and then marched to the Greek consulate to voice their rage against the metropolitan bishop and the *Eforia*. Meanwhile, other students occupied the gymnasium and refused the calls by the communal authorities' to reopen it. They booed the bishop and even threw stones at his servant. The protests continued on the following day and targeted Katsouris's son, who was threatened by students with sticks. The police reported that the students also shouted slogans in favour of the military governor and Italy. This episode ended with a victory for the protesters, since Katsouris was dismissed from the *Eforia* and the headmaster was reintegrated.[141] Metropolitan Bishop Apostolos complained that the Italian police had incited the protesters to attack him by granting them *carte blanche*. He admitted that, as a result, "the Community had to accept the students' demands even at its own damage (*pros tin vlavin autis*)."[142] A new balance of power emerged through this episode: the communal institutions lost prestige in front of both the Greek consul and the Italian authorities, who could more easily place loyal notables in key offices.

The students' unrest did not immediately cease after these protests. A few days later, an anonymous leaflet was found in many corners of the predominantly Orthodox neighbourhood Mitropolis. The *Carabinieri*, who had this message translated into Italian, considered it as related to the incidents at school:

> Fellow townsmen! We cannot stay asleep anymore. We must wake up and care for the interest and the honour of our country (*del nostro paese*). For so long we have been bearing this metropolitan bishop who damaged so much the Orthodox Christians and, as if this were not enough …, he elevated to the post of vice-bishop (*vicario episcopale*) a miserable and immoral man … who cohabits with women in an illegal and obscene way … And we patriots have tolerated this offence! … May all these things end soon and let us fulfil our duty, since it is a shame to bear with such immorality.[143]

Punishments deemed unfair could become a trigger for protest against communal institutions. In turn, disorder in communal structures could trigger attacks based on morality to contest discriminatory punishments. However, the students' horizon expanded beyond local affairs.

A manifesto entitled "Resolution of the Greek student-youth" (*Psifisma tis mathitiotis Ellinikis neotitos Rodou*) appeared a few weeks after the *Venetokleion* protests. "In the name of the Holy Trinity," the signatories claimed that all "Greek young students" in Rhodes looked at the Paris Peace Conference deciding the fate of the Dodecanese. They lamented the "obscure (*skoteia*), devious (*ipoula*), and sinister (*katachthonia*) means" used by the Italians to "change the very Hellenic spirit (*Ellinikotatou fronimatos*)" of the population. The resolution, drafted after a meeting at the *Venetokleion*, is an explicit and reflexive claim of a collectivity defining itself along ethnic (Greek) social (students) and age (youth) criteria:

1) [The Greek student-youth] has declared the union of the very Hellenic island of Rhodes with our sweetest Mother Greece.
2) It firmly declares that it will not accept any other solution to the fate of the very Hellenic and glorious island of Rhodes, as well as the other eleven islands in the same condition of suffering.
3) It strongly protests Italy's attitude as well as its unexpected and arrogant pretensions.
4) It declares that, in case of a condemnation sentence, it will lead the general revolutionary movement of the people that is being prepared spontaneously and resolutely, and that it will turn this beautiful island into ashes and ruins …
5) It sends one last but very warm prayer that the ardent, centuries-long, and rightful claims of the entire population of the Dodecanese be recognized and protected …
   On behalf of more than four hundred students,
   The delegates.[144]

The number of *Venetokleion* pupils was largely below four hundred, which was a hyperbole to strengthen the signatories' claims. In reality, as schools became exposed to political issues, students became factionalized too.[145] At the gymnasium, one group addressed communal issues by attacking the metropolitan bishop and the *Eforia*. Another group tackled diplomatic questions and openly challenged the Italian occupation. During the Greater War, youth became a trope connecting several scales of politics, from the local to the national up to the international level. The students mobilized the notion of youth to legitimize an ethno-national right of self-determination, surfing the wave of the "Wilsonian moment" resonating globally and, in most cases, later ending in disappointment. Yet, the outcome of youth activism is not more important than its origin and purpose. In a moment of rapid political change, mobilizing youth allowed to announce the existence of a new force and to legitimize its future.

The *Venetokleion* and *İdadiye* protests highlight some conditions of possibility for youth politicization. The communalization of secondary schools made them a site of political factionalism. The Italian occupiers' repression marginalized local notables, creating a vacuum of power in which younger individuals could act more autonomously than ever before. Warfare, lastly, caused polarization within the community rather than intercommunal violence.[146] The most active students did not side with notables in power at communal institutions, and no representative of the economic elite took the lead in these actions. Communities were thus not a closed or pyramidal space that neutralized youth-as-students and their activism, but arenas where students could make their voice heard. They expressed "patriotic" feelings either towards the state, the community, a foreign state, or the school itself, and this could coexist with contrasting feelings towards the Italian authorities. The occupiers downplayed the students' autonomy, considering them mere replicators of intercommunal divisions. Military governors were still cautious about meddling in communal affairs in order not to alienate pre-existing Ottoman institutions in light of such factionalism. Yet, students' unrest cannot be reduced to the result of governmental politics. Invested by a broader mission related to new idea of education, secondary schools equally pervaded the political domain to an unprecedented level. Youth-as-students were subject to institutional power dynamics, but they were also autonomous in destabilizing and influencing the negotiations within these dynamics.

***

Secondary schools are arguably the institutions which best reflect the imperial consequence from Ottoman to Italian rule. Founding these schools, defining their curricula and tuitions, and managing their personnel remained an open challenge for governments and communities before and after 1912. Italian sovereignty, though, brought about a greater decisional power assigned to the state. The dilemma of preserving Ottoman diversity or reinforcing an Italianization informed by fascism was a serious challenge related to the transformation of a new colonial territory. First and foremost, this implied removing foreign influence while introducing Italian elements in curricula and especially exams. This aimed at providing advantages to Italian schools and making the communal institutions less attractive. Before 1912, the different schools were a local manifestation of an Ottoman empire-wide diverse educational infrastructure. After 1923, on the contrary, each of them became a quite unique and localized form of accommodation – not without conflict – between communities and the colonial government.

This resumes Rhodes's shift from a provincial to a colonial setting. Pupils and their families were an integral part of this process and not merely its idle targets. This created the multifaceted local configuration of schools and of schooling experiences that the article from 1969 about the reunion at the Italian schools of Rhodes quoted at the beginning of this chapter only superficially mentioned. Interiorizing education received at school in terms of notions and skills, reacting to disciplinary sanctions, and finding the material resources necessary for schooling concerned families in Ottoman and Italian times alike, and they actively negotiated the terms of socialization with school boards and authorities. The most open phase of negotiation corresponded to the decade of the Greater War, precisely because the railroad switch between two sovereign systems lowered the pressure of the Ottoman state and questioned communal authority. This allowed students to partake in discussions concerning the future of Rhodes. Schools had become, and would remain, sites in which discipline, administration, politics, and morality collided in the category of youth-as-students.

These processes heavily depended on material conditions. However solemnly the discourse on education was voiced, all sides were aware that using limited resources, optimizing costs, and coping with scarcity was vital. Students had difficulties converting diplomas into good occupations after school, families often did not have the economic resources necessary for the completion of their children's curriculum, communities did not achieve the monopoly on their coreligionists' educational trajectories, authorities did not obtain the pupils' loyalty as much as they wished. Beyond institutional efforts to impose state and communal control on schooling, the pupils' trajectories largely relied on family resources. Debates concerning schools always implied considerations on the occupational background of the parents and the occupational future of their children. After all, even if all institutions considered schools a factor impacting the local society and economy, they were also aware that the labour and entrepreneurial landscape of Rhodes evolved beyond the reach of school training. Every pupil leaving school to make a living would later be exposed to generational dynamics revolving around the notions of productivity and idleness.

Chapter Four

"Good Conduct" between Work and Leisure

"Cycling is fully flourishing here, and this passion is gradually expanding to the other islands, wherever good roads allow for it." On 28 October 1928, the *Messaggero di Rodi* published these words in a report about the cycling race Rhodes-Lindos-Rhodes, stretching eighty kilometres and requiring more than five hours of endurance. The winner Mustafa Boiagi was "carried shoulder high" by the crowd. He "walked up the balcony of the *Circolo Italia*," a club where the local elite gathered, and the civil and military authorities "handed him the three-coloured jersey [*maglia tricolore*, referring to the Italian flag]" as the "1928 Rhodian cycling champion."[1]

In fascist Italy, cycling and other popular sports were a battleground to reinforce national identity.[2] This race reached beyond the realm of sport and reflected the self-representation of colonial authority, proud of organizing a festive but equally solemn public event. Boiagi won the race on a special day for fascism. For the first time, the race took place on the anniversary of the Blackshirts' March on Rome of 1922 and not of the Italian royal troops' Capture of Rome of 1870 (20 September). This marked a symbolical shift from a celebration of the "old" Italy, united through the *Risorgimento*, to one of the "new" fascist and imperial Italy. Fascist colonialism's modernizing efficiency also appeared in the article, which boasted about the improvement of "good roads" in the Dodecanese. Some lines were dedicated to the military and police who "managed, each in their function, to assure public order in a perfect way."[3] The colonial authorities were delighted to portray themselves as innovators capable of creating the perfect scenography for a celebration of their regime.

This type of sport event would have hardly been thinkable in a late Ottoman provincial setting. Cycling, football, and other leisure activities were fostered by Italian governors as a strategy to bring the state closer to the population. Colonial subjects in Rhodes, indeed, partook in these events as competitors. Legally, they never enjoyed the same rights as their fellow townsmen owning the Italian metropolitan citizenship, but a winning racer like Boiagi could, for a day, literally wear Italy's national flag on his skin and personify Italy's grandeur from the top of the podium. Boiagi dominated the local cycling competitions in 1927 and 1928, when he was 20 years old.[4] It would seem hard to find a better example of an "indigenous youth" racing towards the goal of Lago's "new generation."

But who was Mustafa Boiagi, apart from a popular amateur sportsman? Before those years of glory, he had lost both parents, who did not leave him any resources such as a farm or a shop as inheritance. After some occasional jobs, around 1930 he quit sports and started to work as a public driver. Many young individuals like him in Rhodes faced a fragmented professional landscape marked by familial discontinuity, political transformations, and economic scarcity. Born around the beginning of Italian rule in 1912, Mustafa and others coped with this fragmentation by choosing an occupation not available to their fathers at the same age, since cars also made their appearance, or at least became more accessible, in the 1920s. Mustafa worked as a driver until the Second World War. His job was regularly documented by the police because it required a public license. His personal file in the *Carabinieri* archive contains several traffic offenses, but also reports about a rowdy life including brothels, "neglecting his family," "affairs with women who exploit him," debts and an insolvency trial. The police summarized his character by noting that, despite several warnings, "he never settled himself" (*non si è mai messo a posto*). In 1937, he was even accused by a Blackshirt militant whom he met at work of having "communist" and "revolutionary tendencies," although the police did not pursue these likely groundless allegations.[5] The same person could thus embody a disreputable masculinity, uncapable of building sound family bonds or having a disciplined working life, and a virtuous masculinity as a young athlete acclaimed by crowds and ruling personalities. In contingent situations related to work or sports, this person could be praised during a fascist celebration only to be later accused of being a communist.

This ambivalence reflects a broader issue investigated in this chapter: the intersection between generational dynamics, youth socialization, and new perceptions of work and leisure. Productive and recreative activities redefined relationships in the family and the community, producing outcomes that the authorities had to face, discipline, foster, or repress. This chapter argues that, firstly, communities and their notables tried to gain control over work and leisure socialization emerging from below in Ottoman times. Secondly, the colonial state aspired to discipline these initiatives to minimize dangers of social disorder and to legitimize Italian rule. Thirdly, this control contributed to a polarization based on fascism versus dangerous alternative ideologies. In all cases, generational dynamics and representations of youth were used to profile individuals and determine the criteria for "good conduct," which in turn justified institutional intervention. Although Italian rule brought about considerable innovations in the domains of work and leisure, these domains began to expand in late Ottoman years. Governor Lago accommodated these Ottoman elements into the new circumstances of fascist colonialism. The imperial consequence implied negotiations between the state and local forces that exacerbated when public security was perceived as threatened by initiatives and scandals among the local population.

At different ages and under different circumstances, Rhodians left school to find their place in the adult world. When reconstructing life experiences and social statuses during this passage, information on productive and recreative activities are hard to separate from each other. Whereas institutions were increasingly concerned with how the population of Rhodes made a living, this "living" reached beyond work and economic subsistence. Still, work and leisure were not complementary. Leisure was far for simply meaning a well-deserved "free time" after being absolved of a stable occupation's duties. Work and leisure were concurring references that defined productivity and morality as the result of generational dynamics. Youth appeared in this process as the life stage at stake within the transition from school to work. Yet, youth also mattered as a trope used to connote leisure activities. As Mustafa Boiagi's case shows, colonial sources often provide seemingly contradictory accounts on an actor's lifestyle. By tying work and leisure closer to each other when inquiring into post-school socialization, we can gain a different look on these contradictions. Both work and leisure were discussed to address the stability of the family, the community, and the authorities. Embedded in the imperial consequence linking Ottoman heritage and fascist colonialism, relationships between parents and children as well as among peers marked the tension between norm and transgression, novelty, and tradition. The colonial state was likely to intervene when a judgment on an individual combined with a political assessment. In this case, the authorities increased surveillance and emphasized fascism as a virtuous model in which disciplined work and leisure were harmonized.

In modern history, work and leisure are not easy topics to handle. Since the nineteenth century, they underwent a profound transformation at the global level. Next to the expansion of industrialization and financial capitalism, the early twentieth-century Eastern Mediterranean saw the emergence of sports, gymnastics, theatre plays, and entertainment resorts, but also of cinema and radio, which reached a broad consuming audience especially among the lower classes. In 1921, the director of the *Alliance* school in Rhodes lamented the absence of *"grands cafés with orchestras, as they exist in almost of cities of the Levant."*[6] Only ten years later, the *Messaggero* proudly announced the opening of the orchestra season at the *Café Rodino*, located at the town's outskirts, together with screening at two cinemas, a boxing fight, and an upcoming car race around the island.[7] This range of events accommodated all tastes and classes which, however, did not necessarily mingle when attending them.

Work and leisure were discussed together by contemporary sociologists and economists observing the transformation of capitalism, a symptom of how both terms transformed social relationships and statuses. Diversified forms of leisure were recognized as a factor of social distinction precisely because workers increasingly accessed activities subsumed under the term "free time." Thorstein Veblen's idea of leisure as "abstention from productive work" and as a social demarcation monopolized by the wealthier, formulated in 1899, seemed to no longer keep the pace.[8] In 1930, John Maynard Keynes addressed the same issue through generational dynamics, claiming that increasing "technical efficiency" would create for his contemporaries' grandchildren "freedom from pressing economic cares" but also the challenge of "how to occupy leisure … to live wisely and agreeably as well."[9]

Yet, who was to decide what a "wise" and "agreeable" life consisted of? This is where political circumstances start to matter. The very etymology of "leisure," from Latin *licere*, "to be permitted," reveals that the term is situational, referring to non (regularly) lucrative activities that specific social institutions consider legitimate.[10] Needless to say, when they do not work to earn money for their needs, individuals engage in a number of activities that do not fit this definition of leisure or "free time." In Rhodes, these activities were often stigmatized as "vice," "idleness," or "vagrancy." As the chapter illustrates, all these terms relied on a discourse on productivity and disciplined work. Such discourse, however, did not erase the fuzziness of many situations in which defining an activity's value was a matter of contingent interactions between individuals, communities, and authorities.

In the late Ottoman Empire, the urban upper and middle class interiorized European taste as a distinctive marker of a privileged position in contrast to the working class, all while embracing capitalist modes of production and investment.[11] As Malte Fuhrmann argues, however, "Europeanization" in Ottoman Mediterranean port cities was as effervescent as ambivalent, since it was appropriated and re-elaborated through practices of production and consumption by broader segments of the local society.[12] Although hardly comparable to more vibrant cities such as Smyrna, Beirut, or Salonica, an intensified exchange with the circuits of capitalism was sensed in Rhodes as well. Local traders expanded their business within the densification of the southern Aegean economic space.[13] Rhodes was an insular, provincial town with a smaller volume of affairs. Yet, as a transit port, it was also connected to larger Mediterranean cities, as the local notable Edouard Biliotti wrote as early as 1881.[14] These maritime connections contributed to Western penetration in the Levant, involving large companies as well as familial enterprises. In 1903, the French consul in Rhodes corresponded with a baker from France and illustrated the prospects of this business in town. Most Rhodians, he explained, would not afford *"pain de luxe"* but patisserie would become popular among the upper classes disgusted by the "horrible sweets" prepared by the "Turks." People allegedly complained about the "bad quality" of bread, as only "one messy Jew[ish]" baker prepared "a whitish bread in the European style."[15] This grassroot snapshot captures how social distinction, the Europeanization of taste, and ethnic categorizations were interwoven.

After 1923, the change of sovereignty put actors under pressure in terms of reorientation within a post-Ottoman colonial market and its culture. For instance, movies dubbed in Greek or French were banned at local theatres in the 1930s following complaints by the Fascist Party, although they were popular and cheaper to import. Italian cinema owners showing movies dubbed in other languages were accused of "favouring the Greek and Jewish element," while the import ban economically favoured the Fascist Party's own movie theatre and Italian productions.[16] Even the trajectory of a movie reel could encapsulate traits of Italian colonial rule inseparable from fascism, but equally inseparable from its Mediterranean environment. As Filippo Espinoza has noted, colonial governors ruled the Dodecanese along economic criteria of fascist imperialism (such as "autarchy," the myth of Italy's economic self-sufficiency) but also along the contingencies embedded in the relationships with neighbouring states, most of all Turkey.[17] Unstable politics meant an economic reorientation for families involved in business and new struggles to make both ends meet for those with scarce capital or no property at all.

Italian sovereign rule in Rhodes added on the "ritual colonization of time" that fascism imposed in the metropole.[18] With it came new public performances in the form of politicized parades and ceremonies, like the cycling race mentioned above. Next to an expansion of sport events, fascist colonialism brought about party organizations dedicated to non-productive activities such as the *Opera Nazionale Dopolavoro* (open to colonial subjects), in which voluntarism and coercion had fuzzy boundaries. But this rule also impacted productive activities. Nicholas Doumanis pointed to the perception of "work as normalcy" among many (Greek) Dodecanesians when recalling the period of Italian fascism. They associated this rule with "order" contrasting with precolonial backwardness and subsistence.[19] What happens when we historicize this memorial text by questioning the notion of "normalcy"? As the chapter shows, Italian rule did not imply material improvement or security for the whole colonial population. We can rather speak of "normalization" referring to how notions of productivity and morality converged towards obedience to colonial rule.

Generational dynamics and representations of youth mattered for governmental measures and personal experiences related to work and leisure. The chapter discusses them as combined with two other central factors of social distinction: wealth and gender. Accordingly, the chapter consists of four sections focused on diverse objects: family business, marginalized labour, women's labour, and sports. Some locals, like the Agiakatsikas family, established their trade business in Rhodes already in late Ottoman times. They combined an entrepreneurial activity with a public status achieved through philanthropic commitment and tenures in the communal administration. Whereas recent studies have highlighted how generational continuity in trade intersected with the transition from Ottoman rule to nation-states, post-Ottoman colonial contexts like Rhodes remain underexplored.[20] After 1912, the male descendants of the Ottoman provincial Agiakatsikas dynasty coped with a reconfiguration of the market through a diversification of trajectories and roles within the business. Those entering the business around 1930 embodied new bureaucratic, technological, and managerial competences. But they also followed social innovations in terms of leisure by increasing activism in sports clubs. Especially in the 1930s, though, colonial rule felt challenged by the Agiakatsikas family's public commitment when the governors sought to turn confessional communities into politically neutral instruments of rule. The family's younger generation left communal politics when it took over leading roles in business. The Agiakatsikas family faced the challenge to keep their social capital and respectability upright, between expanding business interests and a negative political profile.

Many families from the lower classes, however, did not have enough capital to secure generational continuity in a time of sociopolitical transformations. A difficult transition from schooling to work prompted their moral stigmatization. Despite material scarcity, schools and philanthropic associations launched initiatives to make this transition smoother already before 1912. During the three decades of their rule, Italian authorities never committed to develop an effective and accessible system of social protection for colonial subjects. Rather, they assumed a criminalizing stance towards youths with weak familial bonds without a stable occupation. At the same time, a new communication emerged between authorities and families when dealing with these "troublesome" children. Quite often, family members took the initiative and demanded the authorities' intervention. In turn, commentators speaking in the name of the community projected these youths' behaviour into virtues and vices of a whole body of coreligionists. The Fascist Party also increased its influence, managing the transfer to reformatories in the Kingdom and offering Italian citizens the opportunity to make up a failed occupational socialization through membership in the paramilitary Blackshirts.

The discourse on productivity concerned mostly young men, although the Italian occupation had implications for young women's labour. Despite recent studies on industrial work, the productive role of women in late and post-Ottoman history remains underexplored, which holds true even more for studies on Italian colonialism.[21] Many Italian families moving to Rhodes employed female domestic servants, while the presence of the military favoured the expansion of sex work.[22] Most domestic servants and sex workers experienced migration and disruption of intergenerational family bonds. Parental control at times persisted and absorbed their revenues, adding on the economic exploitation and psychological harassment by household employers and pimps. Domestic and sex work were described with diverse and ambivalent terms by both authorities and women. Whereas institutions tended to silence it in bureaucratic certificates using the term "housewife," women frequently combined several activities to make a living by preserving their "reputation" as well as social bonds in their environment.

In the case of sport, the last Ottoman years marked the origins of its institutionalization, which colonial rule expanded and profoundly transformed. Ottoman communal institutions absorbed private initiatives to organize teams and games. A club like *Diagoras* was not only a recreational site, but also a platform where Orthodox communal structures put roots in the name of a sound education for the youth. As long as football was perceived as a leisure activity bearing positive effects for the youth's health and socialization, Italian rule encouraged private and communal initiatives. Yet, sport could foster alternative identifications. In this case, state repression and fascist rhetoric lashed back and occupied the stage. After launching a popular football league and trying to keep it under control through team boards dominated by notables considered loyal, the Italian authorities dismembered most teams and reorganized the league within a centralized colonial association. Then and *only* then was sport emphasized as an exclusive element of the fascist "new man," or an exclusive idea of youth based on Italian superiority. Especially for better-off families, however, the main concern was not how their children performed as "new men" on a football pitch. They were more interested in making them ready and fit to take over the business, combining new skills with the continuity of family capital.

A Family of Capitalists in Flux

Wealthy families in Rhodes navigated political, technological, and economic turbulence trying to keep their business afloat. Preserving the family's activity was both a privileged starting point and a responsibility for the new generations of this class. Vittorio Alhadeff narrated the rationalization of his family's business (including banking and trade) along three generational segments. His grandfather Solomon, founder of the proper enterprise, "did not quite feel the need for organization, since he kept all the calculations, all the names in his mind."[23] Vittorio's father Joseph upgraded the business around 1910, as the Alhadeffs' company invited experts from Smyrna to rationalize its management through a modern computing and control system.[24] Vittorio himself entered the company during Italian sovereign administration after completing his studies in law – the first in his family – providing occupational continuity through an additional layer of expertise and academic prestige.

The Italian 1936 census of Rhodes placed "Trade" in a separate category from "Industry and Crafts."[25] However, already in Ottoman times, these sectors could coexist in a family company. In this section, I discuss the trajectory of the Agiakatsikas family of industrialists-traders, chosen due to conspicuous amount of sources available allowing for a detailed account of generational dynamics related to entrepreneurship.

Figure 4.1. The Agiakatsikas family in the early twentieth century.

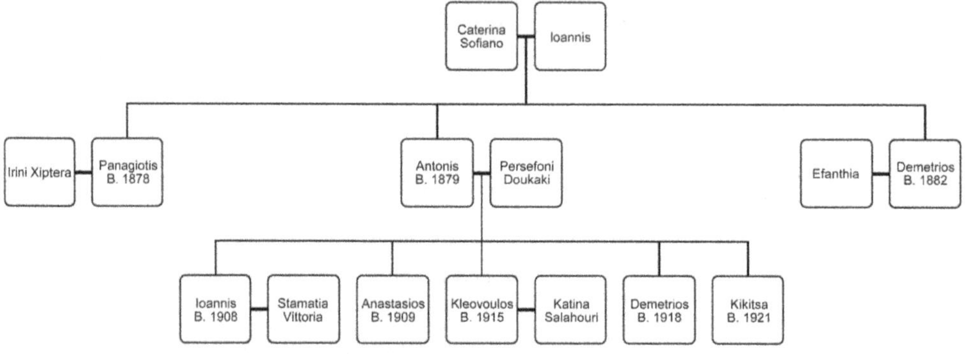

Note: This family tree is limited to those referred to in this section or about whom I could retrieve information. Other relatives and spouses are missing.

Around 1880, Ioannis Agiakatsikas moved to Rhodes from Mytilene. He started a business in olive products and, in 1890, he founded a company called "Kolossos."[26] The Ottoman local authorities described his workshop as a factory producing oil and soap (*yağhāne*) as early as 1905.[27] Ioannis's business grew rapidly and employed around thirty workers, thus being the largest industrial enterprise of Ottoman Rhodes. The French vice-consul mentioned his name to companies from Marseille that "wished to expand ... commercial relationships to the island of Rhodes" in 1910.[28] This is an example of growing economic interactions between late Ottoman provinces and the Western Mediterranean, which later remained a challenge for Italian rule.

While his business flourished, Ioannis became involved in communal institutions. He was a member of the civil jury at the Orthodox tribunal in 1905, and of the *Eforia*, the organ responsible for communal financial and educational issues, in 1906.[29] Meanwhile, new forms of voluntary associations were gaining momentum. Like many upper class entrepreneurs throughout the world, this second Agiakatsikas generation "bought respectability" through investments in philanthropy, an expanding domain in which women played a significant role.[30] Irini Xiptera and Persefoni Doukaki, who had married Ioannis's sons, were members of the society *Ergani Athina*, in which especially the former was active from 1912 to 1934. Irini's husband Panagiotis, who received the Italian title of *Cavaliere* for entrepreneurial merits, was in the society's Examination Committee (*Exelegtiki Epitropi*), a control branch reserved to men.[31] Philanthropic commitment raised the family's public visibility. When Ioannis died in January 1918, the family bought an insertion of the newspaper *Rodiaki* stating that all the association's members, including the female apprentices of its embroidery workshop, would solemnly attend the funeral and pay homage to their patron.[32]

The arrival of Italian military authorities created a new intersection of politics and business. In April 1913, Ioannis Agiakatsikas was among the traders invited by Governor Ameglio and his "commercial delegate" Alfredo Biliotti to discuss the prospects of the local economy.[33] During a decade in which exposing oneself to politics could compromise the relationship with the authorities, the absence of an Agiakatsikas in political actions started by other notables is remarkable. The family does not appear on a petition sent to the Greek foreign minister Nikolaos Politis in August 1919. It was signed by almost all the representatives of the local elite owning the Greek citizenship, but also by those whom the police considered as "well known and outstanding Hellenophiles" suspected of anti-Italian sentiments.[34] The family moved through the uncertainties of the Greater War by keeping a low profile.

Panagiotis, who had inherited the business from his father Ioannis, was both an entrepreneur and a promoter of leisure activities. He was the representative of a Greek shipping company and the vice-president of *Diagoras*, the largest local club dedicated to gymnastics but also to music.[35] The first two Agiakatsikas generations in Rhodes thus obtained their social status mainly through their business activity, later expanding to the philanthropic and cultural domains. The third generation added further innovations. Panagiotis's brother Antonios had four sons: Ioannis, Anastasios, Kleovoulos, and Demetrios. They all graduated from the *Venetokleion* between 1926 and 1934, receiving a communal form of secondary education not available to their parents.[36] The two elder brothers were also active in sports. In his late teens, Anastasios played for the club *Dorieas* between 1927 and 1929, while Ioannis was a member of the *Athlitikos Rodiakos Syllogos/Associazione Sportiva Rodia* (Rhodian Sport Association – ASR).[37]

The four brothers also upgraded the family's business. In 1928, they opened a new company branch called *Rosa di Rodi* specialized in cosmetics and perfumes, while *Kolossos* further expanded in the Egyptian and Turkish markets.[38] Business travels became more frequent as Ioannis visited Syria, Palestine as well as Greece, Italy, and France. He also obtained the exclusive selling license for Italian and German pharmaceutical companies in the Dodecanese.[39] This third generation reflected the professional specialization and diversification of family business which, like for the Alhadeffs, provided for family cohesion around the company. Ioannis was profiled as *commerciante* by the authorities, while Anastasios was chemist and Kleovoulos studied medicine in Athens. For the latter, the Greek capital was only the last stop of an educational trajectory which took him from the *Venetokleion* to colleges in Beirut and Florence. This elitist high school specialization through mobility raised the anxiety of the police, who addressed Kleovoulos with "several warnings" and recommended that he "be treated with distrust."[40]

Through marriage, this generation created further bonds with notables of the Doukakis and Vittorias families.[41] Beyond kinship, though, the creation of political alliances was a more complicated process, given the divisions within the Orthodox community vis-à-vis the Italian authorities. In August 1933, after Lago disbanded the Orthodox Communal Council, two factions concurred for the new elections. Antonios Agiakatsikas led a list containing unreliable elements for the Italian government which was defeated by Athanasios Billis and his successor Giorgios Bekes. This did not prevent Lago from putting the new Council under the control of a commissary.[42]

After these elections, the Agiakatsikas family's social capital decreased despite their prosperous business. Panagiotis and Antonios were open adversaries of the metropolitan bishop Apostolos, who displayed loyalty to Lago. Apostolos was designated as the head of the autocephalous Orthodox church of the Dodecanese, an unfinished project aimed at cutting the ties between the clergy in the Italian *Possedimento* and the Ecumenical Patriarchate.[43] The bishop was criticized by a faction rallied around the Greek consul and his influent agent Nikolaos Karajannis, to which some members of the Agiakatsikas family belonged.[44] They thus did not disappear from local politics but experienced marginalization in communal structures and a reorientation towards notables linked to the Greek state, which exacerbated frictions with the colonial government.

In the mid-1930s, Panagiotis's house was targeted by "some young fascists," who painted Italian flags on the walls, a punishment for not exposing the *tricolore* as a celebration of the Italian victory in Ethiopia.[45] Ioannis was even arrested in 1944 for participating in a "philhellene-Bolshevik" manifestation: he had hosted some individuals who wore a red flower and sang Greek nationalist songs on May Day, preventing the Blackshirts from punishing his guests.[46] Yet, the Agiakatsikas' third generation was not completely alien to fascist institutions. In 1939, Ioannis and Kleovoulos had applied for entering the *Opera Nazionale Dopolavoro* (OND).[47] This was the most important "leisure" organization of fascism, pivotal for the regime to turn "policing" into "persuasion," in the words of Victoria de Grazia.[48] Kleovoulos and Ioannis were not exposed to fascist youth organizations, as the OND targeted adult socialization. They became members when they already owned managerial positions. Since the family's political profile was not optimal after 1933, the focus on economic interests might well have pushed its members towards a compromise. In the eyes of the authorities, in turn, membership in the OND could make up for lack of political trust.

Wealthy families had little interest in changing business when their capital fared well. The Agiakatsikas family adapted the sector of production (olive oil, cosmetics, pharmaceutics) to the evolution of the market, but they kept the company as cohesive as possible in terms of familial management. Entrepreneurial continuity did not imply the replication of professional profiles across generations. The differentiation of tasks was a strategy best handled by a distribution of specializations among younger brothers who co-managed the company. This also allowed the Agiakatsikas family to pursue investments in between industry and commerce continuing after the end of Ottoman rule. Geographically, their market focused on Turkey and Greece, but also included France, Egypt, and Palestine, while it later expanded to Italy.

Politically, the Agiakatsikas kept a complex relationship with the Ottoman and Italian authorities beyond ideal-typic categories used by historians of the modern Mediterranean such as "cosmopolitans," "imperialists," or "nationalists."[49] Keeping family business upright did not exclusively fit any of these categories. Already prior to 1912, the family converted economic into social capital by partaking in communal politics and philanthropic initiatives. More and more recognized as an elite family, they had to find a compromise with Italian colonial rule. The new political setting transformed the very connotations of "philanthropists" and "notables." Unable to maintain a leading position in colonial political institutions, the third generation opted for a limited integration into fascist leisure state organizations to compensate a problematic position within local factionalism. The necessity of this compromise reflects a general pressure posed by fascist colonialism on former Ottoman subjects. For most Rhodians, however, a more modest and even destitute condition made subsistence, and not capital accumulation, the primary concern.

Youth, Productivity, and Idleness

Whereas capitalists like the Agiakatsikas family maintained a privileged social status, a new normative discourse on productivity and idleness appearing in Rhodes in the early twentieth century stigmatized young precarious workers and the unemployed. Abandoned or orphan teenagers made up a large share of cases described by the authorities as "vagrancy," in which the lack of parental bonds exposed them directly to police and juridical authority. As elsewhere, there was no clear demarcation between "honest work" and "illegal trading," "free time" or "vagrancy" in commentaries referring to the lower classes.[50] These youngsters declared to work as water vendors, boatmen, and the like when the authorities arrested them for petty crimes or irregularities and profiled them as vagrants.[51] In 1935, a group of six *"vagabondi"* (vagrants) aged 12 to 14 were arrested for "persistently asking foreign tourists strolling in Rhodes for money." Although half of them were orphans, or at least fatherless, the authorities opted for "taking them to their parents, who have as well been cautioned to exert more surveillance on their children." The police used their authority to impose a sound relationship between children and parents, who were eventually responsible for the former's upbringing.[52]

Already in the late Ottoman Empire, a display of "new techniques of modern governance" related to a "new conception of work" as a "civilizational duty" opposed to (the poor's) idleness.[53] Childhood and youth were a focus of such policies and were targeted by newly established reform houses (*ıslahhane*) meant to create productive manpower in industrializing settings.[54] Anti-vagrancy laws and debates on the imputability of minors equally occurred in Italy before and during fascism. The penal code known as *Codice Rocco*, which entered into force in 1930, raised non-imputability for minors to 14 years of age.[55] If their parents were alive, they oftentimes took the initiative and applied to the courts in Rhodes to send their child to a reformatory (*istituto di rieducazione/casa di correzione*). In other cases, this destination was the result of the court's decision converting a previous prison sentence.[56] At the end of the confinement period (usually two years), the head of the reformatory issued a certificate stating that "the mentioned minor has now achieved the goal of his recovery, he has shown evidence of repentance and profit in vocation and study (*nel mestiere e nello studio*)."[57]

According to the *Codice Rocco*'s age criteria, Demetrio M., son of a mason, was neither sentenced to prison nor to the reformatory in 1938. This is how he was described by his father in a petition asking for Demetrio's confinement: "Demetrio, aged 11, has become the family's trouble and despair due to his bad conduct. Expelled by all schools, he spends all day hanging around in the street with other boys older than him, which leads him to complete perdition. Despite all punishments, he has even beaten his poor mother and his brothers." Demetrio's father described marginalized adolescents as morally dangerous, while invoking state authority to "rescue" parents like him unable to grant a smooth transition from school to work for their children.

Refusing this confinement request, the *Carabinieri* stated that: "Demetrio was indeed expelled from school for his continuous bad conduct, and he was often recognized as culpable of theft without, however, being persecuted through a criminal procedure since he is a minor. On 20 July [1938], the youngster was called to this office. In the presence of his father, he was explained the serious consequences to which he will be exposed if he maintains his reprehensible conduct. He proved to be sensible to this warning, promised not to slip back into evil (*ricadere nel male*) and started an occupation as an apprentice of a local blacksmith." The police then reasserted that virtuous upbringing was not primarily the state's responsibility: "[I]t seems inopportune to back his son's confinement in a reformatory and, instead, as a parent, he has the obligation to place his son under a more accurate surveillance and lead him to the straight and narrow (*sulla via del bene*)."[58]

Three years later, the father of 19-year-old Drosso P. addressed a similar petition directly to the governor, describing the youngster as a: "pervert, useless to himself and his family, dangerous for his family and society. He does not want to work, he constantly argues with his parents, mistreats his relatives, and often steals items from home in order to resell them and then spend the revenue in gambling and in vice with other corrupted companions."[59] By demanding that the authorities "confine him to some reformatory where he can correct himself or enrol him in the army," Drosso's father appropriated the notion of "society," its fate, and the dangers posed to it. Male teens were a particularly sensible reference in this imaginary. The youth's future conflated concerns about a family's well-being, a respectable way to make a living, and the government's capacity to grant both. Yet, another element is striking here. Not only work, but also serving in the Italian army during the Second World War was seen as a remedy for a teenager's bad behaviour. While fascist propaganda cherished this motive in the 1930s, colonial rule often preferred other means when dealing with troublesome youth. Drosso – who, as a colonial subject, could not enrol but only volunteer – was sent to a new, short-lived reformatory in Rhodes run by the local Fascist Party section.

The "vagrancy" of male teens was in the spotlight since authorities and parents situated the inception of "normal" work at the juncture of school and adult breadwinning life as opposed to "hanging around," violence, and theft. Compared to the Ottoman student sent to a reformatory mentioned in the previous chapter, the Italian police established a direct link to both Drosso's parents and the government. The authorities often relied on the familial sphere to reorient "vicious" individuals, oftentimes by reaffirming the principle of *patria podestà* (parental authority). Handing the responsibility of a sound upbringing back to the parental home allowed the state to increase its pressure on the population, merging reliable intergenerational bonds at home with the preservation of fascist colonial order.

Where did youngsters like Drosso hang around? What public sites were considered dangerous for the youth? Discussions on idleness often addressed the cafés of Rhodes. In Ottoman times, next to the traditional *kafeneios/kahvehane*, the *gazino* emerged as the site of a new sociability, more open to women, alcohol beverages, and night-time entertainment.[60] Access to it could imply age limits: an Ottoman bill of indictment (*iddianame*) dated 1912 denounced a popular *gazino* owner, Nikolaos Maltezos, for having let in boys under 16, classified as "beardless youth" (*şāb-ı emred*).[61] Many cafés were visited by the unemployed, and brawls as well as gambling were far from exceptional.[62] Gambling was also a frequent source of revenue in the absence of a "normal" occupation, which confirms that a demarcation between leisure and work is problematic and of secondary importance compared to the different moral connotations attached to this kind of activities.

Cafés were popular among the lower classes, which contrasted to the new bourgeoise sociability observable in clubs. A *Cercle de Rhodes* opened in 1912 and its board included some of the wealthiest personalities of all confessions.[63] Soon after, a *Circolo Italia* was founded along the Mandraki waterfront, showcasing Italian prestige in the most crowded and lively promenade of Rhodes. *Il Messaggero di Rodi* dedicated long descriptions to the *Circolo*'s balls and galas including details on the participants (authorities, military, and private persons) and gastronomy, all aimed to prescribe good taste.[64] Vratsalis's already mentioned short stories describe bars but also less elitist dancehalls open to "both young and old," where: "everyone was enchanted (*xelogiazountan*) to learn the European dances. [To learn to] become ladies (*ntames*) and gentlemen (*kavalieroi*) in order not to be considered as backward (*kathisterimenous*). The traditional local dances, which they learned from the teachers in the schoolyard … were only for the festivities."[65] Both upper and lower class recreational sites could host gambling, dances, talking politics, music, drinking alcohol, and even brawls, but the different social status of their attendees influenced how these sites were represented.

Popular café owners were aware that a doubtful reputation was compatible with good business. The Scalia brothers had moved to Rhodes from Smyrna in the 1920s. They expanded their activities as owners of the movie theatre *San Giorgio*, which had a prominent location next to the *Circolo Italia*. During the summer months, the *San Giorgio* turned into the *Kit Kat*, a summer resort that included a café and hosted evening activities such as movie screenings. Women from Italy were explicitly employed there to entertain and dance with male attendees for the price of some lire. When applying for extending their activity's license in 1937, the owners wrote to the police that: "This is a licit and moral practice which will allow the attendees an honest dance with good looking and well-mannered ladies (*di bella presenza e dai modi corretti*)."[66]

The markers profiling these female workers varied from "girls" to "young ladies," "women" and "ladies," adding to their morality's ambivalence. Their contract stipulated that they had to "be polite to the guests, disciplined and of good conduct, dress properly … [and] return home after closing time for the sake of reputation."[67] Rumours of sexual "promiscuity" and prostitution were frequent in such cafés. One of these waitresses, the sister of a soldier stationing in Rhodes, was fired for her behaviour, judged by the police as inappropriate for "the prestige and the decor of the uniform" worn by her brother.[68] Yet, the authorities had a pragmatic approach meant to guarantee spaces of recreation, to preserve the prestige of the troops and the favour of the population. In 1936, a Jewish waitress at the *Kit Kat*, aged 16, insulted an Italian soldier who had harassed her, after which he slapped her. The *Carabinieri* protested and urged the owners of the bar to fire the "sensitive girl." Soon afterwards, however, the authorities pushed them to hire her anew to avoid discontent among the Jewish community.[69]

Especially cafés attended by the lower classes were described as dangerous by linking immorality and unproductivity to youth. These commentaries were not a monopoly of state authorities. In June 1928, the already mentioned director of the Muslim school Mehmet Kadri wrote these words in a column entitled "On debauchery" (*Sefāhata dā'ir*) for the local newspaper *Selām*: "Those who walk through the old market or the dock in the evening hours looking at the cafes (*ḳahvehāneler*) and saloons (*meyhāneler*) would see that most of their customers are Turkish youth. These youth spend everything they could earn through much trouble and hardship within an hour in the corner of a saloon, while they pay no attention to the families and children yearning to see them at home." Such problems posed to public order were automatically linked to those posed to family bonds and, by extension, to the whole community: "Until night, after partying (*eğlendikden ṣoñra*), they go home completely drunk (*gük ḳandıl bir ḥalde*). They are not at all ashamed of shouting in the streets and the neighbourhoods, singing songs loudly, wrestling and wandering, disturbing the public quiet while reeling from wall to wall (*bir dıvar seniñ, bir dıvar benim*) … Therefore, what could be the benefit that these young men (*delikanlılarıñ*) can provide to their wives and children?"[70] The author, himself described as an "amoral alcoholic" by the Italian police, called these men "youth" not primarily based on age, nor in contrast to adult family life, since they had wives, children, and jobs.[71] What made them young was their overstepping the notion of leisure as both voluntary and licit by show-ing addiction and immoral behaviour such as alcohol abuse. Being involved in a specific activity like drinking or night-time partying was not *per se* a domain of the young. Rather, mobilizing the notion of youth reflected concerns related to these activities. Men from the lower classes were deemed uncapable of caring for their own reputation, the wellness of their families, and the cohesion of their community.

The stigmatization of "debauchery" had its flipside in a positive stance on productivity. Communal institutions and notables had a considerable influence on the normalization of work and of a morally disciplined socialization. Apprenticeship programs or guided inser-tion towards the first employment aimed to assure that, after leaving school, children would still be in the communities' orbit. The *Alliance* was especially active in this regard. In 1904, the first school graduates aged between 15 and 17 pursued the following trajectories: four con-tinued an educational specialization in Paris or Jerusalem, three were employed as accounting assistants in the Alhadeff & Sons or Joseph Notrica companies, and two became apprentices in pharmacies.[72]

The *Alliance* also assisted those who did not complete its curriculum and worked on the brink of poverty, as a director stated in 1908: "The blacksmith apprentice Bohor Hasson has been into apprenticeship for six years now. When I arrived here, I wanted to stop giving him an allowance and clearing his account (*liquider son compte*). However, dur-ing my visits at the atelier where he works, I learned that he is an orphan of father and mother, that he does not earn more than 6.75 fr. per month and that it was a poor uncle of his who hosted him asking for a rent of approximately 10 fr. per month." The director knew the scarcity of resources afflicting Rhodes and asked Paris for support: "Hence, if I cut his monthly handout of 2.50 fr., the youngster would be abandoned by his uncle and would fall from grace (*tomberait bien bas*). For this reason, I have kept [the handout] for this year … [I]t would be good to provide him with … some blacksmith tools in order for him to work from home and to raise his meager salary. Once or twice, you were kind enough to send some tools to the apprentices in Rhodes. I kindly ask you to do the same this time for the apprentice B. Hasson."[73]

For the same purpose, Orthodox notables organized a workshop (*ergastirio*) for girls within the women's society *Ergani Athina*, founded in 1908 short after the Young Turk Revolution. The workshop opened in 1912 and officially functioned as a "professional school" (*epaggelmatiki scholi*), although it also promoted homework for girls whose families did not allow them to work away from home. The artefacts sold widely throughout the networks of Rhodians, especially in Egypt, included embroidery and weaving, and later also carpets, for which the girls received around the half of the purchase price as compensation. These activities continued during Italian rule until Governor De Vecchi shut down the workshop in 1938.[74]

The trajectory of *Ergani Athina* is exemplar for associations navigating through successive regimes and governmental attitudes in the first half of the twentieth century. Still, they did not only face pressure from state authorities. They exerted their own pressure on the population to foster and normalize work and leisure. Marginalized actors were subject to a growing interference of state and communal structures to define the licit boundaries of their recreative activities, often connoted as "idleness" and "vice." The normative discourse on productivity and the stigmatization of idleness were also valid for girls, who obtained valuable working skills and at the same time were channelled towards communal socialization. Many, however, remained outside the community's reach in terms of insertion in the labour market.

All Housewives? Women's Precarious Labour

What labouring women in Rhodes had in common, is that their socialization was influenced by forces dominated by men: the family, the company, the community, and the state. While the 1905 Ottoman census did not record women's occupational status, the 1922 census of Muslim households lists 85 per cent of women as *"ev ḳadını"* (housewife), a category that ranged from 2 (!) to 85 years of age. By contrast, the Italian equivalent *"casalinga"* occurs for only 55 per cent of women in family certificates from the 1930s, mainly because *"scolara"* (female student) grew significantly as a category for girls compared to earlier records.[75] Men working for institutions producing these sources had a biased perception towards breadwinning labour.[76] Normalized occupations were considered a masculine domain, while women – be they schooled or not – were assigned the role of housewives. Still, other sources make clear that many of them earned money as tailors, cashiers, waitresses, midwives, washerwomen, or teachers. The state mostly did not acknowledge their labour in terms of professions, and it remained invisible or only mentioned in their police files.[77] How should we critically assess this age-crossing category of "housewife"? Two marginalized and precarious occupations – domestic servants and sex workers – were often subsumed under that term. Discussing the trajectories of these labouring women reveals the several layers of pressure exerted upon them by older relatives, communities, and authorities.

Not mentioned in the 1905 Hudayi census, domestic servants were present in 10 per cent of the households fifteen years later, amounting to 6 per cent of the total population.[78] These women faced the opportunity – or the necessity – to leave the parental home at an early age. Distance from parental influence collided with disciplining control by their employers. Aged 15 on average, servants were classified with terms such as *hidmetci, besleme or beslenci*, the latter also meaning "foster children." In the 1922 census, *hidmetci* only concerned women, whereas *besleme* and *beslenci* could occasionally apply to male servants. All three terms referred to the relation to the household head and did not appear in the census column reserved for occupations. We rarely know if and how these servants received any salary. Although they performed domestic work in their household, they could be listed as having another occupation, such as fishmonger or "student" (*mektebli*), while "housewife" (*ev ḳadını*) and "unemployed" (*işsiz*) prevailed.

Since the early modern period, wealthy Ottomans acquired un(der)-paid domestic labourers from indigent families as an act of "charity."[79] Nazan Maksudyan, however, has highlighted dynamics of exploitation and sexual harassment of orphans in the nineteenth and twentieth centuries.[80] Indeed, these women's relationship to their patrons were often complicated. Dichea C. came to Rhodes town from her family's village when she was in her teens, and she was sentenced for aggravated theft in 1914. She worked in a doctor's household, himself not native of Rhodes. Her father, who introduced her to the doctor, received the whole of her salary. Living at her employer's house, she was provided with a service uniform. Only two weeks after entering the new household, she decided to quit it without notice, claiming that this was due to a troubled relationship with the *"signora,"* the doctor's wife. According to Dichea, her mistress "was a bit nervous," she "scolded [her] with bad words," and "cursed even the bread [that Dichea] ate." The servant left the house with the garments and some robes that she claimed were a present. Her employers stated that she had stolen them and, in the first instance of the trial, Dichea was sentenced to two years of prison, later suspended, and to the reimbursement of legal expenses.[81]

Intergenerational conflicts between employers and servants could lead to tragic consequences. In May 1920, the corpses of two teenagers were found floating in the sea just outside the town. Since no sign of violence was detected, the police followed two leads: death by accident during a swim or double suicide for an unlucky love affair. Another hypothesis pointed to mobbing by the woman who employed both. Whereas the father of one of the girls denied having heard any complaints by his daughter, her elder sister declared that the two were constantly humiliated by their mistress. The latter used words like "stinking girl," "whore" and accused them of "thinking only about love instead of looking after the children." After a quarrel just before their suicide, the servants allegedly came to wonder: "is this supposed to be a worthy life? It would be better to kill ourselves."[82] Servants stood under significant pressure in terms of responsibility and discipline of free time, without any protection. Love and sexuality were stigmatized as a marker of irresponsible adolescence in conflict with work duties.

Domestic servants – especially Orthodox – often came from villages of the interior of Rhodes or from minor Dodecanese islands, but mobility from Rhodes to other countries was also frequent. In the mid-1920s, Marulli K. from the village of Trianda worked for three years in Alexandria for a landowner's household. Since she was a minor, her father signed the agreement with her employers. Marulli was to receive a salary increasing each year, plus room and board as well as clothes. Despite the geographical distance, her family controlled her by corresponding with the employers, who cosmeticized her labour as an upgrade through socialization in their own middle class milieu: "Our conscience is clean in regard to your daughter because we treat her better than our own children and I do not believe that those who come to Rhodes do not tell you about the position of your daughter Marulli, because we take her out and she lives like a young lady (*signorina*), not a servant."[83] Marulli's employer would have preferred that she keep her salary until the end of the duty, and he claimed that she felt "ashamed" to ask to send the money to her father.[84] Apart from such money issues, the intimacy in the correspondence between the two men suggests that their families' social status was not quite different. Domestic service was not exclusively labour provided by the destitute classes for the elite, but also a formative and – rarely – remunerative experience for women circulating within families of a similar milieu. Yet, adults distinguished between this work and a proper honourable status, as expressed in the opposition between "young lady" and "servant" in the mentioned letter.

While most female domestic servants started to work in their teens, Paraskevi L. began in her thirties to improve her modest revenues. She had gotten married ten years before but, after Paraskevi's husband abandoned her, she had an illicit relationship with a married man from her village.[85] This raised a scandal, due to which she left for Rhodes. Her first occupation was in a tobacco factory, but soon afterwards three male colleagues of hers, with whom she shared the living space, hired her for domestic work. When Paraskevi claimed to have received a marriage proposal from one of them, the man firmly denied this and took legal action against her. His lawyer described her as a tobacco smuggler, referring to a previous fine. He further discredited her by stating that her sister was a "prostitute," and that Paraskevi herself was "of easy virtue and had a reprehensible past ... having sexual intercourses without scruples." These accusations of "bad conduct" had an age-related component, since the man's lawyer exhorted the jury "not to infer that she has been deceived, because, as a woman of over 30 years of age, she had a lot of experience and she was enough mindful not to be caught by surprise ... by a youngster."[86]

Cohabitation between a paid servant and a single man could thus be interpreted as a concubinage-like relationship. Age difference could determine the boundaries between licit and illicit sexual experiences. Sexual harassment against young female servants by their older employers was mostly silenced and tolerated, while older servants could be profiled as vicious "seducers." On the contrary, younger men were mostly absolved from stigmatization precisely because their "youth" was a synonym of innocence. Paraskevi moved across various types of subsistence and precarious work – at the factory, as a servant and, probably, as a smuggler and sex worker – within a few years. She had lost her bonds (and money) in her home village and had to start over in Rhodes. Although she was soon emancipated from marital and parental control, her being married likely prevented the authorities from defining her as youth. Married men, as the *Selām* article on "debauchery" reminds us, could still be profiled as youth in cases of "bad conduct," while stigmatized women were rarely described as such. More often, they were regarded as "whores" or, in official documents, simply as "housewives."

If Paraskevi's case is based on allegations, the police kept track of many sex workers whose trajectories were embedded in the "military-sexual complex" brought about by the presence of Italian soldiers in Rhodes between 1912 and 1945.[87] Yet, sex work was rarely their sole occupation. Judging from *Carabinieri* files of the 1930s, these women changed jobs from year to year, which frequently resulted in the fact that the authorities neutralized their activities under the term "housewife." The police distinguished sex workers in brothels, who had the status of *"ingaggiata"* (employed), from those practicing "clandestine prostitution" at home. The latter raised concerns about public hygiene, and made the notions of "housewife," "servant," or "kept woman" even fuzzier.

Sex work in Rhodes surely existed before 1912, but I have not found any sources dating from the late Ottoman period that mention it explicitly. This contrasts with larger port cities such as Istanbul and Smyrna where the sex market boomed.[88] The *Alliance* school's director claimed in 1913 that: "The customs (*mœurs*) are still quite austere in Rhodes. No prostitution! None of those girls that we encounter in the large cities who, for the love of luxury, enter professions that dishonour the family and Judaism."[89] Here interestingly termed as "profession," sex work might have been recorded by sources to which I had no access, such as the Muslim and Jewish religious tribunals, although I have not found any hint in their Orthodox equivalent or in Ottoman state courts.[90] In July 1913, just prior to the *Alliance* school director's remark, the Italian police in Lecce warned the Ministry of Foreign Affairs and the governor of Rhodes that "white slavery" occurred in the newly occupied territory. A woman from Puglia, Carmela nicknamed "the African," had moved to Rhodes to open a brothel. Her brother-in-law recruited young women who were promised employment and then shipped to Rhodes, where they became sex workers.[91]

Sources often reveal euphemisms for this activity. Duriè K., the orphan of a Cretan refugee policeman, became a sex worker at 18 years of age, around 1910, as a retrospective account by the Italian police alleges. She lived alone in her own house and was reported to: "run a quite carefree life, receiving from time to time youngsters (*giovanotti*) with whom she had intimate relationships. Now, having saved through this life around 200 Turkish liras, which she always keeps with her, her relationships are more limited, but the neighbours agree on condemning her deplorable conduct."[92] Sex work could be a temporary subsistence activity, of which the beginning and end remained difficult to ascertain. In Duriè's case, this resulted from a difficult financial situation after the loss of relatives, but other women remained under parental control. In some cases, young girls were pushed towards sex work by their very parents.[93]

The precariousness of sex work was closely related to mobility. In 1930, the fatherless Violetta B., aged 13, moved with her mother from Milas to Rhodes to join an uncle who owned a little shop at the city market. She found an occupation as a janitress at the Jewish kindergarten, during which she was reported to be a "clandestine prostitute," mostly having intercourses with Italian soldiers. The police accorded her a permit of residence (which she needed as a Turkish citizen's daughter) since she lived in Rhodes "without creating any trouble," reporting that she also worked as a servant for a Jewish family.[94]

Diassino M.'s trajectory is even more complex. Born on the Dodecanese island of Astypalaia in 1912, she started sex work at the age of 17. In the early 1930s, she married a coffee vendor named Teodori on the island of Leros, a favorable setting for the sex market due to its Italian military base. Diassino "abandoned" her husband shortly afterwards to "return to practice prostitution." This led the Orthodox Church to invalidate the marriage. The woman lived on Leros but worked in the brothels of Kos, Kalymnos, and Rhodes throughout the 1930s. In Rhodes, she lived with a Greek citizen who declared his will to "host her as his kept woman (*mantenuta*) pledging to provide her with all she needs."[95]

In 1939, her ex-husband's mother called her back to Leros with a pledge: "My dear daughter Iassemi [*sic!*] ... I, your mother-in-law Lulludia M., beg you to come to Leros where you will live with Teodori. My will is to leave to you and Teodori my coffee-shop, my storehouse, my house and all my estate in Merichia, including several boats. The conditions will be the following: lifelong use of all goods mentioned above and transmission to your heirs in case of death. I await you with the first transport opportunity."[96] Lulludia crossed the matrilineal line of inheritance by promising a dowry to her daughter-in-law Diassino, and this despite the invalidated marriage. Moreover, while Diassino's parents were alive, they never appear in the documents related to her. She probably began sex work just before, or after, an irreversible rupture with them. Although Diassino and Teodori never regularized their union, they occasionally cohabited. Only when the man declared that he did not want to welcome back Diassino did she return to Leros, where she worked in a renowned brothel.[97] This trajectory reminds us that the complex paths to marriage highlighted in chapter 2 could be related to women's precarious labour, a productive activity invisible in most bureaucratic sources produced by the state.

The police gathered information and compiled these reports because the social relationships around sex work, including families and lovers/clients, helped them profile these women's morality and their autonomy in terms of subsistence. Semihe D., aged 16, lived with her widowed mother and her siblings. One evening, her older brother caught her in an intimate encounter with an Italian soldier. Semihe's brother insisted that she follow him back home, but she refused. The two had been to the movies the same evening, but we do not know whether Semihe had received money for sex. If she had, this episode might speak for a gendered work-leisure relation, since a recreational activity for a man would correspond to remunerative sex work for a woman. In any case, her brother's intervention is an example of the constraints faced by young lower class women in terms of leisure activities and sexuality, connected to their relatives' fear that they become "prostitutes." Although Semihe was reported missing from home for several days after this incident, the police listed her as belonging to their household. They classified her as a housewife one year later (1942), when her mother requested – to no avail – a passport to move to Turkey.[98] In 1944, she was again listed as "free prostitute" living apart from her family.[99] Ruptures in kinship bonds due to sex work could be only temporary, especially during wartime, when material solidarity to face poverty could become more urgent than any moral verdict on these women.

The Italian authorities were unwilling to recognize precarious mobility and material scarcity, two of the main motives behind sex work, as social problems. They would have then risked losing a repertoire of sex leisure for the stationing soldiers. The police and colonial bureaucrats used the term housewife because it suspended and silenced the precariousness of these lower class women and because it was far from the idea of lucrative activities and bad reputation. This was also interiorized by many women who knew the consequences of being profiled as prostitutes. In 1939, as the number of soldiers arose due to the tense political configuration on the eve of Italy's entry in the Second World War, the police noted "the necessity" of a new authorized brothel, although they refused an application to open one since its mistress "had induced a woman under 16 years of age to prostitute herself."[100]

This rare reference to an age limit suggests that sex work was per se a licit occupation for female minors, since the age of majority was set at 21, not as 16. Most sex workers – like domestic servants – entered their occupation in their late teens. The length, the modalities, and the association of this activity with youth, however, primarily depended on these women's social status rather than on age. The bonds they kept with their relatives and the extent of the latter's control on them mattered significantly. Besides, their work meant commodified sex leisure for men who could often interchangeably appear as lovers, clients, pimps, and even fiancés and husbands. Indeed, "youth" appeared more often as a term related to these men than to the women they mingled with.

Football and the Normativity of Youth Leisure

If men were more likely to be seen as youth, this was also due to the growing visibility of masculinized and juvenilized sports in Rhodes. Sport per se was a non-productive activity in which women had a marginal place. Yet, from wealthy men like Ioannis Agiakatsikas to lower class men like Mustafa Boiagi, from Italian soldiers to colonial subjects, an important part of the male population practiced it. Sport concurred to create a smooth and virtuous transition from the educational to the occupational domain, since both students and workers participated in it. It was therefore an element of continuity for life trajectories navigating a delicate and uncertain transition.

The 1928 cycling race that opened this chapter combined a disciplined and performative young virility with the symbolism of fascist authority. But the race was also a moment of recreation, fun, spirit of competition, and collective passion. Because of their emotional side, sport events could pose problems to public order causing institutional anxiety and stigmatization of youth's exaltation. The youth in question was also a social marker, since sport engendered distinction: the higher the social position of the people involved, the less a sport was considered "popular."[101] Moreover, the development of sport is embedded in the demarcation between genders. In Rhodes as elsewhere, inducing young men to practice sports countered increasing promiscuity at school, ensuring "the separation of boys from the world of women during the critical transition from childhood to adulthood."[102] In the case of football, the focus of this section, no clubs for women existed in Rhodes during the period analysed. It is no coincidence that football expanded around 1920, when women entered schools such as the *Venetokleion* and the *Regio Istituto* in mixed classes.

In the late Ottoman Empire, Muslims playing football were stigmatized and surveilled, while this sport flourished especially among Christians and foreigners. More generally, though, gymnastics was already part of the curriculum in state schools at the turn of the twentieth century, and sport associations gained momentum after 1908.[103] Athletes and sport entrepreneurs in Smyrna, Salonica, and Istanbul capitalized on the philhellenic revival after the first modern Olympics in Athens in 1896, which also fostered the sympathy for a national community that claimed to bridge classical Hellenism and the modern Kingdom of Greece.[104] Echoes of this spirit also resonated in Rhodes. The first director of the *Venetokleion*, Dimitrios Anastasiadis, attended the Olympics in Athens and recalled his excitement about transmitting "the love for gymnastics, fraternity, and solidarity to young Rhodians." He made gymnastics a mandatory subject, obtained donations for sports equipment installed at school and "gathered many youngsters who expressed a warm interest for athletics in the after-school."[105]

This retrospective narrative relates to the foundation of the most important local club, *Diagoras*, that started from gymnastics but later also expanded to football and other sports. The club's equipment was donated by communal notables, and these activities took place in a site managed by the Orthodox community. Yet, the earliest local football club called *Peisirodos* – after a descendant of the antiquity Olympic champion Diagoras – had been founded already in 1903 on the initiative of its own players. This association appeared in the neighbourhood of Neocori, and all players were Orthodox in their late teens or early twenties.[106] *Peisirodos* only existed for two years and, after its dissolution, the club *Diagoras* was founded in 1905. Diagoras almost monopolized the sport landscape of Rhodes, although one "amateur" (*erasitechnon*) football team is mentioned in 1909 in a newspaper article.[107] Football games remained marginal, informal, and episodic until the end of the First World War, when popular sports in Rhodes gained relevance for colonial rule.

In April 1920, the Italian governor sponsored the first "official" game between soldiers and a team called *Squadra di Rodi* ("Rhodes Team"). The latter consisted of four Jews, three Muslims, three Catholics, and one Orthodox, likely gathered ad hoc. The main novelty was media coverage, as an emphatic report appeared in the *Messaggero di Rodi*. The game took place on an improvised pitch next to military facilities at Kumburnu, the northernmost part of the town, where the glamourous *Grand Hotel delle Rose* would be built a few years later. The players were surrounded by a crowd including "elegant ladies," sitting next to the authorities. The reporter claimed that the atmosphere became "a bit turbulent" due to the passion for the game. This points to the duality of sports that Norbert Elias and Eric Dunning have described as the "quest for excitement":[108] football was considered virtuous for the self-representation of power, but it provoked fears of public disorder associated with its "vulgar" and "mass" nature. As to the *mise-en-scène* of the Italian occupying power, the journalist proudly concluded that: "The goal of an effective propaganda aimed at creating numerous fans of an extremely profitable and interesting physical exercise has been achieved."[109]

In those years, football turned from a sporadic divertissement to a phenomenon with wide public exposure. Voluntary and amateur initiatives increased as well. In 1920, eleven Jews who called themselves "youngsters" (*giovinetti*) asked the military governor for permission to play football "during free time," in order to "develop our body" (*sviluppare le nostre membra*).[110] Two of the signatories, aged 16, graduated with excellent marks from the *Alliance* school.[111] School sociability generally favoured the passion for sport, which led state and community educational institutions to channel football under their control. The *Alliance* school director complained about the competition with the *Frères* school based on the allure of football, since: "two thirds of our pupils left the school immediately after the classes for the outskirts of the town, where a religious teacher trained them in football and taught them many games (*jeux*) during one hour."[112]

In a letter from 1924, the director of the *Regio Istituto* proudly mentioned the school's football team to a fellow friar in Italy. From a photograph he included (figure 4.2), we can infer that the games were played

Figure 4.2. A football game organized by the Italian Regio Istituto, 1924. FSC TORINO 353 1067. Piola to Bigin, 11 April 1924.

in the Old Town, with a few spectators.[113] The school team, called *Veloci* ("The Fast Ones"), also trained with weapons and equipment provided by the Italian military. This team therefore stood at the intersection of school comradeship, healthy free time, and soldiering spirit. Although these three elements were cherished by the Fascist Party's vision of sports, no explicit reference to ideology appeared in the letter.[114] The link between schools and football clubs rather highlights that disciplining work and leisure related to the same challenge. School instructors considered themselves responsible for creating a sound transition from youth to adulthood, be it in the case of apprenticeship initiatives or sport activities.

New sports clubs with prominent football sections were founded in the 1920s. The geographic remoteness of Rhodes did not allow for regular encounters between them and famous Italian teams. Colonial separation was also reflected in the rosters, since the *Fascio*'s team consisted almost exclusively of Italian citizens, while other teams only included Italian soldiers. Some among the most important clubs claimed a confessional/national character, such as the Jewish *Maccabi* and the Muslim *İslam Spor Kulübü*.[115] Indeed, communities continued to participate in the expansion of sports under Italian sovereign rule.

In 1928, the local newspaper *Selâm* published a column praising the benefits of sport in a naturally healthy environment like Rhodes. Mehmet Kadri, who had commented on the "debauchery" of Muslim youth in cafés, welcomed the foundation of a Muslim club by arguing that sport was well part of the *"terbiye"* concept including physical and moral training.[116] The recurring term "youth" in his text further suggests that it was not a leisure activity itself (also practiced by adults), but rather its emphasized positive or negative representation which created a semantic link with youth.[117] As figure 4.3 shows, belonging to these associations was not only a matter of sports. It also shaped representations of masculine youth and a sense of collectivity whenever it appeared in the public space.

Club managers were another novelty of the 1920s. In 1924, Gavriil Misios, a pharmacist from Symi aged 22, founded the club *Dorieas* (Diagoras's son). From its inception, the club developed a rivalry with *Diagoras*, which accused *Dorieas* of being "pro-Italian."[118] There were other important differences between the two clubs. In terms of age, Misios was much younger than the *Diagoras* board members. Moreover, *Dorieas* considered regular training and modern sports as a priority. *Diagoras* placed more emphasis on the cultural, commemorational, and educational components in accordance with the late nineteenth-century Olympic spirit focused on athletics and gymnastics. *Dorieas*

Figure 4.3. Members of the Jewish Sports Club of Rhodes, 1930s. USHMM, Photo 03702, courtesy of Miru Alcana. Among them are Giuseppe Alcanà (third from the left), Alberto Alhadeff (second from the right), and Rahamin Benun (first from the right).

also drew more players from the gymnasium *Venetokleion*, including the already mentioned Anastasios Agiakatsikas but also sons of shopkeepers, masons, or seamen.[119]

Despite their differences, *Diagoras* and *Dorieas* were shut down together in 1929. After a running race, the Italian authorities modified the attribution of points to the clubs and declared *Dorieas* to be the winner. Three members of *Diagoras* aged 15 to 18 staged a protest at the rival club's offices and were arrested for shouting slogans in favour of Greece. The police considered that the "young brats" (*giovinastri*) had been manipulated by irredentist circles of the older generation.[120] Later reports in these youngsters' police files do not mention signs of political activism, insisting, rather, on their rowdy character.[121] The consequences were harsh for both clubs. *Diagoras* could only reopen in Athens as an institution of Dodecanesians expatriates in 1934, while *Dorieas* disappeared until the end of Italian rule.[122]

Politics started to interfere more heavily with sports in the 1930s. Two years after this incident, Lago issued a governmental decree that established the association *FRATRES* (acronym for "Rhodian Federation of Tourism, Recreation, and Sport Associations"), with the aim of "disciplining the practice of sport."[123] Accordingly, it was mandatory for all clubs to submit their statutes to the police and declare that they would not pursue political activities. The authorities worried that the growing followers could develop ethno-national identifications by cheering for a communal-confessional team. Clubs were now accountable if the behaviour of players or followers diverged from the government's aims.

In the new league launched in 1933, *FRATRES* showed a certain tolerance when admitting community-centred societies. The championship gathered a Jewish team, one Muslim, two Orthodox, one represented by the Fascist Party, and one by the *Regio Istituto*.[124] However, the anxious government relied on loyal notables in these clubs' boards instead of welcoming initiatives "from below." The initiators of the club *Gioventù Ebraica di Rodi* (Jewish Youth of Rhodes – GER), were aged between 20 and 25 in 1929 and did not have any public tenure. Yet, *FRATRES* later compelled the GER team to submit a request for affiliation directly to the Jewish Communal Council. In the new 1932 board, only one of the original signatories was present (Isacco Levi). Older and prominent personalities such as Riccardo Pacifici – the president of the *Collegio Rabbinico* – and the doctor Mercado Hasson – member of *Selām*'s editorial board – occupied the main functions.[125]

A similar evolution concerns the ASR, the politically neutralized heir society of *Diagoras* and *Dorieas*. Gavriil Misios remained the club's trainer but he was placed under surveillance. The authorities suspected him of sympathy for Greek irredentism, which eventually led to his banishment to the island of Piscopi in 1938.[126] The notable Giorgios Bekes, considered more loyal, replaced him as the club's president. However, protests aimed at changing the board resulted into the election of another communal notable whom we have already met in chapter 3, the now 50-year-old Emmanouil Kalambichis.[127] Managing or being represented in a club board was thus a factor of social distinction. This held true for those, like Kalambichis, already active in communal institutions who wished to broaden up their visibility as well as for younger professionals like lawyers and doctors.

The authorities at first tolerated and tried to steer the club boards, although a new decree disbanded all societies in 1935. Football was delegated to another umbrella association subordinated to the *FRATRES*, called *Marechiaro*. The authorities continued to promote a discourse on the benefits of sports. Changes are nonetheless striking if we compare the first article on football from 1920 or friar Piola's letter from 1924 to a 1935 column published in the *Messaggero*. This piece attached the virtues of sports not simply to the "development and the empowerment of the human body," but also to the:

> training (*formazione*) of a man, and not a man of a remote past (*di estinta memoria*), but the healthy and strapping (*gagliardo*) man that Mussolini's conception suggests for the continuity of the race (*stirpe*) and the grandeur of the fatherland … [I]t is obvious that all young citizens should follow with fervour all sorts of sport activities … This is why, finally, FRATRES wiped away old local systems and replaced them with the national ones, which, now disciplined and controlled by one single entity, will be able to offer a greater possibility of success in every field of the sport activities in the city. Therefore, it is necessary that all Rhodian sportsmen adhere to the "Polisportiva Marechiaro."[128]

The well-known propaganda motives of fascist youth merged loyalty, race, and sports. For sure, the article was galvanized by a favourable moment. At the apogee of fascist Italy's international prestige in football, the national team won two World Cups and one Olympic gold medal between 1934 and 1938. Nonetheless, sports in Rhodes were not, primarily, aimed to construct a "new man" or to rival with concurring foreign powers. Rather, the reform had local implications as it broke the bonds between the communal boards and the sportsmen. The priority was to normalize football, that is to de-communalize this form of leisure by admitting only interconfessional or purely Italian teams. Youth-as-sportsmen gained visibility in power rhetoric just as initiatives by young actors were hampered. After 1935, the teams had suggestive names such as *Cervo* (Deer, the symbol of Rhodes introduced by Lago), *Lupa* (She-wolf, symbol of Rome and an icon of the fascist imaginary), neighbourhoods of Rhodes (*Acandia, Neocorio, Città Murata*, etc.), or military corps (*Fanteria, Artiglieria*, etc.).[129]

This reform also originated from the attitude towards the clubs' supporters. Football fans were seen as a danger for public order. Especially Orthodox and Jews supporters were considered prone to express an ethno-national identification. The authorities were anxious about any sign of sympathy for collectives outside the claimed hegemony of fascism. In September 1933, the police complained that some "young Jews" cheered for a visiting British team instead of the local Italian one in a friendly football game. In their view, this accident was related to: "youthful naivety [and] … the level of tension reached by the sentiments of those who practice football after the last championship." Thus, the authorities linked a potentially subversive expression to youth, at the same time downplaying and confining it to the realm of sports. They also considered this accident as a reaction by some Jewish supporters who were enraged by a reportage published on the *Messaggero di Rodi*. The newspaper had commented on an earlier skating race in a way that, according to Jewish supporters, discredited the GER, their communal team. The police consequently recommended "the formation of football teams regardless of religious communities."[130] Communal and sport identification eventually came to be two interrelated factors in the eyes of the authorities. Youth was a trope used to disentangle them and establish a new disciplined order.

***

Whereas work and leisure changed in many regards in the first half of the twentieth century, both domains related to a common preoccupation. The threshold between educational and occupational life was the site where different actors voiced anxieties and hopes about youth to assess the condition of the local society. Projections of parent-child relationships onto these emotions were another common trait, although the experiences of Rhodians in work and leisure varied significantly according to class and gender. During the Italian period, the wealthier were less exposed to state interference as long as they refrained from political activities considered suspicious. The focus on productivity targeted especially men from the lower classes while a focus on morality targeted women with precarious family relationships.

Communities channelled and disciplined work and leisure into these normative ideas of productivity and morality to raise their grip on local youth. The Italian colonial regime adopted the same logic and it aimed to raise its control over this communal socialization. From the *Opera Nazionale Dopolavoro* to new reformatories, up to a rhetoric about the virtue of sports converging with racial and militarist ideas, the Fascist Party added a layer to this process, strengthening the bond between ideology, work, and leisure. Both communal and state institutions also recognized that undisciplined remunerative and free-time activities, translated as "vagrancy" and "vice," could pose a danger to their authority. Their capacity to normalize socialization in these domains went hand in hand with these institutions' anxieties and limits. Communal apprenticeship programs remained limited in scope, and the colonial authorities often insisted that the responsibility of disciplining unruly youth remained a prerogative of the parents, thus contrasting the idea of education against parental authorities propagated by school institutions in the earlier decades, as illustrated in chapter 3.

Families and individuals were an active part of this equation. Fathers requested an internment for their unruly sons and women agreed on subsuming "morally" suspicious labour under the term "housewife". Football players also actively partook in the institutionalization of sports, although their passion could expand into a dangerous tension that the authorities interpreted as politically dangerous, which in turn led to changes in the structures aimed at regulating this domain. Even if the population often conformed to communal and governmental ideas on productivity and morality, for most of Rhodians work and leisure remained far from the "normalcy" propagated by this discourse. Material circumstances in the family were stronger than institutional initiatives to shape youth socialization. Non-linear occupational trajectories were the symptom of how the social and political transformations in Rhodes put family bonds under pressure and exposed to scarcity.

Many families responded to such challenges related to making a living with another strategy: mobility. Instead of remaining caught in the local Ottoman provincial or Italian colonial setting, thousands of Rhodians moved to where material opportunities appeared to be more accessible. Others, on the contrary, arrived in Rhodes because an Italian colonial setting seemed the best option to escape poverty and to make the best out of a privileged role as spearhead of *Italianità* in this corner of the Mediterranean.

Chapter Five

Generations, Mobility, and Shifting Limits of Belonging

In September 1910, the inhabitants of Rhodes could read an excerpt from *The New York Herald*, translated in Greek and published in a local newspaper, *Rodos*. The article commented on mass departures from the Aegean island to New York and Buenos Aires as a "feverish tendency of the poorer classes" moved by the "certainty of finding a job or the idea of escaping the military service." The *Herald* characterized the immigrants from Rhodes as mostly "Jews" and "Greeks" but added that "[e]ven the Turks have caught the emigration fever," including reservists of the Ottoman army "disguised as seamen." At the end of the translated excerpt, an anonymous editorialist of *Rodos* added: "[A]part from the causes mentioned by the New York Herald, which compel the villagers of the beautiful Nymph of the Mediterranean to leave their oxen and abandon their spouses, tools, and parents, the first and foremost is the negligence of our agriculture, of that productive force for the whole country."[1]

Some twenty years later, under Italian sovereign rule, Rhodes was still a site of emigration to the Americas and Africa. Yet, it had also become a destination for many Italian citizens who arrived there through military service or to find an occupation. Nicola M. (b. 1896) from Potenza, southern Italy, was discharged from the Italian army at the end of the First World War. He first went to Kuşadası, a town in Asia Minor then under Italian military occupation, where he briefly stayed to work in an oil factory. After moving to Rhodes, in 1924 he married Schilla N., an Orthodox woman. Schilla did not change her confession although the couple baptized their three children with the Catholic rite. In 1928, Nicola's first work contract with the colonial administration in Rhodes expired and he opened a grocery store. The Italian police outlined his socio-economic position: "Not so used to trade, to which he devoted himself … with the insignificant monetary capital available, he had several debts with local, Italian, and even foreign companies … until he had to try to obtain again a stable employment as accountant … Since the time of his employment by the Government, M. passed the [trading] concessions to his wife who keeps running her husband's commercial activity in her name."[2]

These two accounts are separated by chronological distance and by the opposite directions in which the migrants moved. Yet, they reveal similar concerns for changes in the migrants' occupational profile that reflect broader economic and political trends. In the first source, "new jobs" overseas envisioned by Rhodian emigrants were the result of the abandonment of agriculture on their island. This was a problem already highlighted in the late nineteenth century by Ottoman observers, although emigration also concerned the urban poor.[3] In the second source, an Italian metropolitan newcomer in Rhodes is described as "not used" to trade. Neither was Nicola qualified for a stable rank and file occupation within the colonial administration, which offered hundreds of new jobs mostly reserved to Italian citizens like him. Moreover, both accounts describe mobility as a gendered phenomenon. In the first, women are condescendingly situated between the kin and property while, in the second, they are acknowledged as autonomous economic actors. When men and women moved from and to Rhodes, they influenced the economic possibilities of relatives and partners of the other gender. The issue of military service, lastly, points to the role of the Ottoman and Italian states. Many young Rhodians were said to leave in order not to be drafted in the Ottoman army, while many Italians arrived in Rhodes *because* they had been drafted by the new ruling state. Whereas in this politically "quiet" area the Ottoman state did not intervene to hamper the emigration of its subjects as much as it did in other provinces, Italian rulers steered migration flows to consolidate racial hierarchy. They welcomed the arrival of Italian citizens to build a national body in a colonial setting while they discouraged the inflow of Orthodox families, even if they had ties to the Dodecanese, since they were considered potentially dangerous to colonial rule.[4]

In the first half of the twentieth century, hundreds of local families had either a relative who had left Rhodes or one who had arrived during Italian rule, and in many cases both. Considering the thousands of arrivals and departures, the profound consequences for the local society, and the continuity of flows beyond a single ruling system, mobility is a crucial domain to understand imperial transformations in Rhodes. In terms of economy, family bonds, gender relations, and collective identifications, mobility reinforced some pre-existing hierarchies and led to negotiate or even subvert others. Regardless of the commentator's perspective on these hierarchies, representations of mobility usually framed migrants in generational terms through their role as parents, partners, and children. Generational dynamics stressed the importance of the migrants' emotional ties, their economic (in)dependence, as well as categories of belonging based on place of origin, language, confession, or citizenship. Within a wide and dispersed geography of migration flows from and to Rhodes, the chapter prioritizes the two tracks introduced in the opening quotes: Jewish and Orthodox emigration from Rhodes to the United States and Catholic immigration to Rhodes from Italy and Asia Minor.

The first half of this chapter tells the story of how provincial Ottoman subjects turning into American citizens redefined the very notion of "community." Leaving a setting in which community meant a local and empire-wide juridical structure led by notables, the emigrants constructed a community based on attending congregations, educational activities, and youth clubs. The decision to emigrate and the possibility to return to Rhodes or to stay in America engendered negotiations between parents and children, siblings and cousins, betrothed and spouses.

A linear and uniform narrative in retrospective accounts of mobility, especially by the emigrants' descendants, sketches how young single men emigrated to collect some money only to find a spouse in Rhodes who followed him in the new country. A closer look reveals that these trajectories were often far from linear. Keeping the bonds between America and Rhodes produced frictions and conflict as much as solidarity. This explains why commentators speaking on behalf of a whole community often criticized their fellow migrants' behaviour and exhorted them to opt for confessional endogamy. The cause of such anxiety was that the community's boundaries were not stable. Generational dynamics and youth were tropes used by migrants and their descendants to narrate how these boundaries expanded or shrank over time. This section predominantly discusses Jewish emigration due to more abundant sources. It includes, however, accounts on Rhodian Orthodox emigration to show how interactions and proximity between migrants of both confessions short before and after emigration were marginalized as new communities were made from generation to generation. From the 1970s onwards, the Jewish Archives Project of the University of Washington has produced an oral history series including testimonies from Rhodes who settled in Seattle, one of the main destinations in America. These documents ascribe a youth of "hard work" to the ancestors and contrast it with their descendants' youth of "knowledge" and memorial duty. For many of these descendants, youth was the turning point in life in which they became aware of the community's boundaries, often challenging them.

In the second half, the chapter moves to another story merging mobility, generations, and belonging. It investigates how Catholics of different citizenship status came to constitute a privileged national collectivity of *Italianità*, central to the colonial state's legitimacy as its most direct emanation. Generational dynamics established criteria for the sound and solid bonds between Catholic migrant families and the state. These bonds were to last in the future through the socialization of children. However, this vision converging with the discourse on the "new generation" had to face the issue of intermarriage between Catholic Italians and non-Catholic women in Rhodes. From 1912 onwards, this phenomenon increased quantitatively from a narrow group of high-grade officials marrying well-off women to dozens of lower ranks and civilians marrying women with less economic capital. Oftentimes, the Italian husbands lived on a salary within the public sector, while their wives contributed considerably to the couple's capital and real estate through dowry and labour. However, this synergy coexisted with problems related to mobility like changes of occupation, further displacement, the husbands' frequent refusal to maintain their wives and families. Women actively engaged with the authorities to defend their rights, often by highlighting their commitment to a sense of national belonging acquired through marriage with Italian citizens.

Mixed unions were also common among Italians moving to Rhodes from post-Ottoman Smyrna. Their immigration is in itself an imperial consequence. As former residents of the Ottoman Empire, they abandoned their home after the state's collapse in the 1920s. Dozens of Catholic and italophone Smyrniotes did not remain in the Republic of Turkey, nor did they move to the metropolitan Kingdom of Italy. The colonial setting of Rhodes became their new home. Historians have suggested that confessional exogamy was quite exceptional among Catholic families of Ottoman port cities, and that socialization through religious institutions had been the pillar of a "Levantine" identity in the Ottoman Empire.[5] The case of Smyrniotes in Rhodes, however, proves that such pattern could rapidly end when these Catholics moved. Not only they frequently married outside confessional boundaries, but they also increasingly socialized within a new political institution, the Fascist Party. Despite such loyalty towards fascist colonialism, many of these migrants did not enjoy better material and social conditions than their new townsmen and townswomen of other confessions and other citizenship statuses. There existed a gap between the ideal of colonial

Italianità which they represented and many of their individual trajectories marked by material scarcity.

By looking at how the displacement of families intersects with the imperial consequence in Rhodes, two separate historiographies of late Ottoman emigration and Italian colonial mobilities can be connected. Concerning the first field, the pioneer study by Akram Khater on Lebanese migration to the United States (and return) has argued for narrating mobility from the point of view of migrants as actors of social change searching for their "home" in between two or more distant realities.[6] Recent studies expanded the discussion by conflating the experiences of mobility with late and post-Ottoman political transformations. Stacy Fahrenthold highlighted how Lebanese and Syrian emigrants in the "Arab Atlantic" created a political space that took stances on the political developments of the Second Constitutional Period and the First World War.[7] The *mahjar* (an Arabic term only partially corresponding to the notion of diaspora) elaborated visions for post-Ottoman polities that were crashed by the establishment of the French Mandate after the war. David Gutman has focused on Armenians moving to the United States to show how the "paradoxes of Ottoman reforms" inspired by citizenship equality led to emigration bans. These targeted specific persecuted groups like the Armenians at the turn of the twentieth century, especially from eastern Anatolian territories. Ottoman Armenians nonetheless continued to leave by turning to informal and illicit networks that enabled their departure.[8] These migrants' stories are useful to investigate Ottoman politics, which also influenced the provincial society of Rhodes. Yet, looking at Rhodian Jews and Orthodox can decentre the discussion from issues of intercommunal conflict and state-driven persecution and shed light on different, "low-tension" aspects such as the management of money, education, and gender relations.

In the case of Italian mobilities, Donna Gabaccia and other scholars like Franca Iacovetta and Fraser Ottanelli pioneered studies on emigrants. They stressed how the interplay of gender and class did not create a divide between a national feeling of belonging and a transnational socialization culminating in political radicalism.[9] More recently, Mark Choate has addressed a changing geography of Italian emigration from beginnings in African colonial territories to the transatlantic "boom" of departures. Choate has described how late nineteenth-century governments exploited the emigrants' potential to extend "the limits of the imagined Italian nation" through statistics, cultural initiatives, and reports.[10] This aspect also mattered in Italy's own colonies. Alike the settlers in Libya, Italians in Rhodes had complex interactions with the authorities. A favorable position within the racial hierarchy of fascist colonialism coexisted with widespread social marginalization and contacts with colonized subjects.[11] While Italians outside the *"Bel paese"* continued to work as an economic and propaganda reservoir for fascist imperialism, their presence became insidious when Mussolini's empire started to crumble in Africa amid the Second World War. Pamela Ballinger has argued for interpreting the myriad of juridical, bureaucratic, economic, and logistic problems related to the "repatriation" of Italian communities within the former empire, including the Dodecanese, as a factor influencing unstable boundaries of belonging to the national body politic after 1945.[12]

How, then, can imperial histories of mobility collide by placing the map pin on Rhodes? Nancy Green's approach based on comparison – not *between* distant objects of inquiry, but *within* interrelated phenomena – provides an answer to this question.[13] Accordingly, Jewish and Orthodox emigration from Rhodes is a case of *divergent* migration: starting from a situation of proximity, the emigrants' socialization in the United States created two separate memorial narratives which continue to shape the descendants' attachment to Rhodes. In the second part, the chapter analyses a *convergent* migration: arriving from different localities, Catholics in Rhodes were the pivotal representatives of colonial *Italianità*. In both cases, the migrants' stories are so diverse that any golden rule based on a single explicative pattern inevitably becomes a shortfall. At the same time, this variety brings us closer to concurrent motives, subjectivities, and trajectories which reflect the composite social reality of Rhodes.

Using confessional categories of analysis such as "Jewish," "Orthodox," and "Catholics" in this chapter is the starting point to discuss how they interrelate with other collective markers such as *Rodeslis*, Sephardim, Panrhodian, Greek American and Italian citizens. All of them were used and defined as a result of interactions between families, associations, and the state in a transnational space. Kin relations, notions of communal belonging, and population policies mutually transformed each other through mobility inbound and outbound. The main difference between the trajectories of Rhodian emigrants in America and those of Italian immigrants in Rhodes is that the former were concerned by building a community with relatively little interference on the side of the state. The latter, by contrast, did not need to define a community but were directly exposed to how the fascist colonialist state defined national identity in Rhodes.

These mobilities evolved in the broader and longer socio-economic "transformation of the world" of the nineteenth century that led millions of people to move to other states and continents. As Jürgen Osterhammel has argued, a main novelty of that period was that masses of migrants chose to leave "voluntarily", or at least could choose more freely than in past times where to escape from persecution and misery.[14] As other scholars have demonstrated, this global migration momentum reached its peak in the 1920s and experienced a rupture during the Second World War.[15] Rhodes became integrated in a regional and international boom of departures especially around 1910. While emigrants previously reached the Americas from Naples, Marseille, and other Western European ports, the first part of the transatlantic trip became shorter after the Aegean town was directly connected with liners departing from Piraeus. Companies such as the Hellenic National Steamboats (*Ethniki Atmoploia tis Ellados*) were pivotal. Its advertisements appeared in the local newspapers as early as 1909 proposing a trip to New York on the *Patris* liner which lasted "only" thirteen days.[16]

Next to the transatlantic pattern, a vertical route of mobility tied Rhodes to Africa. Already in the nineteenth century, one important destination especially for Aegean Orthodox was Khedivial Egypt with its thriving port cities. Aegean islanders were part of intra-Mediterranean circuits of mobility from the northern to the southern shore.[17] With the increase of imperialist and colonialist projects, these routes expanded further south, although African coastal towns did not disappear from the picture. In 1913, Italian governors recognized that expanding infrastructure in the African transimperial space attracted Rhodians: "once they arrive in the port of our African colony [Massawa], they usually proceed to Port Sudan, where they are easily employed in the railroad construction prompted by the Anglo-Egyptian government. A quite numerous group head for our Libya where they pursue small trade."[18]

Dominant waves and routes of migration conceal diverse and complex trajectories, in Rhodes as elsewhere.[19] The mobility of Aegean islanders implied translocal movements along "transient, non-permanent and unordered" sites used as steppingstones.[20] One such place was the mining town of Penhalonga, at the border between British Rhodesia and Portuguese Mozambique. Marco Alhadeff arrived there from Rhodes in 1905, when he was around 25 years old. Only later did he move to the larger town of Salisbury (Harare). A persisting presence of *Rodesli* Jews emerged there as he invited other islanders to follow him, lending them money for the journey.[21] A similar pattern concerned Elizabethville (Lubumbashi) in the Belgian Congo, another major settlement of *Rodeslis*.[22] More and more workers and employees circulated between Rhodes and Central Africa, and their relationships also extended towards new families through marriage with invited newcomers. Money and manpower thus circulated across empires facilitating the creation of new communities far from the native island.

These trajectories' complexity and the many territorial and legal regimes they crossed implied a range of collective categories to designate migrants. Depending on the standpoint, they could count as "expatriated" (*ekpatrizomenoi*), as in the case of Ottoman emigrants in New York before naturalization, or as "settlers" (*coloni*) in the case of Italian woodcutters from Trentino colonizing the Rhodian interior village of Campochiaro/Eleusa.[23] Moreover, Catholics from Smyrna who arrived in Rhodes after the Great Fire of 1922 were first seen as "refugees" (*profughi*) and then simply as Italian citizens. Jews who left for Africa were described by French consulates in the 1930s as "Italian protégés from Rhodes," including their children, regardless of whether they had ever set foot in the Italian Aegean *Possedimento*.[24] The same Jewish emigrants in Congo, without full Italian citizenship, were considered by an emissary from Rome as "Italians and fascists," whose sentiments were to be mobilized for the construction of the empire during and after Mussolini's Ethiopian campaign.[25] All these terms reflect ideas of "space and territoriality, and their continual revision" observable in Rhodes within the imperial consequence that tied together late Ottoman and Italian rule.[26]

These designations referring to the emigrants' (extra)territoriality prescribed, rather than described the experience of mobility. Institutions tend to see migrants as moving from A (origin) to B (destination), mostly in a single direction. While many left Rhodes never to come back or arrived never to leave, return migration was frequent in this colonial setting.[27] For some, the return could be traumatic and lead to depression, for others it meant a social upgrade transmittable to descendants.[28] A generational perspective blending family and individual experiences allows us to question notions like "origin" or "return." In 1910, Jacob Berro moved from Rhodes to Buenos Aires as a single man aged 20. Ten years later, he returned to his Aegean island with his younger wife and townswoman Rosa (b. 1897), right after the birth of their children Haim and Matilda. Arriving in Argentina as a simple day labourer (*jornalero*), he had accumulated enough capital to be considered of "good economic position" (*buona posizione finanziaria*) by the Italian authorities in the 1930s. His son Haim graduated from the Jewish school in Rhodes and in 1938, at the same age as his father did, he left with his sister for Buenos Aires, where his maternal grandfather lived. This decision compromised the continuity of the family's capital in Rhodes. Yet, taken just after the promulgation of the Racial Laws in Italy, it saved Haim and Matilda, while their parents and their sister Amelia (b. 1921?) were deported from Rhodes and murdered in Auschwitz-Birkenau in 1944. Although the route was the same, the socialization preceding the departure and the political context in which migration happened separated father and son.[29]

For many families, what the state highlighted as origin and destination were but two intermediate stops in a longer journey. Around 1860, Amabile Bogdanich, a boatman from the Adriatic island of Silbe (near Zara), moved to Smyrna. His sons and daughters grew up in the Ottoman city and kept their Austro-Hungarian nationality until both empires collapsed. In the wake of the First World War, some of them took the Italian passport and others opted for the Yugoslav one. A few years after the Great Fire destroyed Smyrna in 1922, a part of the family moved to Rhodes following a brief stay in southern Italy. Later on, one of Amabile's grandsons, Antonio, was sent to Zara, which in the meantime had come under Italian administration, for military service. While some relatives followed him, in the mid-1930s, this branch returned to Rhodes and remained there until the end of the Second World War. The Bogdanich family's trajectory highlights how Italian colonialism in Rhodes intersects with Ottoman and post-Ottoman mobilities. We will meet again the Bogdanich family later in the chapter. Before looking at Rhodes as they and many other Catholic immigrants found it in the 1920s, it is now time to jump back to the beginnings of our chapter's story and outline how new patterns of emigration marked a rupture with the past during the last years of Ottoman rule.

Youth on the Move between Rhodes and America

The population of Rhodes had long been mobile before the twentieth century, but the last years of Ottoman rule saw a massive increase of departures and an unprecedented extension in geographic range. The French vice-consul wrote in 1907 that "four or five hundred inhabitants" per year had left during the previous fifteen years, mostly "illegally" (i.e. making themselves invisible to the state's gaze) due to the difficulty of affording an emigration permit. Earlier on, peasants and workers headed for other provinces of the empire where they could find employment, especially seasonal work in Asia Minor, British-occupied Egypt, and Syria. The turning point towards overseas destinations happened, in the vice-consul's view, because "those displacements were not enough profitable." New routes led to a change in the perception of migrants in social and demographic terms. They were now seen as "young destitute" men allured by the news brought by "the successful ones" (*ceux qui réussissaient*).[30]

In accounts of early twentieth-century emigration from Rhodes, references to youth are indeed widespread. In 1910, the *Alliance* boys school's director commented on "the heroic decision to emigrate," including by "young girls [who] face the hardship of a long trip with courage to join their betrothed." These observations tried to make sense of the motives behind the departures:

> A young man with whom I had the chance to discuss about emigration told me that, despite his good material conditions and his parents' prayers, he was determined to leave with a group of friends for the American Confederation [*sic!*]: How do you think – he told me – I could resist the current that leads towards distant shores so many fellow citizens of mine? ... If I stay here, who says that I – belonging to a distinguished family – will not be forced to ask them for favours in a more or less distant future? This idea does not appeal to me, and I am more than ever convinced about leaving my hometown.[31]

The trope of mobility as a prerogative of youth was appropriated by many voices regardless of the economic or social status at departure. Salomon Notrika, whose father moved to Buenos Aires in 1907, recalled that the wave of emigration "consisted of men, young men almost all single" who "came [to Argentina] to work."[32]

Next to economic prospects, a common motive in these narratives related to youth is the flight from military service. Conscription was extended to Ottoman non-Muslims in 1909 through an imperial reform introduced by the Young Turks, as mentioned in chapter 1. Cynthia Flash Hemphill, a descendant of Clara Barchi (Barkey), who left Rhodes to escape the persecution against Jews in 1939, stated that "young men" compared conscription "to prison and they would do anything to escape."[33] This motive – found in consular reports as well – is only partially cogent.[34] It surely points to a factor increasing departures but less to the original cause of mobility. Ottoman emigration had a longer history in which violence intersected with misery in other provinces like Lebanon and Eastern Anatolia.[35] In Rhodes too, the fear of serving in the army became a trigger because avoiding it through emigration also presented better economic prospects based on the stories of earlier emigrants. Indeed, the accounts emphasizing conscription as a push-factor are often incongruent in their chronology. For instance, Salomon Notrika could not situate exactly when the reform became effective in Rhodes (1909) and his father actually left two years before this happened and before the Young Turks seized power.

Although these accounts portray migrants as youth, this term remained rather vague in terms of age. David Galante, a Jew fleeing Rhodes on the eve of the Second World War, recalled about earlier emigration that "[a]ll those whose economic condition allowed for it (*que estaban en condiciones económicas*) and who had an appropriate age took the decision quickly."[36] Yet, what was an "appropriate age" to emigrate? The thirty-two passengers from Rhodes arriving in New York in June 1909 on the *Patris* liner ranged from 17 to 38 years of age. Almost 20 per cent of them were older than 30, and 25 per cent of them were married. Only two women figure in the list, and all men except one declared their occupation as "workman."[37] The experience of mobility transformed age and wealth markers just as much as these factors could prompt a departure. Being in their late teens and early twenties did not make those who left "young" more than the very decision of leaving. Similarly, the "economic condition" did not make them "poor" or "rich" more than their decision to try their luck overseas. Age translated "experience": being youth meant to be ready to take a risky decision harder to fathom for one's parents. Wealth, in turn, translated "autonomy": by leaving Rhodes, migrants decided to break with economic dependence on their family, if they had one at all. Not alone, yet willing to be autonomous: mobility tales emphasize youth as a reflection of these changing generational relationships.

Emotional conflict within the family when deciding to emigrate was a common feature. Matilda Menashe, born in 1902, spent her childhood away from her parents at her uncle's home in Milas, Asia Minor. Back in Rhodes, Matilda had a troubled relationship with her parents, and after "a big fight," around 1918, she left for Seattle, where she joined her brother Morris.[38] In other cases, though, parents could encourage a boy to emigrate in order to provide resources for his female relatives. Sam Koutouzakis from the village of Lachania was reportedly "sent" to join his brother in America to assure his sister's dowry.[39] Yet, these male migrants were not simple vectors of material aid, but also negotiators of family customs. Ralph Capeluto left Rhodes in 1920 after "planning the trip for quite a long time" and saving "a substantial sum of money" for the journey. A few years later, his relatives from Rhodes asked him to cover the dowry of his sister Esther. Ralph hesitated, and the lack of remittances impacted work and leisure experiences of his young niece in Rhodes, Clara Barkey: "Dear Uncle and Aunt, it appears you have forgotten that you have an orphan girl in Rhodes, and if it were not for us, she would be 'dragged in the sewer.' But now life is not like before, prices are astronomical and Papa can barely make it to support us, so much that I, at the age of 17, when one has fun, am compelled to work in order to help the household."[40]

As a Rhodian Orthodox who settled in Canonsburg recalled, the sense of kinship responsibility coexisted with the ambition to emancipate oneself from it: "Yes, the money paid to us was tempting. Many times I was tempted to go out and spend it as I wanted, but few of us felt free to do this. We realized that our people back in our homeland were counting on us and if we forgot, it wasn't for long. A letter would soon remind us of their suffering."[41] The circulation of resources within the family was even more important in times of crisis such as the First World War.[42] Still, Orthodox and Jewish Rhodians in the Americas perceived themselves and their household as quite autonomous. This holds especially true for younger brothers, who had less pressure in their new environment.[43]

For all unmarried migrants, another delicate issue was the wedding engagement. Whereas many accounts describe a smooth coming of age for "young men" who emigrated overseas, collected money, and then returned to Rhodes or sent for their future wife, migrants oftentimes married contrary to their parents' expectations. At first, Ralph Capeluto considered going back to Rhodes for an "arranged marriage," but his sister Jamila persuaded him to choose a bride in Seattle by arguing that "people in America do not marry that way."[44] At the same time, trans-atlantic engagements increased control on the "reputation" of women who remained in Rhodes. Disputes could escalate up to the tribunal. In 1918, the rumour that Esther M., aged 18 and engaged with a *Rodesli* in America, had spent one or more nights at a hotel in Rhodes "in a dishonest way" spread in the Jewish neighbourhood. Two young men had reported this to her fiancé's mother, and he decided to break up with Esther. She then accused the two men of denigration and stated that, because of that rumour, her "future" was "broken forever."[45] Men in the Americas surely had more freedom than their fiancées in Rhodes. In one account of Orthodox Rhodians based in Pennsylvania, older men even "encouraged" younger migrants to have sexual encounters despite the engagement. However, the settlements where they lived were small, and rumours circulated quickly. In the unfortunate case that intercourses with sex workers or affairs with women in America became known, contrary to the harsh consequences for women described above, these men could allegedly get away through a simple "apology" to the wife's relatives at home in the Aegean.[46]

After the wedding, the relationship between spouses could have complications due to the plurality of legal institutions interacting with migrants. Hizkia A. and Mazaltov M. arrived separately as widows in the United States around 1910. They met in Seattle, where Hizkia worked as a shoeshine and provided for the material sustainment of the household. Although they "spent a conjugal life" and had a daughter, Hizkia married Mazaltov only in 1917 in order not to be drafted after the United States had entered the First World War. Back in Rhodes in the 1920s, he claimed that their union was not legally valid since "he had been forced by the Jewish Community of that city [Seattle] to regularize his position" since Mazaltov had threatened to commit suicide. After the two broke up, Mazaltov accused him of having a concubine, which Hizkia denied.[47]

Whereas previous examples underlined negotiations among partners or within the family, this last case introduces the "Jewish Community" in Seattle as an additional force. Without a formal juridical status – contrary to the Ottoman confessional communities in Rhodes – this community built by migrants in America proved strong enough to pressure those who deviated from an accepted behaviour in terms of sentimental and sexual relationships. Once back in Rhodes during Italian military occupation, the Italian tribunal could not handle the validity of Hizkia and Mazaltov's union, but only the accusation of adultery. The same case could thus involve the family, the community, and the state, although mobility coupled with an unstable territorial status in Rhodes further blurred each entity's domain of authority.

Marriage was used to emphasize the migrants' duty to build families within the boundaries that the same community prescribed. Cementing a Rhodian community in America required commentators publicly stressing a collective "we" and giving authoritative instructions on how a "you" (the migrants) ought to behave. Thus, the newspaper *Nea Rodos* started to print congratulation messages for emigrants' weddings as early as 1911 from remote localities such as Pueblo and Sterling, Colorado.[48] In 1931, *Rodiaki* published a column sent from New York entitled "The question of the Rhodians' marriage in America." The article expressed wishes to the new spouses and stated:

> once again our Rhodian soul feels an indescribable joy since a Rhodian man has married a Rhodian woman! Thus, there are many hopes that one day our unfortunate Rhodes will succeed in seeing its progeny of emigrants (*xeniteumena tekna tis*). When, however, a Rhodian man marries a stranger (*xenin*), as it unfortunately happens sometimes, we have low hopes for a return to Rhodes. The hope for the dream of a Rhodian man abroad must be the quickest possible return to Rhodes! This hope and this dream can be fulfilled when an unmarried Rhodian man here marries a Rhodian woman of America or a Rhodian woman of Rhodes.

Later in the text, the journalist explicitly linked demography in Rhodes and in the United States:

> This duty is even more imperative if one considers that the number of our unmarried young women in Rhodes is incomparably higher than that

of unmarried men. When we forget this fundamental duty of patriotism and of humanity, we marry those who speak a foreign language, those of different confession, of different race, or even of our own [*omogenoi*, Greeks born in America, but not of Rhodian origin].[49]

The letter mentioned that "purely economic reasons" motivated this recommendation. By marrying a woman outside the Rhodian community, a male emigrant would not have access to resources such as a "house, furniture, monetary dowry, buildings" on his home island. This article must be framed within the context of the Great Depression and the change in mobility trends concerning the United States. From 1931 to 1932, the migration ratio switched from a positive net of 35,000 new immigrants to a negative one of 67,000 new emigrants.[50] Such economic considerations provided a bridge towards a discussion on the community's confessional and ethnic homogeneity. *Nea Rodos* argued that a prolonged stay in the United States worsened the unbalance between women and men in Rhodes, already underlined in chapter 2. Women were portrayed as an economic resource for men through their dowry and, at the same time, as a potential threat to the community's cohesion. Just as Orthodox men married non-Rhodians, local women could marry "strangers," most notably Italian (former) soldiers in Rhodes who represented the colonial occupier. The discourse on "dreams," "duty," "hope" and "patriotism" again prescribed the migrants' behaviour at the intersection of the family, the community, and the state.

In most sources, state institutions in America were not perceived as an invasive force in regard to the migrants' familial choices. Still, the United States were imaged as standing in opposition to Rhodes, the haven awaiting the emigrants' return. "America" stood for diversity with its "general law" steering the Rhodians away from the traditions of their home in the Aegean.[51] The return to Rhodes was exalted as a necessary condition to belong to the original community. Seen from the migrants' point of view, however, returning to Rhodes implied negative aspects as well. The regime of colonial citizenship at work under Italian rule would have implied a downgrade: the United States census of 1940 for areas more densely populated by Rhodians reveals that many Orthodox and Jews were either already naturalized or were recorded as "has first papers" status, namely they had started the naturalization procedure. Assuming that this trend had begun a few years earlier, when a return would have been easier than in 1940, once back in Rhodes they would have switched from being citizens in their country of residence to being foreigners in their place of origin. Those who had not yet obtained the American citizenship, if legally recognized as Italian colonial subjects, would have had a second-class status compared to Catholic settlers. There can be little doubts that seeking a quick naturalization in America allured many more than the moralistic call for a return to Rhodes to hamper their female coreligionists from marrying outside communal boundaries.

Reprinted in newspapers in Rhodes under the heavy censorship of the Italian authorities, such articles did not mention any explicit national identification with Greece. Officially, "patriotism" meant attachment to the Orthodox faith and to Rhodes as a homeland. What mostly concerned these commentators was the transmission of capital from parents to children in form of dowry and heritage, as well as the reinvestment of resources accumulated in America once back in Rhodes. Against this backdrop, mobility was often associated with youth, in turn standing for lack of experience and willingness to risk. Youth mattered because of the anxiety about the possibility that emigrants diverge from the older, "customary" family of their parents' generation. Ironically, one wonders how long the anonymous author(s) of the letter printed in *Rodiaki* (signed *X. Dodekanisios*) had been in America and whether this person planned at all his or her return described as the sole purpose for emigrants.

Building a Community of Migrants

In most accounts of emigration, communal institutions in Rhodes do not appear as significantly impacting the migrants' choices. The *Alliance* teacher mentioned above represented an educational institution considered part of the Jewish community. When he heard about his young townsman's decision to emigrate, he did not try to change his mind or help him plan the trip. As early as 1908, the *Alliance* had a mixed stance in regard to emigration, praising its material consequences but fearing that it could become an irreversible trend that would eventually make the community numerically "insignificant."[52] For migrants, these observations were of secondary importance compared to calculations and discussions within the family.

On the contrary, what they meant by "community" was fore and foremost the voluntary effort to keep their coreligionists together once in America. It seems that the less emigrants were actively involved in communal structures in Rhodes, the more they underlined the value of community overseas. This was interrelated with the transmission of economic and intellectual capital across generations. In 1982, Elazar Behar from Seattle commented that: "if our generation today had to be transplanted from this country into a foreign land under the conditions that our parents and grandparents came here, we would not be able to build up a community. We may have the book knowledge and the schooling that they didn't [have], but they had something else that was very much stronger and more far-reaching … They came in here as poor, as if not poorer than the other immigrants in this country." A central element for a new community in Seattle, Behar continued, were religious institutions: "Their function and role was to develop a community here and raise family, get their children educated, and create a religious atmosphere with a religious school and a religious sanctuary, a synagogue, place of worship and a community for their children to belong to. I think they did a terrific job."[53] Converting the parents' "business" into the children's "knowledge" also implied that descendants feel in charge of constructing a story of mobility that stressed their (grand)parents' sacrifices and sense of belonging.

The earlier generations' efforts at communalizing the socialization of their children eventually prevailed over the remembrance of proximity and cooperation between Dodecanesian Orthodox and Jews in America in the early years after the arrival. Traces of this proximity, however, are still visible in several accounts. This is how Charles Alhadeff explains his father Nissim's experience: "When my father was between 18 and 20 years of age he was out with some Greeks on one of the other islands, we believe it was Leros. He and a few Greek friends of his decided to come to America to some relatives. These Greeks had relatives who happened to be in Seattle. They were all Greeks."[54] Friends and co-workers transcended confessional groups and sometimes prepared departure together. Rosa Berro recalled that, in 1908, her husband William was "sent" to America "with a bunch of Greeks" by his father, who knew them from his business.[55] Ralph Cohen was among the first settlers from Rhodes in Montgomery (Alabama) around 1906, travelling with his Orthodox friend John Costarides and "legally sponsored" by the latter's uncle.[56] More in general, in his master thesis dated 1939, one of the earliest detailed accounts of Sephardim immigration to Seattle, Albert Adatto noted that "Greeks" from Marmara were responsible for the arrival of the first Sephardim, and that Ottoman Orthodox and Jews could interact even more than Sephardi and Ashkenazi Jews.[57]

Interconfessional contacts do not imply that Jews and Orthodox left Rhodes in equal numbers on each ship. More than 90 per cent of the thirty-two passengers from Rhodes on board of the *Patris* liner mentioned above were Jews. As is still often the case today, the passengers had to name a contact person in the United States, and among those who had a contact in New York, the following picture emerges:

Table 5.1. Contact person in New York as indicated by at least two passengers from Rhodes, June 1909.

Contact Person	Passengers from Rhodes
Nissim Israel	1 brother-in-law, 1 cousin, 1 friend
Abraham Bevah	2 friends
Bohor Bendicio (Bendicha, Bentista)	1 brother-in-law, 1 cousin, 1 friend
Haim Hasson (Hussion)	2 friends
Mehmet Kadir (Cadir)	1 brother-in-law, 2 friends
Nissim Carafuil	2 friends
Nissim Schahon	1 cousin, 3 friends

Source: EIF PR. From a sample of thirty-two passengers of the liner *Patris* arriving in New York on June 2, 1909.

Note: The role of these contact persons could be described as friend or cousin. At the same time, their function was also that of a broker or middleman. For an insight on this ambivalence: McKeown, "Box."

Many mentioned their address of destination as 176 Chrystie Street or 265 Grand Street in Manhattan where, in 1912, some emigrants founded the society "Brotherhood League of Rhodes" (*Agudath Achim d'Rhodes*). What would become a centre of a *Rodesli* community in New York was, at first, a place where Jews mingled with non-Jews like Mehmet Kadir, with whom they shared friendship and even kin ties.

For most Rhodians, New York was but a stop on the journey. In Seattle, the booming city of the Pacific Northwest where hundreds of them moved, contacts across confessional lines continued. Many Orthodox immigrants there were fish sellers or grocers, and they introduced Jewish newcomers like Nissim Alhadeff to this sector, as his son Charles recalled: "When he got here he worked with these Greeks in their little fruit and vegetable stands and little fish stalls and whatever else the Greek families were doing. He lived with these Greeks."[58]

However, the oral history of migration progressively crystallized around ethno-confessional difference, also because those who left Rhodes together could end up in quite different places within a few years. As a result, Orthodox and Jews only exceptionally and superficially mention each other. Education and schooling were a further factor in this process of separation. Children born or beginning school in the United States experienced a considerably longer schooling than their parents had experienced in Rhodes. Whereas most Jews in Rhodes had attended the communal *Alliance* primary school, migrants arriving in Seattle sent their children to American public schools, while some elders taught Hebrew in the afternoon.[59] This practice was also widespread in the Rhodian Orthodox community of Weirton and Warren (Ohio).[60]

After elementary school, though, access to higher education remained marginal in smaller communities like Canonsburg, where some hundred Orthodox Rhodians from the village of Koskinou had settled. Only one of them, by 1940, had entered college.[61] A different picture emerges for cities with a strong educational infrastructure like Seattle. The gap in schooling years between those born in the United States and those born in Rhodes (or its surroundings) is more striking:

Figure 5.1. Years of schooling for *Rodeslis* in Seattle over 16 years of age, in per cent.

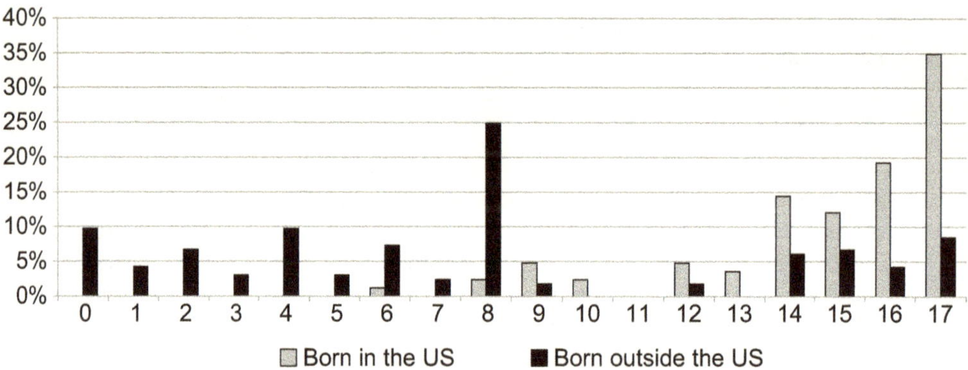

Source: US NA CS 1940 ED 40 162; 165; 287; 288.

Note: I included only individuals above 16 years of age, the first cohort in which both categories can be found. The oldest individuals born in the United States (except a non-Jewish domestic servant) is 31, the oldest one from outside is 90. "Born outside the US" includes individuals whose place of birth is recorded mostly as belonging to Italy (for Rhodes and, possibly, Kos) Turkey (for some Jews who had married an individual born in Rhodes), and in one case, Egypt (idem). Kinship and business bonds led many individuals to either move to Rhodes or leave the island for getting married in surrounding towns such as Milas and Bodrum (but possibly also Smyrna, Salonica, or even Beirut). Once in the United States, since the level of institutionalization and associational life related to those smaller localities was not existent or much lower, they mostly became absorbed in the narrative of the Jews from Rhodes.

A combination of private and public education is nothing unusual among mobile communities of the last two centuries. In the case of Rhodes, this matters since non-curricular education was recalled as a turning point in the young migrants' perception of their community. The orphan Jacob Almeleh graduated from the *Alliance* primary school in Rhodes just before the First World War. In 1920, at 17 years of age, he arrived in Seattle. He first attended some classes of English and then continued with self-teaching at home: "I was from the very beginning interested in the life of the community. From the time I was 17 I got interested in … the [Young

Hebrew Literary Club] … I was active in every office of the organization itself. We had a sort of a debating society. It was an educational organization. We were new in this country and we were trying to get accustomed to the ways of America. So we engaged in public speaking. We engaged in debates. We engaged in lectures. We had speakers from outside … That was for the whole Sephardic community."[62]

What *Rodeslis* like Almeleh referred to as "community" identified a space of socialization permeable to Sephardim from other localities. Yet, this coexisted with frictions. In Seattle, the Sephardim split in two congregations and contacts with Ashkenazim-dominated institutions increased through cultural activities outside religious services. Charles Alhadeff's father reportedly "was [n]ever in the Temple more than once or twice in his life" but, in 1922, he sent his son to the Sunday School since he "felt strongly then that [his children] were not assimilating in the Jewish community."[63] Hence, community had an ambiguous significance. It could emphasize, though not always conflate, Rhodes as the place of origin, Ladino as language of the Sephardim, and Judaism as religion. Many among the first *Rodeslis* in America were not much concerned about this ambiguity. The priority was that their children remain somehow aware of these three levels and socialize within their orbit, even though parents themselves were often not actively taking part in confessional or educational life. This broader notion of Jewish community had three implications. The first related to marriage outside families from Rhodes, the second to a rediscovery of *Rodesli* history, and the third to a more intimate and gendered memory of the Holocaust.

The Seattle sample from the 1940 United States census indicates a striking tendency towards Sephardim endogamy, but intermarriage with Ashkenazim increased among the third generation of descendants for those who arrived in Seattle around 1910, or the second for those arrived around 1920.[64] Mary Capeloto recalled that, in the Seattle Council of Jewish Women in the 1920s, "Ashkenazen [*sic!*] Jews did not have a very good impression of the Sephardic Jews," although at the time of her interview (1982), marriage between them was common.[65] A turning point happened on the eve of the Second World War, as Philip Flash described: "The Temple had a young people's organization going before the war they called the Temple Circle … [A]t that time the community was hungry for young people's social activity, to meet other young Jewish people … They weren't concerned whether you belonged to this group or that group or this synagogue or so on. All they were concerned with is just young Jewish people having good times together. I think that it did more to bind the community than anything that I know of, even today."[66]

At the same time, this expanding notion of community could lead to engage with the particularities of *Rodesli* history, especially for those collecting further intellectual experiences. Marc Angel, born in Seattle in 1945 to *Rodesli* parents, is today rabbi emeritus in New York. His paternal grandfather and eldest uncle Moshe were the first to move to Seattle, as mentioned in chapter 2. At the Hebrew School of Seattle, the predominance of Ashkenazi culture raised his interest in the own Sephardic background.[67] Moving to Yeshiva University in New York, "as a young person," he discovered the heritage and history of the *Rodesli* Jews. Angel wrote a ground-breaking dissertation on this topic in the 1970s and, more recently, his memoirs mobilized generational segments of his family to explain changes from the "Old" to the "New World."[68] In his memoirs and oral history interview alike, youth stands for a series of cognitive experiences that led him to close the circle with his ancestors' origins.

More recently, descendants of *Rodesli*-Ashkenazim families have revived their family story from a gendered perspective. Hannah Pressman, a scholar of Hebrew literature based in Seattle, grew up in Virginia from parents raised in Zimbabwe. In 2014, she recalled discovering her mother's *Rodesli* origins:

> The culture of Ashkenaz [*sic!*] was the one that predominated at home, both linguistically and culinarily, when I was young … Yet somewhere within me there was an awareness that my mother's side of the family had a different story and an alternate set of Jewish cultural accoutrements … And then there was the shoebox, which was kept on an upper shelf in my mother's closet. It held a trove of family memorabilia – postcards, passports, documents, books, and photos. I must have been in college when I first started seriously scrutinizing the box's contents, and it fired up my imagination.

Pressman then stressed elements merging family memory and Jewish history: "the item that changed everything about how I viewed my family's past, and that spurred my quest to know more, was … the document attesting to my great-great-grandmother Rebecca's deportation from Rhodes … [T]he collective Holocaust narratives that I had acquired up until that point felt somehow more distant rather than closer to me. I felt a gap opening up in my heretofore-solid sense of Jewish identity, and an immediate, insatiable craving to know more about Rebecca's life."[69]

Photographs, the Holocaust, and the matrilineal transmission of memory are at the core of Pressman's narrative, one in which the community and its institutions seem to be a more distant reference than the women of her own family. Her account is informed by Marianne Hirsch's notion of "generation of post-memory," the "return of traumatic knowledge and embodied experience" among descendants, for which the Holocaust acts as a "touchstone" connecting personal and collective experiences.[70] Discovering the Holocaust from the standpoint of an unknown trajectory within the family triggered the desire to "re-member, to re-build, to re-incarnate, to replace and to repair" the lost ancestral homeland of Rhodes from abroad.[71]

Family and community seem to reconverge towards the place where it all began. Religious, cultural, or recreational clubs, but also schools, and even the family's house with its closets are described as sites in which young actors make sense of their place within a broader community, a place that usually differs from that of their parents. Be it by narrating the attraction to Ashkenazim, the sense of marginality compared to them or, later, the rediscovery of a silenced *Rodesli* past in the family, youth and generational dynamics have decisively influenced the narratives of mobility and the imagined boundaries of the community abroad.

Today, more than a hundred years after the first arrivals of *Rodeslis* in New York and Buenos Aires, and more than seventy years after the dramatic rupture of the Holocaust, the generation of post-memory involves new media and new connections, which contribute to shift the spotlight back to Rhodes. Already in 1997, Aron Hasson, grandson of *Rodeslis* who settled in Los Angeles in the 1910s, opened the Rhodes Jewish Museum, which has a permanent collection at the Synagogue of Rhodes.[72] In the 2000s, the Rhodes Jewish Museum expanded its website to sections on "genealogy," "family photos," "cemetery" and "Rodesli Diaspora news."[73] More recently, the website is referred to by Facebook groups such as "Children of Rhodes" and "Jews of Rhodes. Family pictures before 1944 – Photos de famille avant 1944."[74] Since users can leave comments, the migrant "community" has now an additional – and very strong – virtual dimension. Old and new generations of *Rodesli* descendants in the Americas, Africa, and Europe exchange greetings on religious festivities, reconstruct family trees, identify relatives in uploaded pictures, and plan get-togethers in Rhodes, especially around 20 July for the annual commemoration of the deportation. For the members of this virtual community, sharing information about *Rodesli* ancestors is more important than sharing details about themselves.

Through all these steps, the narrative of Jewish mobility from Rhodes to the United States made the idea of an original shared experience with Orthodox Rhodians almost irrelevant. The distance between Greeks and Jews is reflected in local histories and memoirs, as well as in the public sphere of today's Rhodes.[75] Moreover, judging from the material available, this sense of distance seems to be shared with descendants of Rhodian Orthodox who remained in America. The latter's associational life emerged quickly after the increase in arrivals in the 1910s. The Panrhodian Society Apollon (founded in 1927 and still existing) had twenty-four sections in both small towns such as Canonsburg and big cities like New York and Detroit between the 1920s and the 1950s. It gathered immigrants from various villages and minor islands and participated in relief initiatives directed to Rhodes, such as donations after an earthquake hit the island in 1926.[76] As in the case of *Rodesli* Jews, several layers of "community" coexisted in these associations. For Rhodian Orthodox, the *topika*, associations referring to the home village or neighbourhood church, rather than Rhodes itself, remained important. Next to them, affiliations to Greek American associations provided a viable connection with Rhodes as an alternative to classifications as Italians while attending naturalization in the United States.

Contrary to *Rodeslis* in Seattle, most Rhodian Orthodox in Canonsburg indicated "Greece" or "Rhodes Isle Greece" as country of origin in the 1940 United States census instead of the expected "Italy," which would have distinguished them from other Greek Americans.[77] In 1942, as Italy was at war with the United States, the Dodecanesian League of America published a pamphlet destined to the government in Washington entitled "The Dodecanesians are not enemy aliens," further stressing their reorientation towards the Greek American space. They also welcomed the Department of Justice's decision to exclude Dodecanesian Greeks from the discrimination measures that affected citizens of enemy states. The authors stated that Dodecanesians were "technically owing allegiance to the Italian state" but were Greek by "blood, religion, language, and tradition."[78]

Contrary to the rupture of the Holocaust for Jews, the annexation by Greece in 1948 increased the perception of Rhodes as an integral part of Greek national and territorial culture. This made it inconvenient to dig for histories of diversity and coexistence in the town's past, including for those writing from America. The first descendant of Rhodian emigrants who dedicated a scholarly work to these communities was the social anthropologist James Kiriazis. His study based on fieldwork in the 1960s explicitly aimed at showing "how much and how often the Rhodian subculture correlates with that of the total Hellenic culture," and that "Rhodians are a sub-culture of both Greek and American cultures."[79] The narrative of mobility and its aftermath, in this case, made Rhodian Orthodox into Greeks and, simultaneously, Greek Americans. Within this dominant interpretation, there was no space left for past or present encounters with Rhodians of a different background.

Is this divergence irreversible? Increased shared initiatives in Rhodes to commemorate the lost presence of the local Jews might resonate among descendants of Rhodian Orthodox abroad. In a recent blog entry written for the association "Greeks in Washington State," the already mentioned Elazar (Elliot) Behar (b. 1923) and his son David (b. 1953), stressed their contacts with Greeks before and after emigration to Seattle at school, in recreational events, and at work. Referring to David, the article stated that: "He shares his religion with any and all Jews, but his culture and traditions are in many respects closer to those of Greeks and Greek-Americans' Mediterranean culture than Jews from Lithuania or other parts of Eastern Europe."[80] The Mediterranean is invoked to bridge this divergence and situate Rhodes in a less exclusive space of Greek history. Highlighting interactions in America after the trauma of the Second World War seems to provide an alternative to the "ghosts" haunting the Mediterranean as a space of lost coexistence.[81] As both Orthodox and Jewish emigrants transformed the institutions and the boundaries of their communities overseas, this proximity has been marginalized by confession-centric narratives. The history of the contacts between Rhodian Orthodox and *Rodesli* Jews in the new world is therefore yet to be written.

Italian Mobilities to Rhodes and the Issue of Intermarriage

While Jews and Orthodox emigration to the Americas redefined the notion of community, the imperial consequence in colonial Rhodes redefined the idea of national belonging. Pivotal in this process was the inflow of Catholics to Rhodes after 1912. The Italian census of 1931 recorded 3,645 "Italian citizens" as residents of Rhodes town, a number quite close to that of Orthodox, of Muslims, and of Jews, the Aegean subjects classified according to their confession. The fascist empire had built its outpost of national settlers in the Aegean, which reinforced the colonial state's claims of legitimacy. Throughout Italian rule, confessional belonging remained the cornerstone to administer local subjects through communal institutions, and it was consistently used by the colonial bureaucracy. Yet, this difference intersected with another distinction separating "Italians" from "Dodecanesians" without full citizenship and from "foreigners."[82]

By discussing the relationship between the metropolitan and the local population, Valerie McGuire has emphasized the hybridity between "otherness" and "familiarity" in Italian citizenship policies in Rhodes. Filippo Espinoza highlighted the political dimension of these policies' selectivity, which favoured elements deemed loyal and excluded those suspected of anti-colonial sentiments.[83] This section provides a different standpoint by exploring personal trajectories of full Italian citizens. While they were overwhelmingly Catholics and most documents refer to them generically as "fellow nationals" (*connazionali*), they came from different localities. Many of them were native of the Italian peninsula (*regnicoli, cittadini metropolitani*), others were born in Ottoman Anatolia. In the latter case, most of them had already upgraded from the "little citizenship" (*piccola cittadinanza*) as former Italian protégés in the Ottoman Empire to Italian full citizenship after the First World War. They saw the colonial setting of Rhodes as a site of economic possibilities related to founding their business, obtaining appointments in the public administration, or pursuing professional careers in demand as lawyers or doctors.

Seen from the point of view of state authorities, these mobile individuals offered an advantage for the three main challenges related to managing a post-Ottoman setting: creating a body of privileged citizens as a counterweight to the preservation of "indigenous" communal structures, establishing a more direct bond between local families and fascism, and redefining the place of Rhodes in the geopolitical environment by reinforcing the town's *Italianità*. Despite this convergence of interests and a favourable citizenship status compared to most of their townsmen in Rhodes, for them too mobility meant the difficult socialization process aimed at inventing "home."

Looking back at the 1931 Italian census, the ratio among sexes shows men outnumbering women by 153 per cent among metropolitan citizens. An implication of this unbalanced demography related to marriage. The "exceeding" Italian men often married non-Catholic women who did not own the full Italian citizenship. Alexis Rappas has argued that regulating these unions across confessional and citizenship categories, although a quantitatively marginal phenomenon, represented a central concern for Italian fascist rule in Rhodes.[84] Fascist colonialism operated within an apparent contradiction: many of those who were committed to keeping the difference between Italian rulers and colonial subjects upright, notably in the ranks of the Blackshirts, often had intimate contacts outside the boundaries of the national body, at a lower level of the hierarchization implied by colonial rule. At the same time, colonial rulers were aware that intermarriage was to some degree inevitable, and even explicitly welcomed it at times.[85]

But the colonial government was not the only force concerned about intermarriage. Communal institutions considered it a threat to their cohesion. Contemporary commentators as well as later ethno-centred historiographic accounts have stigmatized mixed unions as a form of Italian political dominance over the colonized population.[86] Still, many of these unions originated from the demographic (Italian single men for local single women) and economic unbalance (Italian men socially favoured by the state for women providing local resources) that made them pragmatically convenient. Mobility and intermarriage in Rhodes conflate the same generational dynamics highlighted in the previous section: among peers, among parents and children as well as among individuals, communities, and the state. Focusing on these negotiations sharpens the picture of how resources circulated and social relationships changed around the couple. Military service, labour, and ideology will be interwoven threads of this section.

Hundreds of civil wedding records are available at the archives of the Municipality of Rhodes. Especially intermarrying couples recurred to civil certificates given that attestations issued only by one communal religious authority were not easily recognized for both spouses. This applies even more to mixed couples involving Italian citizens after the Treaty of Lausanne. Italian sovereignty implied a different jurisdiction based on "personal status" for Aegean subjects compared to the metropolitan civil law. This had direct consequences for marriage since aspects like polygamy (extremely rare) and especially divorce were not contemplated by the laws of the Kingdom as they were in Ottoman Rhodes. In some cases, if an Italian citizen married at one of the non-Catholic communal institutions, the authorities might claim that the union was not valid.[87] A civil marriage record, in most cases after a Catholic wedding ceremony, was a way to avoid jurisdictional confusion. The municipality archives do not cover all instances of intermarriage, but they allow for a quantitative insight into those involving Italian citizens:

Figure 5.2. Number of civil wedding records of intermarriage in Rhodes, 1912–40.

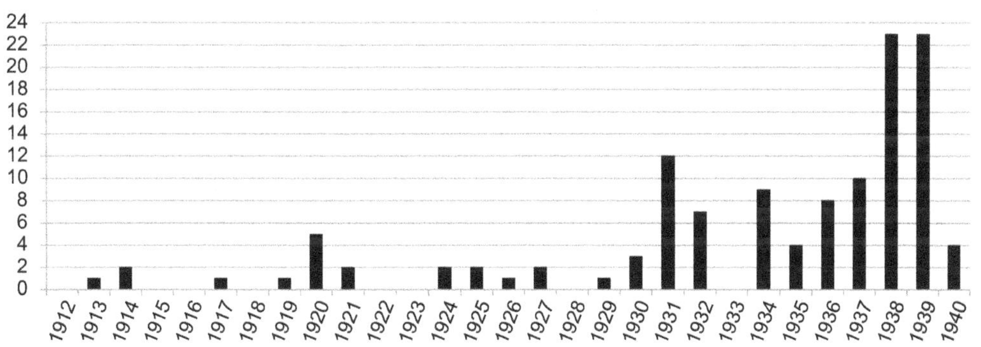

Source: DR LIX GAM, 1913–45. No data could be retrieved for 1933.

The recorded weddings reached a first peak in 1931 and increased between 1935 and the eve of the Second World War. This reflects the increasing presence of Italian soldiers paralleling the revaluation of the Dodecanese in Mediterranean geopolitics.[88] The 1938 boom is in turn linked to De Vecchi's reform which made civil attestations mandatory for all unions. In most cases, Catholic men married Orthodox and, less frequently, Jewish women:

Table 5.2. Intermarriage recorded at the town hall of Rhodes by confession, 1912–40.

Confession (Groom-Bride)	Occurrences	%
Catholic-Orthodox	109	88.6
Catholic-Jewish	7	5.7
Muslim-Orthodox	3	2.4
Catholic-Muslim	2	1.7
Orthodox-Catholic	1	0.8
Orthodox-Muslim	1	0.8
Total	123	100%

Source: These data are based on the same marriage records, integrated with evidence from the family certificates of the late 1930s, DR LIX FF. Where not specified, the following tables and figures also result from these sources.

Jewish and Orthodox predominantly male emigration from Rhodes created a demographic unbalance partly compensated by the arrivals of Italian men. Moreover, compared to data on marriage illustrated in chapter 2, men in mixed unions do not show a significant age gap compared to confessionally endogamous men, contrary to the case of women. For Italian men, therefore, marrying a local woman was not a belated option diverging from the norm. For many local women, in turn, this seems to have been a second choice after difficulties in finding a match within coreligionists.

In terms of occupations, intermarrying husbands show diverse profiles. Although many had previously served in the army, describing intermarriage uniquely as related to the presence of occupying military would be a shortfall.

Lastly, in terms of place of origin, more than two-thirds of men in mixed unions were born in Italy (70 per cent), a few in Rhodes (6 per cent) and the rest – one-fourth – in other former cities of the Ottoman Empire, especially Smyrna (18 per cent).[89] What the citizenship regime in Rhodes tended to subsume under the same category of *connazionali* was therefore a mix of settlers from the Kingdom and of post-Ottoman migration from Anatolia to Rhodes. Even if full Italian citizenship,

Table 5.3. Age characteristics of mixed marriages in Rhodes.

Groom			Bride			Couple
Average	Range	Average gap vs endogamous marriages	Average	Range	Average gap vs endogamous marriages	Average gap (G-B)
30.3	21–54	+0.4	23.8	15–41	+2.1	6.4

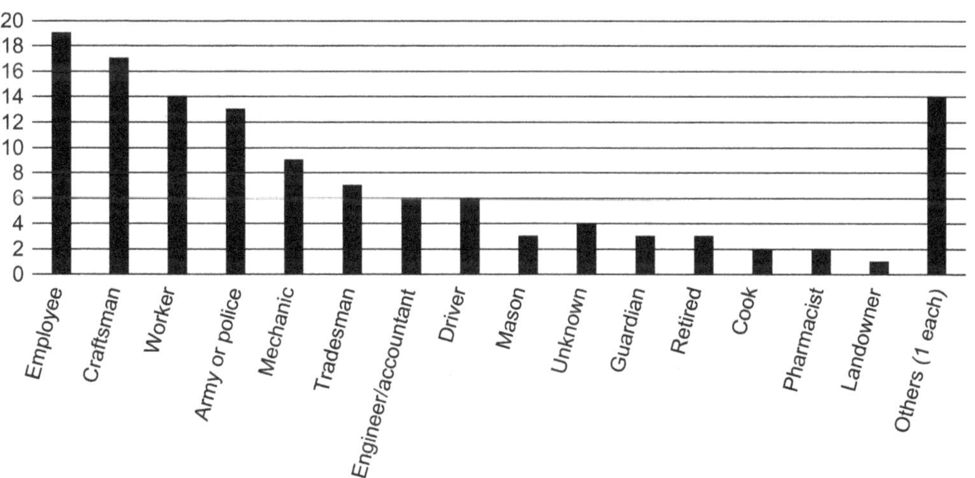
Figure 5.3. Intermarrying grooms' occupations.

intermarriage, and affiliation to fascism were strong markers of convergence between them, it is worth analysing the "metropolitan" and the "Anatolian" immigration separately. They resulted from different motives and often implied different material conditions.

From Soldiers to Settlers

Among the troops stationing in Rhodes between May 1912 and the end of the First World War, many soldiers were single and aged around 20. The end of military service often resulted in the decision to stay in Rhodes and marry local women.[90] In 1913 and 1914 respectively, the sisters Eleni (aged 19) and Anna Caravokyro (21) married an Italian general and a port official (*ufficiale di porto*).[91] Yet, after the First World War, Italians were increasingly civilians at the time of their wedding.

Carlo Gatti arrived in Rhodes just after the end of the war to work as a mechanic and trader. Rosario Rao (brother of Vincenzo, the early fascist leader whom we met in chapter 1), was later employed at the Mail and Telegraphs bureau and had a similar trajectory. On the same day in 1920, they married the Orthodox sisters Crisostomidis.[92] Gatti and Rao were members of the Fascist Party already before the March on Rome and were later awarded the honorific title of *Cavaliere della Corona d'Italia*. The social distinction as Italian citizens favoured a convergence of interest with local resources provided by local women. Arriving in the *Possedimento* as "propertyless" (*nullatenente*), Rao received a house as dowry, which the police mentioned as his main property when they profiled him as being "of good economic condition."[93]

Even though civilian settlers increasingly arrived in Rhodes, many did not come to stay. Marcantonio P., born in Ravenna in 1894, remained in Rhodes after his military service and married the Orthodox Vittoria F. in 1920. During the first years of marriage, Marcantonio allegedly maintained his wife's family. Employed as a civil servant, he was transferred to Libya in 1924, when the couple already had two children. From Tripoli, he sent letters to Vittoria claiming his will to return to Rhodes, and he kept sending money to her family. However, in 1927, he was again relocated to Sondrio, in northern Italy. After hesitating for a couple of months, Vittoria joined her husband in Italy with her mother, only to come back to Rhodes a few weeks later. Vittoria started to reclaim an alimony from Marcantonio while working to finance their daughter's schooling. After a while, she obtained the authorities' attention. The colonial government eventually supported her in name of "the fully Italian education that she provided for her daughter" and sanctioned her husband who "did not show any care."[94]

This story offers several elements to unpack in terms of generational dynamics, both between spouses and between parents and children. For the Italian authorities, the wish to see this "fully Italian education" flourish in Rhodes coexisted with the concern about the management of resources within the couple. The authorities were not keen on giving governmental handouts to help fragile and mobile unions. These were considered at the margins of the "prescribed sexuality" which was accentuated as a marker of colonial and racial separation among the population, albeit to much different extents compared to colonial settings in Africa.[95] As the police noted in 1935:

Unfortunately, many fellow nationals (*connazionali*) have married Orthodox women born in these islands that did not want to follow them in Italy or, after a while, returned here preferring to live, with their children, in misery and privation, often addressing the ruling authorities, rather than remaining in Italy with the head of their family.[96]

Women often did not accept this victim status as abandoned spouses. Vittoria P. insisted on receiving the alimony as a conjugal right. She went back to Italy in 1934 and discovered that her husband was living with another woman. With his own interpretation of the plural legal marriage laws at work in colonial Rhodes, Marcantonio tried to claim that his marriage with Vittoria was not valid, and he refused to give any financial support to his wife. At first, the authorities did not allow Vittoria to return to Rhodes since they feared that she would depend on the state budget as a destitute single parent, but she eventually obtained the permission.[97] Soon afterwards, her daughter married an Italian soldier before turning 20, thus replicating Vittoria's marriage. This man provided for the whole family, and Marcantonio himself later accepted to send a monthly alimony from Italy, where he had settled.[98] Non-Catholic women in mixed marriages, like Vittoria, were particularly affected by the precariousness of social bonds. The authorities intervened only when these women demanded that their rights be respected. Such material support can be understood as a transaction with the state. Some women voluntarily became vectors of *Italianità* through the education they chose for their children. From their perspective, this active commitment entitled them to face the authorities and claim their rights as members of the national body. Even if the authorities remained suspicious of these women, supporting them was a way to avoid scandals when children of Italian men were involved.

An even more complex relationship evolved between the full citizen Antonio T., born in Zara in 1907 (or 1903 according to some documents) and Catina G., born in Istanbul in 1903. Antonio returned to Rhodes shortly after spending his military service there and married Catina in 1930.[99] Back in 1922, Catina had married a man in Istanbul with the Protestant rite, and it was unclear whether she had completed the divorce procedure at the time of her second wedding. Antonio temporarily worked as a plumber before moving to other Dodecanese islands (Kos and Karpathos), where he had found an employment in public works. Antonio and Catina's marriage deteriorated quickly. Some sources relate this to his "character" and her "not quite innocent moral conduct," while others more explicitly mention that he exploited his wife pushing her towards sex work.[100] As argued in chapter 4, a woman's "lack of morality" often implied sex work, while the vocabulary applied to men related to their "idleness." In 1933, the police described Antonio as running "an unruly life," "neglecting his duties, contracting "several debts," loving "vice," "roaming around in town" at night and having concubinage-like relationship with other women."[101] The couple was eventually considered as *de facto* separated. Seizing the opportunity to visit her ill mother in Athens, Catina never came back to live with her husband. Antonio, in turn, moved to his birthplace Zara in 1934. There, a relative informed him that his wife had died in a car accident shortly after their separation.[102]

In most cases of intermarriage, the bride converted to Catholicism or, at least, the wedding was celebrated with the Catholic rite. One remarkable exception is the marriage between a Jewish woman, Eleonora Avzaradel, and Quirino Di Liscia, born a Catholic in 1900 near Isernia, in southern Italy. In 1922, after his military service in Rhodes, Quirino married Eleonora with the Jewish rite after being circumcised and changing his name to Davide. In 1930, however, he reconverted to Catholicism together with Eleonora, and they baptized their three children. Conjugal conflicts marred this mixed marriage. After Di Liscia obtained a managerial position in an agricultural colony on the island of Leros in 1935, his wife demanded a written guarantee by his employer that a part of her husband's salary be reserved for her as alimony, which apparently never materialized.[103] While in Leros, Di Liscia even made a marriage proposal to a local Orthodox woman and, as the police noted, "he did not succeed in realizing his marriage purpose due to the intervention of this Commando, informed by the local Jewish community."[104]

When Quirino and his wife eventually decided to reunite in Leros, the Racial Laws against Jews had already been promulgated. With the recognition of her wedding by state authorities still pending, Eleonora was considered a colonial subject and not an Italian citizen. She was therefore exposed to the "confluence of racist colonial legislation and anti-Jewish legislation" that historians have discussed for the Italian empire after 1938.[105] In February 1940, Quirino and Eleonora eventually celebrated their wedding with the Catholic rite, which granted a swift recognition by the civil authorities and her upgrade to full citizenship. In sources produced during the Second World War, however, she could still be ambiguously labelled as "Catholic Jew" (*ebrea cattolica*), bearing the mark of racial stigmatization. Di Liscia's daughter Carmela, born in 1922 and baptized in 1930, was in turn always officially considered as "Italian citizen, Catholic" and "of Arian race," and even applied for entering the women section of the Fascist Party.[106] In 1943, just before the arrival of German troops and one year before the deportation of Rhodian Jews, Eleonora's husband reenroled in the army and served in Leros, while her citizenship allowed her to leave Rhodes for Italy with her two children at the colonial government's expenses. In the last reports on Eleonora, there are no mentions of her being a convert, just like Zimbul Mizrahi *alias* Maria Cacopardi, a case discussed in chapter 2. Although Eleonora eventually did not leave due to sudden illness, she was not affected by the deportation.[107] In 1949, Eleonora and her children arrived in New York on a ship from Naples and they settled in America. Her brother Baruch, who had remained with her in Rhodes during the war, was deported and murdered in 1944.[108]

This example shows how intermarriage socialization prompted negotiations aimed at determining the boundaries of national belonging in a colonial setting. This process involved the family, communal institutions, and the Italian authorities, three forces who could cooperate in raising and handling legal claims. Yet, the colonial state was the only force determining the rules of the game, tied only to the implications of the personal status applying to Aegean subjects. The framework of the Lausanne Treaty remained the ground upon which Italian sovereignty rested and addressed individual cases. In this game, community, citizenship, and race interplayed while evolving through time. The persecution of the Rhodian Jews after 1938 shows the extreme consequences of such interplay. Whether or not a woman solicited her community to pressure the Italian authorities to eventually recognize a marriage union could be decisive in being considered sufficiently part of the Italian national collective. With the privileged "full" Italian passport and a "half" concealed racial stigma as a Jew that this recognition provided, the validity of a marriage certificate could eventually save this woman's life and make it the only survivor of her family.

The Margins or the Spearhead of *Italianità*? Smyrniotes in Rhodes

For colonial authorities of the late 1930s, racial discrimination was an additional layer that intersected with a bureaucracy based on confessional categories and on the separation between full citizens and Aegean subjects. These distinctions did not only discriminate those at the lower levels of the ladder. They also favoured Italian citizens who invoked a privileged position in their new environment. This appropriation of colonial difference from below contributed to defining the meaning of "Italian" in a colonial setting. The notion of *Italianità*, however, concealed differences in terms of material conditions. Those arriving from the Kingdom of Italy still counted on family bonds and resources there, which could be crucial especially in critical moments such as the Second World War. On the contrary, many newcomers from former Ottoman towns left everything behind and had to socialize from scratch in Rhodes.

A previously occasional mobility between Smyrna and Rhodes increased significantly after the Great Fire of 1922, which led to the displacement of thousands among the city's non-Muslims residents. Among those who relocated from Asia Minor to Rhodes, dozens of

Catholic families had been Italian protégés, a collectivity outside Otto-man *millet* categories identified by historians and descendants associa-tions as "Levantines."[109] After 1922, they were exposed to the loss of capital, networks, and career possibilities caused by the nationalization of Turkish society. The inflow of these migrants continued until the late 1920s and, occasionally, even a few years later. Francesco B. (b. 1899) came to Rhodes in 1922, leaving Smyrna as a "refugee" after killing two Greek soldiers in a brawl.[110] In Rhodes, he worked as a butcher until 1926, when he was drafted in the Italian army. While on service, he was unable to renew his work license and he returned to civil life without a job. At that moment, mobility again became the only survival strategy available, as Francesco recalled in a letter to Governor Lago:

> I ended up working as a daily labourer and then I left for Greece after the job was over. The jobs were meager there, so I returned to Smyrna, again with the aim of struggling for survival. The Turks, however, with Turkish manners (*alla turca*) forced me to leave because that was their policy toward foreigners. So, I went back to Greece but, for the same policy [there] as the Turks had, I was forced to return to Rhodes where, at least, I could be cer-tain to be under the protection of Our Glorious Banner's scepter.

Francesco then asked his former captain to intercede with the *Podestà* (a non-elected mayor in Fascist Italy) of Rhodes in order to obtain the concession for running a storehouse at the town market, to no avail.[111] The "Glorious Banner" he mentioned in his letter was a magniloquent way to address the fatherland. This idealized and impersonal expres-sion also corresponds to an evident lack of support during his mobility. Francesco used the term "return" for Smyrna, Greece, and Rhodes: this difficult search for home reveals his precarious social integration since he, like many newcomers in Rhodes, had no one to support him, and probably no clear destination in mind. Francesco also complained that a local Orthodox man owned the storehouse that he aimed to obtain in Rhodes, calling for Italian rulers to intervene and favour a metropolitan citizen over a colonial subject.

For individuals like him, Rhodes was a colonial setting whose rul-ers were in need of human resources to legitimize their presence in the Aegean territory. This allowed for another transaction between Italian citizens and the state. These Catholic families knew that protection by the "Glorious Banner" was not granted. A factor that enabled it was entering the orbit of fascism.

Figure 5.4 shows a branch of the Bogdanich family, all born in Smyrna, shortly after their arrival in Rhodes: Giuseppe (b. 1899) and his

Figure 5.4. The Bogdanich family around 1935. Giuseppe Bogdanich's (b. 1951) private collection. I thank the owner for allowing me to use this image and, together with his uncle Nicholas, for providing information on this family.

wife Caterina Carakulaki (1904) in the background with their children Pietro (1924) and Antonio (1926) in the middle and the younger Nicholas (1932) and Maria (1928) in the foreground. An ancestor brought the family from Dalmatia to Smyrna, while the demise of the Ottoman Empire and the nationalization of Turkey's economy had brought them to the colonial setting of Rhodes. Shortly after their arrival, the youngest generation of the family was socialized into fascist childhood organizations. From Habsburg subjects to foreigners in the Ottoman Empire and Turkey, the family now found themselves as Italian nationals in Rhodes. The family's portrait puts children in a clearly central position, as if they were heralding the future. The boys' fascist uniform and salute (remarkably, not performed by their father) suggest that fascism appeared as their political horizon in the years to come. According to Lago's vision of a "new generation" of "good fascists," children like them were to take over a leading role among their "indigenous" peers in the making of a future model fascist colony.

Yet, this vision contrasted with precarious material conditions. Another member of the Bogdanich family, Antonio, married the Orthodox Cleanti V. Given their lack of resources, especially during Antonio's service in the army, Cleanti relied on a governmental handout for survival.[112] Another Smyrniote, Giovanni D. (b. 1885), moved to Rhodes in 1925, where he made a living as a carpenter.[113] In the 1930s, his son Antonio (b. 1913) moved to the village of Malona and requested a license to open a grocery store. For this activity, he leaned on the capital provided by Crisafina C., a widow from the village, almost 30 years older than him, with whom he "lived together conjugally" (*maritalmente*).[114] This union, however, was never sealed by a wedding and, in 1939, Antonio married another woman from Malona, who provided him with a dowry consisting of "a vineyard, a garden and a building area for a total value of approximately 4,000 lire."[115] Soon afterwards, Antonio was called to service as a member of the local Blackshirt legion *Conte Verde*. As a Blackshirt of the fascist militia, he assisted the Italian army, while his store was closed since his wife was pregnant. The woman asked for a monthly governmental handout, which she obtained until Antonio's return from the service.[116]

Antonio's brother Carmine (b. 1912) had a similar trajectory, although his profile was strikingly different. Already in 1935, the police described him as an alcoholic who mingled "with the wrong crowd," was not "keen on working" and neglected his parents.[117] Carmine joined the Fascist Party in 1931 and served in the army in 1933–4. Although he adhered to the ruling political order, Carmine continued to cause trouble: he provoked injuries, stole objects from the local *Casa del Fascio*, and was sanctioned for other petty infractions such as pouring water in the wine reserved for the troops he commanded as a corporal. Working as a carpenter like his father, he was said to be surrounded by "persons of good Italian sentiments, but not always of good morality," a profile which applied to him as well.[118] Carmine married an Orthodox woman, Thalia I., registered by the police as "native of the Dodecanese" (*oriunda del possedimento*). During her husband's service in the MVSN's Blackshirts until 1942, Thalia received a military handout of 420 lire per month, despite her husband's recurring problems with the law.[119]

The precariousness of social bonds pushed many Smyrniotes who arrived in Rhodes as kids (whom scholars of migration studies would refer to as "1.5" generation) and those born in Rhodes to join Fascist institutions in their youth.[120] As members of the party, they represented the quintessence of *Italianità* in Rhodes. Their service in the MVSN offered, in most cases, an indemnity which could well be more profitable than unstable jobs. Especially in the second half of the 1930s, the increased militarization of the colony urged the support of these armed forces formed within the Fascist Party.[121] But material resources and a uniform's authority did not compensate weak socialization bonds in Rhodes, which led many to mingle with other marginalized individuals, such as poor Orthodox women from villages around Rhodes. Nor did entering Fascist structures correspond to being considered to have a "good reputation" or be granted access to professionalization with better prospects of income. The authorities needed these individuals to keep the colonial order upright, neutralize signs of dissent among the local population, and reinforce the military. Moralizing the Blackshirts or improving their socio-economic status was far from being the priority.

In some cases, intermarriage with local women could cause political concerns. Roberto D. was born in Foggia in 1912, although his parents came from Smyrna, where they moved back right after his birth.[122] When his parents left for Rhodes in 1930, he stayed in Anatolia and joined them only two years later. Soon afterwards, he entered the fascist youth organization *Fasci Giovanili di Combattimento*, although he was excluded from it in 1935 for "scarce understanding of the … duties and recurring absenteeism."[123] Roberto's family bonds weakened significantly in those years. His mother left his father in 1936 and went to live together with an Orthodox man from a nearby village, while one of his brothers was sent to a psychiatric hospital in Italy in 1939.[124] Moreover, in 1938, Roberto married a local Orthodox woman, the tailor Elena R., whom the police had previously described as of "easy virtue," having "no problems in making love with Orthodox youngsters." She was also stigmatized for resisting her family's pressure to marry Roberto "since he is a Catholic."[125]

Elena's aversion to Catholicism eventually yielded as she converted right before marrying Roberto. This marriage was but the continuation of trouble under one roof. When Italy entered the war in June 1940, Roberto was called back to serve as a Blackshirt. In a letter dated May 1941, he addressed the *Carabinieri* complaining that his wife cheated on him with an Orthodox man, that the whole neighbourhood knew about it, and that Elena's mother encouraged her to continue this extra-conjugal relationship: "I won't even mention – Roberto wrote – all the things [Elena] says against Italy since she is in love with this Greek. If I catch her one day, I do not claim I would kill both … but I am a man and I am not accountable for my deeds in such moments … Therefore, since I am in the army, since the fatherland needs me now and I cannot surveil my wife … I kindly ask this Commando to help me in my pitiful situation by surveilling my wife and catching her in the act."[126]

With a remarkable foresight of later events, Elena boasted about the arrival of British troops in Rhodes in order to humiliate her husband and the occupying power Italy at once. At this point, the Italian police intervened. They warned Elena never again to meet her lover, whom they pushed to move to another neighbourhood. This crisis, however, did not result in a divorce and, at least until 1943, Elena could still receive an alimony provided by the authorities and the company that employed Roberto.[127] His request for intervention confirms that the authorities' growing interference in family issues not only occurred from above, but was also appropriated and invoked from below by migrants to compensate their weak social bonds. In light of the unbalanced ratio between sexes among Italian citizens in Rhodes, it was primarily the "honour" of men which converged with the "honour" of the Italian nation and its imperial legitimacy. However, intermarriage implied increased pressure and surveillance on these citizens' wives. Marginalized by their family and/or their community, they were often stigmatized as a threat to this masculine-cum-national "honour."

As table 5.4 shows, only one-fourth of women who intermarried were born in Rhodes town, and less than half of them on the island. The situation was thus more nuanced than the one described in the 1931 *Rodiaki* article warning about the danger of "virgins" of Rhodes marrying men of other confessions. Many of these women came from smaller islands from which their fathers and brothers had emigrated. They were thus also mobile: they mingled with and possibly married Catholic men after leaving their village to seek economic survival. Marginalized in Rhodes, a marriage outside the community became both a resource and

Table 5.4. Percentage of intermarrying brides according to birthplace.

Birthplace	%
Rhodes town	24
Rhodes (villages)	21
Aegean islands	34
Smyrna	3
Anatolia (others)	13
Egypt	2
Others	3

a necessity. Voluntary initiatives to convert to Catholicism and foster a fascist Italian education on their children coexisted with cases of resilience or overt criticism of the colonial rulers, which conflated family and political issues.

Material conditions were often determinant in terms of marriage possibilities for migrants. This is confirmed by a case from the opposite end of the social ladder, the trajectory of the Aliottis, a wealthy Catholic family from Smyrna. Already in Ottoman years, this family had developed intense contacts with the Italian Peninsula through their business and their consular service. They belonged to the elite of the Anatolian port city, although they had lost a part of their property through the Ottoman authorities' requisitions used as reprisal against Italian enemy citizens in 1911.[128] Their trajectory is quite remarkable, since they managed to keep the family business upright after moving to Rhodes. In 1935, Enrico and Giuseppe Aliotti founded the SAIFE company (*Società Anonima Italiana Fruttindustria Egea*), which almost monopolized the dried fruits trade, one of Rhodes main export produce.[129] Enrico invited his nephew Febo (b. 1908), who was still in Smyrna, to join the company in Rhodes, where he took up a managerial role. Contrary to many lower class Smyrniotes in Rhodes, Febo joined the Fascist Party even before moving to Rhodes, in 1928. In 1937, he married Adriana Corsini, the descendant of another wealthy Smyrniote family, of which a branch remained in Turkey.[130] A privileged economic status coupled with a favourable position vis-à-vis the authorities made mobility to Rhodes a scenario in which their earlier social relationships could be recreated. This included a marriage not only within the national-confessional boundaries, but with a family of the same geographic origin. Marrying a Smyrniote woman and not being affected by significant loss of capital was a pattern out of reach for most individuals discussed in this section.

However fragile, the Smyrniotes' social environment was not confined to the family. Educational, occupational, political, and religious institutions were sites where they had everyday interactions with *regnicoli*. Non-Catholic colonial subjects attended these sites too but, contrary to them, Italian citizens from Anatolia stood on equal footing with metropolitan subjects in the symbolic and bureaucratic hierarchization within *Italianità* in Rhodes. In the rosters of the *Regio Istituto* from the late 1930s, one would find descendants of the Aliotti, Scagliarini, and Ventura families from Smyrna sitting daily next to children of Italians from the Kingdom.[131] The same could be said for a list of *Balilla* from 1937 and for the football club of the fascist youth organization *Gioventù Italiana del Littoro* (GIL) in 1939.[132] On the eve of the Second World War, while some of the locals voiced ominous predictions about the end of Italian rule, the synthesis of a national body in Rhodes brought these migrants of diverse background closer to each other. The "Glorious Banner" referred to by one of them in the 1920s seemed no longer a substitute for personal bonds. These settlers' children were now socialized within structures spanning from childhood to youth to adult militancy in the Fascist Party.

One of the most striking and symbolic performances of patriotism for the empire was the campaign "Gold to the Fatherland" (*Oro alla Patria*) in 1935. *Regnicoli* and Smyrniotes were the bulk of the 1,004 participants who sacrificed golden items such as wedding rings, necklaces, coins, and pins to finance Italy's aggression against Ethiopia.[133] A woman from Smyrna donated one golden "Turkish" (or, rather, Ottoman?) lira. Quite symbolically, she offered a precious keepsake of the world she had left behind to certify her belonging and devotion to the Italian "fatherland" precisely when Mussolini's promise of a grandiose empire seemed to concretize. Most migrants from Asia Minor could not afford to keep golden coins as keepsakes. Still, fascist colonialism promised them to be part of the nation in a post-Ottoman setting that they saw as more familiar than the Italian peninsula. Some of those who donated gold to the "fatherland" without ever setting foot in Italy might have believed in this synthesis of national belonging and imperial expansion. Others might have seen this gold as a necessary transaction with the state, a patron upon whose fate their own precarious livelihood hang together with the future of their children.

***

Reflecting the imperial consequence from Ottoman to Italian rule, mobility from and to Rhodes shaped the notions of family, community, and nation. Emigration overseas and immigration from Italy and from Asia Minor belong together in this regard. They illustrate how the history of an Ottoman province and the history of an Italian colonial possession display connections that reach beyond the respective state polities. Seen from the deck of a steamship leaving or arriving at the city's harbour, the history of early twentieth-century Rhodes can be at once global, transatlantic, imperial, Mediterranean, and translocal. The migrants embodied this connectivity through their trajectories and the narratives they elaborated. Just as Orthodox and Jewish emigrants faced the challenge of handling their kinship bonds across the Atlantic and the Mediterranean, Catholic immigrants from Italy handled the link between the *Possedimento* and the Peninsula. The chapter started from separate confessional categories, but it moved towards discussing shared issues like economic survival, the importance of good moral and political reputation, and the relationship with the authorities.

Especially when considered from the angle of generational dynamics, mobility appears a mosaic of multiple, changing expectations. For the daughter of a *Rodesli* couple who had just been naturalized in the United States in the 1920s, the social environment referred to as "community" could consist of interactions with Sephardic and Ashkenazi elements unknown to her parents. For the son of a Catholic Italian from Asia Minor coming of age in Rhodes in the late 1930s, belonging to the "nation" meant supporting a more aggressive and militarist state compared to the one that had just obtained sovereignty on the island when his father had arrived. Especially in this second case, the discussion on the role of fascism has expanded to active participation in the party's organizations and militias. Italian migrants were on the front row in bringing fascism to the colonies. Even more in the event of intermarriage, upbringing their children in the name of *Italianità* meant to consolidate the government's effort to create the "new generation" of "good fascists."

And yet, only a few years later, these efforts to territorialize Rhodes as a fascist colony would result, for metropolitan citizens and Aegean subjects alike, in displacement. In Ottoman times, the Aegean had already been a site where violence and warfare created waves of expulsions. This ranged from the Muslim refugees fleeing from Crete at the turn of the twentieth century, to the Italian nationals expelled from the Ottoman Empire in 1911, up to the climax of genocidal violence against the Armenian and Orthodox population of Anatolia during the First World War. The socialization of Smyrniotes as settlers embodying the *Italianità* of Rhodes is a further example of this broader history. It confirms how families who had left an empire as unwanted communities could be instrumentalized by another empire to redefine notions of belonging. This reminds us that, although the fascist colonial empire relied on pre-existing politics of difference, the elements and the criteria of this difference could change dramatically.

The process of nationalization in a fascist colonial setting coincided with an acceleration of exclusion based on racial principles. The Italian authorities in Rhodes eventually aligned with the persecution policies emanating from Rome, leading hundreds of Jewish families who had not emigrated before 1938 to seek refuge among their relatives abroad. Those who did not succeed were exposed to the most violent form of displacement of the twentieth century, the deportation to Auschwitz. The construction of a national body in Rhodes largely based on the inclusion of Catholics, formerly residents of the Ottoman Empire, was thus followed by the destruction of the racial enemy based on the exclusion of Jews, formerly a community of Ottoman citizens.

Italy's defeat in the Second World War also meant that precisely those mobile families who had been targeted as champions of *Italianità* came under pressure when the annexation of Rhodes by the Greek state became a reality. Their children had to quickly hide or get rid of their *Balilla* uniform and leave with their relatives to Italy or to other countries. The hardship of the war also led to an increase in the departures of Muslim Aegean subjects towards Turkey. Already in 1942, the Italian police listed 87 families who had migrated there in the previous years, and many more followed, often departing illegally, in the latest and hardest months of the conflict.[134] Once in Anatolia, these Muslims had to enter a new transaction with the Turkish state. This worked at best by concealing the traces of their socialization as colonial subjects that they had experienced in Italian Rhodes and by embracing a new national identification. Insofar, this transaction did not differ much from the highly symbolic participation of Catholic Smyrniotes in the fascist *Oro alla Patria* ceremony.

These experiences of displacement had different motives and, above all, they show significantly different degrees of violence. What they all shared, however, was the fact that mobility unmade imperial categories of belonging and difference just as much as it had consolidated them. For youth of all confessions, then, the Second World War and the end of fascist colonialism would represent a rapid change in socialization compared to those of their parents. The "new generation" envisioned by fascist imperialism would prove its impossibility by bursting into dispersed trajectories and experiences of youth, as Rhodes turned from an Italian colony into a provincial town of the Greek nation-state.

Imperial Coda

Pasquale Cacopardi, son of Antonino and Maria (Zimbul) Cacopardi, whom we met in chapter 2, was only 6 years old when the Second World War broke out. Like many children of Italian metropolitan citizens, he was a member of the fascist childhood organization *Figli della Lupa*. Although fascism in the *Possedimento* had renounced the idea of subverting the colonial separation that excluded the "indigenous" adults from its party structures, it continued to mobilize and discipline youth well into the war years. In January 1943, Pasquale's cohort was promoted to the elder *Balilla* section and, in June, he passed the exams to enter secondary school. Pasquale remembers the tense atmosphere of those summer weeks, with streetlights kept off at night due to the fear of airstrikes by the Allies. When the siren rang, everyone ran to the shelters. In dark and humid underground rooms, a gramophone often entertained the youngsters, who danced to kill boredom and fear.

Socialized in a fascist colonial setting as a child, Pasquale would spend his youth under quite different circumstances. On 1 July 1943, with his mother and his two little sisters, he left Rhodes, never to settle there again. After a stop in Axis-occupied Athens, another plane brought them to Brindisi, where they met up with Pasquale's father Antonino, who was already in Italy. The Cacopardis eventually arrived in Sicily, Antonino's home region, just a few days after the American troops had landed in Gela and started the liberation of southern Italy. Not even one month after Pasquale had arrived in Italy, on 25 July Mussolini was forced to resign through an agreement between King Vittorio Emanuele and high-ranked Fascist Party officials. The regime yielded political and military power to General Pietro Badoglio. A few weeks before the new schoolyear started, on 8 September, Italy had proclaimed the Armistice of Cassibile with the Allies. This shift led to Nazi German reprisals and the occupation of the Italian territory not yet liberated by the Allied troops, who were advancing from the south. The Nazi takeover in Italy also allowed for Mussolini's resurgence as the head of the Fascist "Republic of Salò," causing nineteen months of civil war between partisan resistance and Nazi-fascist counterinsurgency until April 1945. In liberated Sicily, Pasquale went to school, easily met new friends, learned Sicilian but lost command of his Greek, which he used to speak with his housemaid in Rhodes. The beauty of the island's nature, not so different from his birthplace, did not make up for material scarcity. Like thousands of Sicilians, Pasquale eventually emigrated to northern Italy in 1960, at 27 years of age. After the war, his mother frequently wrote to her relatives in America asking for material aid, so crucial in those years. She was heartbroken as she read about the horrors of the Holocaust, and how Nazi Germany, through the help of its fascist Italian allies, had murdered so many of her friends from Rhodes.[1]

Meanwhile, Rosa Hanan and Giuseppe Mallel married in Rhodes in 1947. A Jewish Auschwitz survivor, Rosa had first planned to move to Africa to meet her brothers who had emigrated before the persecutions. But another twist of fate brought her back to her island when she decided to marry Giuseppe, whom she had met in Milan during his convalescence. He was also among the few Rhodian who survived Auschwitz, where his first wife Rebecca had been murdered. In the autumn of 1945, Giuseppe and Rosa returned to Rhodes via Egypt together with a group of *Rodeslis* from the Belgian Congo to rebuild the business that Giuseppe had abandoned in 1944. The former president of the Jewish Community Hizkia Franco, writing for the *Boz de Türkiye*, a Ladino periodical printed in Istanbul, described Rosa and Giuseppe's wedding hosted at Moise Soriano's mansion and attended by the freshly appointed consul of Turkey, Tahsin Bey.[2]

Rhodian Jews of different age appear in figure 6.1 at the wedding reception. Some of them are smiling, maybe since the festive event raised hopes for a merry future on the island. Franco wished to the "unfortunate (*desdichados*) youth" a "perfect happiness capable of erasing the sad remembrance of the past suffering from [their] memory."[3] After the birth of their first son Nissim, the couple eventually left Rhodes but, unlike most survivors, they resettled in Italy.

In a retrospective oral testimony, Rosa stressed her strong feeling of belonging to the Italian national body. Still, she bitterly added that "when it suits (*quando conviene*), we are Jews. When it doesn't, we are not good Italians." These words point to ambivalent identifications during and after the persecutions experienced in the last phase of Italian rule, which partially preserved the dilemma between integration and separation inherent to fascist colonialism. Giuseppe, in turn, recalled "a

Figure 6.1.   Rosa Hanan and Giuseppe Mallel's wedding, 1947. Rosa and Giuseppe stand in the third row right behind the two girls. Courtesy of CDEC Visual Archive, no. 240–022.

memory at every step" as he walked in post-war Rhodes, an unbearable emotional setting described by another Jewish returnee survivor as "just a giant cemetery."[4] Writing before the couple left Rhodes, Hizkia Franco characterized as "youth" a woman aged 29 and a man aged 37. Rather than an age marker, Franco used this term to emphasize his hope that the community, like youth itself, would blossom in the future. He saw this new family as vital for the persistence of the Jewish Community over which he had presided until a few years before the Holocaust destroyed it. Alas, Giuseppe and Rosa's decision to move to Italy confirmed that the Second World War had dealt a fatal blow to this community. Only in 1957 did the Greek state revive it as an official institution, although most of its new members, less than forty between 1966 and 1983, were resettled there from mainland Greece and Egypt, often without any connection to Rhodes.[5]

In 1947, the same year of Giuseppe and Rosa's wedding, the Turkish consul in Rhodes reported to his foreign minister on the condition of his "ethnic kin" (*soydaşlar*) at the end of the British Military Administration, which had taken over local rule after the Italo-German defeat two years earlier. He complained about the "far from unusual occurrence of Turkish girls marrying Italians," resulting from the high degree of "acclimation" (*munasevet, ülfet*) with the "occupier enemy of Turkey." This problem went hand in hand with schooling. The end of the war had caused the degradation of educational institutions ran by the Muslim community, now limited to elementary schools. The consul added that the British had reopened ten schools but the transition towards Greek rule would leave the future uncertain. The main problem was the lack of trained teachers, while only "five or six [Turksih] girls" in the whole Dodecanese were graduating from the Italian secondary schools. This contrasted with the Turkish Republic's efforts to foster female education. In the consul's view, dropouts weakened the Turkish women's "national feelings." They stayed aloof from "communal life" and "intellectual occupations" and were mainly busy with "gossip" (*dedikodu*), while many Turkish men were busy "drinking."

The consul then forwarded some recommendations to improve the situation, which pointed to different forms of demographic engineering. Whereas Rhodian Muslims' visits to Turkey for health, study, and professional reasons were encouraged, permanent settlement and acquisition of Turkish citizenship were to be "obstructed by all means." The first request on the list, however, was to send teachers from Turkey "in order to guarantee the education of children, who are the hope of the future." With this formula, the consul reiterated the trope binding youth (and childhood), education, morality, and mobility. Recovering this generation in post-Italian Rhodes was the last glimmer of hope for "Turkishness" (*Türklük*). The Turkish element had stepped into "decline and had quickly slipped away" vis-à-vis the "Orthodox' (*Rumlar*)" capacity to develop despite "all Italian oppression and fascism's violence."[6] At the time the consul wrote his report, the number of Muslim in Rhodes had indeed significantly shrunk, since many had emigrated to Anatolia before and during the war. In May 1945, as the war was officially still ongoing, the Minister of Health and Welfare Sadi Konuk writing on behalf of the Public Office for Resettlement (*İskan Umum Müdürlüğü*) informed the other ministers about the "race-kin refugees of Italian nationality" (*italyan uyruklu mülteci ırkdaşlarımız*) who were stranded around the Anatolian town of Muğla. They were unable to pursue their valuable professions as electricians or drivers and therefore ought to be transferred to urban settings like Aydın or Smyrna in order to have better prospects without depending on the state's financial aid.[7] Rhodian Muslims were thus part of a much larger process in which Turkey redefined its own post-Ottoman national belonging through resettlement practices targeting Muslim communities, especially from Southeast Europe.[8]

Turkish diplomacy did not elaborate efficient strategies for territorial claims in the post-Italian Dodecanese.[9] The consul in Rhodes was also aware that the end of Italian rule and, implicitly, the catastrophe which had erased the Jewish community, had reshuffled power relations in town. Not anymore negotiable with colonial governors who built their legitimacy on confessional communities, the status of local young Muslims had turned into a minority at risk of being marginalized by the Greek nation-state. Yet in this case, the imperial consequence had some echoes after 1945. As a special status resulting from the Lausanne Treaty which also implied reciprocity of minority politics in Greece and Turkey, the Muslim Community created by the Italians remained in place in Rhodes until the mid-1980s. Mufti Kaşlıoğlu was recognized as its official leader but, after his death in 1974, the office remained vacant and replaced by imams from Western Thrace. The question of schools for the community is still occasionally addressed by Rhodian Muslims, although their number has further shrunk as many of them left for Turkey in the 1970s at the peak of the Cyprus crisis.[10]

The tidal change in the balance of power highlighted by the Turkish consul in the aftermath of the Second World War anticipated the administrative takeover by Greek state authorities, which annexed the Dodecanese and ended British military occupation on 7 March 1948. Three years earlier, only a few months after the end of the Second World War, the sport club *Dorieas* announced its reopening on the new local newspaper *Chronos*.

The president Gavriil Misios, whom we had met in chapter 4, invited all former members to the opening ceremony and stressed that the club's scope was "the gathering and the edification of the suffering youth." Its program consisted in "the fraternization of all classes, before which the corrupt rule (*faulokratia*) withdrew, in addition to the social cohesion and the edification of youth with a Greek education and Christian ethics."[11] Rebuilding an association targeting youth addressed both education and leisure. Under the new circumstances, youth defined the new national boundaries of Greekness. *Dorieas* contributed to turn a community into an integral part of the Greek nation-state by emphasizing an identity based on language and religion.

In the crucial years between 1943 and 1948, many forces continued to stress the importance of youth in Rhodes. From a fascist organization in its twilight to former communal leaders writing from a foreign country, from consuls to local sport entrepreneurs, the motives behind invoking and organizing youth were diverse. Still, they shared the experience of a historic turn: the imperial coda was crossfading into the overture of an epoch dominated by the nation-state. While institutions and boundaries of belonging were heavily affected by this change, youth continued to be a convenient device to address notions such as politics, the family, education, leisure, and mobility.

This book's priority accorded to the transformation from Ottoman to Italian rule left the dramatic years of the Second World War and its aftermath at the margins of the narrative. Their complexity would deserve a separate analysis and a different conceptual approach. Luckily, this has been undertaken by other recent works. Historians have focused on the genocidal violence against the local Jews that culminated with the deportation of almost the entire community on 23 July 1944, commanded by Nazi authorities decisively helped by the persisting Italian administration.[12] Another topic investigated recently is the relationship between Italian and German troops. Ranging from resistance to collaboration, this relationship has produced a particular, albeit marginal, memorialization of the Italian military presence on the islands.[13] From another angle, Pamela Ballinger has included the war aftermath and the decolonization of the Dodecanese in her study centred on Italian repatriated, investigating the redefinition of belonging to *Italianità* and the multiple trajectories of mobility this entailed.[14] Valerie McGuire has emphasized the end of empire and the "sites of selective memory" that relate to the perceptions of Italian rule in the Dodecanese.[15] These studies have offered different interpretations of the end of Italian imperial rule in Rhodes, yet a question remains. What is the historical breadth of the "empire" ending in 1945?

This book argued for considering Italian fascist colonialism as an imperial consequence of the late Ottoman period. By adopting a perspective on the population of Rhodes and its institutions beyond exclusivity based on confession, the view from 1945 suggests that the end of empire was a more profound phenomenon than the Italian royal flag lowering from the governor's palace and being driven off the island. The Ottoman past still echoed at the end of the war as it did during the Italian occupation, although an accelerated transformation would swiftly nationalize the society of Rhodes. It was on this longer, changing but inseparable Ottoman-into-Italian imperial consequence that the curtain fell in 1945.

Pasquale Cacopardi's family is a striking example of interwoven Ottoman and Italian imperial trajectories. While his father settled back in his homeland, Pasquale's Jewish-born mother came to Italy for the first time. She struggled to keep kinship bonds upright far from the *Juderia*, the consequence of emigration starting in the last years of Ottoman rule and continuing until the outbreak of the Second World War. Hizkia Franco writing from Smyrna witnessed the fading link between Jewish communities of Asia Minor and Rhodes, which had been vital in terms of resources and marriage strategies in Ottoman times and persisted, though complicated by the new Italo-Turkish border, during colonial rule. The Turkish consul still referred to schools which the Ottoman state had founded and which the Italians severed from Turkish foreign control. The reopening of *Dorieas* built on religious-ethnic socialization and stressed the same physical activity which had made *Diagoras* a cornerstone for the Orthodox' community in Ottoman times that lasted until the Italians banned it.

Discussing an imperial consequence is not simply a change in periodization but a different angle to look at colonialism in the Mediterranean. It means the search for a delicate balance between a detailed picture of plural forces on the ground and their intersections with a space that transcends territorial boundaries and historiographic domains. The book has shown that colonial sovereignty evolved in constant interaction with its outside. Bonds tying Rhodes to its regional environment in Ottoman times were redefined during Italian rule. Be it in the case of local families involved in disputes processed by foreign tribunals or in the case of the challenges posed by foreign schooling infrastructure, fascist colonialism carved its place in the Mediterranean while this same Mediterranean impacted Italian rule through its changing geopolitical, social, and cultural circulations. It is in this dual process that fascist colonialism's capacity and limits to change personal relationships in Rhodes have been discussed.

The introduction highlighted the coexistence of two factors within the imperial consequence in Rhodes: the question of how to "make Italians" in a colonial setting and the issue of how to "make one's own business" vis-à-vis changing power structures. The variety of life trajectories presented in the chapters demonstrated that these options were not clear-cut, and that the state and families confronted each other through intermediaries. Communal structures were situated in between state authorities and the population, and they followed a winding trajectory. They were galvanized by the early Young Turks' calls for fraternity and equality as politics increasingly addressed youth at school and in newspapers. They were then shaken from within and fragmented by the Greater War as notables conflicted with youth during the Italian military occupation. While emigrants from Rhodes built new institutions overseas and changed the boundaries of the collective called "community" through new forms of youth socialization, Italian colonial rulers after Lausanne reshaped and reinforced communities as an instrument of loyalty. Communal organizers increasingly managed sport clubs and newspapers in which they publicly prescribed youth's behaviour. These same communities, however, later came under attack by fascist bureaucrats and young activists. The former saw them as an obstacle for the ideological assimilation of youth, while the latter considered them inadequate in front of alternative forms of identifications travelling in the post-Ottoman Mediterranean such as Revisionist Zionism, Greek irredentism, and Kemalism.

After the end of Italian rule, youth and generations contributed to determine the bonds tying families and state authority, but they were no longer caught in the tension of empire. In the early post-war years, the new local newspaper *Ethniki Foni* (National Voice) published regular editorials written by the same Giorgios Georgiadis who had spoken at the opening of the *Venetokleion* gymnasium in 1909, and who had been strictly surveilled by the Italian police for his nationalist ideas. In a column dated October 1948, Georgiadis addressed the question of conscription in the Greek army, an effect of the recent annexation. With an appeal echoing Young Turk commentators of forty years earlier, he explained that among the "gifts of freedom" were not only the right to live in a constitutional society, but also the duty to serve the "Holy Fatherland" in arms. Georgiadis invoked patriotism and at the same time created a new image for "the young Dodecanesians." Young soldiers would consider the conscription not as a "tedious task" but as a "just pride, while it meant grief and sorrow for the Dodecanesian elders (*parilikas*) and the undrafted." These elders were not as "young to rush with the same bravery and the same pride" towards this duty, continued the author, likely alluding to himself.[16]

Georgiadis's words confirm the value of youth emphasized in this book. Youth described a contingent situation (a new conscription system), a symbolic correlation (youth-as-patriotism), and a projection into the past and the future (difference from the elders and prospect of freedom). Throughout the period analysed, military service suited well to mobilize a masculine notion of youth. For the Young Turks, the novelty was to extend conscription to non-Muslims. For the Italian governors, the priority was to exclude non-Italian citizens from it, although this exclusion did not happen without exceptions. Despite the rhetoric emphasis shared by Young Turks and fascists, notions of difference crucial to both Ottomans and Italians were of little use for the new Greek administration. Georgiadis traversed the imperial consequence described in this book and he is one of the few voices resonating until the imperial coda. Its vision of young men in arms under the Greek banner appropriately describes the implications of a post-imperial setting embracing the nation-state.

The graffiti hailing the "New Imperial Italy" under Mussolini's portrait with which our journey started had surely disappeared from the alley of Rhodes in 1948. Young Rhodians would now have to become a "new generation" of loyal Greeks. To this end, political rights after the liberation from fascist colonialism, unprecedented in Rhodes, did not only imply military service. They also implied silencing and absorbing ethno-confessional differences in the idea that legitimacy and loyalty were anchored in an exclusive, homogenous, and hegemonic national belonging.

Notes

Introduction

1 I could not retrieve the exact date. The graffiti appears in a photograph on: Booth and Bridge Booth, *Italy*, 273.

2 Bosworth, *Italy*.

3 Micheletta, "Questions," 165; Pasqualini, *Esercito*, 15–69; Bosworth, "Britain," 689; Petricioli, *Italia*, 213–39; Carabott, "Occupation."

4 *"Pur troppo s'è fatta l'Italia, ma non si fanno gl'Italiani."* Azeglio, *Ricordi*, 7.

5 Stoler and Cooper, "Metropole," 1.

6 ASDMAE AAPP 1919–30 992. Lago to Grandi, 29 October 1929.

7 *"Ora che l'Italia è fatta, dobbiamo fare gli affari nostri."* De Roberto, *Viceré*, 440.

8 M. Nuri, "Ṣāḥib-i imtiyāz Süleymān Efendiye ve memleketiñ münevver el-efkār genclerine," *Afitāb*, 27 May 1909.

9 The importance of expanding the periodization of the First World War through the notion of "Greater War" is illustrated in: Gerwarth and Manela, *Empires*.

10 Constant Méheut, "Report for Macron Urges 'Reconciliation of Memories' by France and Algeria," *New York Times*, 21 January 2021.

11 Pamuk and Williamson, *Response*; Isabella and Zanou, *Diasporas*; Khuri-Makdisi, *Mediterranean*; Borutta and Gekas, "Sea"; Fuhrmann, *Cities*.

12 Ghobrial, "Introduction."

13 Clementi and Toliou, *Ebrei*; Clementi, "Fine"; McElligott, "Deportation"; Fintz Menascé, *Buio*.

14 Burbank and Cooper, *Empires (2010)*, 11.

15 Barkey and von Hagen, *Empire*; Brown, *Legacy*. For a pioneering study on Ottoman continuities in Turkey: Zürcher, *Factor*.

16 Todorova, "Legacy."

17 Ginio and Kaser, *Legacies*. For a connected history based on a personal trajectory and its archival trail: Oualdi, *Slave*. For a study on Palestine: Jacobson, *Empire*.
18 Lewis, *Rule*, 3.
19 Amzi-Erdogdular, "Modernities," 915.
20 Andall and Duncan, "Memories," 16.
21 Hom, *Empire*, 1; Ballinger, *World*, 20–1.
22 Pignataro, *Dodecaneso I*, 18.
23 Doumanis, *Myth*; Doumanis, "Italians."
24 Labanca argues that "even if it was not formally a colony, the features of the Italian presence in the Dodecanese were colonial." Labanca, *Oltremare*, 181.
25 Pergher, *Mussolini*.
26 For British Cyprus, Alexis Rappas has underlined the priority given to the neutralization of politics and the international isolation of the island. Rappas, "Polity."
27 Barkey, "Consequences."
28 The vilayet was established in 1867 following the administrative reforms of the *Tanzimat*. On late Ottoman administration in Rhodes: Örenç, *Rodos*.
29 BOA Y MTV 17 28. Census data attached to a letter from the vali of Rhodes to Yıldız Palace, 28 February 1885.
30 GAK DOD IDD 1922 20 21. Census of the Municipality of Rhodes, 1 July 1917; *Censimento 1922*, 179.
31 GAK DOD IDD 1922 20 21. Census of the Municipality of Rhodes, 1 July 1917; GAK DOD IDD 1937 757 572. Census dated 21 April 1937.
32 Aymes, *History*.
33 As two examples: Guerin, *Voyage*; [Tokgöz]Ahmed Ihsan, "Cevelān."
34 Deringil, *Domains*, 150.
35 Eissenstat, "Modernization," 456.
36 *Sālnāme C 1900*, 47.
37 Reinkowski, "State," 199–200.
38 Villa, *Isole*, 19; McGuire, *Sea*, 91.
39 Martinoli and Perotti, *Architettura*; Livadiotti, *Presenza*; Aloi, "Rodi"; Arca Petrucci, "Città"; Ciacci, *Rodi*.
40 For Cyprus, Alexis Rappas argued that the post-Ottoman "transition" was "socially far reaching" in some domains, but also the product of a discursive "overdramatization." Rappas, *Cyprus*, 13–14.
41 Mardin, *Genesis*, 67–77.
42 Deringil, *Domains*, 1–4.
43 Hanioğlu, *Preparation*; Sohrabi, "Waves."
44 Clayer, "Factionalism"; Campos, *Brothers*.
45 "Egklogika," *Nea Rodos*, 24 March 1912; Papachristodoulou, *Istoria*, 481. CADN 569 PO 1 14. Laffon to Bompard, 24 April 1912.

46 Zürcher, "Conscription," 447.

47 Espinoza, "Cittadinanza," 201–4.

48 Hanley, "Nationality," 290.

49 Pignataro, *Dodecaneso I*, 22–6; Donati, *History*, 134–7, 194–8.

50 Pignataro, *Dodecaneso III*, 151–3.

51 Torr, *Rhodes*, 34.

52 Gentile, *Italia*, 62. On the Italian-Ottoman War: Romano, *Sponda*; Del Boca, *Italiani*; Labanca, *Guerra*; Stephenson, *Box*; McCollum, "Spaces." On the Dodecanese within Italy's "Greater War": Wilcox, *Empire*, 36–9; 219–26.

53 Bocquet, "Rhodes."

54 Guidi, "Gefangenen."

55 ASDMAE AAPP 1891–1916 156. Ameglio to Sangiuliano, 6 November 1912.

56 Pignataro, *Dodecaneso I*, 14–15.

57 Melchionni, "Accordi."

58 Gingeras, *Shores*, 6.

59 Hirschon, "Consequences," 14.

60 Rappas, "Formation," 469.

61 Burbank and Cooper, "Empires (2019)," 82.

62 Mosse, *Revolution*, 1–44; Gentile, *Italia*, 164; Matard-Bonucci and Milza, *Homme*; Griffin, "Introduction," 6.

63 Kühn, "Ottomanism."

64 Clementi and Toliou, *Ebrei*, 157.

65 Brubaker, "Aftermaths."

66 Rappas, "Insularity."

67 Grosselli, *Uomini*; Pignataro, *Dodecaneso II*, 549–606.

68 On the newsreels of the fascist Istituto LUCE and tourism: McGuire, "Histories."

69 The first civil governor Alessandro De Bosdari, in charge between 1921 and 1922, did not represent Italian sovereign authority since his tenure preceded the Treaty of Lausanne.

70 Pignataro, *Dodecaneso II*; Pignataro, *Dodecaneso III*.

71 Doumanis, *Myth*, 187; Fintz Menascé, *Buio*, 255.

72 McGuire, *Sea*, 234–45.

73 Espinoza, "Italiani."

74 Scott, *Domination*, 183.

75 Hajdarpasic, *Bosnia*, 127–60.

76 Lüdtke, "Herrschaft."

77 Makdisi, *Culture*; Clayer, "Dimension."

78 Barkey and Gavrilis, "Millet."

79 Kechriotis, "Requiem," 97. Cohen, *Ottomans*.

80 "I epeteios tou Syntagmatos; Didaskalikon synedrion," *Rodos*, 25 July 1909.

81 On Salonica's Jewish community: Naar, *Salonica*.

82 The substance of this "system" has been questioned since the 1980s: Braude and Lewis, *Christians*. For a recent work which also summarizes the state of the art: Michael, Anastassiadis, and Verdeil, *Communities*.

83 White, *Emergence*, 2; Rodrigue, "Millet."

84 Italian historian Giovanni Cecini somehow vaguely writes of "rebellious minorities and … not always keen (*ben disposte*) majorities [which] … led to difficult choices" for the Italian colonial rulers. Cecini, *Guardia*, 12.

85 Manela, *Moment*, 7–13.

86 Doumanis, *Nation*.

87 Pignataro, *Dodecaneso I*, 34–42.

88 Thomas, *Empires*, 4.

89 Rappas, "Soliloquies." Most examples will be cited throughout the book.

90 For a critical assessment: Doumanis, *Myth*, 3; Rappas, "Formation," 468.

91 Georgeon and Dumont, *Empire*; Anastassiadou-Dumont, "Pays"; Smyrnelis, "Empire"; Anastassiadis, *Voisinages*; Doumanis, *Nation*; Bryant, *Coexistence*.

92 Brubaker and Cooper, "Identity," 20. Here, I paraphrase the term "nationalist organizers" found in: Zahra, "Non-Communities," 103.

93 Lüdtke, *Eigen-Sinn*, 13.

94 Thomas, *Empires*, 3.

95 Clementi, "Fondo."

96 Zollmann, "Order."

97 Farge, *Allure*, 6.

98 Mannheim, "Problem"; Pinder, *Problem*. For an overview of recent studies: Jureit and Wildt, "Generationen."

99 Georgeon, "Jeunes-Turcs"; Şeni, "Jeunesse"; Davidova, *Transitions*; Provence, *Generation*.

100 Berghoff et al., "History," 8. Shmuel Eisenstadt and André Burguière inspired me to look at generations as indicators of stability of a given system, the former by stressing the dialectic between age-heterogenous and age-homogenous collectivities, the second by pointing at the ambivalence of intergenerational cohesion and disintegration. Eisenstadt, *Generation*; Burguière, "Rapports."

101 Simmel, *Soziologie*, 5–6.

102 Fanon, *Revolution*, 118.

103 Whelehan, "Youth."

104 Jobs and Pomfret, "Transnationality"; Downs, "Éditorial." On the discrepancies between the official culture of empire and its reception among youth: Bowersox, *Germans*.

105 Reichardt, *Kampfbünde*, 355–89.

106 Ferris, *Life*, 77–82.

107 Bourdieu, *Questions*, 143.
108 Lefebvre, *Introduction*, 162.
109 Passerini, "Giovinezza."
110 Kertzer, "Generation"; Bourdieu, "Famille."

1 The Emergence of Youth as a Political Category

1 Hanioğlu, *Preparation*, 5–6.
2 M. Nuri, "Ṣāḥıb-i imtiyāz Süleymān Efendiye ve memleketiñ münevver el-efkār genclerine," *Afitāb,* 27 May 1909.
3 Georgeon, "Jeunes-Turcs," 161.
4 "L'alta parola del Duce ai giovani," *Il Messaggero di Rodi,* 25 May 1937.
5 "Indimenticabile spettacolo di forza e di giovinezza all'Arena del Sole," *Il Messaggero di Rodi,* 25 May 1937.
6 For a similar discussion on twentieth-century China: Lanza, "Springtime."
7 This was the case for Said Bey, a student from a village around Salonica, banished to Rhodes in 1905. BOA TFR I A 31 3047. Said to the Ottoman grand vizier, 4 November 1906. On the *Mekteb-i Mülkiye*: Clayer, "Students."
8 Demirel, "Implementation."
9 In the case of a certain İbrahim Edhem from Ünye on the Black Sea, the Ministry of the Interior asked for information about his banishment to Rhodes from the directorate of the Imperial School through the Ministry of Education, but this did not bring fruitful results. BOA MF MKT 1079 30. The Ministry of Education to the Ministry of the Interior, 10 November 1908.
10 Şükrü Hanioğlu mentions a local provincial branch of the Committee of Union and Progress settled as early as 1896, which was allegedly important for the distribution of propaganda publications in Western Anatolia, before dissolving one year later. Hanioğlu, *Turks,* 87–8. Erik-Jan Zürcher includes a certain Rodoslu Süleyman among the founding members of the CUP, later establishing a secret society in Syria. Zürcher, "Turks," 275–86, 280. Nathalie Clayer's prosopography on Albanian students at the *Mekteb-i Mülkiye* shows that three graduates who later joined Young Turk circles had spent some years as teachers in Rhodes, where they likely discussed politics with their students outside classes. Clayer, "Students," 311–39.
11 BOA Y PRK AZN 16 7. Report by Public Attorney Hamdi Bey, undated (1896).
12 BOA Y A HUS 413 132. The vali of Rhodes to the Ottoman grand vizier, 15 March 1901.
13 Schmidt, *Orientalist,* 291.
14 [Mumcu], *Vatan,* 184.

15 Flemming and Schmidt, *Diary*, 48.

16 BOA DH SYS 55 97. Telegraph from the Mutesarrif of Amasya, 25 March 1912.

17 Gocek, *Denial*, Appendix B.

18 Büssow, *Palestine*, 63.

19 This person might be Antonios Agiakatsikas, son of Ioannis, who will be mentioned again in chapter 4. While no "Katsikas" appear in later sources, this eventuality is at odds with Antonios Agiakatsikas's young age (20) at the time. It might have been Ioannis's father or brother but, in this case, this would be the only occurrence of this person in the sources in my possession.

20 GAK DOD RRCC 1932 SP 671. Note by the *Carabinieri*, 12 February 1930; Note by the Italian Embassy in Athens, 2 January 1934.

21 GAK DOD ITA DIK (Unclassified). Tribunale Penale di Rodi 1920. [Caritomeni M. against Manoli D.]. Report by the *Carabinieri*, 7 October 1920.

22 Alhadeff, *Chêne*, 72.

23 Galante, *Histoire*, VII: 76.

24 ÖStA HHStA GKA Konstantinopel Gesandtschaftsarchiv 405 1. Barmann to Ekrem Bey, 28 October 1908; AIMR. "Praktika Dimagerontias 1905–1913." Minute of the meeting, 24 August 1912.

25 ASDMAE AAPP 1891–1916 155. Marchi to Sangiuliano, annex, 18 (or 28?) November, 1913.

26 GAK DOD RRCC 1932 15 PS 889. Attestation by Theodoros Frarakis, 18 December 1937; GAK DOD RRCC 1933 2 14 630. Note by the *Carabinieri*, 9 May 1933.

27 GAK DOD RRCC 1933 2 14 64. Mauro to De Vecchi, 16 April 1937.

28 This was a pattern recognizable in many, though not all provinces of the empire, some of which had a special administrative status. Findley, *Reform*; Bragg, *Notables*; Grandits, *Herrschaft*; Ozil, *Christians*.

29 Hanssen, *Beirut*, 74.

30 CADN 569 PO 1 5. The French vice-consul to Constans, 3 August 1908; The French vice-consul to the consul in Smyrna, 4 August 1908.

31 Ibid. The French vice-consul to the consul in Smyrna, 6 August 1908.

32 Ibid. The French vice-consul to the consul in Smyrna, 20 August 1908.

33 Ibid. The French vice-consul to the consul in Smyrna, 2 November 1908.

34 Kalambichis, *Zoi*, 25; Kypriotou, "Drasi," 126. It is unclear when he joined this secret committee, nor in which way he was active.

35 Clayer, "Time." In Rhodes, the vali Ekrem Bey was replaced by Ali Reşad Pasha, previously at Edirne, who was said to be more appreciated by Christians than by Muslims also because of his mildness during the anti-Greek boycott campaign of 1910. He was in turn replaced in 1911 by Ibrahim Soussa, a Chaldean Christian from Mosul. CADN 569 PO

1 5. The French vice-consul to the consul in Smyrna, 8 August 1908; ÖStA HHStA GKA Konstantinopel Gesandschaftsarchiv 405 1. The consul in Smyrna to the Austrian ambassador in Constantinople, 14 January 1911.

36 "To koinotikon zitima," *Rodos*, 20 December 1909.

37 Beşikçi, "Labor"; Peçe, "Conscription," 435.

38 "Stratologia ton mi Mousoulmanon," *Rodos*, 3 January 1910.

39 CADN 569 PO 1 5. The French consul at Smyrna to Constans, undated (16 January 1910?).

40 Zürcher, "Conscription," 449.

41 Alhadeff, *Chêne*, 106.

42 "Stratologika," *Rodos*, 14 March 1910.

43 CADN 569 PO 1 5. Laffon to Bompard, 31 May 1911.

44 For a general account: Çetinkaya, *Turks*, 89–159. For the situation in Rhodes: CADN 569 PO 1 5. Laffon to Bompard, 22 June 1911.

45 AIU FRANCE X F 18 06. The director of the girls school to the AIU in Paris, 23 September 1910.

46 CADN 569 PO 1 5. Laffon to Bompard, 26 October 1911; Laffon to Bompard, 31 May 1911.

47 CADN 569 PO 1 5. Laffon to Bompard, 23 March 1912.

48 BOA DH KMS 4 9. Undated report by Ahmed Fuad Bey annexed to a letter from the Ottoman Ministry of Foreign Affairs to the Ministry of the Interior, 15 October 1913.

49 Luigi Ambrosini, "La mia avventura a Rodi," *La Stampa*, 24 May 1912.

50 ASDMAE GAB 1908–13 50. Amero to Leonardi Cattolica, 8 May 1912; Guidi, "Gefangenen"; Bocquet, "Rhodes."

51 ASDMAE AAPP 1891–1916 154. Report by Ameglio, 19 September 1912. Also quoted in Pignataro, *Dodecaneso I*, 72; Espinoza, "Italiani," 85.

52 ASDMAE AAPP 1891–1916 156. Note by Ameglio, 6 November 1912.

53 Ibid. Report by Ameglio, 10 June 1912.

54 ASDMAE AAPP 1891–1916 156. Report by Ameglio, 13 November 1912.

55 Savva Pavlidis was born around 1860. At 15 years of age he moved to Konya, where he became proficient in Ottoman. After a few years, he moved back to Rhodes and then to other islands where he started to work as a civil servant for several tribunals. In 1902, he obtained the official diploma of lawyer in Istanbul. Then, he moved back to Rhodes and opened his own office. In 1903, the Ottoman government accorded him a third grade honor (*rütbe-yi selāsse*). Kypriotou, "Drasi." See also: BOA DH MKT 705 41, The Ottoman Ministry of the Interior to the Ministry of Finance, 29 April 1903; CADN 569 PO 1 5. The French vice-consul to the ambassador in Constantinople, 28 March 1911.

56 ASDMAE AAPP 1891–1916 151. Tittoni to Sangiuliano, 30 May 1912; "Ḥamiyet-i vaṭaniye," *Ḥakḳ*, 14 May 1912 (erroneously dated 14 March 1912).

57 ASDMAE AAPP 1891–1916 156. The *Dimagerontia* to N. Drakidis and G. Pavlidis, 14 November 1912.

58 ACS AMEGLIO 33 317, Note by the *Carabinieri*, 27 November 1912; Ibid. Pavlidis to Ameglio, undated; ASDMAE AAPP 1891–1916 156. Ameglio to the Sangiuliano, 28 February 1913. CADN 569 PO 1 5. Laffon to Bompard, 28 February 1913.

59 ASDMAE AAPP 1891–1916 156. Ameglio to Sangiuliano, 23 April 1913.

60 Probably the prestigious Robert College.

61 CADN 569 PO 1 5. Laffon to Bompard, 21 April 1913.

62 See his personal file: GAK DOD RRCC 1932 1 1 81.

63 ASDMAE AAPP 1891–1916 156. Report by Ameglio, 12 February 1913.

64 Ibid. Note by the *Carabinieri*, 20 January 1913.

65 CADN 569 PO 1 6. Laffon to Bompard, 4 September 1914.

66 Toprak, "İttihat"; Beşikçi, *Mobilization*, 203–45.

67 CADN 569 PO 1 7. Laffon to Delcassé, 10 June 1915.

68 Ibid. Laffon to Delcassé, 7 June 1915; ASDMAE GAB 1915–18 56. Report by Governor Croce, annex to his letter dated 12 September 1917. These notables were suspected to have corresponded with Istanbul through the Greek consul, and the measure was taken after an air raid of the German *Luftwaffe* on Rhodes wounded three civilians CADN 569 PO 1 7. Laffon to Briand, 6 December 1915; ASDMAE GAB 1915–18 55. Note by Governor Elia, 15 August 1917. See also: CADN 569 PO 1 8. Laffon to Bompard, 9 May 1916.

69 ASDMAE AAPP 1891–1916 171. Garroni to Sonnino, 29 July 1914.

70 CADN 569 PO 1 6. Laffon to Bompard, 6 May 1914.

71 ASDMAE AAPP 1919–30 979. Elia to Sonnino, 13 November 1918.

72 AIU FRANCE X F 18 06. The director of the boys school to the AIU in Paris 15 July 1922.

73 Wolfgang von Weisl, "Reisebriefe Wien-Palästina. Rhodus," *Wiener Morgenzeitung*, 5 August 1922.

74 CZA Z4\40834 BX O106/a, Letters between Bohor Israel and the Executive of the Zionist Organization, 8 June and 4 July 1922.

75 Wolfgang von Weisl, "Reisebriefe Wien-Palästina. Rhodus," *Wiener Morgenzeitung*, 5 August 1922.

76 GAK DOD IDD 1924 29p 203p. Transcription of the grand rabbi's sermon, 15 March 1924.

77 ASDMAE AAPP 1919–30 985. Schanzer to De Bosdari, 22 March 1922.

78 GAK DOD IDD 1922 19p 113p. Strumza to Albertazzi, 25 November 1922; Note by the *Carabinieri*, 9 December 1922.

79 Orakçı, *Rodos*, 80; Papuççular, *Türkiye*, 35–62. ASDMAE AAPP 1919–30 986, Lago to Mussolini, 30 August 1923; The Turkish consul in Rhodes aimed at encouraging the option for the Turkish citizenship well until

1928, and was said to have more success in Kos than in Rhodes. ASDMAE AAPP 1919–30 990. Lago to Mussolini, 20 November 1928.

80 ASDMAE AAPP 1919–30 990, Lago to Baroni, 27 February 1927.

81 Among others: Zervos and Roussos, *Dodécanèse*; Zervos, *Rhodes*; The Executive Committee of the Dodecanesians – Compiled by Skevos Zervos and Paris Roussos, *Book*; Volonakis, *Dodécanèse*.

82 ASDMAE AAPP 1919–30 980. Montagna to Mussolini, 19 May 1922. However, until 1924, these circles were defined as not quite organized and divided along their members' island of origin. ASDMAE AAPP 1919–30 987. The Italian consul in Piraeus to Montagna, 20 December 1923.

83 ASDMAE AAPP 1919–30 989. Resolution dated 23 October 1926.

84 A volunteer during the Greek-Turkish War of 1919–22, Magnataci had been dismissed by Apostolos for an extortion scandal. For a detailed investigation: ASDMAE AAPP 1919–30 990. Lago to Arlotta, 3 November 1927. On the club Dodecanesian Youth in Athens: ASDMAE AAPP 1919–30 991 Lago to Mussolini, 30 September 1928.

85 Heller, "Children"; Şeni, "Jeunesse"; Petrakis, *Myth*.

86 For a detailed discussion: Clementi and Toliou, *Ebrei*, 60–7.

87 Pinto, "Imago"; Bianco, "Sionistes."

88 GAK DOD RRCC 1 1 260. Note by the *Carabinieri*, undated (Aug 1935).

89 Ibid. Copy of the Jewish school headmaster's letter to the President of the Jewish community, 29 November 1935. Even Jabotinsky in person got wind of the tense situation in Rhodes through a letter by Isacco Sciaky, a Revisionist militant and professor in Florence. Jabotinsky and Sciaky, *Stato*, 97–101.

90 GAK DOD RRCC 1932 20 PS 2. Translation of the article's draft, 12 May 1936.

91 This was also the stance of the head of the police, who regretted that "In spite of the warning addressed by this office to the most fervent youth, I note that the Zionist revisionist movement is spreading more and more among the Jewish youth of Rhodes." The *Carabinieri* to the Governor of Rhodes, 2 June 1936.

92 "Un nuovo maestro di Sionismo?" L'idea Sionistica 9, no. 6 (1936): 10–11.

93 GAK DOD RRCC 1935 1 1 260. Mosce Rosio and Giacomo Franco to the *Carabinieri*, 1 June 1936.

94 Ibid. The *Carabinieri* in Rhodes to the *Carabinieri* in Rome, 30 November 1935; Note by Lago, 1 July 1936.

95 Ibid. Note by the *Carabinieri*, 6 June 1936.

96 See his file at: GAK DOD RRCC 1933 2 19 225. Notes by the *Carabinieri*, 3 January 1934; 11 October 1935; 6 December 1935; 1 October 1937; 29.05.1938; "Incontro di boxe," *Il Messaggero di Rodi*, 9 June 1934.

97 BCA 30/10/0/0 237/604/23. The consul of Rhodes to the Turkish foreign minister, 11 August 1934.

98 GAK DOD RRCC 1933 2 12 1039. Note by the Carabinieri, 24 March 1936.

99 GAK DOD RRCC 1934 2 12 1406. Note by the *Carabinieri*, 7 July 1938. GAK DOD RRCC 1933 2 9 24. Note by the *Carabinieri*, 31 October 1937; 30 October 1939.

100 Ibid. Note by the *Carabinieri*, 25 September 1937.

101 GAK DOD RRCC 1933 2 12 1039. Note by the *Carabinieri*, 24 March 1936.

102 Ibid. Banishment decree, 24 March 1936.

103 Ibid. Note by the *Carabinieri*, 29 March 1938; Sünger to Mussolini, 2 June 1936; Sünger to his mother, 31 July 1938; "Fidanzamento," *Il Messaggero di Rodi*, 30 January 1936.

104 "Tragica rissa a Salaco," *Il Messaggero di Rodi*, 12 April 1934.

105 "Le massacre dans l'île de Rhodes ," *L'Humanité*, 3 May 1934. The Palestine Post published the denial by the Italian consul in Jerusalem: "Rioting in Rhodes," *The Palestine Post*, 7 May 1934.

106 "Dodekanisiaki neolaia Aigiptou," *Dodekanisos*, 22 April 1934.

107 GAK DOD RRCC 1934 1 1 120. Article forwarded by the Italian ambassador in Athens, 8 June 1934.

108 "Ai neolaiai mas," *Dodekanisos*, 10 June 1934.

109 GAK DOD RRCC 1934 1 1 120. Note by the *Carabinieri*, 8 June 1934.

110 GAK DOD RRCC 1932 20 PS 1. Note by the *Carabinieri*, 2 February 1935.

111 Ibid. Note by the *Carabinieri*, 30 March 1937.

112 Rainero, "Coup," 438–9.

113 GAK DOD RRCC 1932 20 PS 1. Note by the *Carabinieri*, 21 April 1937.

114 Pignataro, *Dodecaneso III*, 155.

115 Kypriotou, *Venetokli*, 132–6.

116 GAK DOD RRCC 1932 20 PS 1. Report by the director of public education, 22 April 1937.

117 Ibid. Note by the *Carabinieri*, 23 April 1937; VENETOKLEION. "Genikos Elegchos apo 1916.17 eos 1944.1945"; GAK DOD IDD 1937 768 657. List of students, 28 April 1937; "Con una grandiosa manifestazione Rodi italiana celebra il Natale di Roma e la Festa fascista del Lavoro," *Il Messaggero di Rodi*, 22 April 1937.

118 For an account on anti-occupation activities in Rhodes during WWII: Tsalachouris, *Rodos*.

119 Pignataro, *Dodecaneso II*, 88–95; Espinoza, "Italiani," 198–203.

120 "Adunata," *Il Messaggero di Rodi*, 13 October 1921.

121 "Le onoranze al Milite Ignoto," *Il Messaggero di Rodi*, 5 November 1921.

122 ASDMAE AAPP 1919–30 980. De Bosdari to Mussolini, 6 November 1922. Pignataro, *Dodecaneso I*, 231–34.

123 GAK DOD IDD 1922 18p 110p. Biliotti to De Bosdari, 8 October 1922; De Bosdari to Biliotti, 10 October 1922.

124 "Partito Fascista Italiano: Sezione di Rodi," *Il Messaggero di Rodi*, 28 August 1922.

125 Only "Italian" Catholics from Smyrna received this aid. Many Orthodox
families from Makri (Fetihye), Livissi (Kayaköy), Dalyan, and Antalya
arrived and stayed, even if mostly temporarily, mostly aided by their
coreligionists. GAK DOD 1923 21p 152p. Lists of refugees dated
12 October 13, 15, 16 and 19, 1922; "Partito Fascista Italiano: Sezione di
Rodi," *Il Messaggero di Rodi*, 21 September 1922; "Un'altra manifestazione
di gratitudine dei profughi dell'Asia Minore," *Il Messaggero di Rodi*,
30 September 1922; Pignataro, *Dodecaneso II*, 229.

126 "Partito Fascista Italiano: Sezione di Rodi," *Il Messaggero di Rodi*,
23 September 1922.

127 Reichardt, *Kampfbünde*, 355.

128 Ryan, "Violence," 127.

129 "L'inaugurazione della Sede sociale della Lega Italiana," *Il Messaggero di
Rodi*, 14 February 1922.

130 See also Rao's anecdotic portrait as the "Don Juan of the Circolo [Italia]"
in: Vratsalis, *Niochoritika*, 104–6.

131 GAK DOD RRCC 1932 II 641. Note by the *Carabinieri*, 25 June 1932.

132 GAK DOD RRCC 1932 II 601. Note by the *Carabinieri*, 2 May 1937; GAK
DOD RRCC 1932 II 641. Emilia S. to De Vecchi, 21 August 1940.

133 On Mellone: GAK DOD RRCC 1932 II 446. The *Carabinieri* in Maglie to the
Carabinieri in Rhodes, 17 May 1932; Note by the *Carabinieri*, 25 November
1936; DR LIX GAM. 1920 no. 9, 18 November 1920; "Fiori d'arancio." *Il
Messaggero di Rodi*, 22 November 1920; "Cronaca spicciola," *Il Messaggero
di Rodi*, 3 October 1939.

134 GAK DOD RRCC 1938 2 23 659. Note by the *Carabinieri*, 3 December 1938.

135 GAK DOD RRCC 1932 II 446, Note by the *Carabinieri*, 16 June 1937.

136 Ibid. Note by the *Carabinieri*, 17 June 1943.

137 See Cristo M.'s personal file: GAK DOD RRCC 1932 15 PS 711.

138 CADN 569 PO 1 5. Laffon to Bompard, 14 May 1911; ÖStA HHStA GKA
Konstantinopel Gesandtschaftsarchiv 405 1. The consul of Rhodes to the
consul in Smyrna, 3 June 1911.

139 The biographical information is found in Landriscina's personal dossier:
GAK DOD RRCC 1933 2 12 1752. Notes by the *Carabinieri* dated 19 July
1934; 7 April 1936; 27 February 1938; 20 June 1938; 22 May 1940; 14 June
1940; 10 October 1940; GAK DOD RRCC 1933 2 9 15. List of applications
for entering the *Polisportiva Fascio*, 13 March 1933. GAK DOD ITA DIK
(Unclassified). Giudicatura Civile di Rodi 1924. "Ismail K. contro Giacinto
Landriscina." Attestation by Ismail K., 20 November 1924; GAK DOD ITA
DIK (Unclassified). Pretura di Rodi 1933. "Registro Sentenze." Verdict
dated 7 November 1933; GAK DOD ITA DIK (Unclassified). Pretura di
Rodi 1941. "Registro Sentenze." Verdict dated 24 April 1941.

140 GAK DOD RRCC 1935 1 47 994. Note by the *Carabinieri*, 18 November
1935; Verdict dated 13 March 1936.

141 GAK DOD RRCC 1933 2 12 1752. Attestation by Francesco Landriscina, 29 August 1941; Report by the *Carabinieri*, 8 September 1941.

142 Ibid. Note by the *Carabinieri*, date lost (1941–3).

143 ACS MRF 53 123 20. Minute of a meeting between Party Secretary Chiorando and Mussolini, undated (1930).

144 Mahmud Zeki, "Faşizm ve genclik," *Selām*, 7 May 1928.

145 ASDMAE AAPP 1919–30 992. Lago to Grandi, 29 October 1929.

146 FSC ROMA. "Suppléments d'historiques. District de Turin." Entries dated September 1928 and 27 August 1932.

147 GAK DOD IDD 1935 517 290. Leaflet of the Eighth Summer Camp "Ave Dux," 1 August 1935.

148 Downs, *Childhood*, 4–5.

149 "Il ritorno degli Avanguardisti e Balilla da Campo Marzio," *Il Messaggero di Rodi*, 13 August 1935.

150 A short video is available at the archives of the Istituto LUCE: LUCE Giornale A0863, October 1931.

151 GAK DOD IDD 1935 517 290. Lago to Cignolini, 21 January 1935.

152 Concerning the *Balilla*, a roster from 1927 includes fifty-eight names. "Comunicato," *Il Messaggero di Rodi*, 20 March 1927; "Comunicato," *Il Messaggero di Rodi*, 23 March 1927.

153 "Opera Nazionale Balilla: Assegnazione dei graduati," *Il Messaggero di Rodi*, 1 April 1937.

154 GAK DOD IDD 1938 819 170. The commissar of the PNF in Rhodes to De Vecchi, 10 February 1938. In 1940, Romano indicated the presence of 5,090 members of the GIL, of whom, however, only 2,780 were considered regular activists "in uniform" (*in divisa*). Based on the former amount, the male section of the PNF had 224 *Giovani Fascisti*, 327 *Avanguardisti*, 1,459 *Balilla*, 755 *Figli della Lupa*. Concerning female members of the same age groups, there were 170 *Giovani Fasciste*, 213 *Giovani Italiane*, 1,241 *Piccole Italiane*, 701 *Figlie della Lupa*. ACS PNF 1 SIT POL PROV 19. Statistics dated 22 October 1940.

155 GAK DOD IDD 1938 819 170. Cristo P. to the government's delegate in Symi, 12 September 1938. One of the camp organizers gladly commented the letter saying that another participant wanted to volunteer in the Italian army. Ibid. The government delegate in Symi to De Vecchi, 13 September 1938.

156 McGuire, "Fascism," 235.

157 GAK DOD RRCC 1939 2 12 59. Note by the *Carabinieri*, 26 July 1938.

158 GAK DOD RRCC 1933 1 47 2074. Report by the *Carabinieri*, 13 September 1938.

159 Ibid. Note by the *Carabinieri*, 20 September 1938.

160 ACS PNF 1 SIT POL PROV 19. Romano to Starace, 4 January 1939.

161 Pignataro, *Dodecaneso III*, 221.

162 Coverdale, *Intervention*, 158–60.

163 This also applies to Orthodox volunteers. One resident of Kalymnos, after enrolling, served in Ethiopia. After obtaining the Italian citizenship, he ended up collaborating with the British intelligence. Espinoza, "Italiani," 259.

164 Barkey Flash, *Hug* (e-Book).

165 Clementi and Toliou, *Ebrei*, 28–37.

166 See his personal folder: GAK DOD RRCC 1934 2 19 282. Notes by the *Carabinieri* 18 November 1935; 4 June 1937; 14 October 1938; 13 May 1939; 28 May 1939. The *Carabinieri* in Rhodes to the police in Naples, 11 February 1941.

167 Alhadeff, *Sun*, 89. Before the Second World War, Carlo moved to Alexandria, where he later converted to Catholicism.

168 Sciarcon and Nurra, *Pace*, 63.

169 GAK DOD RRCC 1936 1 2 643. Note by the *Carabinieri*, 6 June 1936. The last document from the folder is the application for a passport dated 31 January 1939. He applied for permission of traveling to Italy "and return." No further information on Raimondo (Rahamin) could be found so far. Contrary to most of his close relatives, recorded at the CDEC, he does not appear among the list of victims or the survivors of the deportation of 1944 July nor among the deceased in the records available from 1940 to 1943.

170 "Radiazione," *Il Messaggero di Rodi*, 12 October 1937.

171 CADN 569 PO 1 8. The vice-consul of Rhodes to Reynaud, 16 May 1940.

2 Where Families and Empires Meet

1 Cacopardi, "Souvenirs." Available online at: http://sefarad.org/lm/044/14.html (accessed 20 June 2020).

2 PCPA. Leon Alhadeff to Pasquale Cacopardi, 4 April 1995.

3 GAK DOD RRCC 1932 II 797. Sadoc Mizrahi to Mario Genovesi, 20 April 1933.

4 Ibid. Note by the *Carabinieri*, 27 July 1933.

5 GAK DOD RRCC 1942 1018. Note by the *Carabinieri*, 21 March 1943.

6 Collotti, *Fascismo*; Matard-Bonucci, *Italie*.

7 Hofmeester and van Nederveen Meerkerk, "Family," 3. On family and social change in the *longue durée* see: Sabean, *Property*; Grandits, *Familie*.

8 Barrera, "Sex," 159.

9 Bertola, "Confessione."

10 İnce, *Citizenship*, 53.

11 Doumani, "Introduction," 1.

12 Hartmann, "Portraits," 115.

13 www.rhodesjewishmuseum.org/museum/family-photos/ (accessed 23 July 2019).

14 As I was wrapping up the last pages of this book, I obtained a copy of
    Marc Angel's memoirs. By introducing his ancestors (based on the same
    picture), he informs us that his father Victor was born in Seattle soon after
    the emigration of his grandmother. Angel, *World*, 3.

15 EIF PR no. 103594040062, Liner "Ultonia," arrival 27 November 1911.
    Next to Bohora, other persons travelling together from Rhodes are: Sam
    Angel, a friend, and Bohora's children Victoria, Morris, Albert, Abner
    (name unreadable), and Rachel. Another (?) Sam Angel arrived in New
    York in 1909, and mentioned Bohora's husband as the contact person in
    the US. See EIF PR no. 101643040662, Liner *Patras*, arrival 20 July 1909.

16 DR LIX FF. Angel Giuseppe.

17 Georg Simmel, "Zur Soziologie der Familie," *Vossische Zeitung*, 30 June
    and 7 July 1895.

18 AIU FRANCE X F 18 06. Leon Semach to the AIU in Paris, 28 November 1906.

19 Kampouris, "Gamos," 204.

20 Orakçı, *Rodos*, 67.

21 Altınbaş, "Marriage"; Martykánová, "Sharia."

22 Tucker, "Reform," 5; Metinsoy, *Women*, 188–92.

23 Toprak, "Family."

24 de Grazia, *Fascism*; Seymour, *Divorce*.

25 Reeder, "Making."

26 For a transnational perspective: LaRossa, *Modernization*; King, *Men*.
    More specifically on Italy: Salvante, "Boot-Rag," 103; Ginsborg, *Politics*,
    139–225.

27 On this type of document: Schmelz, "Characteristics," 17–19. On the 1906
    census: Karpat, *Population*, 35.

28 I found the record on this neighbourhood among unclassified and loose
    documents at the Hafiz Ahmet Ağa Islamic Library (ILHAA CENS),
    which holds some sources from the Muslim Community of Rhodes. The
    document related to the other neighbourhood, Abdülcelil, is found in the
    unclassified box: GAK DOD TR 15.

29 On the term *hane*: Duben, "Families," 77–81; Okawara, "Size," 55–7.

30 GAK DOD OTH 113.

31 Akın, *War*, 52–86; Metinsoy, *Women*, 185–98; Dannies, "Gentleman."

32 Unclassified material found at the Registry Office (*Lixiarcheio*) of the
    Town Hall of Rhodes. DR LIX FF.

33 Hirschon, "Jews." Renee Hirschon was the first scholar who used this
    collection, although she only dealt with Jewish households. Hirschon
    dates the records to 1939 and argues that they were related to a census of
    the population. However, family certificates, or at least a register, existed
    as early as 1929. The available collection might consist of certificates

reordered and reprinted in 1936, when the last general census of the
period took place.

34 Kocka, "Family," 421.

35 GAK DOD RRCC 1934 SP 55. Note by the *Carabinieri*, 31 March 1931.

36 Alhadeff, *Chêne*, 99.

37 Ibid., 153.

38 In 1915, Rachel P., aged 14 and from a poor family, was found next to the
corpse of a newborn baby. Her mother was accused of having killed the
baby in accordance with Rachel and her father, a coffeehouse keeper, in
order "to save the honour" of the girl. The midwife's attestation revealed
that, contrary to the claims of the suspects, the neighbours knew that the
girl was pregnant. Rachel confessed to have had an occasional intercourse
with a Muslim man working with her father but argued that she was
asleep while it happened. She claimed that she did not notice being
pregnant until giving birth, and that she dropped the baby inadvertently
as he slipped through her hands, which allegedly caused his death.
GAK DOD ITA DIK (Unclassified). Tribunale Penale di Rodi 1915.
"Procedimento contro M. Matilde … P. Kaim … P. Rachel."

39 GAK DOD ITA DIK (Unclassified). Tribunale Penale di Rodi 1939.
"Procedimento penale contro S. Panaioti," Attestation by Panaiotis S.,
22 February 1939.

40 "Fidanzamento," *Il Messaggero di Rodi*, 20 October 1933.

41 GAK DOD RRCC 1933 2 14 567. "Promemoria," 7 August 1934.

42 DR LIX GAM 1938, 53; GAK DOD RRCC 1933 2 14 567. Visa application
by Francesco V., 6 October 1941.

43 GAK DOD RRCC 1933 1 46 42. Note by the *Carabinieri*, 25 August 1941;
Undated love letter signed by Gino; "I casi della vita," *Il Messaggero di
Rodi*, 3 October 1933.

44 Duben and Behar, *Istanbul*, 87.

45 For instance, in 1929 Suleiman C. tried to break up his niece (or
granddaughter? It. "*nipote*") Bekire's love affair with an Italian man. She
was 14 and was under her uncle's custody. When this man came to the
house gate in a car accompanied by a Muslim youngster and two women,
C. reported to the police that he suspected the preparation of Bekire's
abduction, which eventually did not occur. See GAK DOD ITA DIK
(Unclassified). Tribunale Penale di Rodi 1929. "Corrispondenze." Police
report on C.'s attestation, 28 February 1929.

46 Gutkowski, *Vez*, 28.

47 Ibid., 62.

48 Ibid., 61–70.

49 Alhadeff, *Chêne*, 113; Vratsalis, *Niochoritika*, 383.

50 GAK DOD ITA DIK (Unclassified). Tribunale Penale di Rodi 1918. "Procedimento Penale contro T. Durmusc." Note by the *Carabinieri*, 7 July 1918.

51 Ibid. Minute by the prosecutor of the Civil Tribunal, 9 July 1919.

52 See the examples from 1932–4 in: GAK DOD TR 23.

53 Disposizione Governatoriale [DG] 15 November 1938, no. 324; "Atti Ufficiali," *Il Messaggero di Rodi*, 17 November 1938; Pignataro, *Dodecaneso III*, 161–72.

54 DG 26 November 1938, n. 342. "Atti Ufficiali," *Il Messaggero di Rodi*, 26 November 1938.

55 DG 26 November 1938, n. 343. "Atti Ufficiali," *Il Messaggero di Rodi*, 26 November 1938.

56 GAK DOD IDD 1943 1267 422. Request by Arghirulla M., 18 December 1943.

57 Bourdieu, "Famille."

58 Berkner, "Family," 405.

59 Duben and Behar, *Istanbul*, 49; Okawara, "Size," 62. According to a classification still widely used by historians, household types range from the "solitary," with only one person in the residential unit, to "non-conjugal" cases where siblings, aunts and nephews, one grandparent and grandchildren, or the head and a servant cohabitate. A "simple" (or "nuclear") household consists of a "married couple, or a married couple with offspring, or of a widowed person with offspring," while "extended" households are based on a "conjugal family unit with the addition of one or more relatives other than offspring, the whole group living together on its own or with servants." Lastly, a "multiple" household corresponds to two or more conjugal units "connected by kinship or by marriage," such as two parents, their offspring, and a daughter or a son-in law, two siblings each with their spouse, etc. Laslett, "Introduction," 28–31.

60 Vernier, *Genèse*, 164.

61 Kolodny, *Population*, 309–23; Doumanis, *Myth*, 16–19. See also: Kalafatas, *Bellstone*.

62 DR LIX FF. Cacopardi Antonino.

63 Örenç, *Rodos*, 253–8.

64 BOA DH MKT 2818 64. The Ministry of the Interior to the vali of Rhodes, 20 May 1909. For a similar case see: Türesay, "Victims," 90.

65 GAK DOD IDD 1937 739 444, Petition by Paolina R., 24 April 1937.

66 Ibid., Report by the *Carabinieri*, 3 May 1937.

67 In 1937, Cadigé I., "a poor widow with four children," requested a monthly handout. The Muslim woman had sent two of her children to her mother-in-law's place, she lived together with the other two and her elderly father, who worked as a street candy seller at the age of 85 to maintain the household. Cadigé played with the fuzzy boundaries of household and kin. She staged familial cohesion as good credentials

before the authorities. But she equally stressed the miserable condition of sharing her small apartment with seven other persons. She addressed the governor as "a God, our father, our protector," by which religious, familial, and political unity was invoked. Ibid., Petition by Cadigé I., 27 March 1937.
68 Ibid., Petition by Frosina P., undated [November/December 1936].
69 On the notion of social poetics: Herzfeld, *Poetics*, 11.
70 Guidi, "Inter-Communality," 141–5.
71 GAK DOD IDD 1936 580 33.
72 Toumarkine, *Migrations*; Fratantuono, "Ottomans."
73 BOA A MKT MHM 504 5. The Sublime Porte Secretarial Staff to Halil Rifat Pasha, 2 December 1898; BOA DH MKT 1150 24. The Ministry of the Interior to the vali of Rhodes, 28 February 1907. Örenç, *Rodos*, 236–9.
74 GAK DOD TR 9, "Conclusioni di B. Rebecca vedova di Perahia A.," 25 July 1928.
75 These elements form a "matrix" central to studies on the history of the family. Doumani, "Introduction," 16.
76 GAK DOD TR 9, "Conclusioni di Bohor, Nissim, Elia e Mussani fu Perahia A.," date unreadable.
77 GAK DOD ITA DIK (Unclassified). Tribunale Civile e Penale di Prima Istanza Rodi Egeo 1920. "Nuri Effendi," Declaration by Nuri S., 2 April 1920.
78 CADN 569 PO 1 22. "Succession Étienne M. 2 mars 1933," Copy of the will dated 30 October 1932.
79 GAK DOD ITA DIK (Unclassified). Tribunale Civile e Penale di Prima Istanza Rodi Egeo 1918. "Adolfo P.A.," Declaration of Alice M., 9 January 1918; Testimony of Father Ignazio Beaufays, 21 January 1918.
80 Rubin, *Courts*, 63–8.
81 Marongiu Buonaiuti, *Politica*, 53.
82 Sadi Nasuhoğlu speaks of an "old" and a "modern" version of celebrating marriage among Muslims and suggests that wedding customs in Rhodes "began to be carried out as influenced by the local Greeks and Italians," without elaborating further. Nasuhoğlu, *Rodos*, 56–60; Orakçı, *Rodos*, 145. Avram Galante insisted on early marriages accommodated by the families "according to the custom practiced in the Orient" among Jews and claims that "often, the new spouses did not talk to each other for months and lived at the groom's parents, like sister and brother." Galante, *Histoire*, VII: 123. Other authors further stress the importance of the dowry, regulated by a contract called *kettubah*, positively claiming that, contrary to the *mehr* in Islamic law, it represented a guarantee for women's inalienable property in case of divorce. Angel, *Jews*, 94–100.
83 Herzfeld, "Dowry."

84 Toundassaki, "Pratiques."

85 Kolodny, *Population*, 410–11.

86 Sant Cassia and Bada, *Family*, 184. In 1920, Argiria M. endowed her sister Eleftheria with several real estate properties and, in turn, the latter "committed herself to maintain Argiria for the rest of her life." After her death, Eleftheria resided in Rhodes town and sold a country house "with the consent of her husband, necessary according to the Orthodox religious law," in order to use the money for the maintenance of other properties. GAK DOD ITA DIK (Unclassified). Tribunale Civile e Penale di Rodi 1932. "M. Eleuteria fu Giorgio mar. V. Costantino, residente a Rodi." Request by M. Eleuteria, 27 January 1932.

87 Toundassaki, "Pratiques," 358.

88 AIMR. "Apofaseis Pneumatikou Dikasteiriou," 1914, No. 1, 20 May 1914.

89 Herzfeld, "Dowry," 231. In 1910, Vasilis G. accused his parents-in-law of having delivered only a part of the dowry fixed in his marriage contract. While his bride had received a house, the controversy concerned the 200 *eikosafranga* in cash which the parents added to the contract. The bride's father denied paying the monetary dowry and argued that a part of it was employed for the wedding and for preparing the house included in the contract, although the tribunal rejected his claims. AIMR. "Apofaseis Pneumatikou Dikasteriou," 1911, No. 36, 29 April 1911. See the same case in: AIMR. "Praktika Ekklesiastikou Dikastiriou," Meeting of 26 March 1911.

90 GAK DOD ITA DIK (Unclassified). "Corrispondenza Tribunale Civile e Penale di Rodi 1913." Letter by Paraskevi F. and Yorgi Z., 12 April 1913.

91 GAK DOD ITA DIK (Unclassified). Regio Tribunale di Rodi. "Corrispondenza Evasa 1912–13." Haci H.'s daughter to the Italian Military Governor, 7 September 1912.

92 GAK DOD ITA DIK (Unclassified). Giudicatura Civile di Rodi 1927. "Causa civile – Attore Calegi, figlia di H." Attestation by the mufti of Rhodes, 29 October 1927.

93 Pignataro, *Dodecaneso I*, 56. On the post-Ottoman legal frame for the Muslim population of the Dodecanese see: Tsitselikis, *Islam*, 394–5.

94 GAK DOD TR 6. Translation of a letter from the Civil Court of Köyceğiz, no. 5/3, without date.

95 GAK DOD IDD 1931 152p 1113p. The Secretary General of the Italian Administration to the Metropolitan Bishop of Rhodes, [February] 1931.

96 GAK DOD IDD 1933 187p 332p. Petition by Hüriye M. to the mufti of Rhodes, 15 October 1932.

97 Ibid. The mufti to Lago, 19 October 1932; Note by Vitalis Strumza, 24 December 1932.

98 Martykánová, "Sharia."

99 Rappas, "Marriages."

3 New Schools, or How Youth Became Students

1 Bonetto, "Fermeture."
2 On this concept: Fulbrook, "East Germans," 34.
3 Somel, *Modernization*, 120.
4 Deringil, *Domains*, 93; Evered, *Empire*, 9.
5 Dupont, "Présentation," 7; Somel, *Modernization*, 72; Somel, "Community"; Fortna, *Classroom*, 12; Fortna, "Islamic."
6 AIU GRÈCE VII E 99. The director of the boys school to the AIU in Paris, 30 March 1910.
7 Grange, *Italie*, 645.
8 Turiano and Viscomi, "Immigrants," 5–6.
9 FSC ROMA 565 3. Chronicle of the Community (1925–7), 3.
10 Dogliani, *Fascismo*, 189–92.
11 Tomiak and Kazamias, "Introduction." On the late Ottoman and the Turkish context: Cicek, "Role."
12 Somel, *Modernization*, 5.
13 Ledeen, "Fascism," 142. On state high schools in fascist Italy: Villeggia, *Scuola*; Wanrooij, "Rise."
14 Negash, "Ideology," 115; Pretelli, "Education"; Di Pasquale, "Correlation."
15 ILHAA CENS; GAK DOD OTH 113; DR LIX FF.
16 "L'ordinamento scolastico," *Il Messaggero di Rodi*, 1 May 1926.
17 AIU GRÈCE VI E, 86 bis. The director of the boys school to the AIU in Paris, 7 July 1919.
18 Foucault, *Naissance*, 133–9.
19 Naar, *Salonica*, 140; Ozil, *Christians*, 40–1.
20 Kalambichis, *Zoi*, 15.
21 Der Matossian, "Formation."
22 Kypriotou, *Venetokli*.
23 "Katathesis," 13–14.
24 BOA DH MKT 2676.5. The Ministry of the Interior to the vali of Rhodes, 29 October 1908; BOA DH ID 30–1. The minister of the interior to the vali of Rhodes, 10 October 1910.
25 Papaioannou, *Diagoras*.
26 Kalambichis, *Zoi*, 33; Kypriotou, "Drasi," 119.
27 "Katathesis," 7–8.
28 Kalambichis, *Zoi*, 33–4.
29 "Katathesis," 21–3.
30 Doumanis, *Myth*, 95–103.
31 Frierson, "Women," 150–1.
32 Pernau et al., *Emotions*.

33 Notes on Kaşlıoğlu's biography by John R. Barnes are located the inventory of the material from the Murad Reis Tekke kept at the State Archive of Rhodes. See also: GAK DOD RRCC 1935 RM 4; Nasuhoğlu, *Rodos*, 102.

34 Sertel, *Ḥayāt*.

35 Alhadeff, *Chêne*, 67.

36 Bension Menashe, "Terbiye baḫsı," *Selām*, 23 August 1926.

37 AIU ENIO 2 04. Dissertation by Moise Levy, 2 June 1912.

38 On moral education at *Alliance* schools: Rodrigue, *Instruction*; Benbassa, "Éducation"; Simon, "Education."

39 AIU GRÈCE V E 23. The director of the boys school to the AIU in Paris, 3 June 1912.

40 AIU GRÈCE V E 22. The directress of the girls school to the AIU in Paris, 8 June 1910.

41 Fortna, *Empire*, 16.

42 AIU GRÈCE VI E 92, The director of the girls school to the AIU in Paris, 19 August 1903.

43 AIU GRÈCE VI E 95, Report of June 1909.

44 The first recorded newspaper, *Baḥr-i Sefīd/Aigaion*, was the vilayet's bilingual official bulletin established in 1895. Papachristodoulou, *Istoria*, 506. In 1902, the Ottoman Jewish intellectual Avram Galante asked for permission to open a newspaper called *'Oṣmanlı Musevīleri*, (Ottoman Jews) to be printed in "Turkish," "Greek," and "Spanish," (Ladino), but the Hamidian authorities did not gave their consent. BOA DH MKT 2582 133. The minister of education to the vali of Rhodes, 23 January 1902. Only after the Young Turk putsch of 1908 did other local newspapers appear, this time with a more striking communal feature, such as *Afitāb* (The Sun) and *Rodos*, followed in 1915 by *Rodiaki* and in 1916 by *Il Messaggero di Rodi*. The French vice-consul claimed that the interest of both *Aigaion* and *Rodos* among the local population was "very insignificant, not to say non-existent," suggesting a narrow readership. CADN 569 PO 1 5. The vice-consul to the consul in Smyrna, 30 August 1909. *Sālnāme N 1901*, 520–1. Among the libraries, the still existing Hafiz Ahmed Ağa Library stood out for its precious manuscripts

45 Alhadeff, *Chêne*, 26.

46 Anastassiadou, "Livres."

47 AIU FRANCE X F 18 06. The director of the girls school to the AIU in Paris, 14 December 1905; The director of the girls school to the AIU in Paris, 1 August 1920.

48 Alhadeff, *Chêne*, 123. On the *Venetokleion*: "I anaviosi tis istorikis vivliothikis tou Venetokleiou," *I Rodiaki*, 29 April 2013.

49 Kodaman, *Eğitim*, 198. Örenç refers to 1884 as foundation date. Örenç, *Rodos*, 277.

50 Orakçı, *Rodos*, 20; Örenç, *Rodos*, 271; Nasuhoğlu, *Rodos*, 28.

51 Evered, *Empire*, annex.

52 In 1903, eight students, and among them two Jews, were admitted to the sixth-grade final exams. In 1905, by contrast, eighteen students attended the final exam of the fifth grade, but no one entered the sixth. And yet, in 1909, nine students were enrolled in the sixth grade. See the rosters in: GAK DOD TR 21.

53 *Sālnāme N 1898*, 994; *Sālnāme N 1899*, 1096; *Sālnāme N 1900*, 1237; *Sālnāme N 1901*, 516.

54 GAK DOD OTH B3. Note by the director of the *İdadiye*, 21 December 1909; GAK DOD OTH 145, Notes by the director of the *İdadiye*, 24 December 1911 and 20 March 1912.

55 Kladaki-Menemenli and Freris, *Istoria*, 61–71; Vergotis, *Ekpaideusi*.

56 FSC ROMA Rhodes 561 1. Cirilli to Goblet, 20 February 1889. The consul referred to the short-lived school founded by an Italian resident of Rhodes, Rocco della Cananea, also mentioned in Pignataro, *Dodecaneso I*, 202–3.

57 In 1910, 120 fr., 6 Turkish lira for externs and 24 for boarders some years later. AIU FRANCE X F 18 06. The director of the boys school to the AIU in Paris, 16 August 1910; FSC ROMA 562. Leaflet without date (1922?).

58 19 out of 65 exempted in 1903, 25/128 in 1907, 6/124 in 1908, 20/109 in 1918. CADN 569 PO 1 17. The French vice-consul in Rhodes to the consul in Smyrna, respectively 18 December; 1903, 15 December 1907; 2 December 1908; Note by the director of the *Frères* school, 21 October 1918.

59 CADN 569 PO 1 17. The French consul of Smyrna to the vice-consul of Rhodes, 10 September 1905; Ibid. "Statistique au 1er décembre 1910."

60 AIU GRÈCE V E, 23. Joseph Alhadeff to the AIU in Paris, 21 August 1900.

61 Born in Bodrum and active in different towns of the Aegean region, Galante (often spelled Galanti) maintained his reputation as a public intellectual in republican Turkey. In the 1930s, he wrote a history of the Jews in Turkey widely cited by later scholarship. Sisman, "Galante, Abraham (Avram)"; Galante, *Histoire*, VII: 105; Fintz Menascé, *Ebrei*, 145–9.

62 Rodrigue, *Jews*, 170–2.

63 Molho, "Education," 261.

64 AIU FRANCE X F 18 06. The director of the boys school to the AIU in Paris, 16 August 1910.

65 Galante, *Histoire*, VII: 76–7.

66 AIU FRANCE X F 08 16. The director of the boys school to the AIU in Paris, 11 August 1921.

67 "Dia ta scholeia mas," *Nea Rodos*, 22 July 1911.

68 "Ekpaideutika," *Nea Rodos*, 25 October 1913.

69 "Scholika," *Nea Rodos*, 27 September 1913.

70 GAK DOD IDD 1912–17 6p 37p. Croce to Sonnino, 6 December 1915. See also: McGuire, "Education."

71 GAK DOD IDD 1915–17 6p 37p. Croce to Sonnino, 6 December 1915; "Scuola municipale serale di lingua italiana," 30 November 1915. Pignataro, *Dodecaneso I*, 216–18.

72 GAK DOD IDD 1912–17 6p 44p. Report by Ageo Mancini, 8 July 1917.

73 FSC TORINO 786 3417. In 1945, the last headmaster stated that, until 1924, the Italian government had "ignored the schools just as the Turkish one did." FSC TORINO 786 3419. Scandol to Forrester, 1 June 1945.

74 Di Casola, "Italia."

75 FSC ROMA 565 1. "Cenni sulla fondazione e sviluppo della Comunità di Rodi 1921–1925."

76 FSC TORINO 786 3419. Scandol to Forrester, 1 June 1945; Pignataro, *Dodecaneso III*, 383–416.

77 50 lire per month for externs and 450 for boarders in 1922. FSC ROMA 565.2. Leaflet from 1922. 40–5 (for externs) in 1924. GAK DOD IDD 1924 33p 254p. Piola to Lago, 18 December 1924. 400 (for boarders) in 1926. GAK DOD IDD 1926 55p 474p. Papadimitriou to Lago, 1 November 1926.

78 At times, the "Süleymaniye Medresesi" is mentioned as an institution founded in 1883, one year before the İdadiye. Örenç, *Rodos*, 276. The *salname* of the Vilayet of the Archipelago mentions it in 1903 as a primary school (*mekteb-i ibtidā ʾi*): *Sālnāme C 1903*, 94. A local historian categorizes it as the lower section of the secondary school (*rüşdiye*): Kaşlıoğlu, *Zamanlar*, 121. Finally, an article in *Selām* from 1927 uses this name only as a synonym for the Turkish School in Rhodes: "Medrese-yi Süleymaniye." *Selām*, 10 December 1927.

79 Örenç, *Rodos*, 268–9.

80 See: FSC ROMA 564.1. "Historique du Scolasticat N.D. d'Acandia"; CADN 569 PO 1 17. "Liste des jeunes scolastiques de l'Ecole Normale d'Acandia"; Kladaki-Menemenli and Freris, *Istoria*, 85–108.

81 See a draft in: ASDMAE AAPP 1919–30 990. Lago to Mussolini, 21 June 1927.

82 Rodrigue, "Seminary," 13–15. Since this institution hosted mainly students and personnel from outside Rhodes and has already been analysed by other studies, it is not discussed in this chapter. Pignataro, "Collegio," 49–86; Della Seta, "Ebrei," 1023–5.

83 AIU FRANCE X F 18.06. The director of the boys school to the AIU in Paris, 11 August 1921.

84 For example, the *Alliance* school had some 300 pupils in 1904 and 900 in 1925, when the Italian personnel substituted the French: AIU FRANCE X F

18.06. Yearly reports from 1904; GAK DOD IDD 1925 43p 385p. Lattes to Lago, 2 November 1925. The *Frères* had 45 in 1889 and 209 in 1921: FSC ROMA 560 1. "Diagramme du Collège."

85 FSC ROMA 561 4. Appendix to the school chronicle, "Prix d'excellence et Diplômes décernés depuis leur création 1909 à 1920" [actually 1922].

86 *Sālnāme C 1893*, 93. GAK DOD IDD 1923 20p 136p. Statistics on the local school population for 1922.

87 VENETOKLEIO. "Genikos Elegchos apo 1916.17 eos 1944.45." Prior to 1920, the *Parthenagogeio Kazoulleion* founded in 1887 hosted female students, but only under the age of 14. Papachristodoulou, *Istoria*, 496.

88 Doumanis, *Myth*, 95.

89 GAK DOD IDD 1926 56p 484p. Egidi to Lago, 10 July 1925. For this reason, Lago's reforms made the *Regio Istituto* the mandatory site for the final exam of communal schools candidates in 1928 ASDMAE AAPP 1919–30 992. Lago to Mussolini, 2 June 1928.

90 GAK DOD IDD 1925 43p 385p. "L'insegnamento scolastico nelle Isole Egee."

91 ASDMAE AAPP 1919–30 992. Lago to Mussolini, 2 June 1928.

92 Espinoza, "Italiani," 260.

93 "Atti Ufficiali," *Il Messaggero di Rodi*, 22 July 1937. The *Venetokleion* reopened in 1943 December after the arrival of the German troops, which sought the Orthodox notables' support. Kypriotou, *Venetokli*, 130–6.

94 AIU ENIO 2 01. Results of the admission tests, 1912. Moussafir was naturalized as a French citizen with his wife Mathilde in 1946, after being rescued from the Holocaust by a friend, André Martin. https://yadvashem-france.org/dossier/nom/12726/ (accessed 31 May 2021).

95 Kypriotou, *Venetokli*, 270.

96 However, in 1922 she left Rhodes for Africa, with her fiancé Victor. Benatar, *Rhodes*, 6–10. AIU FRANCE X F 18 06. The director of the boys school to the AIU in Paris, 11 August 1921.

97 FSC ROMA 565 4. Piola to De Bosdari, 12 February 1922.

98 GAK DOD IDD 1923 20p 136p. Piola to Lago, 1 June 1923. The scholarships were awarded to two Italians and one local Jew in the first year. GAK DOD IDD 1924 29p 203p. Piola to Lago, 27 July 1924.

99 GAK DOD IDD 1924 33p 254p. Frascaroli to Lago, 18 December 1924.

100 Ibid. Petition by Markos T., 4 July 1924; Corresponding police report, 9 July 1924; Notification of refusal, 1 August 1924.

101 GAK DOD IDD 1941 1124 325. Note by the director of civil affairs, 12 September 1941. One scholarship was reserved to Jewish students, although the Racial Laws of 1938 had excluded them from Italian schools.

102 GAK DOD IDD 1937 739 444. Petition by Mensure Ö., Feb 1937.

103 Alhadeff, *Chêne*, 146–51.
104 CADN 569 PO 1 6. The school director to the French vice-consul, 12 July 1932; The general inspector of French institutions in Syria and Lebanon to the secretary general of the diplomatic office, 16 January 1933.
105 Pignataro, *Dodecaneso II*, 467–71, 479–81, 484–9.
106 GAK DOD RRCC 1935 2 12 1649. Notes by the *Carabinieri*, 23 February 1938; 28 February 1938; De Vecchi to Galli, 18 May 1938.
107 Fortna, *Classroom*, 164.
108 Alhadeff, *Chêne*, 128.
109 In 1910 May Michail Kaloupaklis was suspended from school for a month after saying to a teacher "I will carve your eyes out!" (*tha sou vgalo ta 'mmatia*) but he was accepted for the September exam session. VENETOKLEIO. "Katoptron Diagogis ton Matiton – 1'Gymnasiou."
110 VENETOKLEIO. "Vivlio vathmologias apo 1912 eos 1917."
111 VENETOKLEIO. "Praktika Venetokleiou Gimnasiou apo 05.05.1924 eos 27.04.1929."
112 Fortna, *Classroom*, 241.
113 GAK DOD OTH 25. Report no. 1, 4 March 1906.
114 Ibid. Appendix to report no. 9, 2 May 1906.
115 Ibid. Report no. 9, 2 May 1906.
116 They bullied him by writing on school walls sentences such as: "Ah! My sweetheart Avram, how nice that would be, if you gave it to me just once" (*Ah! Benim ḳuzum Avram bir kere virsen ne güzel olur*) or "Your beloved eyes and lips Avram, could they not be at our disposal just once? (*Gözlerini dudaḳlarını sevdiğim Avram bize bir kerecik himmet itmeñiz olmaz mı?*). Ibid. Appendix to report no. 1, 5 March 1906; Report dated 15 February 1906.
117 Ibid. Appendix to report no. 3, 28 December 1905.
118 Somel, *Modernization*, 270.
119 GAK DOD OTH 195. Report dated 28 January 1912. On the functions of the *ıslahhane* see: Maksudyan, *Orphans*, 76–115.
120 Fortna, "Education," 18.
121 GAK DOD OTH B3. The Directorate of Education to the İdadiye director, 29 January 1908.
122 GAK DOD OTH 61. Note number 93, 6 June 1910.
123 Ibid. Note number 122, 5 August 1910.
124 AIU GRÈCE V E 23. The directress of the girls school to the AIU in Paris, March 1909; The director of the boys school to the AIU in Paris, January 1909; Benbassa, "Éducation." However, ambivalence as to punishment methods emerges in many reports. As the directress of the girls school noted in 1910: "Very often, what could not be obtained through violence we obtain through mildness." A hint that corporal punishments were tolerated although deemed less effective? AIU FRANCE X F 18.06. The directress of the girls school to the AIU in Paris, 23 September 1910.

125 AIU GRÈCE V E 23. The directress of the girls school to the AIU in Paris, 5 June 1903.

126 Such an attitude had similarities with new Muslim schools in Habsburg Sarajevo. Giomi, "Girls," 288–9.

127 AIU GRÈCE VI E 92. The directress of the girls school to the AIU in Paris, 4 March 1903; 17 January 1904; 12 August 1904.

128 On this association: Kostaridou, *Athina*.

129 AIU GRÈCE V E 81 bis. The directress of the girls school to the AIU in Paris, 27 April 1917.

130 Rodrigue, *Instruction*, 24–30.

131 AIU GRÈCE V E 81. The directress of the girls school to the AIU in Paris, 4 July 1912.

132 Ibid. The directress of the girls school to the AIU in Paris, 2 January 1912.

133 In his memoirs, Vittorio Alhadeff denies the accusations of "pederasty" against the *Frères*. However, he admits to having been the target of sexual abuse by a janitor when he was 11, without denouncing the episode. Alhadeff, *Chêne*, 123.

134 "Rodos ahāli-i hammiyet-mendāni ṭarafindan iʿāne-i ḥarbiyeye iştirāk iden ẓevātiñ isāmılarıla miḳdār-ı iʿānelerini mubīn defterdir." *Ceride-i ʿilmiye* 2 (1915).

135 The seventh grade was the higher in that year at the *İdadiye*. GAK DOD IDD 1915–17 6p 39p. Attestation by Kjanan Efendi, 20 February 1915.

136 Ibid. Petition signed by thirteen students, 21 February 1915.

137 Ibid. Notes by the *Carabinieri* (Annex A and B), 27 February 1915.

138 ASDMAE AAPP 1919–30 979. Elia to Sonnino, 30 April 1919. See also: Pignataro, *Dodecaneso I*, 141; Papachristodoulou, *Istoria*, 541; Doumanis, *Myth*, 39.

139 AIMR. "Praktika Eforias 1914–1922." Minute, 22 February 1919.

140 GAK DOD IDD 1920 10 11. Note by the *Carabinieri*, 25 February 1919.

141 Note by the *Carabinieri*, 27 February 1919. The Italian police mentions a "Turkish student of the third grade" as one of the agitators, although no other source in my possession explicitly refers to him. On Katsouris's expulsion see: AIMR. "Praktika Eforias 1914–1922." Minute, 6 March 1919; "Scholika," *Nea Rodos*, 16 February 1919.

142 CADN 569 PO 1 6. Apostolos to Laffon, 10 March 1919.

143 GAK DOD IDD 1920 10 11. Note by the *Carabinieri*, undated.

144 I have found two copies of this manifesto dated 3/16 April 1919. One is followed by a French translation and is found in CADN 569 PO 1 6. The other is dated 23 April 1919 and is found in GAK DOD ADS MUN 16 0 F 06. Among those students about whom information is available at the *Venetokleion* archives, five of them were sons of traders, three of doctors, and one each of a landowner, farmer, priest, as well as an orphan. Five came from Rhodes town, two from villages, three from other Dodecanese islands,

one from Athens and Istanbul respectively. VENETOKLEION. "Genikos Elegchos apo 1916.17 eos 1944.45."

145 The *Frères* School was less affected by such turmoil, which might also explain why most sons of prominent families were not active in any protest. As the headmaster noted as early as 1912, "Our position is quite delicate. Having been well treated by the Turks, we cannot disown them, nor however sulk over the newcomers. Thus, we have remained quite neutral, preventing any political allusion." This continued until 1923 given this school's bond to France, which was at once Italy's ally in the First World War and its main competitor in terms of educational imperialism. FSC ROMA 561 4. "Historique de notre communauté de Rhodes," 18 May 1912.

146 On the contrary, Apostolos and Ferid, whom the Italian authorities suspected to act in accord, addressed the French vice-consul lamenting that Italian agents were stirring up members of each confession against one another. CADN 569 PO 1 6. Ferid to Laffon, 20 February 1919.

4 "Good Conduct" between Work and Leisure

1 "Il VI Anniversario della Marcia su Roma nelle manifestazioni rodie," *Il Messaggero di Rodi*, 30 October 1928.

2 Foot, *Pedalare*, 5, 57; Cardoza, "Italians."

3 "Il VI Anniversario della Marcia su Roma nelle manifestazioni rodie," *Il Messaggero di Rodi*, 30 October 1928.

4 Sentakis, *Istoria*, 404–5.

5 GAK DOD RRCC 1932 17 PS 343. Notes by the *Carabinieri*, 19 May 1934; 7 May 1936 and 23 November 1936; De Suda to Grassini, 1 August 1937; Note by the *Carabinieri*, 4 August 1937; GAK DOD ITA DIK (Unclassified). "Tribunale Civile di Rodi 1937." Dispute between the *Società Commerciale Italiana* and Mustafa Boiagi.

6 AIU GRÈCE X F 18.06. The director of the boys school to the AIU in Paris, 24 July 1921.

7 See different advertisements and articles in: *Il Messaggero di Rodi*, 29 May 1931.

8 Veblen, *Theory*, 28.

9 Maynard Keynes, "Possibilities," 367.

10 Blackshaw, *Leisure*, 2.

11 Kilinçoğlu, *Economics*, 161–85.

12 Fuhrmann, *Cities*, 118–21; 266–87.

13 Frangakis-Syrret, "Dynamics."

14 Biliotti and Cottret, *Île*, 702.

15 CADN 569 PO 1 17. The French consul to the baker Reynaud, 6 January 1903.

16 GAK DOD RRCC 1933 2 35 2. Note by the *Carabinieri*, 3 September 1935.

17 Espinoza, "Italiani," 162–6; 344–53.

18 Berezin, *Self*, 149.

19 Doumanis, *Myth*, 156.

20 Davidova, *Transitions*.

21 See among others: Quataert, "Women"; Balsoy, "History"; Köksal and Falierou, *History*; Ianeva, "Actors." On Eritrea: Barrera, "Aria."

22 I lean on Kamala Kempadoo's suggestion to use sex work(er) as analytical category instead of "prostitution" or "whore" to decentre the look from a social marker, to highlight the "similarities with other dimensions of working people's lives," and to underline the centrality of precariousness and migration in the trajectories of the working individuals involved. Kempadoo, "Workers," 3.

23 Alhadeff, *Chêne*, 46.

24 Ibid., 81; Espinoza, "Italiani," 324–8.

25 GAK DOD IDD 1936 580 31. "Popolazione Dodecanesina, sudditi italiani e stranieri, di età superiore a 10 anni, secondo le condizioni e la professione del capo famiglia," undated (1936).

26 Arca Petrucci, "Città," 139. The year 1875 as provided by the author for the arrival of the Agiakatsikas in Rhodes needs further cross checking, as it contrasts with the birthplace of Ioannis's sons Panagiotis and Antonios. According to documents from the archive of the *Carabinieri* (see notes below), they were both born in Mytilene, in 1878 and 1879 respectively.

27 BOA BEO 2653 198932. The Sublime Porte to the Customs Department of the Ministry of Commerce, 24 August 1905.

28 CADN 569 PO 1 13. Jules Abril to the French vice-consul in Rhodes, 4 March 1910; The vice-consul's reply, 13 March 1910.

29 AIMR. "Praktika Miktou Ekklesiastikou Dikastiriou 1905–1914"; "Praktika scholon 1901–1914."

30 Adam, *Respectability*.

31 Kostaridou, *Athina*, 172.

32 "Psifisma epi tou thanatou tou K.ou Ioannou Agiakatsika," *I Rodiaki*, 4 January 1918.

33 ACS AMEGLIO 33 299. Ameglio to local traders, erroneously dated "5/18 Avril 1912."

34 ASDMAE AAPP 1919–30 979. Scialoja to the chargé d'affaires in Athens, 24 October 1919; Copy of the letter signed by the notables, 28 August 1919.

35 ASDMAE AAPP 1919–30 980. Draft of a study written by De Bosdari in 1922, 86; GAK DOD IDD 1920 10 11. Note by the *Carabinieri*, 6 December 1920.

36 Kypriotou, *Venetokli*, 54–7.

37 Sentakis, *Istoria*, 95. GAK DOD RRCC 1933 2 9 5. List of the club's members, 13 March 1933.

38 "Le industrie di Rodi," *Il Messaggero di Rodi*, 25 December 1928; Arca Petrucci, "Città," 139–40.

39 GAK DOD RRCC 1932 6 PS 974. Ioannis Agiakatsikas's visa request, 26 September 1934; His application for the commercial license, 23 June 1937.

40 GAK DOD RRCC 1933 2 12 1238. Notes by the *Carabinieri*, 7 December 1937; 7 October 1936; 26 February 1935.

41 GAK DOD RRCC 1932 6 PS 974. Ioannis's marriage certificate, 10 March 1938; For Demetrios: GAK DOD IDD 1935 542 471. Notes on the elections of the neighbourhood Eforia of Neocori, 17 August 1933.

42 "Koinotika," *I Rodiaki*, 28 August 1933. "To neon Koin. Symvoulion," *I Rodiaki*, 7 September 1933; GAK DOD RRCC 1932 20 PS 1. Note by the *Carabinieri*, 23 January 1937; Pignataro, *Dodecaneso II*, 320.

43 Marongiu Buonaiuti, *Politica*, 51–76.

44 GAK DOD RRCC 1933 2 12 598. Note by the *Carabinieri*, 23 November 1934.

45 Ibid. Note by the *Carabinieri*, 8 May 1936.

46 GAK DOD RRCC 1932 6 PS 974. Note by the *Carabinieri*, 1 May 1944.

47 Ibid. Note by the *Carabinieri*, 31 March 1939; GAK DOD RRCC 1933 2 12 1238, Note by the *Carabinieri*, 31 March 1939.

48 de Grazia, *Culture*, 60.

49 Kasaba, Keyder, and Tabak, "Port-Cities"; Fuhrmann, "Imperialists."

50 Muncie, *Youth*, 51.

51 GAK DOD ITA DIK (Unclassified). Tribunale Civile e Penale di Rodi 1916. "Procedimento contro Micali C.C." Attestation by Kirani K., 23 August 1916; Ibid. Attestation by Micali C.C., 9 November 1916; GAK DOD ITA DIK (Unclassified). Tribunale Penale di Rodi 1918. "Procedimento contro Sami I., Recep M., Ali S., Ali H.." Attestation by Recep M., 19 December 1918.

52 GAK DOD IDD 1935 549 516. Daily police report on the infractions committed in Rhodes, 1 April 1935.

53 Hafez, "Lazy," 31; Özbek, "Beggars."

54 Maksudyan, "Children"; Maksudyan, *Orphans*, 12–13.

55 Garfinkel, *Law*, 196–283, 419.

56 These patterns could concern two brothers of the same family: GAK DOD ITA DIK (Unclassified). Tribunale Civile e Penale di Rodi 1930. "Ricovero in casa di correzione del minorenne P. Zambico." Petition by M. Cristina, 13 February 1930; GAK DOD ITA DIK (Unclassified). Tribunale Civile e Penale di Rodi 1930. "Ricovero in casa di correzione del minorenne P. Elefterio." The secretary of the governor of Rhodes to the president of the Civil and Criminal Court, 13 January 1931; The president of the Civil and Criminal Court to Lago, 13 January 1931.

57 Ibid. Certificate issued by the Executive Council of the reformatory of Pisa, 7 October 1932.

58 GAK DOD IDD 1939 974 506. Report by the *Carabinieri* including the copy of the petition, 15 September 1939.

59 GAK DOD IDD 1941 1103 185. Petition by Grigorio P., 15 September 1941.
60 Fuhrmann, "Beer"; Örs, "Coffeehouses"; Georgeon, "Cafés"; Anastassiadou, "Cafés."
61 GAK DOD OTH IN 1327. Bill No. 498, 13 February 1912. In the Ottoman world, "beardless" was not only an age marker, but could also relate to gender and boundaries of homo-erotic male desire. Ze'evi, *Desire*, 77–98.
62 GAK DOD ITA DIK (Unclassified). Tribunale Penale di Rodi 1913. "Procedimento penale contro Zafer I.." Report by the *Carabinieri*, 20 July 1913.
63 "Cercle de Rhodes," *Nea Rodos*, 18 February 1912.
64 "La veglia al Circolo Italia," *Il Messaggero di Rodi*, 6 April 1920.
65 Vratsalis, *Niochoritika*, 119.
66 GAK DOD RRCC 1933 2 35 2. The Scalia brothers to the *Carabinieri*, 22 June 1937.
67 Ibid. Copy of the work contract, 7 June 1937.
68 Ibid. Note by the *Carabinieri* on the margin of a letter by the Scalia brothers, 13 July 1937.
69 Ibid. Notes by the *Carabinieri*, 13 July 1936; 19 July 1936.
70 Kadri, "Sefāhata dā'ir," *Selām*, 4 June 1928.
71 GAK DOD RRCC 1933 2 23 118. Note by the *Carabinieri*, 19 January 1934.
72 AIU FRANCE X F 18 06. The director of the boys school to the AIU in Paris, 26 October 1904.
73 AIU GRÈCE V E 23. The director of the boys school to the AIU in Paris, 11 December 1908.
74 Kostaridou, *Athina*, 29–43.
75 ILHAA CENS; GAK DOD OTH 113; DR LIX FF. See chapter 2 for more information on these censuses.
76 Higgs, "Women," 60.
77 Rose, "Gender," 116; Hill, "Women," 79; Daniels, "Work."
78 In comparative terms this rate is almost three times higher than in early twentieth-century Damascus. Okawara, "Size," 64. In Istanbul, servants were a common element of households, starting to work at an early age and quitting it after marriage. Duben and Behar, *Istanbul*, 67–8.
79 Duben and Behar, *Istanbul*, 167.
80 Maksudyan, "Daughter"; Maksudyan, *Orphans*, 55–78.
81 GAK DOD ITA DIK (Unclassified). Tribunale Penale di Rodi 1914. "Procedimento penale contro C. Dichea di Sava." Attestations by C. Dichea, 17 May 1914 and 20 May 1914; Attestation by Giovanni S., 20 May 1914.
82 GAK DOD ITA DIK (Unclassified). Tribunale Penale di Rodi 1920. "Morte disgraziata di Sotiria C. e Eleni M.M." Report by the *Carabinieri*, 10 May 1920; Attestation by Maria P., 11 May 1920.

83 GAK DOD ITA DIK (Unclassified). Giudicatura Civile di Rodi 1926. "Causa civile, Attore Filippo K.." Letter by Evangelo C., 25 July 1925.

84 Ibid. Request by Filippo K., 22 July 1926.

85 GAK DOD ITA DIK (Unclassified). Giudicatura Civile di Rodi 1926. "Parascheva L. residente a Rodi." Translation of the dowry agreement, 30 September 1917.

86 Ibid. Declaration by Elvio S.C., 7 December 1926.

87 Nagel, *Race*, 191.

88 Fuhrmann, "Perversions"; Fuhrmann, "Quays"; Özbek, "Regulation."

89 AIU FRANCE X F 18 06. The director of the girls school to the AIU in Paris, 15 October 1913.

90 The records of Rhodes's Ottoman Criminal Tribunal (*cezā maḥkemesi*) are unclassified and preserved at the local Greek State Archive. The term *fiʾl-i şeniʿ* (abominable act) recurs often in these documents. Such ambivalent term could relate to rape (especially if preceded by "violently," *cebren*), sodomy, but also adultery. In this case in particular, it might refer to an intercourse with sex workers. See also: Lévy-Aksu, *Ordre*, 99.

91 ASDMAE AAPP 1891–1916 155. Giolitti to Bartolini, 23 July 1913; Giolitti to Sangiuliano, 9 August 1913.

92 GAK DOD ITA DIK (Unclassified). Tribunale Penale di Rodi 1913. "Procedimento penale contro Akmet M.." Report by the *Carabinieri*, 22 July 1913.

93 As was the case for the daughter of Sultana L., who was herself a sex worker. GAK DOD ITA DIK (Unclassified). Copies of sentences of the Civil and Criminal Tribunal in Rhodes. Sentence no. 34, 28 March 1922 and no. 18, 22 June 1927.

94 GAK DOD RRCC 1932 11 PS 71. Notes by the *Carabinieri*, 15 March 1933; 23 December 1936; Personal record dated 24 January 1935.

95 GAK DOD RRCC 1932 11 PS 58. Notes by the *Carabinieri*, 22 December 1932; 10 October 1938; 14 May 1940.

96 Ibid. Lulludia M. to Iassemì M., 2 October 1939.

97 Ibid. Note by the *Carabinieri*, 8 November 1939.

98 GAK DOD RRCC 1939 2 17 39. Notes by the *Carabinieri*, 3 February 1939; 9 March 1942.

99 Ibid. Note by the *Carabinieri*, 9 October 1944.

100 GAK DOD RRCC 1932 11 PS 41. Note by the *Carabinieri*, 16 February 1939.

101 Bourdieu, "Voraussetzungen."

102 Gillis, *Youth*, 111.

103 Okay, "Introduction," 4; Okay, "Sport."

104 Koulouri, "Antiquity."

105 Papaioannou, *Diagoras*, 47.

106 Sentakis, *Istoria*, 40.

107 "Theatron Kalla," *Rodos*, 16 May 1909.

108 Elias and Dunning, *Quest*.

109 "La prima gara di Football," *Il Messaggero di Rodi*, 12 April 1920.

110 GAK DOD IDD 1920 10 11. Letter by David Cohen, 19 November 1920.

111 AIU GRÈCE V E 23. The director of the boys school to the AIU in Paris, 18 July 1920.

112 AIU FRANCE X F 18 06. The director of the boys school to the AIU in Paris, 11 August 1921.

113 FSC TORINO 353 1067. Piola to Bigin, 11 April 1924. The caption reads "Against the Fante [the opponent team]: a moment of the strife."

114 Dogliani, "Sport," 199–206.

115 Fintz Menascé, *Ebrei*, 235; Orakçı, *Rodos*, 97.

116 Mehmet Kadri, "Spora dā'ir," *Selām*, 28 May 1928.

117 This contrasts Jeffrey Hill's claim that "what has primarily identified youth has been its leisure activity": Hill, *Sport*, 115.

118 Sentakis, *Istoria*, 80.

119 VENETOKLEION. "Genikos Elegchos apo 1916.17 eos 1944.45."

120 Papaioannou, *Diagoras*, 125–31.

121 See the *Carabinieri* files: GAK DOD RRCC SP 682; 683; 690.

122 GAK DOD RRCC 1934 1 1 68. Note by the *Carabinieri*, 5 April 1934.

123 GAK DOD RRCC 1933 2 9 14. Decree no. 48, 17 February 1931.

124 Sentakis, *Istoria*, 194–7.

125 GAK DOD RRCC 1932 2 9 2. First application sent to the *Carabinieri*, 21 October 1929; Letter including the first board after the approval by FRATRES, 1 June 1932.

126 GAK DOD RRCC 1932 2 PS 192. Misios's banishment decree, 28 July 1938.

127 GAK DOD RRCC 1933 2 PS 9 5. Notes by the *Carabinieri*, 4 February 1933; 23 February 1933;

128 "Per lo sviluppo dello sport cittadino," *Il Messaggero di Rodi*, 12 June 1935.

129 Sentakis, *Istoria*, 248–69.

130 GAK DOD RRCC 1932 20 PS 2. Note by the *Carabinieri*, 13 September 1933.

5 Generations, Mobility, and Shifting Limits of Belonging

1 "Oi Rodioi ekpatrizomenoi," *Rodos*, 11 September 1910.

2 GAK DOD RRCC 1932 II 445. Note by the *Carabinieri*, 26 January 1933.

3 "La situation politique et économique en Turquie," *Le Yildiz (L'Étoile Orientale)*, 11 May 1893.

4 Espinoza, "Cittadinanza."

5 Smyrnelis, "Colonies," 188; Schmitt, *Levantiner*, 336.

6 Khater, *Home*.

7 Fahrenthold, *Ottomans*, 15.

8 Gutman, *Politics*, 23.
9 Among a long list of works, see: Gabaccia and Ottanelli, "Diaspora"; Gabaccia and Iacovetta, *Women*.
10 Choate, *Emigrant Nation*, 14.
11 Pergher, "Colony."
12 Ballinger, *World*.
13 Green, "Histoire."
14 Osterhammel, *Transformation*, 154.
15 McKeown, "Migration."
16 "Gegonos: Rodos-Ameriki," *Rodos,* 16 May 1909.
17 Clancy-Smith, *Mediterraneans*, 84.
18 ASDMAE AAPP 1891–1916 155. Ameglio to Giolitti, 27 May 1913.
19 Gabaccia, "Time," 56.
20 Freitag and von Oppen, "Translocality," 7.
21 Sephardi Hebrew Congregation of Rhodesia, *History*; Leon, *Anniversary*, 7. In 1913, N. Alhadeff, aged 18, moved to Salisbury as a "very poor" orphan and was employed by Bohor Leon, another pioneer of Rhodian emigration to Salisbury, Rhodesia. After one of his trips to Rhodes, Leon brought a picture of a relative, Behora, to his young employee, who decided to make her a wedding proposal. Behora came to Africa in 1922 to join Jacques, and their daughter married Marco Alhadeff's son. See the biographies of the Jewish Community of Zimbabwe: www.zjc.org.il /showpage.php?pageid=88: "Alhadeff Borthers"; Alhadeff, Solly & Stella"; "Leon, BS" (accessed 4 April 2018).
22 Benatar and Pimienta-Benatar, *Rhodes*.
23 Grosselli, *Uomini*.
24 Stein, *Dreams*, 81.
25 Morelli, "Diplomates."
26 Ben-Ghiat and Hom, "Introduction," 3.
27 More broadly on Italian return migration: Cinel, *Integration*; Douki, "Return."
28 In 1929, Luca P. from Lindos, aged 30, came back after ten years with his savings and settled first in his native village, where he got married, and then to Rhodes at his sister's place, probably because of a quick separation. One year after his return, which his parents interpreted as "need for native atmosphere" (*aria nativa*), he began to show signs of mental disturbances, and attempted suicide. GAK DOD ITA DIK (Unclassified). "Governo delle Isole dell'Egeo, anno 1929, Corrispondenze." Note by the *Carabinieri*, 29 October 1929.
29 See the entry in the arrival records in Buenos Aires from the Latin American Centre for Migration Studies (CEMLA): www.cemla.com/buscador/ "Berro Jacob"; Haim's personal police file GAK DOD RRCC 1936 1 2 639, and his parents' entry: CDEC: "Berro Giacobbe," "Alhadeff Rosa," "Berro Amelia."

30 CADN PO 569 1 17. The French vice-consul to the consul in Smyrna, 13 July 1907.
31 AIU GRÈCE I C 27. The director of the boys school to the AIU in Paris, 30 March 1910.
32 AMIA CMT, Salomon Notrika interview, 28320 n. 135 CD 20.
33 Barkey Flash, *Hug* (e-Book).
34 CADN PO 569 1 5. The French consul in Smyrna to Bompard, date unknown (16 January 1910?).
35 Karpat, "Emigration"; Arsan, *Interlopers*, 23–38; Gutman, *Politics*, 26.
36 Hazan, *Dia* (e-Book).
37 EIF PR. From a sample of 32 passengers of the liner *Patris* arriving in New York on 2 June 1909.
38 UWL OHC, Matilda Menashe interview.
39 Antonakos, *Community*, 115.
40 Barkey Flash, *Hug* (e-Book).
41 Kiriazis, *Children*, 89.
42 In a note from 1917, the Italian military governor wrote of "many millions" sent yearly from abroad to sustain the poorer relatives in Rhodes. ASDMAE GAB 1915–18 56. Elia to Sonnino, 21 June 1917. As an example of aid request: JDC NY AR 1418 7403. Albert J. Amateau to the American Jewish JDC, 5 June 1918.
43 Angel, *World*, 39.
44 Barkey Flash, *Hug* (e-Book).
45 GAK DOD ITA DIK (Unclassified). Tribunale Penale di Rodi 1918. "Procedimento penale contro Nissim C. e Juda N.." Attestation by Esther M., 31 July 1918. Esther does not figure on the list of passengers who arrived in New York in 1921, which included her mother Bulissa. Esther's mother came to join her husband and later moved to Seattle. She came with three daughters, Katina (aged 14) Sara (6) and Tsalia (4). It is possible that Esther changed her name to Katina and declared to be six years younger, but no further information is available: "Polisa M.." Passenger ID 100106010332, Frame 982, Line 24. Arrival date 2 July 1921, Ship *King Alexander* from Piraeus.
46 Kiriazis, *Children*, 66.
47 GAK DOD ITA DIK (Unclassified). Tribunale Civile e Penale di Rodi, 1919. "Procedimento Penale contro Hizkia A. e Estrea A.." Note by the *Carabinieri*, 6 October 1919; Attestation by Hizkia A., 17 February 1920.
48 "Ex Amerikis," *Nea Rodos*, 11 January 1911. *Nea Rodos* was the new edition of the already mentioned paper *Rodos*.
49 "To zitima ton gamon ton en Ameriki Rodion," *Rodiaki,* 22 June 1931.
50 Daniels, *Door*, 59.
51 On the concept of "Homeland" vs. "America" among Greek emigrants: Laliotou, *Subjects*, 100–8.

52 AIU GRÈCE X F 18.06. The director of the boys school to the AIU in Paris, 18 November 1908.
53 UWL OHC, Elazar Behar interview.
54 UWL OHC, Charles Alhadeff interview.
55 UWL OHC, Rosa Berro interview.
56 Kerem, "Settlement," 373.
57 Adatto, "Sephardim," 54–60.
58 UWL OHC, Charles Alhadeff interview. These activities persisted among Jewish *Rodeslis* in Seattle until 1940. In the US general census concerning the districts most densely populated by them around the Synagogue of Yesler Way, more than one third of those who registered their profession (124) were either working at the fish market (23) or selling fruit and vegetables (22). US NA CS 1940 ED 40 162; 165; 287; 288. The sample consists of 79 households including 370 individuals.
59 UWL OHC, Rosa Berro interview; UWL OHC, Elazar Behar interview.
60 YSU SVV, James W. Kiriazis interview.
61 Kiriazis, *Children*, 92.
62 UWL OHC, Jacob Almeleh interview.
63 UWL OHC, Charles Alhadeff interview.
64 Sephardim couples in which both spouses were born in "Italy" (in the 1940 Italian territory, namely the Dodecanese) amounted to 75 per cent. Those in which one spouse was born in "Italy" and the other one in the United States reached 12.5 per cent, the same score as those including a spouse from "Italy" and one from a third country, namely Turkey or Egypt. US NA CS 1940 ED 40 162; 165; 287; 288. This differs from the less endogamous marriage pattern of Rhodian Orthodox in the town of Warren, for which Kiriazis provides data from the period 1919–39. Out of 34 marriages, 50 per cent were of spouses both born in Rhodes, 9 per cent of a Rhodian born and a US born Rhodian, 15 per cent were unions between a Rhodian born and an Orthodox from elsewhere born either in Greece or in the United States, and 26 per cent pertained to a Rhodian born and a non-Greek. Kiriazis, *Children*, 179.
65 UWL OHC, Mary Capeloto interview.
66 UWL OHC, Philip Flash interview.
67 UWL OHC, Marc Angel interview.
68 Angel, *Jews*; Angel, *World*, x.
69 Pressman, "Rhodes." http://jewishstudies.washington.edu/personal-history/remembering-rhodes-sephardic-holocaust/. (accessed 19 March 2020).
70 Hirsch, *Generation*, 5–6.
71 Hirsch, *Family*, 243.

72 Sintès, "Synagogue"; UH MGCJS, Aron Hasson interview. www.youtube
.com/watch?v=dcmKWzARef4. (accessed 19 March 2020).

73 www.rhodesjewishmuseum.org/. (accessed 19 March 2020)

74 www.facebook.com/groups/130804330433532/;www.facebook.com
/groups/546890742472923/ (accessed 19 March 2020). These groups are
"private" and an access permission by their managers is needed.

75 Guidi, "Inter-Communality"; Sintès, *Présence*; Rappas, "Soliloquies."

76 Kiriazis, *Children*, 151–3. See also: Theodoratus, *Community*. GAK DOD
ADS MUN 16 0 F 06 42–3. Undated list of donors (1927); GAK DOD ADS
MUN 16 0 F 06 31–2. Agapitos Tsopannakis to Demetrios Agiakatsikas, 13
March 1927.

77 US NA CS 1940 ED 63 11.

78 National Committee for the Restoration of Greece, *Dodecanesians*, 7.

79 Kiriazis, *Children*, 1, 78.

80 Nicon and Nicon, "Jews." (accessed 19 March 2020).

81 Rappas, "Soliloquies," 101–2.

82 *VII Censimento*, 57.

83 McGuire, *Sea*, 146; Espinoza, "Cittadinanza."

84 Rappas, "Marriages."

85 McGuire, *Sea*, 221–34.

86 Tsirpanlis defines it as "anxiety" (*anastatosi*) vis-à-vis a "deceitful
and dangerous instrument of the conqueror with the purpose of the
de-nationalization (*apo-ethnikopoiisi*) of the population." Tsirpanlis,
Italokratia, 250–1. Doumanis, more accurately, remarks that "patriotic
moral sanctions [against it] did not seem to hinder the frequency of
intermarriage." Doumanis, *Myth*, 171.

87 However, if a local subject was a widow/er or obtained a divorce
certificate from a religious tribunal, he or she was entitled to a second
marriage with an Italian citizen.

88 Pasqualini, *Esercito*, 298.

89 Three per cent came from Istanbul, and 3 per cent from other towns.

90 This kind of post-military colonialism can be observed as well in Italian
East Africa in the direct aftermath of the Ethiopian Campaign of 1935–6.
Barrera, "Mussolini," 429.

91 DR LIX GAM, 1913 no. 1; 1914 no. 2.

92 Ibid. 1920, no. 4; no. 5. For Gatti: GAK DOD RRCC 1932 II 352. Note by
the *Carabinieri* of Torino, 4 June 1932; Note by the *Carabinieri* of Rhodes, 13
September 1938. For Rao: GAK DOD RRCC II 633. Note by the *Carabinieri*
of Castelbuono, 22 June 1932; Note by the *Carabinieri* of Rhodes, 9
September 1935.

93 Ibid. Note by the *Carabinieri*, 9 November 1938.

94 GAK DOD RRCC 1933 1 59 94. Note by the *Carabinieri* of Rhodes, 17 March 1934; Marcantonio to his wife Vittoria, 21 July 1925; 14 April 1928; Note by the *Carabinieri* of Sondrio, 12 May 1930; Note by the *Carabinieri* of Ferrara, 27 March 1934. See the couple's marriage record: DR LIX. GAM 1920, no. 2.

95 Matard-Bonucci, "Fascism."

96 GAK DOD RRCC 1933 1 59 94. Note by the *Carabinieri*, 9 July 1935.

97 Ibid. Vittoria P. to the Ministry of the Colonies, 15 August 1935.

98 Ibid. Note by the *Carabinieri*, 14 December 1938.

99 GAK DOD RRCC 1932 15 PS 282. Note by the *Carabinieri* of Zara, 13 April 1932.

100 Ibid. Notes by the *Carabinieri*, 6 July 1934; 18 January 1933.

101 Ibid. Note by the *Carabinieri*, 18 January 1933.

102 Ibid. Note by the *Carabinieri* 23 May 1934.

103 GAK DOD RRCC 1932 IM 18. Notes by the *Carabinieri*, 14 September 1935; 27 September 1935; 6 March 1936.

104 Ibid. Note by the *Carabinieri*, 3 March 1939.

105 Collotti, *Fascismo*, 38; Matard-Bonucci, "Persécution."

106 GAK DOD RRCC 1936 2 23 1266. Notes by the *Carabinieri*, 6 July 1937; 15 December 1937; 15 July 1940.

107 Ibid. Note by the *Carabinieri*, 20 July 1943. See GC. Interview with Benjamin F. Di Liscia. www.youtube.com/watch?v=G-APPx_nHSs (accessed 20 March 2020).

108 EIF PR, passenger record 9011867028967, ship "Marine Jumper" arriving in New York on 16 May 1949. Only Eleonora and her son Michele are recorded, although Benjamin Di Liscia states that the whole family moved to the United States, after three years spent in Italy. See also: CDEC, "Avzaradel, Baruch."

109 Schmitt, *Levantiner*; Pongiluppi, "Fede."

110 GAK DOD RRCC 1932 6 PS 745. Note by the *Carabinieri*, 12 April 1934.

111 Ibid. Francesco B. to Lago, 18 July 1933.

112 GAK DOD RRCC 1933 1 2 483. Note by the *Carabinieri*, 29 November 1935.

113 GAK DOD RRCC 1933 II 1304. Ferrata to Lago, 18 February 1934.

114 GAK DOD RRCC 1932 6 PS 257. Note by the *Carabinieri*, 19 May 1937.

115 Ibid. Note by the *Carabinieri*, 19 July 1939.

116 Ibid. Antonio D. to the vice-governor of Rhodes, 29 November 1941; Note by the *Carabinieri*, 15 July 1942.

117 GAK DOD RRCC 1933 II 1304. Note by the *Carabinieri*, 9 May 1935.

118 Ibid. Note by the *Carabinieri*, 29 August 1938.

119 One document mentions Smyrna as her birthplace, probably by mistake. Ibid. Notes by the *Carabinieri*, 15 April 1939; 28 August 1941; 24 July 1944.

120 The term "1.5 generation" has appeared in a report for the United States Ministry of the Interior in 1988. The study dealt with immigrant children

conscious enough for being affected by displacement but not autonomous enough to shape their socialization in the new country. Rumbaut and Ima, *Adaptation*. It has been adopted by historians in regards to traumata such as the Holocaust. Suleiman, "Generation."

121 Pasqualini, *Esercito*, 411–12.
122 His parents are said to be "unknown" in Foggia. GAK DOD RRCC 1932 II 1078. Notes by the *Carabinieri*, 8 February 1933; 11 December 1941.
123 "Fasci Giovanili di Combattimento." *Il Messaggero Di Rodi*, 26 April 1935; GAK DOD RRCC 1932 II 1078. Note by the *Carabinieri*, 6 February 1939. Interestingly, he was older than 21, which was usual limit for the membership in this organization.
124 Ibid. Notes by the *Carabinieri*, 8 September 1938; 6 February 1939; 11 December 1941.
125 GAK DOD RRCC 1935 2 23 204. Note by the *Carabinieri*, undated.
126 GAK DOD RRCC 1932 II 1078. Attestation by Roberto D., 16 May 1941.
127 Ibid. Notes by the *Carabinieri*, 27 May 1941; 5 June 1941; 27 August 1942; 25 June 1943.
128 Schmitt, *Levantiner*, 209, 341.
129 Arca Petrucci, "Città," 136.
130 See his personal file: GAK DOD RRCC 1936 2 11 232; "Nozze," *Il Messaggero di Rodi*, 5 July 1937.
131 FSC TORINO 789 3436. "Regio Istituto tecnico commerciale. Registro ammissioni ai corsi superiori dal 1925–6 al 1943–4."
132 "Opera Nazionale Balilla: Assegnazione dei graduati," *Il Messaggero di Rodi*, 1 April 1937; Sentakis, *Istoria*, 305.
133 GAK DOD RRCC 1935 2 23 626. "Elenco nominativo dei connazionali che hanno versato oro alla Patria," undated [November 1935].
134 GAK DOD RRCC 1942 940. List prepared and commented by the *Carabinieri*, 19 October 1942.

Epilogue: Imperial Coda

1 Pasquale Cacopardi kindly agreed to share this account via e-mail.
2 Moise (Maurice) Soriano was among the Jews saved by the Turkish consul Selahettin Ülkümen. Paldiel, *Heroes*, 109. On Ülkümen's rescue operation: Clementi and Toliou, *Ebrei*, 183–91; Guttstadt, *Turkey*, 296–8.
3 Hizkia M. Franco "Entre las ruinas de mi comunidad." *La Boz de Türkiye* 178 (5 January 1947): 245. On Rosa's story: Pezzetti, *Liberazione*, 136.
4 USC SF VHA, Rosa Mallel interview; Antonakos, John, ed. Greek American Community of Essex County, New Jersey. Bloomington: Authorhouse, 2010. et al., Giuseppe Mallel interview; Guttstadt, *Turkey*, 298.
5 Plaut, *Jewry*, 104–10.

6 BCA 30/10/0/0/239/613/25. Saka to Inönü, 24 June 1947.
7 BCA 30/10/0/0/124/882/12. Konuk to Inönü, 2 May 1945.
8 Becan, "Étrangeté."
9 Papuççular, "Balances."
10 On Orthodox-Muslim coexistence after the Second World War: Kaurinkoski, "Communities."
11 Gavriil Misios, "Gymn. Syllogos 'Dorieus' 1924–1945," *Chronos*, 24 August 1945.
12 Clementi and Toliou, *Ebrei*, 175–203; McElligott, "Deportation."
13 Pignataro, *Dodecaneso III*, 241–315. Espinoza, "Lero."
14 Ballinger, *World*, 99–120.
15 McGuire, *Sea*, 251. See also: Papuççular, "Memories."
16 Georgios Georgiadis, "Strateusimoi kai enorkoi," *Ethniki Foni*, 6 October 1948.

Bibliography

Newspaper Articles

"Adunata." *Il Messaggero di Rodi*, 13 October 1921.

"Ai neolaiai mas." *Dodekanisos*, 10 June 1934.

Ambrosini, Luigi. "La mia avventura a Rodi." *La Stampa*, 24 May 1912.

"Atti Ufficiali." *Il Messaggero di Rodi*, 22 July 1937.

"Atti Ufficiali." *Il Messaggero di Rodi*, 17 November 1938.

"Atti Ufficiali." *Il Messaggero di Rodi*, 26 November 1938.

"Cercle de Rhodes." *Nea Rodos*, 18 February 1912.

"Comunicato." *Il Messaggero di Rodi*, 20 March 1927.

"Comunicato." *Il Messaggero di Rodi*, 23 March 1927.

"Con una grandiosa manifestazione Rodi italiana celebra il Natale di Roma e la Festa fascista del Lavoro." *Il Messaggero di Rodi*, 22 April 1937.

"Corrispondenze." *Il Messaggero di Rodi*, 3 October 1933.

"Cronaca spicciola." *Il Messaggero di Rodi*, 3 October 1939.

"Dia ta scholeia mas." *Nea Rodos*, 22 July 1911.

"Didaskalikon synedrion." Rodos, 25 July 1909.

"Dodekanisiaki neolaia Aigiptou." *Dodekanisos*, 22 April 1934.

"Egklogika." *Nea Rodos*, 24 March 1912.

"Ekpaideutika." *Nea Rodos*, 25 October 1913.

"Ex Amerikis." *Nea Rodos*, 11 January 1911.

"Fasci Giovanili Di Combattimento." *Il Messaggero Di Rodi*, 26 April 1935.

"Fidanzamento." *Il Messaggero di Rodi*, 30 January 1936.

"Fidanzamento." *Il Messaggero di Rodi*, 20 October 1933.

"Fiori d'arancio." *Il Messaggero di Rodi*, 22 November 1920.

Franco, Hizkia M. "Entre las ruinas de mi comunidad." *La Boz de Türkiye* 178, 5 January 1947: 245.

"Gegonos: Rodos-Ameriki." *Rodos*, 16 May 1909.

Georgiadis, Georgios. "Strateusimoi kai enorkoi." *Ethniki Foni*, 6 October 1948.

"Ḥamiyet-i vaṭaniye." *Ḥaḳḳ*, 14 May 1912 (erroneously dated 14 March 1912).

"I anaviosi tis istorikis vivliothikis tou Venetokleiou." *I Rodiaki*, 29 April 2013.

"I casi della vita." *Il Messaggero di Rodi*, 3 October 1933.

"I epeteios tou Syntagmatos." *Rodos*, 25 July 1909.

"Il ritorno degli Avanguardisti e Balilla da Campo Marzio." *Il Messaggero di Rodi*, 13 August 1935.

"Il VI Anniversario della Marcia su Roma nelle manifestazioni rodie." *Il Messaggero di Rodi*, 30 October 1928.

"Incontro di boxe." *Il Messaggero di Rodi*, 9 June 1934.

"Indimenticabile spettacolo di forza e di giovinezza all'Arena del Sole." *Il Messaggero di Rodi*, 25 May 1937.

Kadri, Mehmet. "Spora dā'ir." *Selām*, 28 May 1928.

– "Sefāhata dā'ir." *Selām*, 4 June 1928.

"Koinotika." *I Rodiaki*, 28 August 1933.

"L'alta parola del Duce ai giovani." *Il Messaggero di Rodi*, 25 May 1937.

"La prima gara di Football." *Il Messaggero di Rodi*, 12 April 1920.

"La situation politique et économique en Turquie." *Le Yildiz (L'Étoile Orientale)*, 11 May 1893.

"La veglia al Circolo Italia." *Il Messaggero di Rodi*, 6 April 1920.

"Le industrie di Rodi." *Il Messaggero di Rodi*, 25 December 1928.

"Le massacre dans l'île de Rhodes ." *L'Humanité*, 3 May 1934.

"Le onoranze al Milite Ignoto." *Il Messaggero di Rodi*, 5 November 1921.

"L'inaugurazione della sede sociale della lega italiana." *Il Messaggero di Rodi*, 14 February 1922.

"L'ordinamento scolastico." *Il Messaggero di Rodi*, 1 May 1926.

"Medrese-yi Süleymaniye." *Selām*, 10 December 1927.

Méheut, Constant. "Report for Macron urges 'Reconciliation of Memories' by France and Algeria." *New York Times*, 21 January 2021.

Menashe, Bension. "Terbiye baḫṣı." *Selām*, 23 August 1926.

Misios, Gavriil. "Gymn. Syllogos 'Dorieus' 1924–1945." *Chronos*, 24 August 1945.

M. Nuri. "Ṣāḥib-i imtiyāz Süleymān Efendiye ve memleketiñ münevver el-efkār genclerine." *Afitāb*, 27 May 1909.

"Nozze." *Il Messaggero di Rodi*, 5 July 1937.

"Oi Rodioi ekpatrizomenoi." *Rodos*, 11 September 1910.

"Opera Nazionale Balilla: Assegnazione dei graduati." *Il Messaggero di Rodi*, 1 April 1937.

"Partito Fascista Italiano: Sezione di Rodi." *Il Messaggero di Rodi*, 28 August 1922.

"Partito Fascista Italiano: Sezione di Rodi." *Il Messaggero di Rodi*, 21 September 1922.

"Partito Fascista Italiano: Sezione di Rodi." *Il Messaggero di Rodi*, 23 September 1922.

"Per lo sviluppo dello sport cittadino." *Il Messaggero di Rodi*, 12 June 1935.

"Psifisma epi tou thanatou tou K.ou Ioannou Agiakatsika." *I Rodiaki*, 4 January 1918.

"Radiazione." *Il Messaggero di Rodi*, 12 October 1937.

"Rioting in Rhodes." *The Palestine Post*, 7 May 1934.

"Rodos ahāli-i hammiyet-mendāni ṭarafindan i'āne-i ḥarbiyeye iştirāk iden ẕevātiñ isāmılarıla miḳdār-ı i'ānelerini mubīn defterdir." *Ceride-i 'ilmiye* 2 (1915).

"Scholika." *Nea Rodos*, 27 September 1913.

"Scholika." *Nea Rodos*, 16 February 1919.

Simmel, Georg. "Zur Soziologie der Familie." *Vossische Zeitung*, 30 June 1895.

"Stratologia ton mi Mousoulmanon." *Rodos*, 3 January 1910.

"Stratologika." *Rodos*, 14 March 1910.

"Theatron Kalla." *Rodos*, 16 May 1909.

"To koinotikon zitima." *Rodos*, 20 December 1909.

"To neon Koin. Symvoulion." *I Rodiaki*, 7 September 1933.

"To zitima ton gamon ton en Ameriki Rodion." *Rodiaki*, 22 June 1931.

"Tragica rissa a Salaco." *Il Messaggero di Rodi*, 12 April 1934.

"Un'altra manifestazione di gratitudine dei profughi dell'Asia Minore." *Il Messaggero di Rodi*, 30 September 1922.

"Un nuovo maestro di Sionismo?" *L'idea Sionistica*, April 1936.

von Weisl, Wolfgang. "Reisebriefe Wien-Palästina. Rhodus." *Wiener Morgenzeitung*, 5 August 1922.

Zeki, Mahmud. "Faşizm ve genclik." *Selām*, 7 May 1928.

Oral History Documents

AMIA CMT. Salomon Notrika interview, 28320 n. 135 CD 20, 9 August 1988. Giuseppe Mallel interview, 6 October 1998. USC SF VHA.

GC. Interview with Benjamin F. Di Liscia, 20 July 2014. www.youtube.com /watch?v=G-APPx_nHSs. Accessed 20 March 2020.

UH MGCJS. Aron Hasson interview, 21 July 2014. www.youtube.com/watch?v =dcmKWzARef4. Accessed 19 March 2020.

USC SF VHA. Rosa Mallel interview, 14 June 1998. USC SF VHA.

UWL OHC. Jacob Almeleh interview, 23 March 1972.

– Rosa Berro interview, 1 April 1974.

– Marc Angel interview, 18 July 1978.

– Elazar Behar interview, 24 February 1982.

– Charles Alhadeff interview, 3 May 1982.

– Matilda Menashe interview, 17 May 1982.

– Mary Capeloto interview, 15 June 1982.

– Philip Flash interview, 7 January 2002.

YSU SVV. James W. Kiriazis interview, 19 May 1975.

Ottoman Yearbooks (*Salnameler*)

(Salname C)
Cezāyir-i Baḥr-i Sefīd Sālnāmesi. Rodos: Maṭbaʿa-yi Vilāyet, 1893.
Cezāyir-i Baḥr-i Sefīd Sālnāmesi. Rodos: Maṭbaʿa-yi Vilāyet, 1894.
Cezāyir-i Baḥr-i Sefīd Sālnāmesi. Rodos: Maṭbaʿa-yi Vilāyet, 1898.
Cezāyir-i Baḥr-i Sefīd Sālnāmesi. Rodos: Maṭbaʿa-yi Vilāyet, 1900.
Cezāyir-i Baḥr-i Sefīd Sālnāmesi. Rodos: Maṭbaʿa-yi Vilāyet, 1901.
Cezāyir-i Baḥr-i Sefīd Sālnāmesi. Rodos: Maṭbaʿa-yi Vilāyet, 1903.
(Salname N)
Sālnāme-i Neẓāret-i Māʿārif-i ʿUmūmiye. Dār el-Hilāfe el-ʿAlīye (Istanbul): Maṭbaʿa-i ʿĀmire, 1898.
Sālnāme-i Neẓāret-i Māʿārif-i ʿUmūmiye. Dār el-Hilāfe el-ʿAlīye (Istanbul): Maṭbaʿa-i ʿĀmire, 1899.
Sālnāme-i Neẓāret-i Māʿārif-i ʿUmūmiye. Dār el-Hilāfe el-ʿAlīye (Istanbul): Maṭbaʿa-i ʿĀmire, 1900.
Sālnāme-i Neẓāret-i Māʿārif-i ʿUmūmiye. Dār el-Hilāfe el-ʿAlīye (Istanbul): Maṭbaʿa-i ʿĀmire, 1901.

Web Documents

Nicon, John, and Joann Nicon. "Jews and Greeks Together: Sephardic Jews." 1 June 2017. http://greeksinwashington.org/jews-and-greeks-together/. Accessed 19 March 2020.
Pressman, Hannah. "Remembering Rhodes, Family History, and the Sephardic Holocaust," 8 August 2014. https://jewishstudies.washington.edu/personal-history/remembering-rhodes-sephardic-holocaust/. Accessed 19 March 2020.
https://yadvashem-france.org/dossier/nom/12726/. Accessed 31 May 2021.
www.cemla.com/buscador/. Accessed 29 March 2022.
www.facebook.com/groups/130804330433532/. Accessed 19 March 2020.
www.facebook.com/groups/546890742472923/. Accessed 19 March 2020.
www.rhodesjewishmuseum.org/museum/family-photos/. Accessed 23 July 2019.
www.rhodesjewishmuseum.org/. Accessed 19 March 2020.
www.zjc.org.il/showpage.php?pageid=88. Accessed 29 March 2022.

Printed Sources

Adam, Thomas. *Buying Respectability: Philanthropy and Urban Society in Transnational Perspective, 1840s to 1930s.* Bloomington: Indiana University Press, 2009.
Adatto, Albert. "Sephardim and the Seattle Sephardic Community." Master's thesis, Seattle: University of Washington, 1939.

Akın, Yiğit. *When the War Came Home: The Ottomans' Great War and the Devastation of an Empire*. Stanford: Stanford University Press, 2018.

Alhadeff, Gini. *The Sun at Midday: Tales of a Mediterranean Family*. Hopewell: Ecco Press, 1998.

Alhadeff, Vittorio. *Le Chêne de Rhodes: Saga d'une Grande Famille Sépharade*. Paris: Méditerranée, 1998.

Aloi, Virginia. "Rodi: Un posto al sole?: L'identità territoriale dell'isola sotto i governatorati civili di Mario Lago e Cesare De Vecchi (1923–1940)." PhD diss., Università degli Studi di Roma Tre, 2008.

Amzi-Erdogdular, Leyla. "Alternative Muslim Modernities: Bosnian Intellectuals in the Ottoman and Habsburg Empires." *Comparative Studies in Society and History* 59, no. 4 (2017): 912–43.

Anastassiadis, Anastassios, ed. *Voisinages fragiles: Les relations interconfessionelles dans le Sud-Est européen et la Méditerranée orientale 1854–1923*. Athènes: École française d'Athènes, 2013.

Anastassiadou, Meropi. "Les cafés à Salonique sous les derniers Ottomans." In *Cafés d'Orient revisités*, edited by Hélène Desmet-Grégoire and François Georgeon, 79–90. Paris: CNRS Éditions, 1997.

– "Livres et "bibliothèques" dans les inventaires après décès de Salonique au XIXe siècle." *Revue des mondes musulmans et de la Méditerranée*, no. 87–8 (1999): 111–41.

Anastassiadou-Dumont, Méropi. "Vivre ensemble en Pays d'Islam: Territorialisation et marquage identitaire de l'espace urbain." *Revue des mondes musulmans et de la Méditerranée*, no. 107–10 (2005): 9–30.

Andall, Jacqueline, and Derek Duncan. "Memories and Legacies of Italian Colonialism." In *Italian Colonialism: Legacy and Memory*, edited by Jacqueline Andall and Derek Duncan, 10–27. Oxford: Peter Lang, 2005.

Angel, Marc. *The Jews of Rhodes: The History of a Sephardic Community*. New York: Sepher-Hermon Press, 1978.

– *A New World. An American Sephardic Memoir*. Boulder: Albion Andalus, 2019.

Antonakos, John, ed. *The Greek American Community of Essex County, New Jersey*. Bloomington: Authorhouse, 2010.

Arca Petrucci, Marcella. "La città di Rodi tra logiche coloniali e risposte autoctone." In *"Restituiamo la Storia" – Atlante geostorico di Rodi: Territorialità, attori, pratiche e rappresentazioni (1912–1947). Per una geografia del colonialismo italiano*, edited by Marcella Arca Petrucci, 124–47. Rome: Gangemi, 2010.

Arsan, Andrew. *Interlopers of Empire: The Lebanese Diaspora in Colonial French West Africa*. Oxford: Oxford University Press, 2015.

Aymes, Marc. *A Provincial History of the Ottoman Empire: Cyprus and the Eastern Mediterranean in the Nineteenth Century*. New York: Routledge, 2013.

Ballinger, Pamela. *The World Refugees Made: Decolonization and the Foundations of Postwar Italy*. Ithaca, NY: Cornell University Press, 2020.

Balsoy, Gülhan. "Gendering Ottoman Labor History: The Cibali Régie Factory in the Early Twentieth Century." *International Review of Social History* 54, no. Suppl. 17 (2009): 45–68.

Barkey Flash, Claire. *A Hug from Afar: One Family's Dramatic Journey through three Continents to Escape the Holocaust*. Edited by Cynthia Flash Hemphill. E-Book Edition. Bellevue: Flash Media Services, 2016. www.ahugfromafar.com.

Barkey, Karen. "Thinking about Consequences of Empire." In *After Empire: Multiethnic Societies and Nation-Building; the Soviet Union and the Russian, Ottoman, and Habsburg Empires*, edited by Karen Barkey and Mark von Hagen, 99–114. Boulder: Westview Press, 1997.

Barkey, Karen, and George Gavrilis. "The Ottoman Millet System: Non-Territorial Autonomy and Its Contemporary Legacy." *Ethnopolitics* 15, no. 1 (2016): 24–42.

Barkey, Karen, and Mark von Hagen, eds. *After Empire: Multiethnic Societies and Nation-Building; the Soviet Union and the Russian, Ottoman, and Habsburg Empires*. Boulder, CO: Westview Press, 1997.

Barrera, Giulia. "Mussolini's Colonial Race Laws and State-Settler Relations in Africa Orientale Italiana (1935–41)." *Journal of Modern Italian Studies* 8, no. 3 (2003): 425–43.

– "Sex, Citizenship and the State: The Construction of the Public and Private Spheres in Colonial Eritrea." In *Gender, Family, and Sexuality: The Private Sphere in Italy 1860–1945*, edited by Perry R. Willson, 157–72. New York: Palgrave Macmillan, 2004.

– "L'aria di città rende liberi?: Appunti sulla storia delle donne sole nell'Eritrea coloniale." In *Colonia e postcolonia come spazi diasporici: Attraversamenti di memorie, identità e confini nel Corno d'Africa*, edited by Uoldelul Chelati Dirar, Silvana Palma, Alessandro Triulzi, and Alessandro Volterra, 93–111. Rome: Carocci, 2011.

Becan, Elif. "Une familière étrangeté: L'accueil des immigrants musulmans des Balkans en Turquie (1923–1964)." PhD diss., EHESS, 2021.

Benatar, Isaac. *Rhodes and the Holocaust: The Story of the Jewish Community from the Mediterranean Island of Rhodes*. New York: iUniverse, 2010.

Benatar, Jacqueline, and Myriam Pimienta-Benatar. *De Rhodes à Elisabethville: L'odyssée d'une communauté sépharade*. Paris: SIIAC, 2000.

Benbassa, Esther. "L'éducation féminine en Orient: L'école de Filles de l'Alliance Israélite Universelle à Galata, Istanbul (1879–1912)." *Histoire, Économie et Société* 10, no. 4 (1991): 529–59.

Ben-Ghiat, Ruth, and Stephanie Malia Hom. "Introduction." In *Italian Mobilities*, edited by Ruth Ben-Ghiat and Stephanie Malia Hom, 1–19. London: Routledge, 2016.

Berezin, Mabel. *Making the Fascist Self: The Political Culture of Interwar Italy*. Ithaca: Cornell University Press, 1997.

Berghoff, Hartmut, Uffa Jensen, Christina Lubinski, and Bernd Weisbrod. "Introduction." In *History by Generations: Generational Dynamics in Modern*

History, edited by Hartmut Berghoff, Uffa Jensen, Christina Lubinski, and Bernd Weisbrod, 1–12. Göttingen: Wallstein Verlag, 2013.

Berkner, Lutz K. "The Stem Family and the Developmental Cycle of the Peasant Household: An Eighteenth-Century Austrian Example." *American Historical Review* 77, no. 2 (1972): 398–418.

Bertola, Arnaldo. "Confessione religiosa e statuto personale dei cittadini italiani nell'Egeo e Libici: A proposito del R.D.L. 19 ottobre 1933, n. 1379." *Oriente Moderno* 14, no. 3 (1934): 105–11.

Beşikçi, Mehmet. *The Ottoman Mobilization of Manpower in the First World War: Between Voluntarism and Resistance.* Leiden, NL: Brill, 2012.

– "Mobilizing Military Labor in the Age of Total War: Ottoman Conscription before and during the Great War." In *Fighting for a Living: A Comparative History of Military Labour 1500–2000*, edited by Erik Jan Zürcher, 547–80. Amsterdam: Amsterdam University Press, 2013.

Bianco, Alberto. "Les Sionistes Révisionnistes et l'Italie. Histoire d'une amitié très discrète (1932–1938)." *Bulletin du Centre de recherche français à Jérusalem* 13 (2003): 22–45.

Biliotti, Eduard, and Pierre Marie Cottret. *L'île de Rhodes: Ouvrage traduit en Grec moderne, avec le concours des auteurs par Marc Malliaraki.* Rhodos: Thorin, 1881.

Blackshaw, Tony. *Re-Imagining Leisure Studies.* Abingdon: Taylor and Francis, 2017.

Bocquet, Denis. "Rhodes 1912: Les mésaventures du Général d'Ameglio [*sic !*]." *Cahiers de la Méditerranée*, no. 68 (2004): 133–52.

Bonetto, Beniamino Giuseppe. "22 ans après la fermeture de leurs écoles, les anciens élèves de Rhodes constituent à Rome leur association." *Informations lasalliennes*, 1969, 15–19.

Booth, Charles Douglas, and Isabelle Bridge Booth. *Italy's Aegean Possessions.* London: Arrowsmith, 1928.

Borutta, Manuel, and Sakis Gekas. "A Colonial Sea: The Mediterranean, 1798–1956." *European Review of History: Revue Europeenne d'histoire* 19, no. 1 (2012): 1–13.

Bosworth, Richard J.B. "Britain and Italy's Acquisition of the Dodecanese (1912–1915)." *The Historical Journal* 13, no. 4 (1970): 683–705.

– *Italy and the Approach of the First World War.* New York: St. Martin's Press, 1983.

Bourdieu, Pierre. "Historische und soziale Voraussetzungen modernen Sports." In *Sport, Eros, Tod*, edited by Gerd Hortleder and Gunter Gebauer, 91–112. Frankfurt am Main: Suhrkamp, 1986.

– "À propos de la famille comme catégorie réalisée." *Actes de la recherche en sciences sociales* 100, no. 1 (1993): 32–6.

– *Questions de Sociologie.* Paris: Les éditions de minuit, 2002.

Bowersox, Jeff. *Raising Germans in the Age of Empire: Youth and Colonial Culture, 1871–1914.* Oxford: Oxford University Press, 2013.

Bragg, John. *Ottoman Notables and Participatory Politics: Tanzimat Reform in Tokat, 1839–1876*. New York: Routledge, 2014.

Braude, Benjamin, and Bernard Lewis, eds. *Christians and Jews in the Ottoman Empire: The Functioning of a Plural Society*. New York: Holmes & Meier Publishers, 1982.

Brown, Carl Leon, ed. *Imperial Legacy: The Ottoman Imprint on the Balkans and the Middle East*. New York: Columbia University Press, 1996.

Brubaker, Rogers. "Aftermaths of Empire and the Unmixing of Peoples: Historical and Comparative Perspectives." *Ethnic and Racial Studies* 18, no. 2 (1995): 189–218.

Brubaker, Rogers, and Frederick Cooper. "Beyond 'Identity.'" *Theory and Society* 29, no. 1 (2000): 1–47.

Bryant, Rebecca, ed. *Post-Ottoman Coexistence: Sharing Space in the Shadow of Conflict*. New York: Berghahn Books, 2016.

Burbank, Jane, and Frederick Cooper. *Empires in World History: Power and the Politics of Difference*. Princeton: Princeton University Press, 2010.

– "Empires after 1919: Old, New, Transformed." *International Affairs* 95, no. 1 (2019): 81–100.

Burguière, André. "Les rapports entre générations: Un problème pour l'historien." *Communications* 59 (1994): 15–27.

Büssow, Johann. *Hamidian Palestine: Politics and Society in the District of Jerusalem 1872–1908*. Leiden, NL: Brill, 2011.

Cacopardi, Pasquale. "Mes premiers souvenirs du Quartier Juif de Rhodes." *Los Muestros*, no. 44 (2001, first printed in March 1995). http://sefarad.org/lm/044/14.html.

Campos, Michelle Ursula. *Ottoman Brothers: Muslims, Christians, and Jews in Early Twentieth-Century Palestine*. Redwood City, CA: Stanford University Press, 2011.

Carabott, Philip J. "The Temporary Italian Occupation of the Dodecanese: A Prelude to Permanency." *Diplomacy & Statecraft* 4, no. 2 (1993): 285–312.

Cardoza, Anthony. "'Making Italians?': Cycling and National Identity in Italy: 1900–1950." *Journal of Modern Italian Studies* 15, no. 3 (2010): 354–77.

Cecini, Giovanni. *La Guardia di Finanza nelle Isole Italiane Dell'Egeo, 1912–1945*. Rome: Gangemi, 2014.

Censimento della popolazione delle colonie italiane al 1 dicembre 1921 e rilevazione degli abitanti del Possedimento delle Isole Egee al 20 agosto 1922. Rome: Istituto Poligrafico dello Stato, 1930.

Çetinkaya, Y. Dogan. *The Young Turks and the Boycott Movement: Nationalism, Protest and the Working Classes in the Formation of Modern Turkey*. London: I.B. Tauris, 2014.

Choate, Mark I. *Emigrant Nation: The Making of Italy Abroad*. Cambridge, MA: Harvard University Press, 2008.

Ciacci, Leonardo. *Rodi Italiana: 1912–1923: Come si inventa una città*. Venezia: Marsilio, 1991.

Cicek, Nazan. "The Role of Mass Education in Nation-Building in the Ottoman Empire and the Turkish Republic, 1870–1930." In *Mass Education and the Limits of State Building, c. 1870–1930*, edited by Laurence Brockliss and Nicola Sheldon, 224–50. Basingstoke, UK: Palgrave Macmillan, 2012.

Cinel, Dino. *The National Integration of Italian Return Migration, 1870–1929*. Cambridge: Cambridge University Press, 1991.

Clancy-Smith, Julia Ann. *Mediterraneans: North Africa, Europe, and the Ottoman Empire in an Age of Migration, c. 1800–1900*. Berkeley, CA: University of California Press, 2012.

Clayer, Nathalie. "The Albanian Students of the Mekteb-i Mulkiye: Social Networks and Trends of Thought." In *Late Ottoman Society: The Intellectual Legacy*, edited by Elisabeth Özdalga, 289–339. London: Routledge/Curzon, 2005.

– "The Dimension of Confessionalisation in the Ottoman Balkans at the Time of Nationalisms." In *Conflicting Loyalties in the Balkans: The Great Powers, the Ottoman Empire and Nation-Building*, edited by Hannes Grandits, Nathalie Clayer, and Robert Pichler, 89–109. London: I.B. Tauris, 2011.

– "Local Factionalism and Political Mobilization in the Albanian Province in the Late Ottoman Empire." In *Popular Protest and Political Participation in the Ottoman Empire: Studies in Honor of Suraiya Faroqhi*, edited by Eleni Gara, Erdem M. Kabadayı, and Christoph K. Neumann, 197–208. İstanbul: İstanbul Bilgi University Press, 2011.

– "The Time of Freedom, the Time of Struggle for Power: The Young Turk Revolution in the Albanian Provinces." In *The Young Turk Revolution and the Ottoman Empire: The Aftermath of 1908*, edited by Noémi Lévy-Aksu and François Georgeon, 113–52. London: I.B. Tauris, 2017.

Clementi, Marco. "Il fondo dei Carabinieri Reali di Rodi e la Comunità Ebraica: Dal controllo alla deportazione." In *L'Europa e il suo Sud-Est: Percorsi di ricerca: Contributi italiani all'XI Congresso Internazionale dell'Association internationale d'études du Sud-Est européen, Sofia, 31 agosto – 4 settembre 2015*, edited by Antonio D'Alessandri and Francesco Guida, 37–54. Ariccia: Aracne editrice, 2015.

– "La fine della Comunità Ebraica di Rodi." In *REMSHOA. L'Italia, la Shoah, la Memoria. La deportazione degli Ebrei in Grecia*, edited by Luca Micheletta, 73–80. Rome: La Sapienza, 2017.

Clementi, Marco, and Eirini Toliou. *Gli ultimi Ebrei di Rodi: Leggi Razziali e deportazioni nel Dodecaneso italiano (1938–1948)*. Rome: DeriveApprodi, 2015.

Cohen, Julia Phillips. *Becoming Ottomans: Sephardi Jews and Imperial Citizenship in the Modern Era*. Oxford: Oxford University Press, 2014.

Collotti, Enzo. *Il Fascismo e gli Ebrei: Le Leggi Razziali in Italia*. Rome: Laterza, 2003.

Coverdale, John F. *Italian Intervention in the Spanish Civil War*. Princeton Legacy Library. Princeton: Princeton University Press, 1975.

Daniels, Arlene Kaplan. "Invisible Work." *Social Problems* 34, no. 5 (1987): 403–15.

Daniels, Roger. *Guarding the Golden Door: American Immigration Policy and Immigrants since 1882*. New York: Hill and Wang, 2005.

Dannies, Kate. "'A Pensioned Gentleman': Women's Agency and the Political Economy of Marriage in Istanbul during World War I." *Journal of the Ottoman and Turkish Studies Association* 6, no. 2 (2019): 13–31.

Davidova, Evguenia. *Balkan Transitions to Modernity and Nation-States: Through the Eyes of Three Generations of Merchants, (1780s–1890s)*. Leiden, NL: Brill, 2012.

d'Azeglio, Massimo. *I miei ricordi. Volume I*. Firenze: Barbera, 1867.

de Grazia, Victoria. *The Culture of Consent: Mass Organization of Leisure in Fascist Italy*. Cambridge: Cambridge University Press, 1981.

– *How Fascism Ruled Women: Italy, 1922–1945*. Berkeley, CA: University of California Press, 1992.

Del Boca, Angelo. *Gli Italiani in Libia. Vol 1. Tripoli bel suol d'amore, 1860–1922*. Rome: Laterza, 1986.

Della Seta, Simonetta. "Gli Ebrei del Mediterraneo nella strategia politica fascista sino al 1938: Il caso di Rodi." *Storia Contemporanea* 17, no. 6 (1986): 997–1032.

Demirel, Fatmagül. "The Implementation of the General Pardon after the Proclamation of the Second Constitution and the Reactions in the Prisons." In *The Young Turk Revolution and the Ottoman Empire: The Aftermath of 1908*, edited by Noémi Lévy-Aksu and François Georgeon, 97–109. London; New York: I.B. Tauris, 2017.

Deringil, Selim. *The Well-Protected Domains: Ideology and the Legitimation of Power in the Ottoman Empire, 1876–1909*. London: I.B. Tauris, 1998.

Der Matossian, Bedross. "Formation of Public Sphere(s) in the Aftermath of the 1908 Revolution among Armenians, Arabs, and Jews." In *"L'ivresse de la liberté": La Révolution de 1908 dans l'Empire ottoman*, edited by François Georgeon, 189–219. Leuven: Peeters, 2012.

De Roberto, Federico. *I Vicerè*. Milano: Galli, 1894.

Di Casola, M. Antonia. "L'Italia e il Trattato di Losanna del 1923." *Il Politico* 58, no. 4 (167) (1993): 679–94.

Di Pasquale, Francesca. "The Spiritual Correlation: The Perception and the Response of Libyan Muslims to the Educational Fascist Policy (1931–1940)." *Oriental Institute Studies* 1 (2012).

Dogliani, Patrizia. "Sport and Fascism." *Journal of Modern Italian Studies* 5, no. 3 (2000): 326–48.

– *Il Fascismo degli Italiani: Una storia sociale*. Torino, IT: UTET libreria, 2008.

Donati, Sabina. *A Political History of National Citizenship and Identity in Italy, 1861–1950*. Redwood City, CA: Stanford University Press, 2013.

Douki, Caroline. The "Return Politics" of a Sending Country: The Italian Case, 1880s–1914." In *A Century of Transnationalism: Immigrants and Their Homeland Connections*, edited by Nancy L. Green and Roger Waldinger, 35–55. Urbana, IL: University of Illinois Press, 2016.

Doumani, Beshara. "Introduction." In *Family History in the Middle East: Household, Property, and Gender*, edited by Beshara Doumani, 1–19. Albany, NY: State University of New York Press, 2003.

Doumanis, Nicholas. *Myth and Memory in the Mediterranean: Remembering Fascism's Empire*. New York: St. Martin's Press, 1997.

– "Italians as 'Good' Colonizers: Speaking Subalterns and the Politics of Memory in the Dodecanese." In *Italian Colonialism*, edited by Ruth Ben-Ghiat and Mia Fuller. New York: Palgrave Macmillan US, 2006.

– *Before the Nation: Muslim-Christian Coexistence and its Destruction in Late Ottoman Anatolia*. Oxford: Oxford University Press, 2013.

Downs, Laura Lee. *Childhood in the Promised Land: Working-Class Movements and the Colonies de Vacances in France, 1880–1960*. Durham, NC: Duke University Press, 2002.

– "Éditorial: Vers une histoire transnationale des mouvements de jeunesse." *Le Mouvement Social* 267, no. 1 (2019): 3–8.

Duben, Alan. "Turkish Families and Households in Historical Perspective." *Journal of Family History* 10, no. 1 (1985): 75–97.

Duben, Alan, and Cem Behar. *Istanbul Households: Marriage, Family and Fertility, 1880–1940*. Cambridge: Cambridge University Press, 1991.

Dupont, Anne-Laure. "Présentation." *Cahiers de la Méditerranée*, no. 75 (2007): 7–16.

Eisenstadt, Shmuel N. *From Generation to Generation: Age Groups and Social Structure*. Brunswick, NJ: Transaction Publishers, 2003.

Eissenstat, Howard. "Modernization, Imperial Nationalism, and the Ethnicization of Confessional Identity in the Late Ottoman Empire." In *Nationalizing Empires*, edited by Stefan Berger and Alexei Miller, 429–59. Budapest, HU: Central European University Press, 2015.

Elias, Norbert, and Eric Dunning. *Quest for Excitement: Sport and Leisure in the Civilizing Process*. Oxford: Blackwell, 1986.

Espinoza, Filippo M. "Fare gli Italiani dell'Egeo: Il Dodecaneso dall'Impero Ottomano all'impero del Fascismo." PhD diss., Università degli Studi di Trento, 2017.

– "Una cittadinanza imperiale basata sul consenso: Il caso delle Isole Italiane dell'Egeo." In *Sudditi o cittadini? L'evoluzione delle appartenenze imperiali nella Prima Guerra Mondiale*, edited by Sara Lorenzini and Simone A. Bellezza, 187–202. Rome: Viella, 2018.

– "'Lero attende tutti.' Memoria della Resistenza e pellegrinaggi patriottici nel Dodecaneso." *E-Review. Rivista degli Istituti Storici dell'Emilia-Romagna in rete* 7 (2020).

Evered, Emine. *Empire and Education under the Ottomans: Politics, Reform and Resistance from the Tanzimat to the Young Turks*. London: I.B. Tauris, 2012.

Executive Committee of the Dodecanesians – Compiled by Skevos Zervos and Paris Roussos. *White Book: The Dodecanese. Resolutions and Documents Concerning the Dodecanese 1912–1919*. London: A. Page, 1920.

Fahrenthold, Stacy D. *Between the Ottomans and the Entente: The First World War in the Syrian and Lebanese Diaspora, 1908–1925*. Oxford: Oxford University Press, 2019.

Fanon, Frantz. *Toward the African Revolution: Political Essays*. New York: Grove Press, 1988.

Farge, Arlette. *The Allure of the Archives*. New Haven, CT: Yale University Press, 2013.

Ferris, Kate. *Everyday Life in Fascist Venice, 1929–40*. Basingstoke, UK: Palgrave Macmillan, 2012.

Findley, Carter V. *Bureaucratic Reform in the Ottoman Empire: The Sublime Porte, 1789–1922*. Princeton: Princeton University Press, 1980.

Fintz Menascé, Esther. *Gli Ebrei a Rodi: Storia di un'antica comunità annientata dai Nazisti*. Milano: Guerini e associati, 1992.

– *Buio nell'isola del sole. Rodi 1943–1945. I due volti di una tragedia quasi dimenticata. Il martirio dell'Ammiraglio Campioni e dei militari italiani in Egeo, e lo sterminio degli Ebrei di Rodi e Coo*. Firenze: Giuntina, 2005.

Flemming, Barbara, and Jan Schmidt. *The Diary of Karl Süssheim: (1878–1947): Orientalist between Munich and Istanbul*. Stuttgart, DE: Steiner, 2002.

Foot, John. *Pedalare! Pedalare!: A History of Italian Cycling*. London: Bloomsbury, 2012.

Fortna, Benjamin. "Education and Autobiography at the End of the Ottoman Empire." *Die Welt des Islams* 41, no. 1 (2001): 1–31.

– *Imperial Classroom: Islam, the State, and Education in the Late Ottoman Empire*. Oxford: Oxford University Press, 2002.

– "Emphasizing the Islamic: Modifying the Curriculum of Late Ottoman State Schools." In *Enfance et jeunesse dans le monde musulman*, edited by François Georgeon and Klaus Kreiser, 193–209. Paris: Maisonneuve & Larose, 2007.

– *Learning to Read in the Late Ottoman Empire and the Early Turkish Republic*. Basingstoke, UK: Palgrave Macmillan, 2011.

Foucault, Michel. *Surveiller et punir: Naissance de la prison*. Paris: Gallimard, 1974.

Frangakis-Syrret, Elena. "The Dynamics of Economic Development: Izmir and Western Anatolia, late 19th/early 20th centuries." *T.C. Mersin Üniversitesi Yayinlari* 7 (2020): 65–72.

Fratantuono, Ella. "Producing Ottomans: Internal Colonization and Social Engineering in Ottoman Immigrant Settlement." *Journal of Genocide Research* 21, no. 1 (2019): 1–24.

Freitag, Ulrike, and Achim von Oppen. "'Translocality': An Approach to Connection and Transfer in Regional Studies." In *Translocality: The Study of Globalising Processes from a Southern Perspective*, edited by Ulrike Freitag and Achim von Oppen, 1–21. Leiden, NL: Brill, 2010.

Frierson, Elizabeth B. "Women in Late Ottoman Intellectual History." In *Late Ottoman Society: The Intellectual Legacy*, edited by Elisabeth Özdalga, 135–61. London: Routledge/Curzon, 2005.

Fuhrmann, Malte. "Cosmopolitan Imperialists and the Ottoman Port Cities: Conflicting Logics in the Urban Social Fabric." *Cahiers de la Méditerranée* 67 (2003): 149–63.

– "Down and Out on the Quays of İzmir: 'European' Musicians, Innkeepers, and Prostitutes in the Ottoman Port-Cities." *Mediterranean Historical Review* 24, no. 2 (2009): 169–85.

– "'Western Perversions' at the Threshold of Felicity: The European Prostitutes of Galata-Pera (1870–1915)." *History and Anthropology* 21, no. 2 (2010): 159–72.

– "Beer, the Drink of a Changing World." *Turcica* 45 (2014): 79–123.

– *Port Cities of the Eastern Mediterranean: Urban Culture in the Late Ottoman Empire.* Cambridge: Cambridge University Press, 2020.

Fulbrook, Mary. "East Germans in a Post-Nazi State: Communities of Experience, Connection, and Identification." In *Becoming East German: Socialist Structures and Sensibilities after Hitler*, edited by Mary Fulbrook and Andrew I. Port, 33–55. New York: Berghahn Books, 2013.

Gabaccia, Donna R. "Time and Temporality in Migration Studies." In *Migration Theory: Talking across Disciplines*, edited by Caroline B. Brettell and James F. Hollifield, 33–66. New York: Routledge, 2015.

Gabaccia, Donna R., and Franca Iacovetta, eds. *Women, Gender, and Transnational Lives: Italian Workers of the World.* Toronto: University of Toronto Press, 2002.

Gabaccia, Donna R., and Fraser Ottanelli. "Diaspora or International Proletariat?: Italian Labor, Labor Migration, and the Making of Multiethnic States, 1815–1939." *Diaspora: A Journal of Transnational Studies* 6, no. 1 (1997): 61–84.

Galante, Avram. *Histoire des Juifs de Turquie.* Vol. VII. Istanbul: İsis, 1985.

Garfinkel, Paul. *Criminal Law in Liberal and Fascist Italy.* Cambridge: Cambridge University Press, 2016.

Gentile, Emilio. *La Grande Italia: The Myth of the Nation in the Twentieth Century.* Madison, WI: University of Wisconsin Press, 2009.

Georgeon, François. "Les cafés à Istanbul à la fin de l'Empire ottoman." In *Cafés d'Orient revisités*, edited by Hélène Desmet-Grégoire and François Georgeon, 39–78. Paris: CNRS Éditions, 1997.

– "Les Jeunes Turcs étaient-ils jeunes? Sur le phénomène des générations, de l'Empire ottoman à la République turque." In *Enfance et jeunesse dans le monde musulman*, edited by François Georgeon and Klaus Kreiser, 146–73. Paris: Maisonneuve & Larose, 2007.

Georgeon, François, and Paul Dumont, eds. *Vivre dans l'Empire ottoman: Sociabilités et relations intercommunautaires (XVIIIe – XXe Siècles).* Paris: L'Harmattan, 1997.

Gerwarth, Robert, and Erez Manela, eds. *Empires at War: 1911–1923.* Oxford: Oxford University Press, 2014.

Ghobrial, John-Paul A. "Introduction: Seeing the World like a Microhistorian." *Past & Present* 242, Suppl. 14 (2019): 1–22.

Gillis, John R. *Youth and History: Tradition and Change in European Age Relations 1770–Present*. New York: Academic Press, 1974.

Gingeras, Ryan. *Sorrowful Shores: Violence, Ethnicity, and the End of the Ottoman Empire, 1912–1923*. Oxford: Oxford University Press, 2009.

Ginio, Eyal, and Karl Kaser, eds. *Ottoman Legacies in the Contemporary Mediterranean: The Balkans and the Middle East Compared*. Jerusalem, IL: The European Forum at the Hebrew University, 2013.

Ginsborg, Paul. *Family Politics: Domestic Life, Devastation and Survival, 1900–1950*. New Haven, CT: Yale University Press, 2014.

Giomi, Fabio. "Forging Habsburg Muslim Girls: Gender, Education and Empire in Bosnia and Herzegovina (1878–1918)." *History of Education* 44, no. 3 (2015): 274–92.

Gocek, Fatma Muge. *Denial of Violence: Ottoman Past, Turkish Present, and Collective Violence against the Armenians, 1789–2009*. Oxford: Oxford University Press, 2014.

Grandits, Hannes. *Familie und sozialer Wandel im ländlichen Kroatien: (18.–20. Jahrhundert)*. Wien: Böhlau, 2002.

– *Herrschaft und Loyalität in der spätosmanischen Gesellschaft: Das Beispiel der multikonfessionellen Herzegowina*. Wien: Böhlau, 2008.

Grange, Daniel J. *L'Italie et la Méditerranée (1896–1911): Les fondements d'une politique étrangère*. Rome: Ecole française de Rome, 1994.

Green, Nancy L. "L'histoire comparative et le champ des études migratoires." *Annales. Histoire, Sciences Sociales* 45, no. 6 (1990): 1335–50.

Griffin, Roger. "General Introduction." In *Fascism: The Nature of Fascism*, edited by Roger Griffin and Matthew Feldman, 1–16. New York: Routledge, 2004.

Grosselli, Renzo Maria. *Gli uomini del legno sull'isola delle rose: La vicenda storica del villaggio italiano di Campochiaro a Rodi 1935–1947*. Trento, IT: Curcu & Genovese, 2012.

Guerin, Victor. *Voyage dans l'île de Rhodes et description de cette île*. Paris: Durand, 1856.

Guidi, Andreas. "Defining Inter-Communality between Documents, Tradition and Collective Memory: Jewish and Non-Jewish Capital and Labor in Early Twentieth Century Rhodes." *Southeast European and Black Sea Studies* 17, no. 2 (2017): 165–80.

– "Die osmanischen Gefangenen vom Dodekanes: An der Schnittstelle von kolonialer und kriegerischen Gewalt während des Italienisch-Osmanischen Krieges von 1911–1912." *Zeitschrift Für Genozidforschung* 16 (2019): 6–29.

Gutkowski, Hélène. *Erase una vez ... Sefarad: Los Sefaradíes del Mediterráneo. Su historia, su cultura, 1880–1950*. Buenos Aires, AR: Editorial Lumen, 1999.

Gutman, David. *The Politics of Armenian Migration to North America, 1885–1915: Sojourners, Smugglers and Dubious Citizens*. Edinburgh: Edinburgh University Press, 2019.

Guttstadt, Corry. *Turkey, the Jews, and the Holocaust*. Cambridge: Cambridge University Press, 2013.

Hafez, Melis. "The Lazy, the Idle, the Industrious: Discourse and Practice of Work and Productivity in Late Ottoman Society." PhD diss., Los Angeles: UCLA, 2012.

Hajdarpasic, Edin. *Whose Bosnia? Nationalism and Political Imagination in the Balkans, 1840–1914*. Ithaca, NY: Cornell University Press, 2015.

Hanioğlu, Şükrü M. *The Young Turks in Opposition*. Studies in Middle Eastern History. Oxford: Oxford University Press, 1995.

– *Preparation for a Revolution: The Young Turks, 1902–1908*. Oxford: Oxford University Press, 2001.

Hanley, Will. "What Ottoman Nationality Was and Was Not." *Journal of the Ottoman and Turkish Studies Association* 3, no. 2 (2016): 277–98.

Hanssen, Jens. *"Fin de Siècle" Beirut: The Making of an Ottoman Provincial Capital*. Oxford: Oxford University Press, 2005.

Hartmann, Elke. "Family Portraits: Visual Sources for a Social History of the Late Ottoman Empire." In *Ways of Knowing Muslim Cultures and Societies*, edited by Bettina Gräf, Birgit Krawietz, and Schirin Amir-Moazami, 111–31. Leiden, NL: Brill, 2018.

Hazan, Martín. *Un día más de vida: Rodas, Auschwitz, Buenos Aires: La odisea de David Galante*. E-Book Edition. Buenos Aires, AR: Lumiere, 2007.

Heller, Daniel Kupfert. "Obedient Children and Reckless Rebels: Jabotinsky's Youth Politics and the Case for Authoritarian Leadership, 1931–1933." *Journal of Israeli History* 34, no. 1 (2015): 45–68.

Herzfeld, Michael. "The Dowry in Greece: Terminological Usage and Historical Reconstruction." *Ethnohistory* 27, no. 3 (1980): 225–41.

– *The Poetics of Manhood: Contest and Identity in a Cretan Mountain Village*. Princeton: Princeton University Press, 1985.

Higgs, Edward. "Women, Occupations and Work in the Nineteenth Century Censuses." *History Workshop Journal* 23, no. 1 (1987): 59–80.

Hill, Bridget. "Women, Work and the Census: A Problem for Historians of Women." *History Workshop Journal* 35, no. 1 (1993): 78–94.

Hill, Jeffrey. *Sport, Leisure and Culture in Twentieth-Century Britain*. Basingstoke, UK: Palgrave Macmillan, 2002.

Hirsch, Marianne. *Family Frames: Photography, Narrative, and Postmemory*. Cambridge, MA: Harvard University Press, 1997.

– *The Generation of Postmemory: Writing and Visual Culture after the Holocaust.* New York: Columbia University Press, 2012.

Hirschon, Renée. "The Jews of Rhodes: The Decline and Extinction of an Ancient Community." In *The Last Ottoman Century and Beyond: Proceedings of the International Conference on "The Jewish Communities in the Balkans and Turkey in the 19th and 20th Centuries through the End of World War II," June 5–8, 1995,* edited by Minna Rozen, 291–307. Tel Aviv, IL: The Chair for the History and Culture of the Jews of Salonika and Greece The Goldstein-Goren Diaspora Research Center, 2002.

– "The Consequences of the Lausanne Convention. An Overview." In *Crossing the Aegean: An Appraisal of the 1923 Compulsory Population Exchange between Greece and Turkey,* edited by Renée Hirschon, 13–20. New York: Berghahn Books, 2003.

Hofmeester, Karin, and Elise van Nederveen Meerkerk. "Family, Demography and Labour Relations." *The History of the Family* 22, no. 1 (2017): 3–13.

Hom, Stephanie Malia. *Empire's Mobius Strip: Historical Echoes in Italy's Crisis of Migration and Detention.* Ithaca, NY: Cornell University Press, 2019.

Ianeva, Svetla. "Female Actors, Producers and Money Makers in Ottoman Public Space: The Case of the Late Ottoman Balkans." In *Ottoman Women in Public Space,* edited by Ebru Boyar and Kate Fleet, 48–90. Leiden: Brill, 2016.

"I katathesis tou themeliou lithou tou 'Venetokleiou Gymnasiou' en Rodo. Genomeni ti 18i Ianouariou 1909." Athinai, GR: Athinaiko Typografeio, 1909.

İnce, Başak. *Citizenship and Identity in Turkey: From Atatürk's Republic to the Present Day.* London: I.B. Tauris, 2012.

Isabella, Maurizio, and Konstantina Zanou, eds. *Mediterranean Diasporas: Politics and Ideas in the Long 19th Century.* London: Bloomsbury, 2015.

Jabotinsky, Vladimir, and Isacco Sciaky. *Stato e libertà: Il carteggio Jabotinsky-Sciaky: 1924–1939.* Edited by Vincenzo Pinto. Soveria Mannelli: Rubbettino, 2002.

Jacobson, Abigail. *From Empire to Empire: Jerusalem between Ottoman and British Rule.* Syracuse: Syracuse University Press, 2011.

Jobs, Richard I., and David M. Pomfret. "The Transnationality of Youth." In *Transnational Histories of Youth in the Twentieth Century,* edited by Richard I. Jobs and David M. Pomfret, 1–19. Basingstoke, UK: Palgrave Macmillan, 2015.

Jureit, Ulrike, and Michael Wildt. "Generationen." In *Generationen: Zur Relevanz eines wissenschaftlichen Grundbegriffs,* edited by Ulrike Jureit and Michael Wildt, 7–26. Hamburg, DE: Hamburger Ed., 2005.

Kalafatas, Michael N. *The Bellstone: The Greek Sponge Divers of the Aegean; One American's Journey Home.* Lebanon, NH: Brandeis University Press, 2003.

Kalambichis, Emmanouil. *Apo tin zoi mou.* Rhodos, GR: I Rodiaki, 1968.

Kampouris, Christodoulos. "O gamos." *Rodiakon imerologion* 1, no. 1 (1912): 203–9.

Karpat, Kemal H. "The Ottoman Emigration to America, 1860–1914."
    International Journal of Middle East Studies 17, no. 2 (1985): 175–209.
– *Ottoman Population, 1830–1914: Demographic and Social Characteristics.*
    Madison, WI: University of Wisconsin Press, 1985.
Kasaba, Reşat, Çağlar Keyder, and Faruk Tabak. "Eastern Mediterranean Port
    Cities and Their Bourgeoisies: Merchants, Political Projects, and Nation-
    States." *Review (Fernand Braudel Center)* 10, no. 1 (1986): 121–35.
Kaşlıoğlu, Şahap. *Rodos'ta saklı zamanlar.* İstanbul, TR: Doğu Kütüphanesi, 2007.
Kaurinkoski, Kira. "The Muslim Communities in Kos and Rhodes: Reflections
    on Social Organization and Collective Identities in Contemporary Greece."
    In *Balkan Encounters: Old and New Identities in South-Eastern Europe*, edited
    by Jouko Lindstedt and Max Wahlström, 47–78. Helsinki: Department of
    Modern Languages University of Helsinki, 2012.
Kechriotis, Vangelis. "Requiem for the Empire: 'Elective Affinities' Between
    the Balkan States and the Ottoman Empire in the Long 19th Century." In
    Beyond the Balkans: Towards an Inclusive History of Southeastern Europe, edited
    by Sabine Rutar, 97–121. Wien: LIT, 2014.
Kempadoo, Kamala. "Introduction: Globalizing Sex Workers' Rights." In
    Global Sex Workers: Rights, Resistance and Redefinition, edited by Kamala
    Kempadoo and Jo Doezema, 1–28. New York: Routledge, 1998.
Kerem, Yitzchak. "The Settlement of Rhodian and Other Sephardic Jews in
    Montgomery and Atlanta in the Twentieth Century." *American Jewish History*
    85, no. 4 (1997): 373–91.
Kertzer, David I. "Generation as a Sociological Problem." *Annual Review of
    Sociology* 9 (1983): 125–49.
Khater, Akram Fouad. *Inventing Home: Emigration, Gender, and the Middle Class
    in Lebanon, 1870–1920.* Berkeley, CA: University of California Press, 2001.
Khuri-Makdisi, Ilham. *The Eastern Mediterranean and the Making of Global
    Radicalism, 1860–1914.* Berkeley, CA: University of California Press, 2010.
Kilinçoğlu, Deniz T. *Economics and Capitalism in the Ottoman Empire.* London:
    Routledge, 2015.
King, Laura. *Family Men: Fatherhood and Masculinity in Britain, 1914–1960.*
    Oxford: Oxford University Press, 2015.
Kiriazis, James W. *Children of the Colossus: The Rhodian Greek Immigrants in the
    United States.* New York: AMS Press, 1989.
Kladaki-Menemenli, Foteini, and Timotheos Ad. Freris. *Apo tin ekpaideutiki
    istoria tis Rodou: 1889–1989.* Siros, GR: Dimos Rodion, 2002.
Kocka, Jürgen. "Family and Class Formation: Intergenerational Mobility and
    Marriage Patterns in Nineteenth-Century Westphalian Towns." *Journal of
    Social History* 17, no. 3 (1984): 411–33.
Kodaman, Bayram. *Abdülhamid devri eğitim sistemi.* İstanbul, TR: Ötüken, 1980.

Köksal, Duygu, and Anastasia Falierou, eds. *A Social History of Late Ottoman Women: New Perspectives*. The Ottoman Empire and Its Heritage. Leiden, NL: Brill, 2013.

Kolodny, Émile Yerahmiel. *La population des îles de la Grèce: Essai de géographie insulaire en Méditerranée orientale*. Aix-en-Provence, FR: Edisud, 1974.

Kostaridou, Athina P. *Ergani Athina: Adelfotis kirion Rodou 1908–1938*. Rodos, GR: Sfragida Erganis, 1998.

Koulouri, Christina. "From Antiquity to Olympic Revival: Sports and Greek National Historiography (Nineteenth-Twentieth Centuries)." *International Journal of the History of Sport* 27, no. 12 (2010): 2014–52.

Kühn, Thomas. "Shaping and Reshaping Colonial Ottomanism: Contesting Boundaries of Difference and Integration in Ottoman Yemen, 1872–1919." *Comparative Studies of South Asia, Africa and the Middle East* 27, no. 2 (2007): 313–29.

Kypriotou, Platonos K. *I Venetokli kai to Venetokleion: I symvoli ton eis tin paideian tou ethnous. I zoi kai to ergon ton adelfon Dimitriou kai Minoos megalon euergeton*. Athinai, GR: Stegi Grammaton kai Technon Dodekanisou, 1973.

– "I drasi ton dimogeronton tis Ellinikis Orthodoxou Koinotitos Rodou kata ta prota eti tis italikis katochis 1912–1914." *Dodekanisiaka chronika* 9 (1983): 95–136.

Labanca, Nicola. *Oltremare: Storia dell'espansione coloniale italiana*. Bologna, IT: Il Mulino, 2002.

– *La guerra italiana per la Libia: 1911–1931*. Bologna, IT: Il Mulino, 2012.

Laliotou, Ioanna. *Transatlantic Subjects: Acts of Migration and Cultures of Transnationalism between Greece and America*. Chicago: University of Chicago Press, 2004.

Lanza, Fabio. "Springtime and Morning Suns: 'Youth' as a Political Category in Twentieth-Century China." *Journal of the History of Childhood and Youth* 5, no. 1 (2012): 31–51.

LaRossa, Ralph. *The Modernization of Fatherhood: A Social and Political History*. Chicago: University of Chicago Press, 1997.

Laslett, Peter. "Introduction: The History of the Family." In *Household and Family in Past Time*, edited by Peter Laslett, 1–90. Cambridge: Cambridge University Press, 1972.

Ledeen, Michael A. "Italian Fascism and Youth." *Journal of Contemporary History* 4, no. 3 (1969): 137–54.

Lefebvre, Henri. *Introduction à la modernité, préludes*. Paris: Les éditions de minuit, 1962.

Leon, Benny, ed. *60th Anniversary 1931–1991 of the Sephardi Hebrew Congregation of Zimbabwe*. n.p., 1991.

Lévy-Aksu, Noémi. *Ordre et désordres dans l'Istanbul ottomane (1879–1909)*. Paris: Karthala, 2012.

Lewis, Mary Dewhurst. *Divided Rule: Sovereignty and Empire in French Tunisia, 1881–1938*. Berkeley, CA: University of California Press, 2013.

Livadiotti, Monica. *La presenza italiana nel Dodecaneso tra il 1912 e il 1948: La ricerca archeologica, la conservazione, le scelte progettuali*. Catania, IT: Edizioni del Prisma, 1996.

Lüdtke, Alf. "Einleitung: Herrschaft als soziale Praxis." In *Herrschaft als soziale Praxis: Historische und sozial-anthropologische Studien*, edited by Alf Lüdtke, 9–63. Göttingen, DE: Vandenhoeck & Ruprecht, 1991.

– *Eigen-Sinn: Fabrikalltag, Arbeitererfahrungen und Politik vom Kaiserreich bis in den Faschismus*. Hamburg, DE: Ergebnisse-Verlag, 1993.

Makdisi, Ussama S. *The Culture of Sectarianism: Community, History, and Violence in Nineteenth-Century Ottoman Lebanon*. Berkeley, CA: University of California Press, 2000.

Maksudyan, Nazan. "Foster-Daughter or Servant, Charity or Abuse: Beslemes in the Late Ottoman Empire." *Journal of Historical Sociology* 21, no. 4 (2008): 488–512.

– "Children as Transgressors in Urban Space: Delinquency, Public Order and Philanthropy in the Ottoman Reform Era." In *Violences juvéniles sous expertise(s) XIXe–XXIe siècles. Expertise and Juvenile Violence 19th–21st Centuries*, edited by Aurore François, Veerle Massin, and David Niget, 19–37. Louvain, BE: Presses universitaires de Louvain, 2010.

– *Orphans and Destitute Children in the Late Ottoman Empire*. Syracuse: Syracuse University Press, 2014.

Manela, Erez. *The Wilsonian Moment: Self-Determination and the International Origins of Anticolonial Nationalism*. Oxford: Oxford University Press, 2007.

Mannheim, Karl. "Das Problem der Generationen [1928]." In *Wissenssoziologie: Auswahl aus dem Werk*, by Karl Mannheim, 509–65. Berlin: Luchterhand, 1964.

Mardin, Şerif. *Genesis of Young Ottoman Thought*. Princeton: Princeton University Press, 1962.

Marongiu Buonaiuti, Cesare. *La politica religiosa del Fascismo nel Dodecaneso*. Napoli, IT: Giannini, 1979.

Martinoli, Simona, and Eliana Perotti. *Architettura coloniale italiana nel Dodecaneso 1912–1943*. Torino, IT: Edizioni Fondazione Giovanni Agnelli, 1999.

Martykánová, Darina. "Combinando la Sharia y la 'gubernamentalidad': Los cambios de la legislación matrimonial en el Imperio Otomano." *Tiempos Modernos* 18, no. 1 (2009).

Matard-Bonucci, Marie-Anne. "D'une persécution l'autre: Racisme colonial et antisémitisme dans l'Italie Fasciste." *Revue d'histoire moderne et contemporaine* 55–3, no. 3 (2008): 116–37.

– "Italian Fascism's Ethiopian Conquest and the Dream of a Prescribed Sexuality." In *Brutality and Desire: War and Sexuality in Europe's Twentieth Century*, edited by Dagmar Herzog, 91–108. Basingstoke, UK: Palgrave Macmillan, 2009.

– *L'Italie Fasciste et la persécution des Juifs*. Paris: Presses universitaires de France, 2012.

Matard-Bonucci, Marie-Anne, and Pierre Milza, eds. *L' Homme nouveau dans l'Europe fasciste (1922–1945): Entre dictature et totalitarisme*. Paris: Fayard, 2004.

Maynard Keynes, John. "Economic Possibilities for Our Grandchildren." In *Essays in Persuasion*, 358–73. New York: W.W. Norton & Co, 1963.

McCollum, Jonathan. "Reimagining Mediterranean Spaces: Libya and the Italo-Turkish War, 1911–1912." *Diacronie. Studi di Storia Contemporanea* 23, no. 3 (2015).

McElligott, Anthony. "The Deportation of the Jews of Rhodes, 1944: An Integrated History." In *The Holocaust in Greece*, edited by Giorgios Antoniou and A. Dirk Moses, 58–86. Cambridge: Cambridge University Press, 2018.

McGuire, Valerie. "Arcadian Histories: Italian Encounters in the Eastern Mediterranean." In *New Perspectives in Italian Cultural Studies: Definitions, Theory, and Accented Practices*, edited by Graziella Parati, 231–58. Madison, NJ: Fairleigh Dickinson University Press, 2012.

– "Fascism's Mediterranean Empire: Italian Occupation and Governance in the Dodecanese Islands (1912–43)." PhD diss., New York University, 2013.

– "An Imperial Education for Times of Transition: Italian Conquest, Occupation and Civil Administration of the Southeast Aegean, 1912–23." In *Italy in the Era of the Great War*, edited by Vanda Wilcox, 145–63. Leiden, NL: Brill, 2018.

– *Italy's Sea: Empire and Nation in the Mediterranean, 1895–1945*. Liverpool: Liverpool University Press, 2020.

McKeown, Adam. "Global Migration 1846–1940." *Journal of World History* 15, no. 2 (2004): 155–89.

– "How the Box Became Black: Brokers and the Creation of the Free Migrant." *Pacific Affairs* 85, no. 1 (2012): 21–45.

Melchionni, Maria Grazia. "Accordi Italo – Greci a Parigi (1919–1920)." *Rivista di Studi Politici Internazionali* 48, no. 3 (191) (1981): 465–80.

Metinsoy, Elif Mahir. *Ottoman Women during World War I: Everyday Experiences, Politics and Conflict*. Cambridge: Cambridge University Press, 2017.

Michael, Michalis N., Anastassios Anastassiadis, and Chantal Verdeil, eds. *Religious Communities and Modern Statehood: The Ottoman and Post-Ottoman World at the Age of Nationalism and Colonialism*. Berlin: Klaus Schwarz, 2015.

Micheletta, Luca. "The Questions Raised by the Occupation of the Dodecanese: Thoughts on the Foreign Policy of Liberal Italy." In *The Libyan War 1911–1912*, edited by Andrea Ungari and Luca Micheletta, 159–74. Newcastle Upon Tyne, UK: Cambridge Scholars Publishing, 2014.

Molho, Rena. "Education in the Jewish Community of Thessaloniki in the Beginning of the Twentieth Century." *Balkan Studies* 34, no. 2 (1993): 259–69.

Morelli, Anne. "Les diplomates Italiens en Belgique et la 'Question juive,' 1938–1943." *Bulletin de l'Institut Historique Belge de Rome* 53–54 (1983): 357–407.

Mosse, George L. *The Fascist Revolution: Toward a General Theory of Fascism.* New York: H. Fertig, 1999.

[Mumcu], İsmail Hakkı Paşa. *Vatan uğrunda yahut Yıldız Mahkemesi: Amasya mebusu İsmail Hakkı Paşa'nın hatıraları,* edited by Orhan Sakin. İstanbul, TR: Bilge Kültür Sanat, 2014.

Muncie, John. *Youth and Crime: A Critical Introduction.* London: Sage, 1999.

Naar, Devin E. *Jewish Salonica: Between the Ottoman Empire and Modern Greece.* Redwood City, CA: Stanford University Press, 2016.

Nagel, Joane. *Race, Ethnicity, and Sexuality: Intimate Intersections, Forbidden Frontiers.* Oxford: Oxford University Press, 2003.

Nasuhoğlu, Sadi. *Rodos: Anılar ve tarihçe.* Muğla, TR: Muğla Üniversitesi Basımevi, 2004.

National Committee for the Restoration of Greece, ed. *The Dodecanesians are not Enemy Aliens: A Memorandum submitted to the U.S. Dept. of Justice by the National Committee for the Restoration of Greece.* New York: The Dodecanesian League of America, 1942.

Negash, Tekeste. "The Ideology of Colonialism: Educational Policy and Praxis in Eritrea." In *Italian Colonialism,* edited by Ruth Ben-Ghiat and Mia Fuller. New York: Palgrave Macmillan US, 2006.

Okawara, Tomoki. "Size and Structure of Damascus Households in the Late Ottoman Period as Compared with Istanbul Households." In *Family History in the Middle East: Household, Property, and Gender,* edited by Beshara Doumani, 51–75. Albany, NY: SUNY Press, 2003.

Okay, Cüneyd. "Sport and Nation Building: Gymnastics and Sport in the Ottoman State and the Committee of Union and Progress, 1908–18." *The International Journal of the History of Sport* 20, no. 1 (2003): 152–6.

– "The Introduction, Early Development and Historiography of Soccer in Turkey: 1890–1914." *Soccer & Society* 3, no. 3 (2010): 1–10.

Orakçı, Meryem. *Rodos Müslümanları: Selam Gazetesi 1926–1936.* İstanbul, TR: Kitap Yayınevi, 2012.

Örenç, Ali Fuat. *Yakındönem Tarihimizde Rodos ve Oniki Ada.* İstanbul, TR: Doğu Kütüphanesi, 2006.

Örs, İlay. "Coffeehouses Cosmopolitanism and Pluralizing Modernities in Istanbul." *Journal of Mediteranean Studies* 12, no. 1 (2002): 119–45.

Osterhammel, Jürgen. *The Transformation of the World: A Global History of the Nineteenth Century*. Princeton: Princeton University Press, 2014.

Oualdi, M'hamed. *A Slave Between Empires: A Transimperial History of North Africa*. New York: Columbia University Press, 2020.

Özbek, Müge. "The Regulation of Prostitution in Beyoglu (1875–1915)." *Middle Eastern Studies* 46, no. 4 (2010): 555–68.

Özbek, Nadir. "'Beggars' and 'Vagrants' in Ottoman State Policy and Public Discourse, 1876–1914." *Middle Eastern Studies* 45, no. 5 (2009): 783–801.

Ozil, Ayse. *Orthodox Christians in the Late Ottoman Empire: A Study of Communal Relations in Anatolia*. New York: Routledge, 2013.

Paldiel, Mordecai. *Diplomat Heroes of the Holocaust*. Jersey City, NJ: KTAV Publishing House, Inc., 2007.

Pamuk, Sevket, and Jeffrey G. Williamson, eds. *The Mediterranean Response to Globalization Before 1950*. London: Routledge, 2000.

Papachristodoulou, Christodoulos. *Istoria tis Rodou: Apo tous proistorikous chronous eos tin ensomatosi tis Dodekanisou (1948)*. Athina, GR: Stegi Grammaton kai Technon Dodekanisou, 1972.

Papaioannou, Manoli. *Diagoras olympionikis o Rodios. Gymnastikos Syllogos "Diagoras."* Athina, GR: Zaharopoulos, 2005.

Papuççular, Hazal. "Fragmented Memories: The Dodecanese Islands during WWII." In *Heritage and Memory of War: Responses from Small Islands*, edited by Gillian Carr and Keir Reeves, 36–55. New York: Routledge, 2015.

– "Fragile Balances: Turkish Foreign Policy on the Sovereignty of the Dodecanese Islands (1940–1947)." *Journal of Balkan and Near Eastern Studies* 20, no. 5 (2018): 405–19.

– *Türkiye ve Oniki Ada 1912–1947*. Istanbul, TR: Türkiye İş Bankası Kültür Yayınları, 2019.

Pasqualini, Maria G. *L'Esercito Italiano nel Dodecaneso 1912–1943: Speranze e realtà*. Rome: Stato Maggiore dell'Esercito Ufficio Storico, 2009.

Passerini, Luisa. "La giovinezza metafora del cambiamento sociale: Due dibattiti sui giovani nell'Italia Fascista e negli Stati Uniti degli anni cinquanta." In *Storia dei giovani: II. L'età contemporanea*, edited by Giovanni Levi and Jean-Claude Schmitt, 383–459. Roma: Laterza, 1994.

Peçe, Uğur Z. "The Conscription of Greek Ottomans into the Sultan's Army, 1908–1912." *International Journal of Middle East Studies* 52, no. 3 (2020): 433–48.

Pergher, Roberta. "Between Colony and Nation on Italy's 'Fourth Shore.'" In *National Belongings: Hybridity in Italian Colonial and Postcolonial Cultures*, edited by Jacqueline Andall and Derek Duncan, 89–106. Oxford: Peter Lang, 2010.

– *Mussolini's Nation-Empire: Sovereignty and Settlement in Italy's Borderlands, 1922–1943*. Cambridge: Cambridge University Press, 2017.

Pernau, Margrit, Helge Jordheim, Emmanuelle Saada, Christian Bailey, Einar Wigen, Orit Bashkin, Mana Kia, et al., eds. *Civilizing Emotions: Concepts in Nineteenth-Century Asia and Europe*. Oxford: Oxford University Press, 2015.

Petrakis, Marina. *The Metaxas Myth: Dictatorship and Propaganda in Greece*. London: I.B. Tauris, 2011.

Petricioli, Marta. *L'Italia in Asia Minore: Equilibrio mediterraneo e ambizioni imperialiste alla vigilia della Prima Guerra Mondiale*. Firenze, IT: Sansoni, 1983.

Pezzetti, Marcello, ed. *La liberazione dei campi nazisti*. Rome: Gangemi, 2015.

Pignataro, Luca. "Il Collegio Rabbinico di Rodi." *Nuova Storia Contemporanea*, 2011.

– *Il Dodecaneso Italiano 1912–1947: I lineamenti giuridici, l'occupazione iniziale 1912–1922*. Chieti, IT: Solfanelli, 2011.

– *Il Dodecaneso Italiano 1912–1947: Il governo di Mario Lago 1923–1936*. Chieti, IT: Solfanelli, 2013.

– *Il Dodecaneso Italiano,1912–1947: De Vecchi, guerra e dopoguerra 1936–1947/50*. Chieti, IT: Solfanelli, 2018.

Pinder, Wilhelm. *Das Problem der Generation in der Kunstgeschichte Europas*. Leipzig, DE: Seemann, 1928.

Pinto, Vincenzo. "Between Imago and Res: The Revisionist-Zionist Movement's Relationship with Fascist Italy, 1922–1938." *Israel Affairs* 10, no. 3 (2004): 90–109.

Plaut, Joshua Eli. *Greek Jewry in the Twentieth Century, 1913–1983: Patterns of Jewish Survival in the Greek Provinces before and after the Holocaust*. Madison, NJ: Fairleigh Dickinson University Press, 1996.

Pongiluppi, Francesco. "Tra fede Cattolica e legame nazionale: L'identità degli Italo-Levantini di Turchia negli anni 1923–1933." *Storia e problemi contemporanei*, no. 72 (2017): 63–77.

Pretelli, Matteo. "Education in the Italian Colonies during the Interwar Period." *Modern Italy* 16, no. 3 (2011): 275–93.

Provence, Michael. *The Last Ottoman Generation and the Making of the Modern Middle East*. Cambridge: Cambridge University Press, 2017.

Quataert, Donald. "Ottoman Women, Households, and Textile Manufacturing, 1800–1914." In *Women in Middle Eastern History: Shifting Boundaries in Sex and Gender*, edited by Nikki R. Keddie and Beth Baron, 161. New Haven, CT: Yale University Press, 1991.

Rainero, Romain H. "Le coup d'État de Metaxas et ses échos dans l'Italie fasciste." *Revue d'histoire moderne et contemporaine* 36, no. 3 (1989): 438–49.

Rappas, Alexis. "The Elusive Polity: Imagining and Contesting Colonial Authority in Cyprus during the 1930s." *Journal of Modern Greek Studies* 26, no. 2 (2008): 363–97.

– *Cyprus in the 1930s: British Colonial Rule and the Roots of the Cyprus Conflict*. London: I.B. Tauris, 2014.

– "Insularity and Ethnicity in the Eastern Mediterranean: The Dodecanese under Italian Colonial Rule." In *Mediterráneos: An Interdisciplinary Approach to the Cultures of the Mediterranean Sea*, edited by Arturo Echavarren and Esther Fernández Medina. Newcastle Upon Tyne, UK: Cambridge Scholars Publishing, 2014.

– "The Transnational Formation of Imperial Rule on the Margins of Europe: British Cyprus and the Italian Dodecanese in the Interwar Period." *European History Quarterly* 45, no. 3 (2015): 467–505.

– "Memorial Soliloquies in Post-Colonial Rhodes and the Ghost of Mediterranean Cosmopolitanism." *Mediterranean Historical Review* 33, no. 1 (2018): 89–110.

– "Mixed Marriages in the Fascist Aegean and the Domestic Foundations of Imperial Sovereignty." In *New Perspectives on the History of Gender and Empire: Comparative and Global Approaches*, edited by Ulrike Lindner and Dörte Lerp, 31–58. London: Bloomsbury, 2018.

Reeder, Linda. "The Making of the Italian Husband in Nineteenth-Century Italy." In *Italian Sexualities Uncovered, 1789–1914*, edited by Valeria P. Babini, Chiara Beccalossi, and Lucy Riall, 272–90. London: Palgrave Macmillan UK, 2015.

Reichardt, Sven. *Faschistische Kampfbünde: Gewalt und Gemeinschaft im italienischen Squadrismus und in der deutschen SA*. Köln, DE: Böhlau, 2009.

Reinkowski, Maurus. "The State's Security and the Subjects' Prosperity: Notions of Order in Ottoman Bureaucratic Correspondence (19th Century)." In *Legitimizing the Order: The Ottoman Rhetoric of State Power*, edited by Hakan T. Karateke and Maurus Reinkowski, 195–212. Leiden, NL: Brill, 2005.

Rodrigue, Aron. *De l'instruction à l'émancipation: Les enseignements de l'Alliance Israélite Universelle et les Juifs d'Orient, 1860–1939*. Paris: Calmann-Lévy, 1989.

– *French Jews, Turkish Jews: The Alliance Israélite Universelle and the Politics of Jewish Schooling in Turkey 1860–1925*. Bloomington, IN: Indiana University Press, 1990.

– "From Millet to Minority: Turkish Jewry." In *Paths of Emancipation: Jews, States, and Citizenship*, edited by Pierre Birnbaum and Ira Katznelson, 238–61. Princeton: Princeton University Press, 2014.

– "The Rabbinical Seminary in Italian Rhodes, 1928–38: An Italian Fascist Project." *Jewish Social Studies* 25, no. 1 (2019): 1–19.

Romano, Sergio. *La Quarta Sponda: La Guerra Di Libia, 1911–1912*. Milano, IT: Bompiani, 1977.

Rose, Sonya O. "'Gender at Work': Sex, Class and Industrial Capitalism." *History Workshop Journal* 21, no. 1 (1986): 113–32.

Rubin, Avi. *Ottoman Nizamiye Courts. Law and Modernity*. New York: Palgrave Macmillan, 2011.

Rumbaut, Ruben G., and Kenji Ima. *The Adaptation of Southeast Asian Refugee Youth: A Comparative Study. Final Report to the Office of Resettlement.* Washington, DC: Office of Refugee Resettlement (DHHS), 1988.

Ryan, Eileen. "Violence and the Politics of Prestige: The Fascist Turn in Colonial Libya." *Modern Italy* 20, no. 2 (2015): 123–35.

Sabean, David Warren. *Property, Production, and Family in Neckarhausen, 1700–1870.* Cambridge: Cambridge University Press, 1990.

Salvante, Martina. "'Less than a Boot-Rag': Procreation, Paternity, and the Masculine Ideal in Fascist Italy." In *Masculinities and the Nation in the Modern World: Between Hegemony and Marginalization,* edited by Simon Wendt and Pablo Dominguez Andersen, 93–112. Basingstoke: Palgrave Macmillan, 2015.

Sant Cassia, Paul, and Constantina Bada. *The Making of the Modern Greek Family: Marriage and Exchange in Nineteenth-Century Athens.* Cambridge: Cambridge University Press, 1992.

Schmelz, Uziel O. "Population Characteristics of Jerusalem and Hebron Regions according to Ottoman Census of 1905." In *Ottoman Palestine, 1800–1914: Studies in Economic and Social History,* edited by Gad G. Gîlbar, 15–68. Leiden, NL: Brill, 1990.

Schmidt, Jan, ed. *The Orientalist Karl Süssheim meets the Young Turk Officer Isma'il Hakki Bey: Two Unexplored Sources from the Last Decade in the Reign of the Ottoman Sultan Abdulhamid II.* Leiden, NL: Brill, 2018.

Schmitt, Oliver Jens. *Levantiner: Lebenswelten und Identitäten einer ethnokonfessionellen Gruppe im osmanischen Reich im "langen 19. Jahrhundert."* München, DE: Oldenbourg, 2005.

Sciarcon, Andrea, and Fabrizio Nurra. *Io desidero la pace: Vita di Morris Sciarcon, Ebreo di Rodi sopravvissuto alla Shoà.* Milano, IT: Guerini e associati, 2017.

Scott, James C. *Domination and the Arts of Resistance: Hidden Transcripts.* New Haven, CT: Yale University Press, 1990.

Şeni, Nora. "La Jeunesse, une 'non-génération': Rhétorique éducative dans la Turquie des années trente." In *Enfance et jeunesse dans le monde musulman,* edited by François Georgeon and Klaus Kreiser, 233–57. Paris: Maisonneuve & Larose, 2007.

Sentakis, Giorgos M. *I istoria tou rodiakou athlitismou (464 p.Ch. – 1945).* Rodos, GR: Techni, 1987.

Sephardi Hebrew Congregation of Rhodesia. *A Brief History of the Congregation on the Occasion of the Twenty-Fifth Anniversary and the Consecration of the New Synagogue.* Salisbury, RI, 1958.

Sertel, Zekeriya. *Ḥayāt ve şebāb – Liberalizm.* Selanik, GR: Rumeli Maṭbaʿasi, 1911.

Seymour, Mark. *Debating Divorce in Italy: Marriage and the Making of Modern Italians, 1860–1974.* New York: Palgrave Macmillan, 2006.

Simmel, Georg. *Soziologie: Untersuchungen über die Formen der Vergesellschaftung.* Leipzig, DE: Duncker und Humblot, 1908.

Simon, Rachel. "Jewish Female Education in the Ottoman Empire." In *Jews, Turks, Ottomans: A Shared History, Fifteenth through the Twentieth Century*, edited by Avigdor Levy, 127–52. Syracuse: Syracuse University Press, 2002.

Sintès, Pierre. "La Synagogue au musée." *Ethnologie Française* 43, no. 4 (2013): 679–90.

– *En présence du passé: Géopolitique de la mémoire aux frontières de la Grèce.* Aix-en-Provence, FR: Presses universitaires de Provence, 2017.

Sisman, Cengiz. "Galante, Abraham (Avram)." In *Encyclopedia of Jews in the Islamic World*, edited by Norman A. Stillman. Leiden, NL: Brill, 2010.

Smyrnelis, Marie-Carmen. "Colonies européennes et communautés ethnico-confessionelles à Smyrne: Coexistence et réseaux de sociabilité (Fin du XVIIIe – milieu du XIXe Siècle)." In *Vivre dans l'Empire ottoman: Sociabilités et relations intercommunautaires (XVIIIe–XXe Siècles)*, edited by François Georgeon and Paul Dumont, 173–94. Paris: L'Harmattan, 1997.

– "Vivre ensemble dans l'Empire ottoman: XIIIe – XIXe Siècles." *Siècles* 26 (2007): 55–66.

Sohrabi, Nader. "Global Waves, Local Actors: What the Young Turks Knew about Other Revolutions and Why It Mattered." *Comparative Studies in Society and History* 44, no. 1 (2002): 45–79.

Somel, Selçuk Aksin. *The Modernization of Public Education in the Ottoman Empire, 1839–1908: Islamization, Autocracy, and Discipline.* Leiden, NL: Brill, 2001.

– "Christian Community Schools during the Ottoman Reform Period." In *Late Ottoman Society: The Intellectual Legacy*, edited by Elisabeth Özdalga, 254–73. London: Routledge/Curzon, 2005.

Stein, Sarah Abrevaya. *Extraterritorial Dreams: European Citizenship, Sephardi Jews, and the Ottoman Twentieth Century.* Chicago: University of Chicago Press, 2016.

Stephenson, Charles. *A Box of Sand: The Italo-Ottoman War 1911–1912.* Ticehurst, UK: Tattered Flag, 2014.

Stoler, Ann Laura, and Frederick Cooper. "Between Metropole and Colony: Rethinking a Research Agenda." In *Tensions of Empire: Colonial Cultures in a Bourgeois World*, edited by Frederick Cooper and Ann Laura Stoler, 1–56. Berkeley, CA: University of California Press, 1997.

Suleiman, Susan Rubin. "The 1.5 Generation: Thinking about Child Survivors and the Holocaust." *American Imago* 59, no. 3 (2002): 277–95.

Theodoratus, Robert James. *A Greek Community in America: Tacoma, Washington.* Sacramento, CA: Sacramento Anthropological Society, Sacramento State College, 1971.

Thomas, Martin. *Empires of Intelligence: Security Services and Colonial Disorder after 1914.* Berkeley, CA: University of California Press, 2008.

Todorova, Maria. "The Ottoman Legacy in the Balkans." In *Imperial Legacy: The Ottoman Imprint on the Balkans and the Middle East*, edited by Carl Leon Brown, 45–77. New York: Columbia University Press, 1996.

[Tokgöz], Ahmed Ihsan. "Süriye'ye Bir Cevelān." *Servet-i Fünun*, no. 299 (12 March 1896).

Tomiak, Janusz, and Andreas Kazamias. "Introduction." In *Schooling, Educational Policy and Ethnic Identity: Comparative Studies on Governments and Non-Dominant Ethnic Groups in Europe 1850–1940*, edited by Janusz Tomiak, Knut Eriksen, Andreas Kazamias, and Robin Okey, 1–11. New York: New York University Press, 1990.

Toprak, Zafer. "İttihat ve Terakki'nin paramiliter gençlik örgütleri." *Boğaziçi Üniversitesi Dergisi: Hümaniter Bilimler* VII (1979): 95–113.

– "The Family, Feminism, and the State during the Young Turk Period, 1908–1918." In *Première rencontre internationale sur l'Empire ottoman et la Turquie moderne*, edited by Edhem Eldem, 441–52. Istanbul, TR: İsis, 1991.

Torr, Cecil. *Rhodes in Modern Times*. Cambridge: Cambridge University Press, 1887.

Toumarkine, Alexandre. *Les migrations des populations musulmanes balkaniques en Anatolie (1876–1913)*. Istanbul, TR: İsis, 1995.

Toundassaki, Irini. "Pratiques coutumières de succession et structures parentales dans la mer Égée (Cyclades-Dodécanèse)." In *Parenté et société dans le monde grec de l'antiquité à l'âge moderne: Colloque international, Volos (Grèce), 19–20–21 juin 2003*, edited by Alain Bresson, Marie-Paule Masson, Stavros Perentidis, and Jérôme Wilgaux, 12:351–66. Pessac, FR: Ausonius Éditions, 2006.

Tsalachouris, Kostas F. *Rodos '43-'44: Meres antistasis kai prodosias*. Athina, GR: Trochalia, 1997.

Tsirpanlis, Zacharias. *Italokratia sta Dodekanisa: 1912–1942: Allotriosi tou anthropou kai tou perivallontos*. Rhodos, GR: Zete, 1998.

Tsitselikis, Konstantinos. *Old and New Islam in Greece: From Historical Minorities to Immigrant Newcomers*. Leiden, NL: Nijhoff, 2012.

Tucker, Judith E. "Revisiting Reform: Women and the Ottoman Law of Family Rights, 1917." *The Arab Studies Journal* 4, no. 2 (1996): 4–17.

Türesay, Özgür. "Political Victims of the Old Regime under the Young Turk Regime (1908–1911)." In *The Young Turks and the Ottoman Empire: The Aftermath of 1908 Revolution*, edited by Noémi Lévy-Aksu and François Georgeon, 67–95. London: I.B. Tauris, 2017.

Turiano, Annalaura, and Joseph John Viscomi. "From Immigrants to Emigrants: Salesian Education and the Failed Integration of Italians in Egypt, 1937–1960." *Modern Italy* 23, no. 1 (2018): 1–17.

Veblen, Thorstein. *The Theory of the Leisure Class: An Economic Study of Institutions*. Oxford: Oxford University Press, 2007.

Vergotis, Giorgios. *I ekpaideusi sto "Koino" tis Rodou kata tin Othomanokratia*. Rodos, GR: Rodos, 1995.

Vernier, Bernard. *La genèse sociale des sentiments: Aînés et cadets dans l'île grecque de Karpathos.* Paris: Éditions de l'EHESS, 1991.

VII Censimento della popolazione. 21 aprile 1931 – IX. Volume V: Colonie e Possedimenti. Rome: Failli, 1935.

Villa, Andrea. *Nelle isole del sole: Gli Italiani nel Dodecaneso dall'occupazione al rimpatrio (1912–1947).* Torino, IL: Edizioni Seb 27, 2016.

Villeggia, Nemo. *La scuola per la classe dirigente: Vita quotidiana e prassi educative nei licei durante il Fascismo.* Milano, IT: Unicopli, 2007.

Volonakis, Michel. *Le Dodécanèse vers l'union: Avec un avant-propos de M.E. Denis.* Paris: Éditions de l'Orient illustré, 1919.

Vratsalis, Antonis. *Niochoritika.* Rhodos, GR: Techni, 1990.

Wanrooij, Bruno. "The Rise and Fall of Italian Fascism as a Generational Revolt." *Journal of Contemporary History* 22, no. 3 (1987): 401–18.

Whelehan, Niall. "Youth, Generations, and Collective Action in Nineteenth-Century Ireland and Italy." *Comparative Studies in Society and History* 56, no. 4 (2014): 934–66.

White, Benjamin Thomas. *The Emergence of Minorities in the Middle East.* Edinburgh: Edinburgh University Press, 2012.

Wilcox, Vanda. *The Italian Empire and the Great War.* Oxford: Oxford University Press, 2021.

Zahra, Tara. "Imagined Non-Communities: National Indifference as a Category of Analysis." *Slavic Review* 69, no. 1 (2010): 93–119.

Ze'evi, Dror. *Producing Desire: Changing Sexual Discourse in the Ottoman Middle East, 1500–1900.* Berkeley, CA: University of California Press, 2006.

Zervos, Skevos Georges. *Rhodes, capitale du Dodécanèse.* Paris: Leroux, 1920.

Zervos, Skevos Georges, and Paris Roussos. *Le Dodécanèse: L'histoire du Dodécanèse à travers les siècles, les services qu'il a rendus à l'humanité, ses droits.* London: A. Page, 1919.

Zollmann, Jakob. "Communicating Colonial Order: The Police of German South-West-Africa (c. 1894–1915)." *Crime, Histoire & Sociétés* 15, no. 1 (2011): 33–57.

Zürcher, Erik Jan. *The Unionist Factor: The Role of the Committee of Union and Progress in the Turkish National Movement, 1905–1926.* Leiden, NL: Brill, 1984.

– "The Ottoman Conscription System, 1844–1914." *International Review of Social History* 43, no. 3 (1998): 437–49.

– "The Young Turks – Children of the Borderlands?" *International Journal of Turkish Studies* 9, no. 1–2 (2003): 275–86.

Index